This is Charles Dawson's handwriting and refers to the discovery of the tooth with the second Piltdown Skull 30th July. 1915

(A S Woodward)

I am sorry I shall not be able to come to Keith's demonstration. I wonder if he has seen the new paper on Pleistocene & Pliocene primates in the Indian Govt. Geol publication. The writer sent me a separate but I forget his name. Boule has been writing to me about Starch & flints & I have sent him a sample of them. He has promised to send me a separate of some new paper he has written about Eoanthropus. Teilhard wrote yesterday – he is quite well & in a quiet spot at present. I have got a new molar tooth (Eoanthropus) with the new series, but it is just the same as the others as to wear. It is a first or second right m. the root broken. At Piltdown the road is falling in at the edge where we got too close & Kenard has put up a fence.

C.D.

Frontispiece
A postcard [4.1.21] from Charles Dawson to Arthur Smith Woodward announcing the discovery of the Piltdown II molar. Courtesy of Trustees of the British Museum (Natural History).

THE
PILTDOWN PAPERS
1908–1955

*The correspondence and other documents
relating to the Piltdown Forgery*

FRANK SPENCER

Natural History Museum Publications
Oxford University Press
LONDON OXFORD & NEW YORK

First published 1990 by
British Museum (Natural History)
Cromwell Road, London SW7 5BD

&

Oxford University Press, Walton Street, Oxford OX2 6DP
Oxford New York Toronto
Delhi Bombay Calcutta Madras Karachi
Petaling Java Singapore Hong Kong Tokyo
Nairobi Dar es Salaam Cape Town
Melbourne Auckland

and associated companies in
Beirut Berlin Ibadan Nicosia

Oxford is a trade mark of Oxford University Press

Published in the United States
by Oxford University Press, New York

© Frank Spencer
Department of Anthropology
Queens College CUNY, NY 11367–0904

British Library Cataloguing in Publication Data
Spencer, Frank, 1942–
The Piltdown papers: the correspondence and other
documents relating to the Piltdown forgery 1908–1955.
1. Piltdown man
I. Title
573.3
ISBN 0–19–858523–3

Library of Congress Cataloging-in-Publication Data
Spencer, Frank, 1942–
The Piltdown papers, 1908–1955: the correspondence and other
documents relating to the Piltdown forgery / Frank Spencer.
p.   cm.
Includes bibliographical references.
ISBN 0–19–858523–3
1. Piltdown forgery.   I. Title.
GN282.5.S64   1990
573.3—dc20
90–32881
CIP

Typeset in Palatino by J&L Composition Ltd, Filey, North Yorkshire
Printed by Staples Printers Kettering Ltd.

Contents

In Memoriam

IAN LANGHAM
(1942–1984)

Introduction

On 18 December 1912, details of a remarkable ancient human skull reportedly recovered from a gravel pit at Piltdown in East Sussex were unveiled before a crowded meeting of the Geological Society of London, at Burlington House. These remains consisted of nine cranial fragments, plus the right half of a seemingly ape-like mandible (with two molars *in situ*), and an assortment of fossil animal bones and stone artifacts. When fitted together the cranial fragments made up the greater part of the left side (and a portion of the right mid-section) of an essentially modern-looking human braincase, which was articulated with the incomplete lower jaw. This pairing rested largely on two major considerations: first, while recognizing that the configuration of the mandibular body did resemble that of an ape, the molars nevertheless had flat crowns with nonaligned occlusal surfaces, indicating a wear-pattern that was decidedly human and quite uncharacteristic of ape dentition; second, the stratigraphical circumstances in which these remains had been reportedly found supported the argument of association. Although this interpretation was contested, the argument advocating the separation of the jaw from the skull did not prevail either at the Geological Society meeting in December 1912 or subsequently, despite repeated attempts by various workers between 1913 and 1917 to demonstrate the anatomical falsity of the monistic interpretation. Similarly, there was clearly an incipient difference of opinion regarding the geological interpretation of the assemblage. Some contended the evidence pointed to the skull belonging to a horizon of the Lower Pleistocene, while others favoured a much earlier date. But in spite of the patently controversial nature of these remains, it was the considered opinion of those in attendance at Burlington House on 18 December that they constituted "the most important discovery in England ... [and] ... if not of greater importance than any other yet made at home or abroad." And during the next four years, further discoveries were made at Piltdown which served to consolidate this point of view.

Although this initial enthusiasm had embodied a palpable sense of national pride, this emotion had not been a primary factor in determining the successful launching of the Piltdown skull. Rather, the key to this success resided, so it seems, in the timing of its entry onto the scientific stage and the encoded messages it delivered to an expectant and confused scientific community.

Palaeoanthropological theory was at this time in a critical state of flux. While most workers of the period subscribed to the thesis that modern human anatomy was the evolutionary product of a development from an as yet unknown, ancestral anthropomorphous ape, opinion diverged dramatically on the details of this process. Indeed, since the closing decades of the nineteenth century, there had been mounting resistance to the simplistic Darwinian assumption that the hominoid-hominid transition and the subsequent refinement of human anatomy to its modern form had been a gradual and orderly process. As it appeared to many the accumulated evidence on extinct and extant forms of humanity did not accord well with this viewpoint. Consequently, where scientific opinion had previously been inclined to a simple unilineal interpretation of the existing human fossil record, there had been during the first decade of the twentieth century a steady retreat from this position, with a growing support for schemes that promoted a more complex and branching view of the evolutionary process.

In the absence of a more suitable candidate, the hominid remains found in Java during the early 1890s, which had been fittingly dubbed *Pithecanthropus erectus* (now known as *Homo erectus*), had been retained by many workers as the progenitor of the human lineage. Found in association with fauna that placed it on the boundary between the Lower Pleistocene and Upper Pliocene, this specimen, consisting of a heavily mineralized and undistorted skullcap (calotte) and a complete femur, was seen to possess a mosaic of ancient and modern features. Unlike the thigh bone, which was remarkably human-like, the skullcap displayed a suite of "primitive" characters. Although the frontal portion was incomplete, enough remained of it to appreciate the existence of a heavy, overhanging eyebrow ridge (supraorbital torus), a cranial character that had been found in all the fossil hominids prior to Piltdown and only hinted at in the most "primitive" modern human crania. Beyond this bony ledge, the forehead, instead of rising sharply as it does in modern crania (as well as Piltdown), recedes at a dramatically low angle; while the occipital bone is bent sharply down and forward, resulting in a cranial profile that is quite different from the modern rounded form.

Subsequent restoration of the Java skull enabled anatomists to determine that its cranial capacity hovered in the region of 900 cubic centimetres, which served to reinforce its presumed transitional status. But while some workers continued to endorse this specimen as an ancestral hominid, and its presence on the mainline leading to the subsequent emergence of modern *Homo sapiens*, there were many who disputed this. Some had gone so far as to reject its hominid status, claiming it to be nothing more than the calotte of an extinct hominoid ape; while others assumed a more prudent posture, arguing that *Pithecanthropus* represented either an evolutionary cul-de-sac or at best the progenitor of the equally controversial hominid form known as Neanderthal, whose remains had been found in association with fauna belonging to the Middle–Upper Pleistocene of Europe.

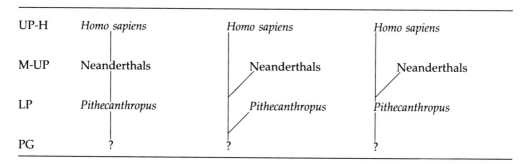

Competing views on human phylogeny at the beginning of the twentieth century. UP-H: Upper Pleistocene-Holocene (Recent); M-UP: Middle-Upper Pleistocene; LP: Lower Pleistocene; PG: Pre-Glacial (Tertiary: Pliocene, Miocene etc.).

Where previously the Neanderthals had been considered to stand on the periphery of the modern range of human variation, comparative anatomical studies had progressively peeled away the veneer of their humanity. The Neanderthal skeleton was found to be peppered with structural peculiarities which, when considered together, were thought to preclude all possibility of it being an antecedent form to modern *Homo sapiens*. Among other things, these studies showed that their hindlimbs had retained the anthropoid disproportion between the lengths of the thigh and shin bones, and that their curiously curved thigh bones must have prevented them from standing absolutely erect, requiring them to walk with a bend at the knees. But perhaps more than any other finding, the declaration that their brains lacked the proportions characteristic of the "superior organization" of the modern human brain, had served to reduce the Neanderthals to a lowly, shambling race of moronic brutes— a decision endorsed by the dull visage of their massively built and heavy-browed crania.

The possibility of Neanderthals having been a precursor of modern *Homo sapiens* was further undermined by the increasing number of reports of anatomically modern human skeletal material being found in geological horizons that either matched or predated those in which the Neanderthals had been recovered. Besides fuelling the argument for the pre-eminence of the brain in human evolution and the resident claim for the great antiquity of modern human cerebral and neurocranial morphology, these discoveries, in demanding an expansion of the chronological framework for human evolution, also had served to support the controversy that had raged in archaeological circles since the mid-1800s over the interpretation of material known as eoliths.

Just as the human fossil record could be used to demonstrate the gradual evolution of human anatomy, so the archaeological record provided evidence to document the progressive improvement of human industry through a sequence of periods in which stone had been the primary material for tool-making. Although, as in palaeontology, there was at this time considerable confusion and uncertainty regarding the interpretation of the evidence, it was generally agreed that this stone age could be divided into two major industrial periods: the Palaeolithic (or old stone age, the period of chipped or flaked stone tools); and the Neolithic (or new stone age, the period of polished stone). The transition from the Palaeolithic to the Neolithic was generally thought to have coincided with the onset of the modern geologic epoch (Holocene). Furthermore, by the turn of the century, there was fairly wide agreement that the Palaeolithic sequence could be broken down into three major subdivisions: the Lower Palaeolithic (Chellean and Acheulian), Middle Palaeolithic (Mousterian) and Upper Palaeolithic (Aurignacian, Solutrean and Magdalenian); and that these subdivisions corresponded roughly with specific geological phases in the Pleistocene. Although it had been recognized since the middle of the nineteenth century that the Pleistocene had been affected by an ice age, it was not until the late 1870s that it was finally understood that there had been not one, but rather four successive glaciations, punctuated by three warm (interglacial) periods. During the first decade of the twentieth century these four glaciations became widely known by the terms Günz, Mindel, Riss and Würm.

In the case of the Lower Palaeolithic, represented by implements of chipped stone known as "core-tools" (made by striking flakes from a flint nodule or pebble so that the residual core forms the implement), it appeared to be confined to the Lower Pleistocene (specifically the Second Interglacial, or Mindel-Riss); whereas the Middle Palaeolithic was associated with the horizons of the Third Interglacial or Riss-Würm. The Middle Palaeolithic period or Mousterian industries was distinguished by tools made from stone flakes. The Upper Palaeolithic period was characterized not only by the use of flint flakes or blades, but also bone, antler and ivory, all of which were worked extensively and frequently displayed a high level of workmanship. The successive industries of the Aurignacian on through the Solutrean to the Magdalenian were regarded as being contemporaneous with the "Last Glaciation" or Würm.

While many archaeologists of the period believed the industrial sequence of the

Palaeolithic defined the boundaries of the human evolutionary scenario, there were others who claimed that the Palaeolithic addressed only the gradual refinement of the human species to their modern form, and said nothing of the earlier stages of human evolution, namely the hominoid-hominid transition. According to this viewpoint, the core-tools of the Lower Palaeolithic had been preceded by an industrial tradition whose roots lay buried in dark recesses of the Tertiary era. As might be expected, this industry, which had come to be known as the Eolithic (meaning the dawn of tool-making), was characterized by flints whose natural form was judged to have been crudely, and often only slightly, altered to make it more useful as a tool. In spite of the continuing efforts of sceptics to demonstrate that eoliths were nothing more than the natural products of geological processes, the movement had survived and retained a significant following in Britain and on the Continent.

The archaeological and palaeontological assemblages recovered from the Piltdown site appear to have been designed to promote not only the eolithic cause, but also to provide a compelling vehicle for an ancestral hominid that had been carefully tailored to satisfy scientific expectations and thereby to fill the hiatus created by the theoretical expulsion of the Neanderthals and *Pithecanthropus* from the human lineage.

Between the two World Wars, however, a number of new additions were made to the human fossil record which prompted a growing number of workers to reconsider *Pithecanthropus* and Neanderthals as possible ancestors. This revisionary trend progressively undermined the evolutionary propositions demanded by the Sussex skull. Thus, while there was still a number of influential workers during this period who continued to regard Piltdown as a pivotal specimen, the general tendency was either to ignore the specimen or, at best, to relegate it to a position of relative unimportance in the reconstruction of human phylogeny.

It was in this context that Kenneth Oakley of the British Museum (Natural History) began his work in 1947 on the development of a chemical technique of relative dating. The initial results of Oakley's chemical analysis of the Piltdown remains, while supporting the possibility of their belonging to a single individual, also revealed that their age was much younger than previously imagined. To many this latter finding simply cast doubt on the validity and utility of the technique, but to Joseph Weiner (then a Reader in physical anthropology at Oxford University), these findings were "astonishing", since, as he later wrote: "a composite, primitive man-ape would be even more incongruous at the end of the Pleistocene in England than two separate fossil individuals" (Weiner, cited in Harrison 1982: 47). Thus, Oakley's work triggered a line of thinking which ultimately led Weiner to doubt the authenticity of the Piltdown remains.

In August 1953, a full-scale investigation of the Piltdown remains was sanctioned by the British Museum (Natural History). The preliminary results of this investigation (published in November 1953), demonstrated that the respective ages of the cranium and jaw were different, and that these remains had been deliberately stained and the teeth artificially remodelled. Later, it was shown that the entire assemblage was bogus.

Following these sensational disclosures, Weiner launched a systematic inquiry aimed at discovering who had been responsible for this scientific forgery, the conclusions of which were published in his book *The Piltdown Forgery* (1955). At that time, Charles Dawson, a country solicitor and principal discoverer at Piltdown, was regarded by many as the prime suspect. Although favourably inclined to this hypothesis, Weiner nevertheless admitted in his book that the case against Dawson was largely circumstantial and clearly "insufficient to prove beyond all reasonable doubt" that he had been the culprit. To the majority of professional scientists, however, the identity of the forger(s) was of secondary importance. Much more important was that the spurious skull had been detected and discarded. Furthermore, in the light of Weiner's seemingly thorough inquiry, there appeared to be little prospect of solving this mystery. Evidently the forger(s) had been careful to cover his tracks, but in spite of this speculation continued and during the past 30 years Piltdownian sleuths have brought forth a dozen or more possible suspects, ranging from the illustrious to the obscure, many of whom (though not all) are known to have been associated with Dawson, or had collaborated with him on his work at Piltdown. But without exception, the respective cases brought against these suspects have rested exclusively on suspicion rather than evidence.

To a large extent, this proliferation of suspects has been due to a limited knowledge of the primary archival materials and a corresponding lack of detailed information on the activities of those individuals who were either directly or indirectly involved in the events that transpired at Piltdown between 1912 and 1916. Thus, one of the aims of the work at hand is to provide a more complete account of this episode and the means by which past and future suspects might be more objectively evaluated.

While recognizing that the mystery of the forger's or forgers' identity is not without its attractions, this preoccupation has nevertheless been allowed to obscure the value of the Piltdown episode as a case study in the history of science. Given the extent of the available primary archival material related to this event, an admirable opportunity exists to examine how scientists, under prescribed conditions, go about their business of formulating, debating and resolving their problems. With this in mind the following collection of some 500 letters, many of which until now, have never been published, has been assembled to provide those scholars interested in the history of science with a convenient source for future study.

The work is divided into six sections covering the period immediately preceding the announcement of the discovery in 1912 through to the publication of Weiner's book in February 1955.

The opening subsection provides background information on the relationship between the two principal discoverers at Piltdown, namely Charles Dawson and [Sir] Arthur Smith Woodward, former Keeper of Geology at the British Museum (Natural History). The remaining two subsections document events leading to the official unveiling at Burlington House on 18 December 1912, providing at the same time more insights into the socio-scientific network to which Dawson and Woodward belonged.

The second section deals with events in 1913, and is subdivided into four subsections. Although the content of these subsections is apparent from their respective titles, Section 2.2 requires some explanation. While serving to demonstrate the extent of the interest provoked by the discoveries at Piltdown in 1912, this subsection also indicates that after 1913 all enquiries relating to the availability of Piltdown casts went directly to the company responsible for their production and distribution. Hence the absence of a similar subsection elsewhere in the catalogue.

The third and fourth sections map the broad contours of the Piltdown debate as it developed between 1914 and 1917.

The fifth section is subdivided into two subsections, covering the period from 1918 to 1939, and 1946 to 1952 respectively. While these divisions are arbitrary, they nevertheless serve to reflect the shifting focus of scientific attention during these years. In the former subsection, the selected correspondence highlights some of the developments occurring in palaeoanthropology between the two World Wars. This period terminates, conveniently, with the discovery by Alvan Marston of the fossil hominid at Swanscombe (Kent) in the mid-1930s and his initial attempt to equate this find with that at Piltdown (Sussex). Indeed, Marston's work serves as a convenient bridge to the period following World War II when Oakley began his investigations which ultimately led to the debunking of Piltdown in 1953.

The correspondence in the last section documents the chronology of those events which delivered the *coup de grâce* to the Piltdown enigma and the investigation that was subsequently mounted to discover the perpetrator.

To assist the reader in tracking certain individuals as well as specific themes and events, extensive cross-referencing has been employed throughout. A separate name and subject index has also been provided.

The primary source of the manuscripts presented in this volume is the British Museum (Natural History), London. However, in an effort to provide a more complete narrative of events, sources from several other archives have been employed, in particular those of the Royal College of Surgeons of England (London), the American Museum of Natural History (New York) and the Smithsonian Institution (Washington, D.C.)—see my note on manuscript sources for complete details.

During the preparation of this work for publication I received information and assistance from a number of people whom I would like to thank. They include: Ms Stella Bellem (Curator, Bexhill Museum); Mr Geoffrey T. Denton (Uckfield, Sussex); Mr K. W. Dickins (Archivist, Sussex Archaeological Society); Ms Penny Gavaris (Queens College CUNY); Mr Leslie V. Grinsell (Bristol, Somerset); Professor J. de Heinzelin (Institut Royal des Sciences Naturelles de Beligique, Bruxelles); Professor G. Ainsworth Harrison (Oxford University); Mrs Margaret Hodgson (Canterbury, Kent); Mrs Robin Kenward (Piltdown, Sussex); Mr Giles Oakley (London); Dr David B. Scott (Sun City, Arizona); Ms Jennifer Stewart (Curator of Archaeology, City of Bristol Museum & Art Gallery); Professor Phillip V. Tobias (University of the Witwatersrand, Johannesburg); Sig. Franco Vivarelli (Livorno, Italia); Professor Sherwood L. Washburn (Berkeley, California); Professor Richard G. West (Cambridge University); and Mr Lionel Woodhead (Brighton, Sussex).

I also take pleasure in recording the enthusiasm and ungrudging assistance of the librarians and archivists at the Smithsonian Institution; the American Museum of Natural History; and the Royal College of Surgeons. Likewise, I wish to convey my sincere gratitude to the numerous people at the British Museum (Natural History) who have assisted me from time to time in the compilation of this work. Of these many generous and kind individuals, I must thank personally several members of the Department of Palaeontology, namely William Ball (former Keeper), Theya Molleson, Chris B. Stringer, Peter Andrews and Robert Kruszynsky, as well as Paula Jenkins of the Zoology Department and Dorothy Norman formerly of Library Services. I also would like to express my deep gratitude to Ann Lum of the Palaeontology Library for her undying commitment to the project, and to Myra Givans and her editorial staff for their patient assistance in bringing this work to its finished form. Finally, I am deeply indebted to my wife, for without her support this work would have never been completed.

1 The Arrival Of Piltdown Man, 1908–1912

1.1 Before The Unveiling 1908-1911. The Dawson-Woodward Connection and Other Relationships

The principal discoverers at Piltdown were Charles Dawson (1864-1916), a solicitor and well-known amateur palaeontologist and antiquarian, and Arthur Smith Woodward (1864-1944), then Keeper of Geology at the British Museum (Natural History) in South Kensington, London. As the preserved correspondence at the Natural History Museum indicates, these two men had enjoyed a friendly professional relationship that well preceded the events of 1912. Furthermore, it is evident from the published writings of Woodward (1911, 1916, 1948), that Dawson had Woodward's confidence and respect as a palaeontologist; a view also shared by others in the British scientific establishment [1].

Although sharing similar social backgrounds, the two men were quite different in terms of temperament and physique (Fig 1.1). In many respects Dawson could be the miller in Chaucer's *Canterbury Tales*. He was a bald, short "stout fellow," with a large pointed moustache that harmonized with his energetic and jovial disposition. In direct contrast, Woodward with his pince-nez and well-groomed Edwardian beard was a more reserved personality. Indeed, many, considered him cold and aloof, even those who retained his friendship.

At the time of Piltdown, Dawson was a senior partner in a solicitor's firm located in Uckfield, Sussex, which from all indications was a successful one. In this connection, Dawson was active in local civic affairs as Clerk to the Magistrates for the Uckfield Petty Sessional Division and Clerk to the Urban Council. In addition to these duties, he also held the Stewardships of several local Manors, namely those of Hetherall, Tarring Camois, and Barkham. It was on the latter estate that the Piltdown remains were found.

As the senior partner in the firm Dawson was provided with the opportunity to indulge his primary avocation, which was palaeontology, an interest he had nurtured since childhood. Indeed, it was while growing up in St. Leonards, near Hastings that Dawson began collecting and studying Wealden fossils under the guidance of a local palaeontologist Samuel H. Beckles F.R.S. (d. 1890). The result was the assembly of a sizeable and valuable collection of Wealden fossils which Dawson donated to the British Museum in 1884. Included in this collection is one of the finest extant examples of ganoid fish, *Lepidotus mantelli*. In recognition of this work, the Museum installed Dawson as an honorary collector. The following year (1885), he was elected to the prestigious Geological Society of London [2], a notable achievement for a young amateur investigator.

In the years immediately preceding the events of 1912, as will be seen in the correspondence below, Dawson made a number of important additions to his collection at the British Museum, the most notable being his discovery of a new species of dinosaur, *Iguanodon dawsoni* and a previously unknown Wealden mammal: *Plagiaulax dawsoni* [3]. Dawson had also by this time acquired a local reputation as a

Fig. 1.1 The principal investigators at Piltdown (circa 1912). Arthur Smith Woodward (foreground) and Charles Dawson (background). Courtesy of Mrs Margaret Hodgson.

geologist and antiquarian, and while clearly well-versed in Wealden geology (see Dawson 1898c, 1913, 1915), it appears his reputation as a geologist was based largely on his discovery of a natural gas deposit at Heathfield in 1898 (see Dawson 1898a, 1898b), which was later used for many years to light the local railway station and hotel[4]. As for his antiquarian interests, besides being an acknowledged authority on old iron work[5], his large two-volume *History of Hastings Castle* (1909) was regarded as the standard work. In addition to being a Fellow of the Society of Antiquaries (1895), Dawson was also a member of the Sussex Archaeological Society (1892).

Likewise, on the eve of Piltdown, Woodward was at the peak of his career, enjoying an international reputation as a leading authority on fossil fish.

As the son of a prosperous dye manufacturer in Macclesfield, Cheshire, Woodward had attended the local grammar school[6] and from there in 1880 he went to Owen's College of the newly established Victoria University of Manchester to study geology and palaeontology under William Boyd Dawkins (1837-1929)[7]. In 1882, while at Manchester, Woodward published his first scientific paper. In that same year he decided to apply for the post as an assistant in the Geology Department of the British Museum (Natural History)[8], before completing his degree.

Competing successfully against fourteen other candidates, Woodward began his career as a professional scientist on 12 August 1882. During the first years of his appointment at the British Museum (Natural History), Woodward endeavoured to devote as much time as he could to completing his formal scientific education[9]. His plans to complete his degree, however, were skotched by a request to undertake the preparation of a catalogue of the Museum's extensive fossil fish collections. This resulted in a four-volume catalogue (1889-1901), which represents the corner-stone of Woodward's developing international reputation as an ichthyologist[10]. Within the time period embraced by the *Catalogue*, and indicative of his growing stature in the scientific community, are the various awards he began to accumulate. In particular one can cite his receipt of the prestigious Wollaston (1889) and Lyell (1896) Medals from the Geological Society, followed by the honorary degree of LL.D. from the University of Glasgow in 1900. Likewise, he made progress at the Museum, beginning first with his promotion to Assistant Keeper in 1892, and finally, in 1901, to Keeper, when he succeeded Henry Woodward (1832- 1921) on his retirement. That same year he was elected a Fellow of the Royal Society.

By 1901 Woodward had several hundred scientific publications to his credit, many of which represented the product of extensive fieldwork conducted in various parts of Europe and North America (Cooper 1945). Although now known primarily as an ichthyologist, Woodward did not confine himself exclusively to fossil fish. He had also produced a number of studies on higher vertebrates; a notable example is the *Catalogue of British Fossil Vertebrates* (1890). Also worthy of note is his popular textbook *Outlines of Vertebrate Palaeontology* (1898), written for students of zoology. This latter work is of interest since it reveals a latent interest in palaeoanthropology, and more particularly his sympathetic inclination to the theories of Benjamin Harrison (1857-1921) and Joseph Prestwich (1812-1896) regarding eoliths (see Harrison 1899; Prestwich 1889, 1891, 1892). These controversial objects were considered by some to be nothing more than the *caput mortuum* of natural processes, whereas Harrison and his disciples believed they represented the precursors of the stone tool industries of the Palaeolithic period (see Woodward 1898:410). Indeed, Woodward is known to have made several scientific excursions to Ightham in Kent to visit Harrison and to examine such evidence (Spencer 1990).

Contrary to expectations, however, this interest and connection with Harrison and other known members of the Ightham Circle are not reflected in Dawson's early letters to Woodward. In fact, prior to 1912, Dawson's letters to Woodward are surprisingly dull, concerned largely with the collection and preservation of specimens for the Museum, with little or no mention of anthropology[11]. But despite their apparent dullness, these letters are nonetheless valuable documents, for several reasons. First, they throw some light on Dawson's relationship with Woodward, supporting the view that while their association was long standing, it was not until 1909 that their relationship deepened. Prior to 1909, Dawson's contact was seemingly sporadic; there is only one letter in 1903, a request for Woodward to examine some material; then in 1907 a single letter regretting Woodward's failure to attend a party at his new home at Castle Lodge in Lewes. After 1909, however, the correspondence becomes regular. Second, they provide information on Dawson's movements and activities in the period immediately preceding the events at Piltdown, early in the spring of 1912. And third, they throw some light on his association with other individuals, some of whom were later involved in the Piltdown episode. Of particular interest is his developing relationship with the French Jesuit novice and then amateur palaeontologist, Pierre Teilhard de Chardin (1881-1955)[12]. Later, in the summer of 1913, Teilhard was to discover at the Piltdown pit a canine tooth which proved to be crucial to the resolution of a debate that had arisen over the accuracy of Woodward's reconstruction of the Piltdown skull.

NOTES

[1] See particularly Arthur Keith's foreward to Woodward's posthumous Piltdown text *The Earliest Englishman* (1948: ix-xiii), and his *An Autobiography* (1950: 328-329, 654). See also the various obituary notices in: *The Times* (1916) August 11, p 3b; *The Manchester Guardian* (1916) August 11; *The Morning Post* (London) (1916) August 11, p 4g; *The British Medical Journal* (1916) August 19, p 265. For an impression of Dawson's stature prior to Piltdown, see comments by the palaeontologist Henry Woodward *et al.* appended to Woodward (1911: 68).

[2] Dawson's election to the Geological Society coincided with that of Woodward's, see Weiner (1955:83).

[3] For further details on these and related discoveries, see Seward (1911) and Dawson's 1911 correspondence with Woodward.

[4] See DF 100/26 Dawson 28 March (Letter 1.1.1), and note entitled "Piltdown skull anniversary" by the editor [Arthur Beckett] of the *Sussex County Magazine*, in column "Country Notes" (1941), Vol 15, p 243.

[5] Dawson is mentioned as such in Straker's text on *Wealden Iron* (1931).

[6] For details of Woodward's early years see the unpublished manuscript "Early Memories of Arthur Smith Woodward", transcribed by Lady Woodward (DF 114).

[7] Prior to 1880 the Governors of Macclesfield Grammar School had awarded scholarships to Oxford and Cambridge, but in that year it was decided to add a scholarship to Manchester. The first award was made to Woodward. It is not known to what extent Dawkins' presence at Manchester prompted Woodward's decision to go there, rather than to Oxford or Cambridge (see Spencer 1990).

[8] As indicated by the following letter Dawkins supported Woodward's ambition: "I have great pleasure in testifying that you are a most energetic student of nature, and that you were the best of the students in Geology and Palaeontology of your year in the College. If you succeed in being chosen for the post which you desire, I am sure that you will do honour to the choice . . . " (DF 114 Dawkins 20 April 1882).

[9] Woodward's academic achievements prior to 1887 consisted of a first class pass in the London University matriculation examination, and a first in the Intermediate B.Sc. of London University. He was also the recipient in 1886 of a prize for "comparative anatomy and biology" awarded by King's College.

[10] According to William Dickson Lang (1878-1966), former Keeper of Geology (1928- 1938), this work stands out "not only as a monument of meticulous accuracy, of intense research, but also as a source of many other ichthyological publications." Cited in Stearn (1981: 235).

[11] With few exceptions (see 4.1.37) Woodward's correspondence with Dawson has not survived (see Note C: 6.3.4).

[12] A Jesuit's training is a lengthy process. In Teilhard's case he entered the order in 1898 at Aix-en-Provence. From 1902-1905 he was stationed in Jersey, followed by a stint in Egypt (1905-1908) and his sojourn at Ore House, Hastings, where he completed his training. He was ordained on 24 August 1911 (Cuénot 1965:11).

CORRESPONDENCE

1.1.1 DF 100/26 Dawson 28 March 1909

(a) Charles Dawson (1864-1916); (b) handwritten letter to Woodward on printed stationery: "The Castle Lodge, Lewes"; (c) –.

This letter was a response to Woodward's reply to an earlier inquiry made by Dawson regarding some mammoth bones.

. . . I go to Hastings [A] occasionally and am on the Museum Committee there but the introduction of foreign road metal has rather curtailed our chances of much increasing our stock of bones. I have several good ones by me, small bones chiefly Iguanodon; and someday if you think of setting up I. Hollingtonensis, I will pack them up for you, but I have been waiting for the big "find" which never seems to come along. . . . . The Natural Gas site goes on undiminished at Heathfield [B] but no one has yet attempted to fathom its source and the [Gas] Company which took it up did it a bad turn and now, beyond the [railway] station lamps being lit by it, it is allowed to waste . . . [C] I hope to meet you soon but have been very busy professionally lately. Don't forget to look us up when this way.

[A] See 1.1.2-1.1.4 and 1.1.17-18.

[B] See footnote 4, and Dawson (1897, 1898a, 1898b).

[C] This appears to be a tangential reference to Dawson's on-going battle with the geochemist John Th. Hewitt (1868-1955) over the nature and source of the Heathfield gas deposit (see Hewitt (1898). For further details on Hewitt and this debate, see Costello (1985) and Daniel (1986). Peter Costello has argued that that it was this animosity between Dawson and Hewitt that led the latter to fabricate the Piltdown hoax (in conjunction with Samuel Woodhead) in an effort to humiliate Dawson. For further details on the Dawson-Woodhead connection, see Note C: 1.2.2, 1.2.22 and Note A: 2.3.49. See Letter 1.1.11 for further reference to the Heathfield gas deposit.

1.1.2 DF 100/26 Dawson 4 April 1909

(a) Charles Dawson (1864-1916); (b) extract of handwritten letter to Woodward, on printed stationery: "The Castle Lodge, Lewes"; (c) annotated by Woodward: "8th".

We have got on the track of a Dinosaur (at Hastings), rather an extensive series of bones . . . At present we seem to be upon the pelvic region and I arrived in time to superintend getting out the sacrum but the mud was so awful that I could hardly see them well enough to judge what we had got; but I believe it is of the Iguanodon type . . .

The remainder of this letter is devoted to an explanation of difficulties attending the recovery of this specimen and asking if Woodward is interested in securing it for the Museum. As indicated by subsequent letters, Woodward was, and promptly arranged for the delivery of shipping boxes. The location of the site in question is identified in Letter 1.1.3: "The Old Roar Quarry, Silverhill, Hastings." It is believed that it was at this quarry, and during the recovery operation of the above specimen, that Dawson first met Teilhard de Chardin. See Weiner's (1955: 90) account of this meeting, as well as notes appended to 1.1.10.

1.1.3 DF 100/26 Dawson 26 May 1909

(a) Charles Dawson (1864-1916); (b) extract of handwritten letter to Woodward, on printed stationery: "The Castle Lodge, Lewes"; (c) annotated by Woodward: "27th".

The opening portion of this letter deals with the business of recovering the dinosaur remains from Roar Quarry in Hastings, see 1.1.2.

The foreman of the quarry [Mr. W. Taylor] is in distress about boxes, so will you send him three large boxes by goods train and (prepaid) suitable for carrying fossil bones! They are finding more bones, but not so freely and I fear not so many . . .
I am interested in what you say about Crowborough and the the footprints [A] . . . I shall be very pleased to make Sir A. Conan Doyles acquaintance. If I am in Crowborough first I will call on him or if he comes to Lewes I hope he will come and see me. Tell him if you write that I am Capt. F.J.M. Postlethwaites's stepfather, as he knows him [B].

[A] Referring to the physician and well-known novelist, Sir Arthur Conan Doyle (1859-1930) who evidently had reported to Woodward the discovery of dinosaur footprints near his home in Crowborough, Sussex. This incident is of interest for several reasons. First, because Conan Doyle has been implicated as the forger of the Piltdown remains (Winslow & Meyer 1983). Second, as this letter indicates Dawson had not yet met the illustrious author. And third, later in 1911, another rumour was circulated (1.1.36), again emanating from Conan Doyle, regarding the discovery of a complete Iguanodon skeleton in Crowborough.

[B] Postlethwaite was the son of Hélène Postlethwaite, whom Dawson married in 1905, see notes appended to 1.2.9.

1.1.4 DF 100/26 Dawson 26 May 1909

(a) Charles Dawson (1864-1916); (b) handwritten letter to Woodward, on printed stationery: "The Castle Lodge, Lewes"; (c) –.

This brief letter, written after 1.1.3, reports on the discovery of another Iguanodon specimen at the Roar Quarry, which Dawson said was similar to *Iguanodon dawsoni* (Lydekker).

1.1.5 DF 100/26 Dawson 13 June 1909

(a) Charles Dawson (1864-1916); (b) handwritten letter to Woodward, on printed stationery: "The Castle Lodge, Lewes"; (c) –.

This communication is concerned with Dawson's handling of a dispute at the Roar Quarry regarding payment of the quarrymen who had been responsible for discovering the above Iguanodon remains.

You will be wondering what has happened to your bones and cases. I was over there [at the quarry] again yesterday and assisted in getting out what will be the last of them for a little time, and I hope 5 cases will go off to you next Tuesday . . . I rather expect to be in Town on Wednesday so I will call and see if all has arrived . . . I have had some trouble in dealing with the contractor who works the quarry; an old quarryman himself and who still retains a thirst, for he claims a share in the proceeds. The quarrymen are very indignant about it . . . I have been trying to settle things and hope it is now all right and it is rather important that it should be so for the future.

1.1.6 DF 100/26 Dawson 13 July 1909

(a) Charles Dawson (1864-1916); (b) handwritten letter to Woodward, on printed stationery: "Town Hall Chambers, Uckfield"; (c) annotated by Woodward: "15th".

A brief covering letter accompanying a specimen of fish caught in a "local" pond (? Piltdown) which Dawson thought was unusual and might interest Woodward.

1.1.7 DF 100/26 Dawson, July 25, 1909

(a) Charles Dawson (1864-1916); (b) handwritten letter to Woodward, on printed stationery: "The Castle Lodge, Lewes"; (c) annotated by Woodward: "Retd. Others Oct.26th"

A short note evidently accompanying a number of specimens sent to Woodward, that included one molar reminiscent of *Plagiaulax*.

1.1.8 DF 100/26 Dawson 25 October 1909

(a) Charles Dawson (1864-1916); (b) handwritten letter to Woodward, on printed stationery: "Town Hall Chambers, Uckfield"; (c) annotated by Woodward: "Retd. 26th".

The primary objective of this letter was to inform Woodward of the shipment of "a box of miscellaneous specimens" from the Roar Quarry. Later in the letter, Dawson informs Woodward that he has "some friends" assisting him in his search for Wealden fossils. It is believed that these friends are Teilhard de Chardin and his companion Félix Pelletier, see 1.1.10 for further details.

1.1.9 DF 100/26 Dawson 4 December 1909

(a) Charles Dawson (1864-1916); (b) handwritten letter to Woodward, on printed stationery:

"The Castle Lodge, Lewes"; (c) annotated by Woodward: "8th ackn!" Retd. 14th."

A brief covering note to an unspecified number of Wealden fossils submitted to Woodward for examination. It is believed that these specimens are the subject of the next communication.

1.1.10 DF 100/28 Dawson 15 January 1910

(a) Charles Dawson (1864-1916); (b) handwritten letter to Woodward, on printed stationery: "The Castle Lodge, Lewes"; (c) –.

This letter is of particular interest because it provides the first direct mention by name of Dawson's developing relationship with Pierre Teilhard de Chardin (1881-1955).

. . . I am very glad to hear that the Fairlight tooth [A] is going to turn out so interesting and I have written to my friends at Hastings to tell them about it and cheer them along to fresh onslaughts.

I think you had better say in the descriptive note that "this specimen (the Dipriodon) was discovered by Messieurs P. Teilhard de Chardin and Felix Pelletier [B] who have been rendering Mr. Ch. Dawson great assistance in collecting specimens for the British Museum, especially by systematic search in the bone-beds of the Hastings Beds for smaller palaeontological specimens." Or words to that effect [C]. The horizon may be described as a bone-bed near the base of the Ashdown Sands at Fairlight Cliffs, near Hastings . . . I hope you will make an excursion with me someday to this bed, when the circumstances warrant!

Perhaps you can help us by sending some sort of solution for preserving the specimens when they are just found. The specimens have a way of scaling and cracking on drying, especially when they occur on the weathered edges of those blocks exposed to the sea salt. We have several times lost specimens . . . [D]

I hope to come and see you soon and all what you have done. With best wishes for a happy new year to you all.

[A] For further information on the Fairlight Clays, see Edmunds (1935).

[B] From all indications Pelletier was one of several people who were assigned to accompany Teilhard on his occasional nature rambles into the district surrounding Ore House in Hastings. According to Teilhard's biographer, Cuénot (1965: 7), Pelletier was "a graduate in chemistry and mineralogy" and that since 1904 the two men had been frequent companions and had collaborated together in a "preliminary geological and mineralogical note of the island [of Jersey]." Teilhard had been a junior novice on Jersey from 1902 until his departure for Cairo in September, 1905. Evidently his relationship with Pelletier was renewed in Hastings in 1909, at which time they presumably resolved to write the above report which was published in the Jersey Society's annual bulletin of 1910 (Cuénot 1965:7). According to Teilhard's "Letters from Hastings 1908-1912" it appears that he and Dawson first met in May while he (in the company of Félix Pelletier) was looking for fossils. In a letter dated 31 May, 1909, Teilhard wrote to his parents:

In the past two weeks, I've become acquainted with Charles Dawson, a geologist in the area. It happened under amusing circumstances. While visiting a quarry close by, we [presumably referring to Pelletier] were surprised to see the "manager" take on an understanding attitude when we discussed fossils with him. He had just discovered an enormous pelvis bone from an iguanodon [see 1.1.2] and was very anxious to talk about it. I knew then that it was almost a whole iguanodon being found piece by piece, and the fragments . . . are piling up one by one in a crate destined for the British Museum. Mr. Dawson always arrived when we were on the grounds and immediately [sic], he would come over to us full of joy and say, "Geologists?" (Letter No 14, in Teilhard (1965) 1968: 47-48 [see Note E]),

Although it remains unclear how often and when Teilhard met with Dawson in the remaining months of 1909, it appears that they occasionally exchanged letters (see Teilhard

(1965) 1968: 53, Letter No 16, dated 1 July, 1909 [see Note E]) and that Dawson visited Teilhard in July (1.1.29) and December (1.1.23). Also, it should be noted that Pelletier was not Teilhard's only companion. As indicated in notes to 1.1.29, he occasionally went on excursions with a Father de Bélinay whom he had apparently known since his time in Egypt (see 1.1.29).

[C] Woodward's communication to the Geological Society read as follows: "Mr. Charles Dawson, F.S.A., F.G.S., has obtained two imperfect molars apparently of *Plagiaulax*, from the beds of grit in the Wealden near Hastings; and his associates in the work of exploration, Messrs. P. Teilhard de Chardin and Félix Pelletier, have found a well-preserved multituberculate molar of the form named *Dipriodon* by Marsh" (1911: 67).

[D] Woodward apparently sent Dawson a supply of preservation fluid (potassium dichromate solution) prepared by Frank Orwell Barlow (1880-1951), a technician in the Geological Department of the Museum. For further information on Barlow see Note B: 1.2.23.

[E] Teilhard's letters from the Hastings and Paris period (1908-1914) were published in 1965 (French edition). The English translation of this volume became available in 1967 and 1968. The former collection is composed primarily of letters from the Paris period, 1912-1914, while the latter contains letters essentially from the Hastings period. Unless otherwise stated, the letters in this catalogue are from the 1967 or 1968 English editions.

1.1.11 DF 100/28 Dawson 15 February 1910

(a) Charles Dawson (1864-1916); (b) handwritten letter to Woodward, on printed stationery: "Town Hall Chambers, Uckfield"; (c) annotated by Woodward: "16th. Fossils retd. personally Ap. 13th. 1910".

This letter deals with a number of unconnected issues, beginning with the matter of a number of fossils (from the "Wealden Purbecks of Netherfield, Sussex") he had sent Woodward under separate cover for identification. For further details on this site, see Dawson (1898c). He then goes on to thank Woodward for assisting him in a "private matter" (details of which are not given), noting that: ". . . I have no definite news, but believe it is receiving influential support, nous verrons!" In the last paragraph he makes mention of new developments on the Heathfield gas front [see 1.1.1], noting that a syndicate has been formed (with Dawson being hired as a "consultant") and that explorative drilling is about to commence.

1.1.12 DF 100/28 Dawson 21 February 1910

(a) Charles Darwin (1864-1916); (b) handwritten letter to Woodward, on printed stationery: "The Castle Lodge, Lewes"; (c) annotated by Woodward: "26th Thanks".

A brief note accompanying photograph of *Iguanodon* ilia; the photograph is not in the collection.

1.1.13 DF 100/28 Dawson 6 March 1910

(a) Charles Dawson (1864-1916); (b) handwritten letter to Woodward, on printed stationery: "The Castle Lodge, Lewes"; (c) annotated by Woodward: "7th".

In this letter Dawson relays to Woodward news of the discovery of a cache of palaeolithic implements in a "deposit of Glacial Drift" at Northfleet [near Gravesend], Kent, and suggests: "If you have not heard of it I think you should make inquiries and see to it." See 1.1.15.

1.1.14 DF 100/28 Dawson 14 May 1910

(a) Charles Dawson (1864-1916); (b) handwritten letter to Woodward, on printed stationery: "The Castle Lodge, Lewes"; (c) annotated by Woodward: "21st."

On May 13, Dawson received a telegram [attached to Letter 1.1.14] from Mr Taylor at the Roar Quarry (Silverfield, near Hastings) informing him that more bones had been found. Dawson's letter of May 14, following an urgent visit to Roar Quarry, confirms the recovery of further *Iguanodon* remains. The letter ends: "I am glad that the season has opened so well . . ."

1.1.15 DF 100/28 Dawson 21 May 1910

(a) Charles Dawson (1864-1916); (b) handwritten letter to Woodward, on printed stationery: "The Castle Lodge, Lewes"; (c) annotated by Woodward: "Ack! 24th".

This communication notes Woodward's recent visit to the Middle Purbeck Beds of Swanage (Kent), where he found a maxilla of *Triconodon*. Woodward (1912) later described this visit and the specimen in the *Proc Geol Assoc*. This excursion, however, seems unrelated to Dawson's mention in an earlier letter (1.1.13) to the discovery of palaeolithic implements in the vicinity of Northfleet (Kent). The remainder of the letter is concerned with the recovery of the *Iguanodon* remains at the Roar Quarry, see 1.1.14.

1.1.16 DF 100/28 Dawson 24 May 1910

(a) Charles Dawson (1864-1916); (b) handwritten letter to Woodward, on printed stationery: "The Castle Lodge, Lewes"; (c) annotated by Woodward: "27th".

A brief note indicating that he had been searching for Wealden mammals in a "bone-bed (Wadhurst Clay) at Uckfield," and evidently without much success.

1.1.17 DF 100/28 Dawson 27 May 1910

(a) Charles Dawson (1864-1916); (b) handwritten note to Woodward, on plain stationery: "The Castle Lodge, Lewes"; (c) annotated by Woodward: "Ackn. 31st".

A note referring to his visit (on May 27) to Roar Quarry and that some of the bones found on May 13 (see 1.1.14 and 1.1.15) had been shipped.

1.1.18 DF 100/28 Dawson 31 May 1910

(a) Charles Dawson (1864-1916); (b) handwritten note to Woodward, on plain stationery: "The Castle Lodge, Lewes"; (c) annotated by Woodward: "June 2nd".

A further brief note on additional specimens retrieved from Roar Quarry, which Dawson believed would interest Woodward.

1.1.19 DF 100/28 Dawson 8 June 1910

(a) Charles Dawson (1864-1916); (b) handwritten letter on printed stationery: "Town Hall Chambers, Uckfield"; (c) annotated by Woodward: "9th. Asked whether from bottom of [word unclear: ? strike]".

A brief note accompanying a specimen of "globular lightning" found near Uckfield, which Dawson felt Woodward might be interested in.

1.1.20 DF 100/28 Dawson 13 June 1910:

(a) Charles Dawson (1864-1916); (b) handwritten letter to Woodward, on printed stationery: "The Castle Lodge, Lewes"; (c) annotated by Woodward: "21st".

Another brief note relating to further recovery of bones from the Roar Quarry. Accompanying this note, Dawson apparently sent a collection of "cigarette cards" for Woodward's son, see 1.2.20.

1.1.21 DF 100/28 Dawson 10 July 1910

(a) Charles Dawson (1864-1916); (b) handwritten letter to Woodward, on printed stationery: "The Castle Lodge, Lewes"; (c) –.

Before you go off on your annual tour I think I had better write to you for the return of some tuberculated bits of bone . . . and tooth [fossil fish] . . . (I believe) in a glass tubes. They will be of no value to you and my two friends at Hastings would be glad to have them back [A]. . .
   I have been very busy lately attending to the last details of my book on Hastings Castle etc (2 vols) which is published tomorrow (Monday). I am glad it is off my hands [B]. . .

[A] A reference to Teilhard de Chardin and Félix Pelletier.

[B] This reference is of interest since the book, published by Constable (London), bears the date 1909! However, according to *The English Catalogue of Books* Volume VIII (January 1906-December 1910), page 335, Dawson's book was not published until July 1910. The reason for the delay in publication is not known.

1.1.22 DF 100/28 Dawson 7 September 1910

(a) Charles Dawson (1864-1916); (b) handwritten letter to Woodward, on printed stationery: "Town Hall Chambers, Uckfield"; (c) annotated by Woodward: "Get back Mammal book 14.9.10" [A].

This letter is concerned largely with Woodward's pending field trip to Spain, and is of interest since it supports the view that while Dawson had known Woodward for some time, his familiarity with the latter was quite recent. For example he does not seem to have been aware of the fact that Woodward had visited Spain before, namely in 1902, and again in 1905. In 1910 Woodward went back to Tarrega which he had visited in 1905 (see Cooper 1945).

[A] The title of the book he had loaned to Dawson is not known.

1.1.23 DF 100/28 Dawson 16 December 1910

(a) Charles Dawson (1864-1916); (b) handwritten letter to Woodward on printed stationery: "The Castle Lodge, Lewes"; (c) annotated by Woodward: "17th".

. . . I am going down to Hastings to see my fossil hunters during Xmas . . . They were rather disappointed at having no more definite news [about their fossils] . . . and I think if you did something . . . it would assist me in reassuring them for the Museum.

To what extent, if any, Dawson was using Teilhard and Pelletier as an excuse to secure a firm commitment from Woodward to report on the Wealden fossils in question is not clear. However, as indicated by Letter 1.1.24, Dawson was anxious about the matter.

1.1.24 DF 100/30 Dawson 19 January 1911

(a) Charles Dawson (1864-1916); (b) handwritten letter to Woodward, on printed stationery:

"The Castle Lodge, Lewes"; (c) annotated by Woodward: "21st. 'broken ?'".

After dealing with a problem related to a crumbling specimen, Dawson writes: "I send you the mammal tooth and think that Mr. Barlow's solution [see Note D: 1.1.10] will act very well." Following this Dawson adds: " Please arrange to get a few "separates" [reprints] for the note when published for my friend's edification" (see Woodward 1911). From this it is evident that Woodward had responded positively to Dawson's appeal in 1.1.23.

1.1.25 DF 100/30 Dawson 22 January 1911

(a) Charles Dawson (1864-1916); (b) handwritten letter to Woodward, on printed stationery: "The Castle Lodge, Lewes"; (c) annotated by Woodward: "24th"

This short note deals with the mammalian tooth mentioned in 1.1.24, which Dawson sent to Woodward for examination.

1.1.26 DF 100/30 Dawson 27 January 1911

(a) Charles Dawson (1864-1916); (b) handwritten letter using stationery of the "Hans Crescent Hotel, Belgravia, London". This printed address is deleted, and written above is "The Castle Lodge, Lewes"; (c) annotated by Woodward: "28th"

More about the above mammalian tooth.

1.1.27 DF 100/30 Dawson 29 January 1911

(a) Charles Dawson (1864-1916); (b) handwritten letter to Woodward, on printed stationery: "The Castle Lodge, Lewes"; (c) –.

This letter informs Woodward that the Roar Quarry in Hastings has yielded the remains of a number of fossil fish, namely *Lepidotus*. While aware that Woodward is now probably "full up with Lepidotus," he suggest that it would be "unadvisable" to abandon the specimens and "disappoint" the quarrymen, and perhaps thereby risk "draw[ing] other people to the spot."

1.1.28 DF 100/30 Dawson February 1911

(a) Charles Dawson (1864-1916); (b) undated letter (see Woodward's annotation) and handwritten on stationery of "Law Society's Hall, Chancery Lane, London." This printed address has been deleted, and written above is "The Castle Lodge, Lewes"; (c) annotated by Woodward: "Feb. 10th 1911".

On Sunday I expect to be seeing my friends the priests at Hastings and should like to return to them the specimens of reptile teeth which you have . . . I should be glad if you would post them to me in a wooden box.

In a letter to his parents (Letter No 43, dated February 16, 1911, in Teilhard (1965) 1968: 134), Teilhard indicates that this meeting took place. In this letter Teilhard writes:

Last Sunday, Mr. Dawson, my geologist friend, paid me a visit. In regard to our offer to send the British Museum our last fern (imprinted in a block of about 12 kilograms) he said he would take the responsibility of carrying it, and left here carrying it under his arm, with vigor at that."

1.1.29 DF 100/30 Dawson 14 March 1911

(a) Charles Dawson (1864-1916); (b) handwritten note to Woodward, on plain stationery: "The Castle Lodge, Lewes"; (c) annotated by Woodward: "15th Yes"

This note is in reference to photograph(s) believed to have been taken by Dawson of *Iguanodon* footprints. As indicated by 2.3.5, Dawson possessed a camera and facilities for developing his own pictures. He asks Woodward if the footprints are deserving of preservation. The photograph in question is not in the collection. It is conjectured that these photographs were of footprints discovered by Teilhard and Pelletier. In a letter written to his parents, dated 25 July 1909 (Letter No 18, in Teilhard (1965) 1968: 58), Teilhard writes:

Thursday, I took my new friend, Dr. Dawson [sic], the geologist to the cliffs to show him the iguanodon tracks. So high was the tide, and so violent the wind, that the expedition was heroic. Mr. Dawson isn't very used to the rocks, and both Father de Bélinay and I had to help him over the obstacles. I had all the trouble in the world rescuing his hat from the ditch. Finally, it was decided not to remove the prints that weren't clear enough . . .

On this occasion, Dawson is also said to have requested a supply of small crocodile teeth, which Teilhard reports he dutifully gave Dawson the next Tuesday (Letter No 18, *Ibid*). The location of the above site is not known. It is conjectured that it might be this site or another Teilhard had shown Dawson which led to the Dawson-Woodward excursion mentioned in Letter 1.2.1.

1.1.30 DF 100/30 Dawson 24 March 1911

(a) Charles Dawson (1864-1916); (b) handwritten letter to Woodward, on printed stationery: "The Castle Lodge, Lewes"; (c) –.

This communication refers to the *Dipriodon* specimen found by Teilhard and Pelletier. Dawson asks if these could be returned: ". . . for the present, as my friends would like to have it till their visit to England is concluded." Evidently a request emanating from Dawson's meeting with Teilhard and Pelletier in mid February (see 1.1.29). Dawson concludes with a reference to Woodward's pending trip to Turkey [see Note A: 1.1.31].

1.1.31 DF 100/30 Dawson 13 May 1911

(a) Charles Dawson (1864-1916); (b) handwritten letter to Woodward, on printed stationery: "The Castle Lodge, Lewes"; (c) annotated by Woodward: "15th"

This letter provides some insight into Dawson's earlier activities, as well as his familiarity and knowledge of local palaeontological activities.

I am glad you have returned intact from Constantinople [A].

The "Crowhurst Iguanodon" story which you asked about, I suppose has its origin in a large series of fossil bones (mostly Iguanodon) found in a small quarry adjoining the first bridge over the railway, going towards Hastings (along the railway) from Battle.

The quarry was only open a short time but an unusually large number of bones were found about the years 1885-87. The late Mr. Lambert of Telham Court, Battle wrote Dr. H[enry] Woodward about them and suggested that the Brit[ish]. Mus[eum]. should send someone to look after the finds, but as he had no one else available and Mr. Lambert did not take sufficient interest in it, most of the bones were lost and a very promising series unfortunately. Dr. Woodward told me about it but I could not leave London at the time, but when I returned to Hastings in 1887 I visited the quarry several times but found that most of the bones had been dispensed and no great number were then being found [B].

There was a wild story about the discovery of a whole Iguanodon at Crowborough the other day, but it turned out to be untrue and due to the fancy of someone who had been listening to Conan Doyle's [word unclear] on his finds of footprints [C] and the description of the animal, or what he remembered of it, after your visit. Anyhow it brought the poor Curator of the Hastings Museum up to Crowborough on a bicycle at moments notice – On his arrival he was shown a rock supposed to have a resemblance to a curled up Kangaroo, understood to be a type of Iguanodon! [D]

[A] A reference to Woodward's recent field trip to Turkey, where he examined a number of collections of fossil fishes, and secured for the Museum a number of Devonian specimens.

[B] According to Weiner (1955: 84), when Dawson was articled to F.A. Langham's law firm in 1880, he had "spent some years in London at the head office, then went in 1890 to a branch at Uckfield . . ." On the basis of Letter 1.1.31 it would seem that Dawson was in London from at least 1885 on through into 1887, and thereafter at Hastings until 1890 when he moved to the Uckfield branch, where he subsequently became a partner in the firm.

[C] See 1.1.3.

[D] The Curator at that time was W. Ruskin Butterfield (1872-1935), an ornithologist by inclination, and a known friend of Dawson's. Later, Dawson had an opportunity to view this "fossil" himself when he visited Conan Doyle at his home, see 1.1.36.

1.1.32 DF 100/30 Dawson 25 July 1911

(a) Charles Dawson (1864-1914); (b) handwritten letter to Woodward, on printed stationery: "Town Hall Chambers, Uckfield"; (c) annotated by Woodward: "28th acknd. by postcard."

This letter relates details of further finds made at the Roar Quarry. The specimens included a "complete" *Iguanodon* tarsal bone which Dawson believed belonged to the same individual recovered earlier (see 1.1.14), and remains of a new species of *Lepidotus*.

1.1.33 DF 100/30 Dawson 11 November 1911

(a) Charles Dawson (1864-1916); (b) handwritten letter to Woodward, on printed stationery: "The Castle Lodge, Lewes"; (c) annotated by Woodward: "Nov. 17th".

This letter notes that Seward (Note F: 1.2.1) is interested in seeing the fossil Wealden plants collected by Teilhard and Pelletier from the Fairlight Clays. He also notes that he is anxious to photograph the *Lepidotus* specimen found earlier in the season, before it is placed in the Museum's collections.

1.1.34 DF 100/30 Dawson 13 November 1911

(a) Charles Dawson (1864-1916); (b) handwritten letter to Woodward, on plain stationery: "Uckfield"; (c) annotated by Woodward: "Nov. 17th"

Note on a plaster cast of *Iguanodon* footprint, see Letter 1.1.29.

1.1.35 DF 100/30 Dawson 21 November 1911

(a) Charles Dawson (1864-1914); (b) handwritten letter to Woodward, on printed stationery: "Town Hall Chambers, Uckfield"; (c) annotated by Woodward: "Mr. Thomas [A] kindly tell me how to reply 23.11.11."

A brief note indicating his intention of calling at Museum to photograph the *Lepidotus* found earlier in the year, see 1.1.33.

[A]: Probably Michael Rogers Oldfield Thomas (1858-1929) in the Museum's Department of Zoology.

1.1.36 DF 100/30 Dawson 30 November 1911

(a) Charles Dawson (1864-1916); (b) handwritten letter to Woodward, on printed stationery: "The Castle Lodge, Lewes"; (c) –.

This letter relates details of a visit to Sir Arthur Conan Doyle's home in Crowborough,

Sussex. How this invitation came about is not known, but possibly related to events mentioned in Letter 1.1.31.

My wife and I went to lunch with the Conan Doyles at Crowborough today and to see the great fossil! [A].

I regret to say it was a mere concretion of oxide of iron and sand. Sir Conan and the ladies pointed out several "striking resemblances" to the "carcasses" of various animals, all ultimately destructive! [B].

But the visit was not altogether lost for as I was trying to draw Sir Conan away from the hope of finding much in the sandstone and directing his attention to the drift deposits above I espied a beautiful flint arrowhead embedded, and in view of us all.

Subsequently we found washed flints; and so I started him off on a new and I hope more fruitful enterprise.

I was so sorry at his disappointment – he is such a good fellow – but the neo-[lithic] find revived him a lot. Of course, I have given him the arrowhead.

Do not trouble to answer this. I hope to get something better worth your attention someday [C].

[A] Evidently is a reference to the rock Butterfield said resembled a "curled-up Kangaroo, see 1.1.31.

[B] This incident does not reflect well upon the notion that Doyle had an informed interest in palaeontology, and the perpetrator of the Piltdown hoax, see Note A: 1.1.3. It does, however, reinforce the view that he was extremely gullible.

[C] To those scholars who are convinced of Dawson's involvement in the forgery this sentence is regarded as being highly significant.

1.1.37 DF 100/30 Dawson 23 December 1911

(a) Charles Dawson (1864-1916); (b) handwritten letter to Woodward, on stationery of the "Lansdown Grove Hotel, Bath [Somerset]"; (c) annotated by Woodward: "28th."

In this letter, Dawson relates details of a "hitherto unidentified tooth" in the C. Moore Collection at the Literary Institute in Bath (Somerset), and notes that he had made arrangements for a cast of the tooth and related details to be sent directly to Woodward. As indicated by 2.3.70, Dawson invariably spent Christmas with his "parson Brother" [Rev. H.L. Dawson] in Bath.

1.2 1912: The Piltdown Site and Events Leading to The Unveiling of *Eoanthropus dawsoni*

From all indications in the years immediately preceding 1912, Charles Dawson's fossil-hunting activities in the neighbourhood of Uckfield were intensified by the discovery of human cranial fragments in a gravel pit located on the estate of Barkham Manor in the parish of Piltdown.

When Dawson and Woodward commenced their exploration of this gravel pit in 1912, it is important to note that there had been no formal geological survey of the superficial deposits of the Wealden district (see White 1925). Thus, while such deposits were known to be widely distributed throughout the region, their geologic significance was unclear. By and large, they were considered to be either "plateau" or "river" gravels. The former occurring usually about 300-ft above sea-level, while the latter are found at lower elevations. The gravel deposits at Piltdown that had reportedly yielded the fossil hominid and faunal remains fall into this latter category. They are situated on a well-defined plateau, dissected by two rivers, the Ouse (east) and the Uckfield (west), that meet several miles south of Piltdown (Fig 1.2). Dawson had estimated that the elevation of the gravel terrace at Piltdown was about 80-ft, and thereby equivalent to the 100-ft terraces of the Thames valley and other rivers of Europe. The work of the Geological Survey in 1924 (see White 1925), however, revealed that the true elevation of this terrace was well below the 50-ft mark, which supported the later view that the deposit had undergone geologic reconstruction at the close rather than the beginning of the Pleistocene.

The gravel terrace at Piltdown is shallow, occurring only a few inches from the surface. This stratum overlays the hard yellow sandstone of the Tunbridge Wells Sands (Hastings Beds). For the most part, these gravels are composed of dark-brown Wealden ironstone pebbles that are derived from the underlying Hastings Beds. Not infrequently, however, brown flints are also found in such deposits. These flints originate from the Chalk formations that encircle the Weald. Often, and particularly in horizons near the base of these deposits, the constituent materials are cemented together by iron oxide forming an extremely hard matrix; hence the mention in the published reports of the employment of pickaxes. It is from this basal stratum that the Piltdown "fossil remains" were supposedly extracted.

In the official account of the discoveries made at the Piltdown gravel pit, published in the *Quarterly Journal of the Geological Society of London*, Dawson stated that his interest in the site had been aroused some years prior to 1912:

Several years ago I was walking along a farm-road close to Piltdown Common, Fletching (Sussex), when I noticed that the road had been mended with some peculiar brown flints not usual in the district. On enquiry I was astonished to learn that they were dug from a gravel-bed on the farm [Barkham Manor], and shortly afterwards I visited the place, where the two labourers were at work digging the gravel for small repairs to the roads. As this excavation was situated about 4 miles north of the limit where the occurrence of flints overlying the Wealden strata is recorded, I was much interested, and made a close examination of the bed. I asked the workmen if they had found bones or other fossils there. As they did not appear to have noticed anything of the sort, I urged them to preserve anything they might find. Upon one of my subsequent visits to the pit, one of the men handed me a small portion of an unusually thick human parietal bone. I immediately made a search, but could find nothing more, nor had the men noticed anything else.

It was not until some years later, in the autumn of 1911, on a visit to the spot, that I picked up, among the rain-washed spoil-heaps of the gravel-pit, another and larger piece belonging to the frontal region of the same skull, including a portion of the left superciliary ridge. As I had examined a cast of the Heidelberg jaw, it occurred to me that the proportions of this skull were similar to those of the specimen. I accordingly took it to Dr. A. Smith Woodward at the British Museum (Natural History) for comparison and determination. He was immediately impressed with the importance of the discovery, and we decided to employ labour and to make a systematic search among the spoil-heaps and gravel, as soon as the floods had abated; for the gravel-pit is more or less under water during five or six months of the year. We accordingly gave up as much time as we could spare since last spring (1912), and completely turned over and sifted what spoil-material remained; we also dug up and sifted such portions of the gravel as had been left undisturbed by the workmen" (Dawson & Woodward, 1913a: 117-118).

There are, however, some discrepancies between this account and what Dawson is reported to have said at the meeting of the Geological Society of London on the evening of 18 December 1912. According to the various newspapers that covered the story, Dawson is quoted as saying that he was first handed a fragment of a human cranium "four years ago." And more particularly, that this and subsequent fragments constituted the remains of a skull which had been accidently broken and then discarded by labourers working at the gravel pit[1], because to them it looked like a "cocoa-nut." The original notes to his portion of the Geological Society paper, while making no mention of date, do provide confirmation of the "coconut" story. Under the heading "Brief Story of Discovery" he writes:

Human skull found and broken by workmen. Hence subsequent digging both in spoil-material and in bottom layer of gravel left untouched by them" (DF 116/16 [14]).

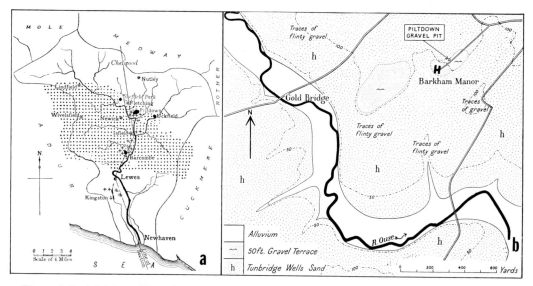

Figure 1.2: (a) Map of East Sussex, showing the location of Piltdown in relation to Lewes and the Sussex coast. The stippled area indicates the distribution of iron-stained flints, and (+) flint-bearing gravels. The Piltdown II remains (see Section 4) were thought to have been recovered from a site in "Sheffield Park", a few miles north of Piltdown. The site at which the so called Barcombe Mills skull was supposedly found (2.3.21; 5.2.10) is also uncertain (see Weiner 1955 and Spencer 1990). (b) Geology of the Piltdown district (based on Edmunds in Weiner et al. 1955:274).

Further support for this comes from the dentist, Arthur Underwood in a letter to Woodward (1.3.1) in which details of the December 18th meeting are recounted. Dawson's reasons for omitting the "coconut story" from the official report are no longer clear, but whatever they might have been, no significance was attached to the decision at the time. Now, in light of the knowledge that the remains are bogus, this omission, compounded with the palpable vagueness of his recounting of the chronology of events has served to reinforce the case against him as a possible suspect in the forgery. But be this as it may, it nevertheless appears that there is no major conflict in the general substance of his various accounts of the events prior to 1911. Correlating Dawson's various published accounts of these events with the testimony of other witnesses, it appears that farm labourers while working in the gravel pit at Barkham Manor, uncovered and accidently shattered a human skull, which they likened to a "cocoa-nut," and that two versions of this story exist (see fn 1). The evidence seems to favour the view that this event occurred in 1908 (Spencer 1990). Then, in the autumn of 1911, following further investigations at the pit, Dawson claims to have recovered a second, and larger cranial fragment. Impressed by the robusticity of these fragments and the apparent antiquity of the gravel deposit, Dawson then informed Woodward of his discoveries.

The surviving correspondence indicates that Woodward was first informed of Dawson's discovery on 14 February 1912[2]. Evidently impressed by what he saw, Woodward agreed to visit the site, and as a consequence it was decided that the pit warranted further investigation. Thus, throughout the summer of 1912, they worked at excavating and sifting through the earth previously removed from the gravel pit, assisted on occasions by a few trusted colleagues that included Teilhard de Chardin. This "first season" of digging was done mostly on weekends, with Woodward coming down from London and lodging either at the railway hotel in Uckfield or with Dawson at his home in Lewes. From all indications the cost of the excavations were shared by Dawson and Woodward. These labours yielded a further seven cranial fragments, plus the right half of a seemingly apelike jaw with two molars *in situ*, and a modest assortment of fossil animal bones and stone artifacts. (For further details on the assemblage, see Table 1.1).

Although all of this activity was supposedly conducted under a veil of secrecy, rumours of the "remarkable skull" found at Piltdown appear to have begun circulating by late September. It was not, however, until mid November that the story was finally picked up and reported in the national press, by which time arrangements had been made to present the full story before the Geological Society at Burlington House on Wednesday evening, 18 December 1912.

NOTES

[1]   Two versions of the "coconut" story appear in the newspapers. (I) Relates how Dawson is handed a fragment of the broken skull, and his subsequent efforts to retrieve the other discarded pieces. The second (II) reports that all of the fragments were discarded, and then goes on to tell of his efforts to recover them. Version I: *The Times* (1912) 19 Dec; *Daily Chronicle* (1912) 19 Dec; *The Globe* (1912) 19 Dec; *Sussex Daily News* (1912) 19 Dec; *Manchester Guardian* (1912) 19 Dec; and for version II, see *Westminster Gazette* (1912) 19 Dec; *Daily Graphic* (1912) 19-21 Dec; *East Anglian Times* (1912) 21 Dec; *Hastings and St.Leonards Observer* (1913) 1 Feb.

[2]   From all indications this is the first communication of 1912. There are, however, two letters which precede it, one dated 1 January, and the other 4 February 1912, but the contents of both strongly suggest the dates are incorrect. These letters, 2.1.1 and 2.1.4 respectively, are assumed to have been written in 1913, see text for further explanation.

CORRESPONDENCE

1.2.1 DF 100/32 Dawson 14 February 1912

(a) Charles Dawson (1864-1916); (b) handwritten letter to Woodward on printed stationery: "The Castle Lodge, Lewes"; (c) annotated by Woodward: "Feb 15th. Say £3 all". Underlining in original by Dawson.

I am afraid I have not kept account of expenditure but I do not think it has been much. I think our trip to Cliff End cost 25/- for carriage and the man, and I say £1 for the quarrymen. £2.5.0 total. (I have got some odds and ends to send you) [A]. It will pay for my photo of the fish [B].

   I have come across a very old Pleistocene (?) bed overlying the Hastings Bed between Uckfield and Crowborough which I think is going to be interesting. It has a lot of iron-stained flints in it, so I suppose it is the oldest known flint gravel in the Weald [C].

   I [*] portion of a human (?) skull [sic] which will rival H. Heidelbergensis [sic] in solidity [D].

   I have been very busy with work at the Office and have lost one of my French priests at Hastings who has gone to Jersey but hopes to be back for a short spell in July when I hope to visit Ore [House] with you to take your pick of their collection [E].

   We have not heard anything from Seward [F] about the plants [G]. Yes, C[onan] Doyle is writing a sort of Jules Verne book on some wonderful plateau in S. America with a lake which somehow got isolated from "Oolitic" [H] times and contained old the [sic] fauna and flora of that period, and was visited by the usual "Professor [I]." I hope someone has sorted out his fossils for him!

[*] Unclear word: either "thick" or "think". It is conjectured that Dawson had intended to say either "I have a thick …" or "I think I have a …"

[A] The purpose of this excursion and when it had been arranged is not known. It is conjectured that Dawson and Woodward may have visited Teilhard's site mentioned in 1.1.29, which from all indications is believed to be in the neighbourhood of Cliff End, a small coastal town situated a few miles east of Hastings. What is more important here is the fact that the two men had recently been together, and evidently Dawson had not (for some reason) broached the subject of the Piltdown site.

[B] Possibly related to the photograph mentioned in 1.1.35.

[C] See introduction to subsection 1.2 for a discussion of these formations. The lack of specificity regarding the actual location of the site is not considered highly significant in the circumstances.

[D] This refers to the Mauer mandible (i.e *Homo heidelbergensis* now known as *Homo erectus*) that was found by a workman at the Rösch sand pit at Mauer, six miles southeast of Heidelberg on 21 October 1907, and subsequently described in 1908 by the German anatomist, Otto Schoettensack (1850-1912). See Day (1986: 72-77) for a detailed description and evaluation of the specimen.

[E] This is a reference to Félix Pelletier, see 1.2.5.

[F] Albert Charles Seward (1863-1941), a palaeobotanist, who until 1906 was professor of botany at Cambridge. See 1.2.5 for Seward's response.

[G] Dawson is probably referring to the specimen he had received from Teilhard earlier in 1911, see 1.1.28.

[H] "Oolitic" is a geological term, that came into use during the late eighteenth century, and technically is used either to describe a series of fossiliferous rocks lying between either the Chalk and Wealden formations of S.E. England, or the Lias formations of S.W. England. Sometimes the term is employed with a more inclusive meaning that implies the whole series of limestones, sandstones, and clays to which these belong, as part of the Jurassic system.

[I] Recently it has been suggested by Winslow & Meyer (1983) that Conan Doyle had been responsible for the deception at Piltdown, and that a number of the characters appearing in his novel *The Lost World* are modeled closely on several of the central figures in the Piltdown episode. For example, they claim that Professor Summerless "bears a close resemblance" to Woodward, and that Professor Challenger is Edwin Ray Lankester. For further discussion of this subject, see Langham (1984).

1.2.2. DF 100/32 Dawson 24 March 1912

(a) Charles Dawson (1864-1916); (b) handwritten letter to Woodward, on printed stationery: "The Castle Lodge, Lewes"; (c) annotated by Woodward: "25th". Underlining in original by Dawson.

I find that our excursion to Holland is not coming off yet, so that I expect to be home round about Easter.
    Painters and builders will be more or less in possession of my little house and the whole place turned up-side down, but I hope to see something of you.
    Our visit to the gravel bed will depend on the weather. At present the roads leading to it are impassable and excavation is out of the question [A].
    Edgar Willett [B] kindly offered to motor us there on Good Friday if you can come – picking us up at Lewes?

I will have a look at the place, if the weather improves, and see if things are possible, but I feel sure nothing short of four fine days would set matters straight enough to even see the gravel . . . I have not told Willett anything about the situation of the gravel [C].

[A] As this suggests Woodward's response to Letter 1.2.1 was both positive and prompt – he apparently replied on 15 February. Furthermore, contrary to the impression received from the dates of Letters 1.2.1 and 1.2.2, the opening paragraph of 1.2.2 suggests an intervening letter that has not survived in which Woodward had presumably indicated his desire to examine the site. It is not, however, at all clear from the surviving correspondence when Woodward first saw the cranial fragments, though judging from Letters 1.2.4 and 1.2.5 it was not until late May (see 1.2.8).

[B] Edgar [William] Willett M.D. (1856-1928), was an associate of Dawson, who lived at Worth Park, Crawley, Sussex. The extent of their friendship is uncertain. From all indications, Willett was, like Dawson, a member of the Sussex Archaeological Society, as well as being a friend of Edwin Ray Lankester, see 1.2.9.

[C] At this juncture Woodward was evidently labouring under the impression that only he knew of the discovery, see 1.2.4. In reality, however, there were several others privy to Dawson's secret. This initial circle is known to have included the Kenward family at Barkham Manor and the farm labourer, Alfred Thorpe. It is also known that Samuel Allinson Woodhead (1862-1943), a close friend and chemistry instructor at Uckfield Agricultural College had been intimately involved in Dawson's activities at Piltdown. In addition to their original fruitless search of the gravel pit circa 1908 (Dawson 1913: 75-76), Woodhead later carried out a chemical analysis of the "first" cranial fragment (see Dawson & Woodward 1913a: 121). In addition to Woodhead it also appears that prior to Woodward's first visit to the Piltdown site, Dawson showed the cranial fragments to a friend in Lewes, namely a Mr. Ernest Victor Clarke (1868–1954). During an interview with Joseph Weiner on Friday, 12 February 1954, Clarke said that Dawson had shown him "several" pieces of "skull bone," and that Woodward was soon to take an active interest in the material, see 6.3.41. Two weeks after the interview Clarke died. Similarly, during the same time period, Henry Sargent (1891-1983), former Curator of the Bexhill Museum (near Hastings) later reported (see 6.3.48) that Dawson had shown him the cranial fragments also. During the coming months this circle was enlarged further, and by June is known to have included Teilhard de Chardin (see notes 1.2.5) and W.J. Lewis Abbott, (see Note A: 1.2.11) among others.

1.2.3 DF 100/32 Dawson 26 March 1912

(a) Charles Dawson (1864-1916); (b) handwritten note to Woodward, on printed stationery: "Town Hall Chambers, Uckfield"; (c) annotated by Woodward: "28th Premolar of *Hippopotamus* and piece of a sandstone concretion. Retd. ASW"

Will you very kindly identify enclosed for me. I think the larger one is hippo'?"

From all indications the *Hippopotamus* molar was found, along with the frontal cranial fragment, in the autumn of 1911 (see Table 1.2, and appended notes). From all indications the hippo tooth in question was a lower pre-molar. Since this specimen had been returned by Woodward, it can be inferred that the hippo tooth mentioned by Teilhard in a letter (dated April 26) refers to the same specimen [see, Table 1.1, and notes to 1.2.5).

1.2.4 DF 100/32 Dawson 28 March 1912

(a) Charles Dawson (1864-1916); (b) handwritten letter to Woodward, on printed stationery: "The Castle Lodge, Lewes"; (c) –.

Very many thanks for your determination of the tooth. I quite agree as to the other fragment.

I will of course take care that no one sees the pieces of skull who has any knowledge of the subject [A] and leave all to you. On second thoughts I have decided to wait until you and I can go over by ourselves to look at the bed of gravel. It is not very far to walk from Uckfield and it will do us good! [B]

[A] It is inferred from this that Woodward's reply to 1.2.3 had included a note on the need for secrecy. Aside from the question of priority, it appears that Woodward was also anxious that the site not be disturbed by amateurs looking for spoils. These anxieties were later relayed during the course of an interview he gave to a reporter from the *Manchester Daily Dispatch* 22 November 1912.

[B] While it is possible that Woodward may have visited Piltdown between 28 March and 18 April, there is every indication that his first visit to the Piltdown site was in late May, see 1.2.9. This is based largely on the fact that on 19 April, Dawson was still in possession of the remains (see notes to 1.2.5), and it is assumed that had Woodward visited Dawson earlier, he would have in all probability taken the remains back with him to London for further study.

1.2.5 DF 100/32 Dawson 18 April 1912

(a) Charles Dawson (1864-1916); (b) handwritten letter to Woodward, on printed stationery: "The Castle Lodge, Lewes"; (c) annotated by Woodward: "19th Regret cannot"

I am arranging to go to Hastings to the monastery as my friend, remaining there, has some new things he wishes to show me. Perhaps you could arrange to accompany me? If you could lunch here about 1.00 we could go on by the 1.53 (Lewes to Hastings). Drop me a line if this is suitable. We could go by the 12 o'cl[lock] from Lewes train if you like but I leave that to you.

As indicated by Woodward's annotation, Friday, April 19th was not possible. It appears Dawson's plans to visit Teilhard [see Note E: 1.2.1] clashed with those of Woodward, who was about to leave for Berlin to study specimens collected by recent expeditions in East Africa. The London Chapter of the German Colonial Society had invited Woodward to lecture on the dinosaurs of East Africa. His visit to Germany was in preparation for this lecture. According to Teilhard's correspondence, however, Dawson visited him alone on Saturday, 20 April. Writing of this visit to his parent's he notes:

Last Saturday, my geologist friend, Mr. Dawson, came for a visit. He brought [? to show] me some prehistoric remains (silex [flint tools], elephant and hippopotamus, and especially, a very thick, well-preserved human skull) which he had found in the alluvium deposits not far from here; he did this in order to stir me up to some similar expeditions; but I hardly have the time for that anymore" (Letter No 65: 26 April 1912, see Teilhard (1965) 1968:190-191).

Further information on Dawson's visit can be gleaned from a letter Teilhard wrote later to Pelletier in Jersey on 18 May:

I forgot to tell you that when Dawson came along the last time [20 April] he appeared with a large carefully wrapped box from which he excitedly drew one third of the skull of the "Homo Lewensis" found by him during these last years in some alluvia (reposing on Wealdian) near Uckfield. The skull is certainly very curious, of deep chocolate colour and especially of a stupefying thickness (about one centimetre at the thinnest points); unfortunately the characteristic parts, orbits, jaws etc. are missing. Dawson brought along a sample of the alluvium (small pebbles stripped bare by rolling, such as you find on the bottom of a stream) and species of what is found there: teeth of hippopotamus, elephant (fragments) and one or two very beautiful silex [flint tools], which were covered with a compact patina. I would like to work there for an hour or two; perhaps that can be arranged . . . (quoted in Schmitz-Moormann 1981:9).

As this indicates the Piltdown cranial fragments were not at this time in Woodward's possession. In fact it appears that Woodward did not see these remains until at least 24 May [1.2.8]. In the above letter, Teilhard also notes that Dawson brought with him Seward's "conclusion" (see 1.2.1):

Voici la conclusion: Professor Seward remarks that . . . the material, though it does not afford evidence of many new form, adds to our knowledge of several species and is an important contribution to the Wealden Flora.

See also Teilhard's Letter No 66 (10 May) in which he tells his parents:

I received news from Cambridge [Seward]; without disclosing any great new things, my plant collections constitute an "important contribution to botany," especially in making knowledge of several species more precise . . . A study with photographic reproductions and drawings will be published (Teilhard (1965) 1968: 193-194).

1.2.6 DF 100/32 Dawson 20 April 1912

(a) Charles Dawson (1864-1916); (b) handwritten letter to Woodward, on plain stationery: "The Castle Lodge, Lewes"; (c) –.

I am very sorry that you cannot come today [A].
     Re: Red Crag shells. I enclose you Major Molineux's letter [B] which you see is not very much use.
     I am asking the farmers to report to me any brown flints in the plough-fields or gravels north of the spots where we know they are. Yesterday I found another bed close to Uckfield out of which I took two similar flints but there did not seem to be many. The occurrence of the London Clay and other Tertiary beds on the west side of New Haven Harbour is worth noting in connection with [?our] subject. The whole subject wants sorting out. Tomorrow I shall be at Framfield and will have a look round for gravels.

[A] An acknowledgement of Woodward's reply to 1.2.5.

[B] Major HP Molineux (d.1923), was honorary Treasurer of the Sussex Archaeological Society. The following letter enclosed with 1.2.6 is written on printed stationery headed: "Old Bank, Lewes." The letter is addressed to Dawson, dated 16 April 1912 and signed H. P. Molineux:

All that I can tell you about the 'Red Crag' incident is that some workmen who were engaged in making the line from Uckfield to Lewes, about 1860, brought my father 2 or 3 unmistakable large Red Crag shells, which they said they had dug out between Isfield and Uckfield or Tunbridge Wells – at least that was my impression. I showed one of the shells to a Geological expert at Sandhurst College [C], and there is no doubt whatever as to their being of Red Crag derivation. I am afraid that is now impossible to find one of the shells, as I have never seen them since our Lewes house was sold in 1880 and I daresay they were thrown away, or sold with other debris that was cleared out at that time. The shells were full of red earth very like the deposits on the top of Newhaven Cliffs, but I think rather more gritty. I do not know of any flint gravels about Isfield . . ."

[C] It is conjectured that this expert might be Major Wade interviewed by Weiner in 1955, see 6.3.42.

1.2.7 DF 100/32 Dawson 12 May 1912

(a) Charles Dawson (1864-1916); (b) handwritten letter to Woodward, on stationery embossed: "The Castle Lodge, Lewes", marked "PRIVATE" and dated "Sunday 12 May 1912"; (c) annotated by Woodward: "Retd 18th".

Many thanks for your wire. I hope you and Mrs Woodward have had a good time abroad [A].

I expect to be in London tomorrow (Monday), at the Law Courts, and hope to have a chance of of [sic] getting to see you during the day or next day.

Since I saw you I have been writing on the subject of "The 13th Dorsal Vertebra," in certain human skeletons, which I believe is a new subject [B].

I send you the result and if you think well enough of it I should be very much obliged if you would introduce the paper for me at the Royal Society [C]. I am very anxious to get it placed at once because I have had to work the photographs under the nose of Keith and his assistant.

I gather from the latter person that Keith is rather puzzled as to what to make of it all, and I want to secure the priority to which am entitled . . . I have had no further opportunity of doing more work in our gravel bed, but I am tracing the same deposit to various other points in the Weald, which may help our determination of the geological horizon, someday [D].

[A] See Letter 1.2.5.

[B] From the texts of the surviving letters of 1912, there is every reason to suppose that Dawson had not met with Woodward since there excursion to "Cliff End" in January (1.2.1). Hence it is inferred that Dawson was implying that he had been working on the subject of "13th Dorsal Vertebra" since the beginning of the year. The original handwritten draft, and a typed draft of his paper, entitled "On the persistance of a 13th Dorsal Vertebra in Certain Human Races" has been preserved, see DF 116/16 (No 97-105). The photographs which Dawson said he "took under the nose of Keith and his assistant", make it clear that what he did was to take photographs of the relevant human skeletons displayed in glass cabinets in the museum exhibition halls of the Royal College of Surgeons. The photographs are somewhat marred by the glare of the flash reflected in the glass of the museum cases. It should be noted that during May Keith was away on a field trip. This curious episode and its relevance to events unfolding at Piltdown is discussed in Spencer (1990).

[C] One of Dawson's burning ambitions was to become a Fellow of the Royal Society, see 3.1.6.

[D] Although referring to the pit as "ours" it is evident that Woodward had yet to inspect the site. Furthermore, he had not, so it would seem from 1.2.8, examined the cranial fragments.

1.2.8 DF 100/32 Dawson 23 May 1912

(a) Charles Dawson (1864-1916); (b) handwritten letter to Woodward, on printed stationery: "The Castle Lodge, Lewes"; (c) annotated by Woodward: "24th" Underlining in original by Dawson.

Sometime – tomorrow (Friday), probably after lunch, I will bring the pieces of skull and a few odd [sic] and ends found with it, or near it, in the gravel-bed [A].

I cannot hear of any [?more] flint gravel to the North [sic], only to the South, but I have got a lot of farmers to report to me, and they keep bringing in specimens of what "gravels" they can find. Most of it seems to be "Kernel stone" and flakey iron-stone, which they call "gravel", but which is not so. There are however very ancient beds of ironstone gravels to the north in which no flint is found. These may yield some bones, someday –

[A] As indicated earlier, this passage seems to imply that Woodward had not yet seen the cranial fragments. It is conjectured that the cranial fragments may have been the two occipital fragments (Table 1.1), and possibly included the left temporal fragment as well. Likewise the "odds and ends" to which Dawson nonchantly refers, are in all probability those he had shown to Teilhard at Ore House in April (see Teilhard's letter to Félix Pelletier, in notes to 1.2.5), which included a number of flint implements, and molars of *Stegodon* and *Hippopotamus*.

1.2.9 DF 100/32 Dawson 27 May 1912

(a) Charles Dawson (1864-1916); (b) handwritten letter to Woodward, on plain stationery: "The Castle Lodge, Lewes"; (c) annotated by Woodward: "28th <u>Yes</u>"

Next Saturday (2 June) I am going to have a dig at the gravel bed and Father Teilhard will be with me [A]. He is quite safe. Will you be able to join us? [Edgar] Willett has had Ray Lankester [B] with him this Whitsuntide but I have remained obdurate! We shall be arriving at Uckfield at 10.00 am.

[A] From all indications the planned meeting took place. Although Teilhard's correspondence does not confirm this date, it certainly is not at variance with the known facts. On 10 May 1912, Teilhard wrote to his parents that he would be spending a "couple of weeks [at Bramber] near Brighton in a convent which doesn't have a chaplain" (see Letter 66 Teilhard (1965) 1968: 192 and Section 1.1, fn. 12.). On 3 June, he wrote his parents, this time from Bramber, saying:

I am living an ideal little life of a hermit. Separated from the highly populated Brighton coast by the downs, Bramber is right in the country [1] . . ."

Later in this letter, Teilhard relates to his parents details of his recent visit to the Piltdown site:

I haven't told you about the day I spent in Lewes (near Newhaven) at my friend Mr Dawson's home; it was on my way here [to Bramber]. For that day, we planned an excursion to the famous alluvial deposits at Uckfield (north of Lewes); the prehistoric remains I mentioned in one of my letters over a month ago came from there. I began with a hearty English breakfast in Mr. Dawson's very tidy home; it's a very comfortable dwelling nesting right in the middle of the ruins of the old castle which overlooks Lewes.

Mrs. Dawson is an Irish woman born in Bordeaux. One son is in the colonial army in the Sudan, and is cluttering the house with antelope heads [2].

I was received cordially. Around 10 o'clock, we were in Uckfield where Professor Woodward joined us. He is director of the British Museum's palaeontology division, and is a little man with salt-and-pepper hair, plus a rather cold appearance . . . At three o'clock [sic], armed with all the makings for a picnic, we started off in the car [3]. After going across Uckfield Castle's grounds, we were left off on the hunting ground: a grassy strip 4-5 metres wide, which skirts a wooded path leading to a farm. Under this grass, there's a 50 centimetre layer of gravel which is gradually being removed to be used for roads. A man was there to help us dig [4]; armed with picks and sieves, we worked for several hours and finally had success. Dawson discovered a new fragment of the famous human skull; he already had three pieces of it, and I myself put a hand on a fragment of an elephant's molar; this made me really worth something in Woodward's eyes. He jumped on the pieces with the enthusiasm of a youth and all the fire that his apparent coldness covered came out. To meet my train, I had to leave before the other two were to abandon their search" (Letter No 67, Teilhard (1965) 1968: 195, 197-198).

[1]: According to Letter No 68, dated 16 June 1912 (Teilhard (1965) 1968: 199), Teilhard remained at Bramber until 17 June. In this letter to his parents, he writes: "Tomorrow, I am leaving . . . I shall arrive in Hastings just in time to make a triduum for vows (until the 21st) . . ."

[2] Captain F.J.M. Postelthwaite, see Note B: 1.1.3 and Section 6.2, fn 1. In addition to the son, Hélène Dawson (1859-1917), also had a daughter, named Gladys (see Note C: 6.3.4).

[3]: From Teilhard's subsequent remark, "we were left off" suggests that the car was not driven by someone in the party. Neither Dawson nor Woodward owned a car. Since he does not speak of anyone else at the dig besides the farm-labourer (see below), this rules out the possibility that they had been driven to the site by an intimate associate of Dawson's, such as Edgar Willet (Note B: 1.2.2). In all probability Dawson had pre-arranged with a local

garage to hire a car and chauffeur to ferry the party from Uckfield to Piltdown, or simply picked up a taxi at Uckfield railway station. Evidently leaving early, Teilhard presumably walked the few miles back to Uckfield railway station.

[4]: It is conjectured that the labourer was "Venus" Hargreaves (d. 1917), who is known to have been regularly employed after 1912, and is featured in several photographs taken at the site in 1913 (Note B: 2.3.50).

[B] Edwin Ray Lankester (1847-1929) was Director of the British Museum (Natural History) from 1898 to 1907, during which time he became embroiled in a dispute with the Principal Librarian and Director of the British Museum, Sir E. Maunde Thompson (1840-1929) and with the Museum's Trustees. For further details on this affair, see Stearn (1981: 77-96).

1.2.10 P.MSS.KPO Piltdown File II: Teilhard de Chardin 21 June 1912

(a) Pierre Teilhard de Chardin (1881-1955); (b) handwritten letter to Dawson on plain stationery: "Ore Place [Hastings, Sussex]"; (c) –.

It has been decided that my theological studies will end on the 14th of July. After that day, I may leave Hastings at any time. So, if you wish to come, with Dr. Woodward, and pick some specimens of my collection, it would be better not to delay too long. You have only to let me know beforehand the moment of your visit, and any day will suit me.

See Letter 1.2.11 and notes to 1.2.12.

1.2.11 DF 100/32 Dawson 30 June 1912

(a) Charles Dawson (1864-1916); (b) handwritten letter to Woodward on printed stationery: "The Castle Lodge, Lewes"; (c) annotated by Woodward: "July 1st".

I was at Hastings yesterday and called to see Abbott [A] and showed him two of our specimens of flints. He says they are "man – man all over." Certainly, one large one you have not seen, is a primitive hand-axe. Abbott says it is equal to Moir's best and of the same age - but -! [B]

Yesterday I heard from Butterfield [C] that the remainder of the Jesuit's collection is to go to the Hastings Museum and so that I think we must very soon go and make the selection [D]. Possibly Wednesday next week could suit me.

Do you think you could meet me at Lewes at 1.51 pm and I could come from Uckfield by then? If that day does not suit it will have to be in the week following, as I am quite booked up.

I traced the yellow flints in a motor [car] two miles to the north of our digging place near Uckfield and I expect to trace them quite another mile [E]. I have also heard of other river flint gravels running to the ridge. I begin to think I have started a big [?] which will end in some considerable modification of the theories of Wealden denudation [F].

Don't forget to see the skull in the Aylesford Museum [G], if possible. I enclose you a picture of the skull at Cheddah [sic]. The chin is nearly straight and massave [sic: ? massive] . . . [H]. The squamosal bone has a ridge, behind the ear, at the point of attachment of the squamosal bone to the skull but I think that there are modern examples as to this [I]. No more luck at the diggings yet.

[?] word unclear.

[A] William James Lewis Abbott (1863-1933), the former London jeweller who moved his business to Hastings [8 Grand Parade, St. Leonards-on-Sea] at the close of the nineteenth century. By this time Abbott had already established a reputation as an amateur prehistorian (e.g. Abbott 1892a, 1892b, 1893, 1894, 1895, 1897a, 1911) and a known member of the Ightham Circle (Spencer 1990). As the above letter indicates Woodward and Abbott had an established relationship. In fact Woodward had known him since the late 1880s. According to Lady Woodward, it was from Abbott that her husband purchased her 21st birthday brooch and engagement ring, as well as other jewellery that she still wore (6.3.30). It is conjectured that this meeting might account for Abbott's later contention that he had been responsible for persuading Dawson of the importance of the Piltdown remains, see 2.3.28. It is interesting to note that when Abbott wrote Woodward in August (1.2.13), he made no mention of Dawson's recent visit.

[B] James Reid Moir (1879–1944), a businessman and amateur prehistorian from Ipswich, Suffolk. In 1910, Moir had caused a minor sensation when he announced that he had found evidence supporting the existence of preglacial man in East Anglia (see Letter to Editor *London Times* 17 October 1910, and his publications 1911, 1913a, 1913b, and 1916a). Although Moir's claim was met with stiff opposition, he received considerable support from several members of the Ightham Circle, most notably Edwin Ray Lankester (1912).

[C] See Note D:1.1.31.

[D] See letters 1.2.4 and 1.2.5.

[E] It is conjectured that Dawson had used Edgar Willett as chauffeur, see Note B: 1.2.2, 1.2.19 and 1.2.23.

[F] See notes to Letter 1.2.30.

[G] There is no museum at Aylesford, Kent. However, as the author and museologist Ronald Jessup pointed out to Weiner, 4 January 1954 [MSS WEI 3.18.1], this is probably a confusion with Aylesbury Museum.

[H] Sandwiched between this and the following sentence, Dawson has drawn a small sketch of the jaw (unlabelled), indicating the position of the anterior teeth and mental foramen.

[I] It is conjectured that Dawson is referring to the mandible of the skeleton found in 1903 at Cheddar cave, situated in a gorge on the southern flanks of the Mendip Hills, near Bristol (see Davies 1904). Further reference to the Cheddar specimen is made in Letter 2.3.70. For further details on this specimen, see Seligman & Parsons (1914). Weiner (1955:89) surmises on the basis of this reference that the Piltdown mandible had been found and was already in Woodward's possession. If this is the case, it appears that both Woodward and Dawson refrained from telling Teilhard about the discovery when they visited him early in July, just prior to his departure for France (see notes appended to Letter 1.2.12). Teilhard's apparent ignorance of this discovery is supported by a letter to Pelletier, dated 1 January 1913, in which he says:

The last news from Dawson is a letter card announcing to me the measurements of his skull of Lewes "Eoanthropus Dawsoni" (woodw.), which were presented to the Geological Society on 18 December. To know the exact importance of the discovery, one must await some time for the publication of the memorandum and for the criticisms that will follow. Stratigraphically the pebble cannot but be Chellean (the elephant and mastodon must have been introduced to the site) for, anatomically it seems that the form of the skull and especially the jaw (which I have not seen) is very remarkable; I am in the position to have the opinion of Boule and Obermaier [1], who are not easily taken in, especially if the finds are English" (in Schmitz-Moormann 1981:10).

[1] Marcellin Boule [1861-1942], French palaeontologist and professor at the Muséum d'Histoire Naturelle de Paris. See section 2 for further details on Boule. Hugo Obermaier [1877-1946], an Austrian priest, specializing in the prehistoric archaeology of Spain and North Africa. In 1912 he had just published his *Der Mensch der Vorzeit*, the first of a 3 volume work: *Der Mensch aller Zeiten, Natur und Kultur der Völker der Erde*. He was a member of the Institut de Paleontologie Humaine (Paris), which had been founded (though not officially inaugurated until after the First World War) by the Prince of Monaco under Boule's direction.

1.2.12 P.MSS.KPO Piltdown File II Teilhard de Chardin 10 July 1912

(a) Pierre Teilhard de Chardin (1881-1955); (b) handwritten letter to Dawson on plain stationery: "Ore Place [Hastings, Sussex]". For reasons probably related to Teilhard's postscript, this letter was passed along to Woodward; (c) annotated by Woodward: "18th".

I am sorry to tell you that it is impossible for me to go to Lewes, next week, because I have to start from Hastings on Tuesday! I hope, nevertheless, that we will again dig together the Uckfield's gravel: next year, I am likely to study Natural History in France, and to spend my holidays in England. If so, I will surely do my best to see you. Until I give you my definitive address, you can write me at: Château de Sarcenat, par Oreines, Puy-de-Dôme.

I am very thankful to you for your kindness towards me during this last four years. Lewes will certainly be one of my best remembrances of England, and you may be sure that I shall often pray God to bless the Castle Lodge.

[Post-script]: I sent yesterday the fossils to Dr.Woodward.

According to a postcard mailed on 12 July, Teilhard actually sent them on the 11th: DF 100 Teilhard de Chardin 12 July 1912, annotated by Woodward "July 18th". On 13 July, Teilhard informed his parents that:

Last Wednesday, Dr. Woodward of the British Museum paid me a visit; he has "plundered" my collection enough to make me feel flattered. I now have free access to South Kensington, if ever I need it (Letter No 70, Teilhard (1965) 1968:206).

Dawson kept in touch, and apparently alerted Teilhard to the pending announcement of the Piltdown discoveries. "The day before yesterday a good letter from Dawson," Teilhard told Pelletier, "full of the Homo Valdensis [sic] which is to be announced in November" (letter dated 13 October 1912. The full text of which can be found in Schmitz-Moorman (1981: 10).

1.2.13 DF 100/32 Abbott 28 August 1912

(a) William James Lewis Abbot (1853-1933); (b) handwritten letter to Woodward on printed stationery: "W.J. LEWIS ABBOTT Jeweller [etc] . . . 8 Grand Parade, St. Leonards-on-Sea [Hastings], Sussex." Abbott lived on the premises; (c) annotated by Woodward: "29th. Lateral scale of Lepidotus. ASW".

A general letter evidently written in response to an enquiry made by Woodward regarding a reptilian fossil tooth in Abbott's collection. Having noted his inability to locate the specimen, he refers Woodward to another specimen sent for identification [see Woodward's annotation]. Abbott also makes a tangential reference to his recent activities in the district of Ightham. This letter is included here largely because of its timing and Abbott's failure to note Dawson's recent visit (see 1.2.11) to which he later attached considerable importance (Abbott 1913).

1.2.14 DF 100/32 Dawkins 6 October 1912

(a) William Boyd Dawkins (1837-1929); (b) handwritten letter to Woodward on stationery embossed: "Fallowfield House, Fallowfield, Manchester" [Dawkins' home address]; (c) annotated by Woodward: "8th".

. . . Concerning your wonderful find – I think that the absence of well defined hollows for the reception of the convolutions of the brain, on the inner wall of the skull is of first rate importance.

As noted in the introduction to Section 1.1, Boyd Dawkins was Woodward's mentor at Manchester University. It is not known if Boyd Dawkins was responding to a description given him by Woodward or whether he had actually examined the Piltdown cranial fragments. Judging from Letter 1.2.18, it would appear to have been the latter rather than the former. It is conjectured that Boyd Dawkins was responsible for securing Grafton Elliot Smith's assistance in describing the Piltdown endocranial cast, see 1.2.27 and 1.2.31.

1.2.15 DF 100/33 Lankester [27] October 1912

(a) Edwin Ray Lankester (1847-1929); (b) undated handwritten letter to Woodward on printed stationery: "29 Thurloe Place, South Kensington [London]." Beneath the address Lankester had originally written "Friday Eve." This is crossed-out and written above is "Sunday". Based on this and Woodward's annotation, this letter was probably written on Sunday 27 October; (c) annotated by Woodward: "Oct. 28th. 1912". Underlining in original by Lankester.

For background information on Lankester, see Note B: 1.2.9.

I have been thinking of nothing else but that splendid human fossil all day. Don't you think the quarto plates of the Phil[osophical]. Trans[actions, Royal Society] are necessary to illustrate it satisfactorily? You want perfect drawings or photos of every possible point of view of each piece – and it would be well to give them all at once – not a little bit at a time – with also comparative views for the lower jaw of chimpanzee and normal man.

Also ought you not at once to see about getting – say £500 from the Gov[ernmen]t. grant reserve fund – so as to start future digging and secure the sifted (by legal assignment from the landlord) to completely turn over the whole area in which this gravel occurs.

It seems to me it would be worth spending thousands on this – a regular systematic and complete sifting of every hatful of gravel in the neighbourhood.

Some German or American will come and buy the estate – if you don't secure the option on rights of digging. I feel sure the whole family are there leg bones and all of a dozen individuals!

As Lankester predicted the matter of digging rights became an issue, see the Woodward-Dawsons correspondence with Maryon-Wilson, the owner of Barkham Manor (2.1.1-2.1.11). At this juncture Lankester had evidently not seen the Piltdown site. His first visit was on 9 November in the company of Dawson and Edgar Willett, see 1.2.19.

1.2.16 HP/NAA Hrdlička 30 October 1912

(a) Aleš Hrdlička (1869-1943); (b) typewritten carbon-copy from Hrdlička at the U.S. National Museum of Natural History (Smithsonian Institution), Washington, D.C. to Arthur Keith at the Royal College of Surgeons of England. The original letter is not preserved in KP/RCS.

Hrdlička, was Curator of the Division of Physical Anthropology at the U.S. National Museum in Washington D.C. from 1903 through to the early 1940s. In this brief note, Hrdlička indicated that rumours were circulating in Washington regarding the discovery of a "remarkable" human fossil skull in England, and wondered if there was any truth in these stories. Arthur Keith (1866-1955), Conservator at the Royal College of Surgeons in London, however, did not reply to this enquiry until December 23, by which time the essential facts were public knowledge. Considering the apparent importance of the Piltdown finds, Hrdlička could not understrand why Keith, and more particularly Woodward had not mentioned it when he was in London attending the International Congress of Americanists during the summer (Spencer 1979, II:436-437). In replying to Hrdlička in December, Keith said that he had not been privy to events leading up to the historic meeting at the Geological Society of London (HP/NAA Keith 23 December 1912). Hrdlička, however, found this hard to believe and was evidently hurt by the fact Keith had not taken him into his confidence. But as indicated by Letters 1.2.17 and 1.2.27 Keith had not been entirely open with Hrdlička on this matter. Indeed during the next year Hrdlička became increasingly irritated by the visible reluctance of both Keith and Woodward to share information with him. Three weeks after Hrdlička wrote to Keith, the *The Manchester Guardian* (Thursday, November 21) gave the first printed (and somewhat speculative) account of the discovery, and as indicated by Letter 1.2.25 it was an "unofficial" leak (Spencer 1990). The story was subsequently picked by most of the major national and provincial newspapers e.g. *Evening News* [London] 21 Nov; *Daily Sketch* 22 Nov; *Manchester Daily Despatch* 22 Nov; *Liverpool Echo* 23 Nov; *The Times* 23 Nov; *Brighton Herald* 23 Nov; *Glasgow Evening Times* 23 Nov; *Dundee Evening Telegraph* 23 Nov; *Sussex Daily News* 23 Nov; *Southern Weekly News* 23 Nov (see Woodward's scrapbook: DF 116/1).

1.2.17 DF 100/33 Keith 2 November 1912

(a) Arthur Keith (1866-1955); (b) handwritten note to Woodward on printed stationery: "Royal College of Surgeons of England, Lincoln's Inn Fields, London W.C."; (c) –.

I should very much like to have a glimpse of that wonderful find – of which rumours have reached me from time to time. It bucks me up to think England is yielding up trumps and that the specimens have reached the right hands – send me a p[ost]. c[ard]. when I may come.

From all indications (see 1.2.27), Keith did not get to see the Piltdown remains until 2 December.

1.2.18 DF 100/32 Dawkins 7 November 1912

(a) William Boyd Dawkins (1837–1929); (b) handwritten letter to Woodward on stationery embossed: "Fallowfield House, Fallowfield, Manchester"; (c) at the side of the embossed address (top right hand corner), Dawkins has written "En route → York".

This brief note refers to some fossil specimens found in Kent and sent to Woodward for identification, see Letter DF 100/32 Dawkins 23 October 1912 for further details. The letter concludes with: "If I can steal away from politus next week in London, I will come to the Museum to refresh my soul."

1.2.19 DF 100/32 Dawson 9 November 1912

(a) Charles Dawson (1864-1916); (b) handwritten letter to Woodward on stationery embossed: "The Castle Lodge, Lewes"; (c) annotated by Woodward: "11th". Underlining in original does not appear to have been done by Dawson.

Lancaster [sic] came to the gravel pit with Willett today and seemed very satisfied with it all, and thinks as you do that the age of the human remains are probably late Pliocene or early Pleistocene. We looked over our diggings but found nothing, but there was a lot of water there and all the lower side was deep with it. We went in the plough[ed] fields both there and at <u>Barcombe Mills</u> [A]. I found a very early looking implement in the middle of the plough[ed] field adjoining our gravel pit and Willett found another in the plough [sic] at Barcombe Mills [B]. Lancaster [sic] loaded himself with samples of flints [C]. He said he had imagined it all just as he found it, from your description, but the beds did not contain quite so much flint as he thought they would. He said he should very much like to see a restoration of the jaw (both sides) if you can manage it. I suppose this can be done with a reverse model of the one side.

Please remember that the two implements found today are to be handed to you by Lancaster [sic]. He is going to give them to C.H. Read at the B.M. [D]

I so much enjoyed the dinner and meeting the other night and to find all my old geol[ogy] friends so interested in our discoveries [E]. May I ask you to kindly get several spare copies of the abstract of the paper on Teilhard and Pelletier's plants for them.

They tell me it will help them as an introduction to other geologists abroad.

I thought Seward's paper most admirably expressed [sic] and only wished the poor French priests had been there to hear it [see E].

[A] This is the first mention of the Barcombe Mills site by Dawson, which is situated south of Barkham Manor, on the west bank of the River Ouse (Fig 1.2a). It was in this general region that the so-called Barcombe Mills cranial fragments were reportedly found by Dawson, see 2.3.21. The provenance and dates of discovery of this assemblage is largely unknown, see 5.2.10 for further details. With the exception of this artifact and the frontal bone mentioned by Dawson in 1913, there existence was not known until after Dawson's death in 1916 (4.2.22). At this time these remains along with an assortment of other fossils in Dawson's collection were handed over to Woodward. The Barcombe Mills material consists of a large piece of frontal bone [E 644a], a fragment of a right parietal [E 644b], a pair of zygomatic bones [E 644 (left) c/(right) d], and a mandibular 2nd molar tooth [E 645]. These remains were later described by Robert Broom (1950) and Ashley Montagu (1951b). According to Montagu, the cranial remains belong to at least two individuals. Morphologically they are indistinguishable from modern human bones and are not as thick as those belonging to the Piltdown specimen. It should be stressed, however, that neither Dawson nor Woodward claimed anything of special interest for these remains.

[B] The identity of these artifacts (and if represented in the BMNH collections) is unclear.

[C] It is presumed that Lankester wanted these specimens to compare with the flint samples collected from Reid Moir's site at Ipswich, see DF 100/33 Lankester 15 April 1912.

[D] [Sir] Charles Hercules Read (1857-1929), Keeper of the Ethnological Department, British Museum at Bloomsbury. See Lankester (1912).

[E] A reference to Teilhard de Chardin and Félix Pelletier, see notes to Letters 1.2.1 and 1.2.5. Seward's (Note F: 1.2.1) communication on Wealden flora was presented to the Geological Society on 6 November 1912. In this paper he made special reference to the collections made by Teilhard and Pelletier (Seward 1913).

1.2.20 DF 100/32 Dawson 11 November 1912

(a) Charles Dawson (1864-1916); (b) Handwritten letter to Woodward on printed stationery: "The Castle Lodge, Lewes"; (c) –.

Thank you for your kind invitation for the 5 Dec[ember] for the private R[oyal]. S[ociety] [? view] which may be useful [A] . . . I will bring up a selection of sample matrices which I showed Lankester and which he thought should be at the G[eological] S[ociety] show.

I shall be glad to see your outline sketch of the proposed G[eological] S[ociety] paper.

I have still got several tough field days to go through before I shall feel safe on the subject of the gravels. I find it a little difficult to account for our gravels at 100 feet being so very like the Ight[h]am gravels at 500 feet. This appears to be so both as to size and wear. I suppose the reason is that the process of denudation has been gentle, a mere "letting down," except where the flints have got into the main current of the stream. In the new section of the small gravel pit, close to Uckfield (which you saw once), there is shown a very finely laminated deposit of gravel. It is almost an ironstone silt, the layers are so fine in places. I am going to give old Frisby a job of photographing the section [B]. I will get a few general lantern slides made for the G[eological] S[ociety] lecture and I think you would find it easier to explain some points if you do so with the bones and casts? I may be in town in a few days and if so will call.

[A] Details of this "private view" are not known. See Abbot 1.2.24.

[B] See *Quart J Geol Soc Lond* LXIX, Plate XV: "Flint-bearing gravel-bed overlying the Tunbridge Wells Sands (Hastings Beds) at Piltdown, Fletching, Sussex. This photograph (Fig. 1.2a) is one of several taken by the Uckfield photographer J.S. Frisby. The little boy

Fig. 1.2 Piltdown Photographs c. 1912 [DF 116/42]. (a) Photograph taken by Frisby of Uckfield, and used to illustrate Dawson & Woodward (1913a). According to Letter 1.2.20, this photograph was commissioned by Dawson. N.B. The skull and mandible were reportedly found in the lower layers of the dark basal stratum. (b) Photograph attributed to Frisby showing Dawson and Woodward at work in the pit. (c) Frisby's postcard: "Searching for the Piltdown man", see Note B:1.2.20.

(presumably included to indicate scale) has been identified as Woodward's son Cyril [Randulph]. It appears that Frisby had taken a number of photographs showing Dawson and Woodward working at the pit (Fig 1.2b). The date of this photograph (b) is unknown, and was later used in an article that appeared in *The Illustrated London News* on December 28, 1912. In this version (Fig 1.2c), "Cyril Woodward" has been obliterated, and portraits of Dawson and Woodward have been inserted. Later, Frisby produced a postcard from this version which he entitled "Searching for the Piltdown Man" (Fig 1.2c). Given the boy's identity and the apparent similarity of the clothes he is wearing, as well as the general appearance of the hedgerow in the background, it seems safe to suggest that the two photographs are contemporaneous. If this is the case, then this could imply that Woodward arranged, subsequently with Dawson, to visit the site [with his son] and supervise the photographic session with Frisby. It should be noted that Dawson and Woodward also employed the photographic services of E.J. Bedford of Lewes.

1.2.21 DF 116/46 Moir 12 November 1912

(a) James Reid Moir (1879-1944); (b) handwritten letter to Woodward on printed stationery: "12 St. Edmund's Road, Ipswich [Suffolk, East Anglia]; (c) annotated by Woodward: "13th"

For background information on Moir, see Note B: 1.2.11.

I have been thinking a great deal about that wonderful find of yours since you so kindly showed it to us, and wondering as to the age of the human remains [A].
  If we are to judge of the age of a deposit by the latest implement or bone found in it, then this Sussex

gravel will put down as of the Chellean period, because you have undoubtedly got implements of that type in it.

The question then is as to whether the skull and jaw are of the same age as these Chellean flints.

In the first place I noticed that the flints were stained yellow and the human bones a dark red, and thus one would imagine the latter to be older. But then flint may stain only yellow while porous bone is turned red. My experience of Crag bones is that the specimens which are stained the deepest red are most mineralised and therefore most probably older. The Elephas remains you found appeared to me to be in a similar condition to the human relics, and therefore the weight of evidence seems to point to a pre-Chellean date for the latter.

But some of our friends will I am sure say that Chellean man has been found and nothing more [B].

Then there is another interesting point – The Harrisonian implements [C] have always been put aside as worthless by some people because they have never been found in association with human bones – well here you have found these specimens [and] the bones lying together, and it will be open for the "Eolithic" men to say that the conditions required have now been found! [D]

[A] As noted in Note B: 1.2.11 Moir was an avid eolithophile, and had the support of Ray Lankester, who in an effort to circumvent antieolithic sentiment had coined the term "rostro-carinate" to describe the "implements" Moir had discovered. Moir was also the discoverer to the Ipswich skeleton in 1911.

[B] For example Boyd Dawkins who favoured a more orthodox view of human origins, had long been an antagonist of the British eolithic movement (Spencer 1990).

[C] A reference to Benjamin Harrison and the eoliths that he and Joseph Prestwich had found and described from the district surrounding Ightham in Kent. For further details on this movement, see introduction to Section 1.1.

[D] Indeed this is precisely the posture assumed by Abbott (see 3.1.1) and other eolithophiles.

1.2.22 DF 100/33 Lankester 13 November 1912

(a) Edwin Ray Lankester (1847-1929); (b) handwritten letter to Woodward on printed stationery: "29 Thurloe Place, South Kensington [London]"; (c) –.

It seems to me that it might be very important if you have a small piece of the human bone from Piltdown – not yet treated with gum or gelatine – to have its specificity taken by Herbert Smith – in the simple way they now use for bits of crystal etc.

Possibly an identity in spec[ific] grav[ities] of the human bone and a bit of the accompanying elephant bone might furnish some evidence of their contemporaneity. I think that some simple test should also be applied to an untouched piece of the human bone – to show whether all traces of animal matter has gone or whether a little still remains.

Although heeding Lankester's advice, the analyses undertaken were surprisingly modest and confined exclusively to "a small fragment of the skull." This chemical examination was performed by Samuel Woodhead, then Public Analyst for East Sussex & Hove and close friend of Dawson (see Note C: 1.2.2). Woodhead reported that "the specific gravity of the bone (powdered) is 2.115 at 5 C. as standard. No gelatin or organic matter is present. There is a large proportion of phosphates (originally present in the bone) and a considerable proportion of iron. Silica is absent" (Dawson & Woodward 1913a: 121). For information on subsequent investigations along this line, see 5.1.28. Regarding Lankester's view of Woodward's reconstruction of the Piltdown remains, see Table 1.2, and Letters 1.3.9 and 4.1.39.

1.2.23 DF 100/32 Dawson 21 November 1912

(a) Charles Dawson (1864-1916); (b) handwritten letter to Woodward on stationery embossed: "The Castle Lodge, Lewes"; (c) annotated by Woodward: "29th"

I am glad you have arranged for the 18th Dec[ember]. After much reading and running about over the country I begin to feel the path clearing and when I get your [*/plan] scheme I will set to work.

Willett has kindly put his motor at my disposal next Saturday and we are to trace the upper reaches of the Ouse down to East [Mascalls?] where you and I went that Sunday in a motor [A]. So far the whole region seems unproductive of flints and I am glad it is so, because I had an idea that the Ouse might me responsible for the drift as well as the beds of gravel, but all points to our flints having come from the chalk plateau and to have altered very little if at all in the process of coming down [see Fig 1.2].

Has Ray Lankister [sic] sent you the two rough implements which Willett and I found? I have got three Rostro-carinate implements from the Chalk plateau to show him at our meeting. The flint is just the same as at Barkham. I am glad Barlow [B] is getting on well [C]. We ought to get some photographs ready [D].

If you have not sent Teilhard the abstracts already send them to me and I will send them to Pelletier and Teilhard [E]. The former is now at Brest.

I have got a series of yellow stained flints from Fairlight Down (overlying the Fairlight Clays) also one or two "Eoliths" from there [F]. I am going to exhibit them as examples of what we can produce in the Weald!

[*] Word "plan" written and deleted by Dawson.

[A] The date of Dawson's motor excursion with Woodward is unknown.

[B] Frank Oswell Barlow (1880-1951) was a technical assistant in the BMNH Department of Geology whose forte was making casts and models of fossil remains. He had entered the Department in 1896 where he was trained by his father Caleb Barlow (1840-1908). Barlow was a partner in the Damon (Weymouth) Co. contracted to make and distribute the Piltdown casts.

[C] This runs contrary to Woodward's later remark to Boyd Dawkins (1.2.25) that the reconstruction had presented a number of difficulties (see also 1.2.27).

[D] Evidently nothing in this regard had been done since November 11th (1.2.20) in which he mentioned commissioning Frisby of Uckfield to photograph the site.

[E] See Note E, 1.2.19.

[F] These Fairlight (Sussex) "eoliths" [E.609] are described and figured in Plate XVII, figs 4.5. Dawson & Woodward (1913a: 122).

1.2.24 DF 100/32 Abbott 24 November 1912

(a) William James Lewis Abbott (1853-1933); (b) typewritten letter to Woodward on plain stationery: "8 Grand Parade, St. Leonard's O/S"; (c) annotated by Woodward: "29th"

I am sure you are inundated with enquiries for information about the skull which I hear you had on view; you will realize what special interest this is to me, since I have been working these Sussex gravels, and trying to awaken an interest in them in others. Did Mr. Dawson show you the fragments of one he has got? [A] I have been trying to make him realize how wrong our old ideas of Wealden geology are, and the startling nature of some of these gravels! And I have no doubt that some of the flints he has brought me are really man's work, while the fragment of skull was very remarkable, thicker than anything I have ever seen before. If you can possibly spare me a minute or two to tell me anything of your new addition, I shall be very much obliged to you. Since I saw you I have correlated our various glacial deposits in the South (and Thames) with those Penck [B], and they will, I have no doubt prove very interesting, and also stimulate a lot of controversy. But of this I am sure, they will introduce a lot of unknown matter, that fits in with nothing on the old lines . . .

[A] From this it would appear that Abbott was either being discrete or completely innocent of the connection between what Dawson had shown him earlier (1.2.11) and the specimens now in Woodward's care.

[B] See Abbott's Letter 1.2.30 and appended notes for further details on his view of Wealden geology; and Penck & Bückner (1900).

1.2.25 BDC/LP Woodward 25 November 1912

(a) Arthur Smith Woodward; (b) photocopy of handwritten letter to Boyd Dawkins at Manchester, on printed stationery: "Department of Geology, British Museum (Natural History), Cromwell Road, South Kensington"; (c) –.

Very many thanks for your kind letter and the verbosity of the Manchester Guardian [A]. I suspect I can identify the thief and shall treat him cautiously in the future [B]. If I am right, the man has not seen the specimens – has only asked me questions. Both Dawson and I have told the reporters they must wait until December 18th. We are having much trouble putting the skull together, but I think by the end of this week we shall have a satisfactory reconstruction [C]. It is true that the bits of Stegodon and Mastodon are much more rolled than the Chellean implements, so it is quite likely there is a mixture. Still the man cannot be later than Chellean.

[A] See notes appended to Letter 1.2.16.

[B] For further details, see Spencer 1990.

[C] See Note D: 1.2.27.

1.2.26 DF 100/32 Dawson [?28] November 1912

(a) Charles Dawson (1864-1916); (b) undated [see (c)], handwritten letter to Woodward on stationery embossed: "The Castle Lodge, Lewes"; (c) annotated by Woodward: "29th".

I forgot to show you the enclosed worked flint from Fairlight. You see that the inside when broken is quite grey. I exposed one side for a few weeks and it has begun to go yellow. The other piece not exposed remains grey. I think that the flint is more or less charged with iron which goes yellow by oxidation on exposure. It was originally a beach flint. I think all the other Fairlight ones made from these iron charged flints are yellow outside for the above reason.

Conan Doyle has written and seems excited about the skull. He has kindly offered to drive me in his motor next week anywhere.

See Note I: 1.2.1.

1.2.27 DF 116/25 Keith 2 December 1912

(a) Arthur Keith (1866-1955); (b) handwritten copy of a letter from Keith (Royal College of Surgeons of England) to Grafton Elliot Smith (Professor of Anatomy at Manchester University) on private stationery: "17 Aubert Park, Highbury [London] N." Original in the files of Warren R. Dawson, biographer of Elliott Smith (1938). In 1959, Warren Dawson sent this copy to Sir Gavin Rylands de Beer (1899-1972), then Director of the British Museum (Natural History) because: "It is interesting historically as recording Keith's first sight of the Piltdown Skull around which so much controversy was destined to arise" (DF 116/25 Dawson 10 November 1959).

. . . I took [in] S[outh]. K[ensington Museum]. on my way to the Zoological Tea tonight and saw the Sussex man, or woman rather, for the size of the teeth and small size of the temporal muscles and the occipital markings best fit with that idea [A].

The mastoid, ear and temporo-maxillary joint and zygoma are absolutely of the modern type; the wear on the teeth, the temporal muscle – the form of joint are incompatible with a big canine. I think they are construing the symphysis region wrongly in supposing they have left ½ as far as the middle line [sic]. I'm sure there is 8-10 mm missing – even if it were ultra anthropoid that would be the case. The occipital region: the manner in which the head is hafted to the neck is of the modern form. But the thickness of the bone, the flattening and width of the cranial cavity are neanderthaloid – except La Quina was a thin-walled skull [B].

I think the c[ranial]. c[apacity]. will turn out to be about 1200 cc [C] – not a small brain is it? I found Barlow trying to reconstruct – 2nd attempt [D]. In the present attempt they have the petrous bones directed almost horizontally inwards with the apices 2½ inches apart an absolutely impossible distance unless the basilar plate were twice the width of that of the gorilla. At present they are making the skull 150 mm wide. I think the real width should be 10 or 15mm less but cannot tell until they get the occip[ital] bone in its right place. Of course I couldn't keep quiet and probably gave more advice than was welcome. But it is a great find: a revelation and a verification all combined.

[A] Keith's friendship with the Elliot Smith dates from the 1898 meeting in Cambridge of the International Zoological Congress. At that time Elliot Smith was a Fellow of Johns College, and Keith reports in his autobiography that "I saw much of him" (1950: 202). From the above letter (and confirmed by Keith's diary entry for 30 November) it appears Elliot Smith had been a weekend house guest at Keith's home in Highbury. In a letter from Elliot Smith to the French neuroanatomist Raoul Anthony (1874-1954) it appears Elliot Smith had been asked by Woodward (sometime in mid November) to report on the Piltdown endocranial cast. In this letter, dated 21 November, Elliot Smith wrote: "I do not know whether you have heard that a very (pre-Heidelberg, said to be Pliocene) skull has been found in England and I want to be able to compare the brain-cast with your La Quina [see Note B] cast next week" (Dawson 1938:59, fn 3). Keith's communication strongly suggests that Elliot Smith had yet to see the celebrated remains. See Letter 1.2.31.

[B] The La Quina skeleton, referred to here, was found in September 1911 by Henri Martin. For an account of its discovery, see Martin in *Rev Scientifique* (1912:49).

[C] This is a particularly interesting statement since Keith later agitated against Woodward's reconstruction noting the modern braincase and the apelike jaw was incompatible with anatomical knowledge. In arguing for a new assembly, Keith raised the cranial capacity upwards to 1400 cc (1915) – close to the approximate average of modern humans. Recalling this visit in his autobiography, Keith wrote: "On reaching Highbury I went to my diary and noted the various points that had surged through my head during those twenty minutes I spent at South Kensington. On re-reading my notes today I am pleasantly surprised to see that had carried away with me all the essential features of the Piltdown race" (1950: 325).

[D] Shortly after this, Woodward informed Keith:

The 3rd edition of the lady is now ready and the base now fits the mandible beautifully. I have made a fine theory which I think will please you." (KP/RCS/KL2 Woodward 6 December 1912).

1.2.28 DF 100/32 Dawson 10 December 1912

(a) Charles Dawson (1864-1916); (b) handwritten letter to Woodward on stationery embossed: "The Castle Lodge, Lewes"; (c) annotated by Woodward: "12th". Underlining in original by Dawson.

I have had Strahan here today and took him [on] a complete tour in motor car in the rain [A]!
I had some profitable discussion with him and in result have made a slight alteration in the proof

abstract sent to me by Belinfaunte [sic] this morning [B].

The alteration I have made is at the end of the <u>second</u> paragraph of the abstract 4 lines from its end and reads now: "It may be assumed that <u>they have been derived from a plane formerly existing between these two points</u>." [C]

This is in place of the four last lines of that paragraph. I have also taken out the following words in the last but one of the abstract: "Considerable recession of the Chalk escarpment" and it now reads: "by the subsequent deepening of the valley of the Ouse to the amount of 80 feet."

This is as you originally drafted it. I have sent the proof back to Belinfaunte [sic].

I think Stranhan [sic] was much interested in his visit and has got a good grip of the whole situation.

[A] [Sir] Aubrey Strahan [1852-1928], Director of the Geological Survey of Great Britain and then President of the Geological Society of London.

[B] Leo Louis Belinfante (d.1937). At this time Belinfante was Librarian of the Geological Society (1890-1916) and editor of its *Quarterly Journal.* (1890-1930). From 1916, until his retirement in 1936, Belinfante was permanent secretary of the Society.

[C] See Dawson & Woodward (1912: 21).

1.2.29 DF 100/33 Lankester 11 December 1912

(a) Edwin Ray Lankester (1847-1929); (b) handwritten letter to Woodward on printed stationery: "29 Thurloe Place, South Kensington"; (c) annotated by Woodward: "12th."

With the greatest pleasure I will lend you my Heidelberg jaw – and the flint implement I got from Piltdown for the eve of Wednesday next. I am anxious to see your results and to see the re-construction of the lower jaw – for I have doubts as to it being of the chinless type like the Neanderthal jaws and Heildelberg one.

This is rather curious since the British Museum (Natural History) had its own cast; acquired from Schoettensack in July 1909 [No. E558]. For a discussion of this incident, see Spencer 1990.

1.2.30 DF 100/32 Abbott 15 December 1912

(a) William John Lewis Abbott (1853-1933); (b) typewritten letter to Woodward on plain stationery: "8 Grand Parade, St. Leonard's O/S."; (c) annotated by Woodward: "19th". Underlining in original by Abbott.

I deeply regret that business will not allow me to be present at the meeting on Wednesday , the more so as I have paid such a lot of time to the Wealden gravels, bringing to light a new set of facts which will fit in nowhere with the old ideas, but find a place for the flint-bearing gravels of the Weald a necessity – and also because I feel that my work in this line has stimulated Mr.Dawson, without which, it is quite possible that these important things would never have been brought to light, as Mr. Dawson knew of the existence of the gravel many years, without following it up. I don't know if you ever saw the accompanying little paper? It does not go very deeply into the subject but it shows sufficient to explode that greatest nightmare of geology the "Wealden Dome" 6000 feet high which some tell us was planed down by the sea, but what sea, and at what time, or what became of the rest of Europe when the ocean rolled 6 or 7 thousand feet above O.D. [A] neither legend nor theory telleth us! Then the subaerial denudationists tell us that it was not a sea, but subaerial denudation; and this since man sat upon the "Dome." But what was done with the waste is also a mystery; nor is there any record of what the almighty navvy was doing with the rest of the British Islands all the time.

The conclusions to which a re-study of Wealden geology has led me, may be summarized as follows: The Wealden dome bringing up the oldest beds in the centre of the area, and each of the newer beds upon its flanks <u>with absolute bi-semmetry</u> [sic] is perfectly untenable. The claim that a mountain ridge 6000 feet high has been planed off by marine action was made without considering what would have been the *state of the other part of the country, or Europe in general with an ocean 6 or 7 thousand feet above present O.D. or, at what geological period this occurred, or the possibility of such an ocean existing over an area of deep hollows without leaving a vestage [sic] behind it.*

The claim that it has been planed down by sub-aerial denudation since "man sat upon the dome" is equally ridiculous, as sub-aerial denudation would not have been so selective in its action upon one locality regardless of others and the vast mass of removed material be found somewhere, and <u>all traces of River Deposits older than later Pleistocene would have been destroyed</u>.

On the other hand evidence points to it being more probable that, towards the close of the Chalk period elevation set in the west, travelling somewhat eastward, which continued for a long time, so that the further east we go the newer beds that are represented, until we reach a formation (the Maestrichean) that was not deposited in this country at all. Subsequently great – but slow – earth movements set in giving rise to NW and SE ridges (the Wealden of the future); these were attacked by the succeeding Thanet sea. The chalk was removed, and the flints on this island – shingle – beach were ground to rounded pebbles. Upon elevation rivers flowed southwards to Newhaven and northward over Kent to Woolwich, Thanet, and East Anglia (the Woolwich and Blackheath Beds). Then followed the Miocene period (vide page 7). Once more depression sets in bringing in the Deistian [sic] Sea, which did not stop at Lenham, but extended over at least a greater part of Sussex (Eastbourne).

With the elevation of this old sea-bottom rivers ran down depositing drifts of early Pliocene age = the Coralline, Red and Norwich Crags being deposited as described (p.7). The moot point now is at what period the first Glacial Phase appeared. The finding of ice scratched flints at the base of the Red Crag suggests that it was at the close of the Coralline Crag, a hypothesis hinted at by Prestwich many years ago. This would correspond to the Günz of Penck. It is also certain that the idea of a single Glacial period, with glacial deposits stopping north of the Thames, must be abandoned, as we now have a number of well-marked phases in the Thames Valley, some extending over Sussex; one at least reaching the other side of the channel, each marked by its characteristic fauna and flint implements, a number of which I showed you the last time you were here. Under the new reading the Meridionalis gravels of the South of England fall into a logical position and become of great importance. From the really good parallel flaking that has been found in the Cromer Forest Bed it is highly probable that a flint-working creature was here much earlier; and for the evidence of this we must look to these Wealden gravels.

This long letter indicates that Abbott was opposed to the traditional "Dome hypothesis" as an explanation of the geology of SE England. Succinctly this hypothesis popularized by the geologist William Topley (1841-1894) claimed that southern England, including a portion of the present northwest coast of France (south of the Bas Boulonnais), had originally been covered by a dome of chalk. Deposited during the Cretaceous period, this dome had been progressively planed down, so it was contended, during the immense interval of time that separated the Cretaceous and Recent geologic periods, leaving in England only the bordering rims of the North and South Downs, while the remnants of its eastern rim could be found across the Channel. For a discussion of the relevance of this hypothesis to Wealden palaeoanthropological studies, see Spencer 1990. While Abbott was not alone in his opposition to the "Dome hypothesis" there were many who continued to support it, including Woodward (1948) and Keith (1915). Later, in 1918, Marriott (6.3.31) published a paper that embodies the Abbott viewpoint. See Wooldridge (1949) for a recent assessment of Wealden geology. Regarding his support of Albrecht Penck's (1858-1945) view of Pleistocene chronology (see Penck & Brückner 1900), there were at this time few serious geologists who supported the old monoglacial theory. Indeed by the mid 1890s most professional geologists were advocating a rejection of the monoglacial model (e.g. Geikie 1894, Penck & Brückner 1900). According to Penck & Brückner there had been four distinct glacial advances, which they named after the Bavarian valleys where the respective moraines and outwash gravels were well-developed: Günz, Mindel, Riss, and Würm. These were considered synonymous with the First, Second, Third and Fourth Glaciations recognized by James Geikie (1839-1915). See Letter 1.3.12.

[A] Ordnance Datum line.

1.2.31 DF 116/5 Elliot Smith 16 December 1912

(a) Grafton Elliott Smith (1871-1937); (b) handwritten letter to Woodward on printed stationery: "The University, Manchester"; (c) underlining in original by Elliot Smith.

With such an out-and-out simian jaw it seems impossible to avoid making a new form.

The brain is certainly lowlier and more ape-like than anything I have yet seen in real Homo: *but on the cerebral features alone I would not have felt justified in according separate generic rank to the new creature. But I think the jaw settles it.*

Our examinations have made such inroads into my time that I have not had the leisure to write *any report in time to send off; but if you wish it I shall come prepared to make a preliminary verbal report on Wednesday.*

This letter appears to support the conjecture made earlier (1.2.27), that Elliot Smith did not get to examine the Piltdown endocranial cast until after 2 December. Indeed Woodward's letter to the *Manchester Guardian* on December 21 seems to suggest a considerably later date, see Note A: 1.2.32. Furthermore, it is evident from the above that he did not submit a written report until after the 18 December meeting.

1.2.32 DF 116/5 Elliot Smith 21 December 1912

(a) Grafton Elliot Smith (1871-1937); (b) handwritten letter to Woodward on printed stationery: "The University, Manchester"; (c) –.

I am very much obliged to you writing the note that appears in today's "Manchester Guardian." [A] It is not that I minded the omission of any reference in the newspaper report to my small contribution to last Wednesday's proceedings, so much as the misunderstanding such omission had given rise to here. There was a very important meeting of the University Council on Wednesday, and I excused myself on the ground that I had to present a report upon the brain cast at the Geological Society's meeting in London.

When I reached home yesterday I found that enquiries were being made as to whether I had really been present, as the newspapers had no reference to my contribution to the discussions.

For this reason your note is very welcome and I thank you for it, and again for the the opportunity of studying the wonderful brain cast.

[A] In his letter to the Editor of the *Manchester Guardian*, Woodward wrote:

Permit me to supply an omission in your report of the meeting of the Geological Society at which Mr. Charles Dawson and I exhibited the Piltdown human skull. At the last moment, after the notice of the meeting had been published, we were able to prepare a cast of the brain-cavity of the specimen, which we had the pleasure of submitting to our friend Professor G. Elliot Smith, of the University of Manchester.

Professor Elliot Smith came to the meeting, and after the reading of our paper gave a short account of the principal characters of the brain . . . We hope that at a later date he will be able to prepare a detailed memoir on the subject for the Royal Society."

1.3   December 1912: The Unveiling and The Initial Response

An indicated by the Geological Society's *Minute Book* the meeting room at Burlington House on the evening of Wednesday, 18 December was packed to capacity to witness the unveiling of the Piltdown skull (see Fig 1.4).

The brain-case consisted of four large pieces of bone (reconstructed from nine fragments) that provided information on the "shape and natural relations of the frontal, parietal, occipital and temporal" regions, which Woodward reported, justified "the reconstruction of some other elements by inference" (Dawson & Woodward 1913a:124). Neither Dawson nor Woodward seem to have questioned the association of the cranial fragments and jaw. The latter consisted of a right mandibular ramus, which Woodward contended, exhibited "the same mineralized condition as the skull, and corresponds sufficiently well in size to be refered to the same specimen without hesitation" (Dawson & Woodward 1913a:129). Both Woodward and Dawson seemed clearly convinced that the remains constituted the long awaited "Plateau Man," the

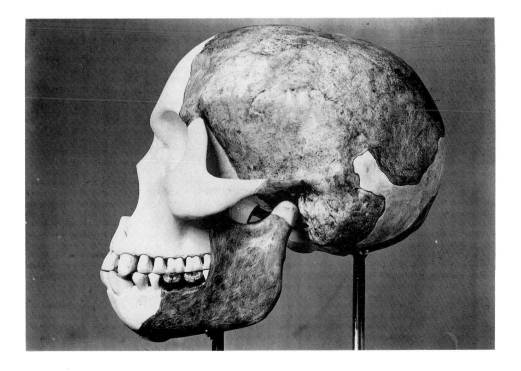

Fig. 1.3 Woodward's restoration of the Piltdown skull (1912). A left lateral view of the cast produced by the R.F. Damon Company of Weymouth, England. The dark areas represent the original bone fragments. The reconstructed regions are white. N.B. The left mandibular ramus shown here is in fact a reconstruction, based on the original right mandibular fragment. Note also the large projecting (reconstructed) canine in the lower jaw. This expectation was satisfied by the discovery of the canine tooth by Teilhard de Chardin in the summer of 1913 (see 2.3.35). Courtesy of the British Museum (Natural History).

author of the much disputed eoliths that had been found littering the "high gravels" of southeast England. To this reconstruction Woodward gave the name *Eoanthropus dawsoni* the "Dawn Man." Indeed this diagnosis was strongly supported by Elliot Smith, who testified that his preliminary examination of the endocranial cast of *Eoanthropus* indicated that it was "the most primitive and most simian brain so far recorded" (Dawson & Woodward 1913a:147).

Along with the hominid remains, the Piltdown gravel pit had yielded a miscellaneous collection of stone artifacts and a suite of mammalian fauna (Table 1.1). In their interpretation of the human remains, Dawson and Woodward were clearly guided by this attending assemblage. While the fragments of *Stegodon* and *Mastodon* pointed to the Pliocene, specimens of *Castor* and *Cervus* were typically Pleistocene. Likewise, the archaeological artifacts, consisting of a mixture of "eoliths" (= Pliocene) and "Chellean" (= Lower Pleistocene) palaeoliths, presented a similar picture. In a nutshell, the assemblage was equivocal on the question of age of the site. Similarly the stratigraphical circumstances in which these remains had been found provided considerable room for debate.

In the discussion that followed the presentations of Dawson, Woodward, and Elliot Smith respectively, it became apparent that opinion was split on two major issues, namely the age of the specimens (i.e., whether they belonged to the Pliocene or Pleistocene), and the association of the jaw and cranium.

The discussants (in order) included: Sir Edwin Ray Lankester (Note B:1.2.8); Arthur Keith (1.2.16/17); William Boyd Dawkins (1.2.14); Wynfrid L. H. Duckworth (1.3.11), an anatomist from Jesus College, Cambridge; Clement Reid (1853-1916), a geologist attached to the Survey of England; David Waterston (1871-1942), an anatomist at King's College, London; Alfred S. Kennard (1870-1948), an amateur malacologist; [Allender] Reginald Smith (1873-1940), a professional antiquarian employed at the Bloomsbury branch of the British Museum with a specific interest in British prehistory; and Edwin Tully Newton (1840-1930), a palaeontologist. The views expressed by these individuals are summarized in Table 1.2 [1].

In the public domain, interest in these proceedings was fuelled by an avalanche of newspaper articles. The story was immediately picked up by the wire services and by weekend the story had circled the globe [2]. During the remaining days of 1912 three major articles appeared in the popular British press which capture the essence of the controversy that was to slowly envelop the Piltdown remains. The first was an anonymous article published in *The Graphic* [3] (28 December) under the pregnant title: "A Hard Nut to Crack for Christmas: Have we really found the 'missing link' at last?" The second, also anonymous, appeared in *The Sphere* [4] (Vol 51 (Oct-Dec 1912). In comparison to the story in *The Graphic* this article took an essentially neutral position. The third was a lavish three-page article in the national glossy magazine *The London Illustrated News* (which also appeared on Saturday, 28 December). Written by William Plane Pycraft (1868-1942), a zoologist at the British Museum (Natural History) and former assistant of Ray Lankester, the tone of this latter article is, by contrast to the others, more reverential. Woodward's incoming correspondence during the same period reflects, though somewhat more diluted, the emerging controversy.

TABLE 1.1 Material recovered from Piltdown 1908-1912

Date	Material	Finder
	"Human" Remains	
1908 *	left parietal	Dawson [1,2,3]
1911 *	left frontal	Dawson [1,2,3]
1912 **	left temporal	Dawson [3,4]
1912 ***	occipital (2 fragments)	Dawson [3]
1912 ***	right parietal (3 fragments)	Dawson [3,5]
1912 ***	occipital (3rd fragment)	Woodward [1,2,3]
1912 ***	right mandibular ramus	Dawson [1,2,3]
	Mammalian Fauna	
1912 **	*Hippopotamus amphibius* lower premolar	Dawson [1,2,3,6]
1912 **	*H. amphibius* left lower molar	Dawson [3]
1912 *	*Mastodon arvernensis* molar	Woodward [3]
1912 *	*Stegodon* sp. molar	Dawson [3]
1912 ***	*Stegodon* sp. molar	Teilhard [a,1]
1912	*Cervus elaphus* antler	Dawson & Woodward [1]
1912	*C. elephus* metatarsal proximal end	Dawson [1]
1912	*Equus* sp. left upper molar	Dawson & Woodward [1]
1912	*Castor fiber* lower molar	Dawson & Woodward [1]
1912	*C. fiber* lower 4th premolar	Dawson & Woodward [1]
	Implements	
1912	Palaeolith E605	Woodward [1,5,A]
1912	Palaeolith E606	Teilhard [1,B]
1912	Palaeolith E607	Dawson [3,C,X]
1912	Eolith scraper, rolled	Dawson [1,5,D]
1912	Eolith scraper, unrolled	Dawson [1,5,E]
1912	Eolith scraper, rolled	Dawson [1,5,F]
1912	Eolith drill, rolled	Dawson [1,5,G]
1912	Eolith drill, unrolled	Dawson [1,5,H]
1912	Eolith scraper, rolled	Dawson [1,5,I]
1912	Eolith scraper, rolled	Dawson [1,5,J]
1912	Eolith scraper, unrolled	Dawson [1,5,K]
1912	Eolith (chipped), rolled	Dawson [1,5,L]

* See text, Section 1.2; * * found before June 1912, see 1.2.5; * * * Summer season (June-? September); 1: Dawson & Woodward (1913a); 2: Dawson (1913); 3: Woodward (1948); 4: see Morning Post and Sussex Daily News 11 July 1916. Both papers mention that a third piece was found by Dawson in Winter 1912; 5: based on notes prepared by Woodward for Henry Fairfield Osborn in September 1933, see DF 116/46; 6: see Letter 1.2.3; (a) see Notes to Letter 1.2.9; A-L refer to plate and figure numbers in Dawson & Woodward (1913a) showing respective implements: A (XVI-1/fig 9); B (XVI-2/fig 8); C (XVI-3/fig 7); D (XVII-1); E (XVII-2); F (XVII-3); G (XVII-6); H (XVII-7); I (XVII-8); J (XVII-9); K (XVII-10); L (XVII-11); X: see Letter 1.2.11.

NOTES

[1]   Notes taken by unknown recorder tally with the discussion summaries appended to the Woodward & Dawson paper published the following spring in the *Quart J Geol Soc Lond* (1913a:147-151). These "summaries" are not in either Woodward's or Dawson's handwriting (see DF 116/16).

[2]   For example: *Australian Melbourne* 21 Dec; *New York American* 22 Dec; *New York Times* 22 Dec; *Le Journal des Débats* (Paris) 22 Dec; *The Advertiser* [Adelaide] 28 Dec.

[3]   A London based newspaper that was active until April 1932, whereupon it became the *National Graphic*. Later that year (December) it was absorbed by the *Sphere* .

[4]   A London based magazine which ceased publication in June 1964.

TABLE 1.2: Position taken by respective discussants on the issues of the age of the Piltdown deposits and the association of the mandible and skull.

	Age Issue		Association Issue	
Discussant	PLE	PLI	M	D
Lankester	E	E	R	N
Keith	N	+	R	N
Dawkins	+	N	+	N
Duckworth	E	E	+	N
Reid	E	E	N	N
Waterston	N	N	N	+
Kennard	E	E	N	N
Smith	E	E	R	N
Newton	N	+	N	N

PLE: Pleistocene; PLI: Pliocene; M: monist; D: dualist; E: Equivocal; +: favoured without reservation; R: accepted proposition with reservation; N: no opinion expressed.

CORRESPONDENCE

1.3.1 DF 116/9 Underwood 19 December 1912

(a) Arthur Swayne Underwood (1854-1916); (b) handwritten letter to Woodward on printed stationery: "26 Wimpole Street [London]; (c) annotated by Woodward: "9/1". Underlining in original by Underwood.

Underwood was Professor of Dental Surgery at King's College, London, with a private practice in Harley Street. Underwood appears to have been Woodward's primary advisor on dental matters, see 1.3.13.

I must send you a line to say how greatly I enjoyed the "historic occasion" – I did not disturb you to say my good byes as you were all so like lumps of sugar in a flies' festival. I had the good luck to be near Mrs Woodward during the meeting and with Dawson at the delightful dinner. I thought that Elliot Smith was very useful, the middle meningeal running back is just as simian as the chin so the enemy are left to the hypothesis that a workman's pick burst the remains into two animals as well as many fragments and caused all duplicate pieces to disappear *[A] and that both skull and mandible were human with ape characteristics, a bit thick! (as the skull is).*

I do feel that Keith is right and that the thing is Tertiary Man, but your point about the brain and face development is quite brilliant and seems to light-it-up all round. Only grant her to be Pliocene and all of us may live happy ever afterwards, but ought we to be so happy? Perhaps not.

What awful rot the papers have got! The Daily Chronicle seems the best [B].

Lankester in the Telegraph has a very poor picture of a modern mandible . . ." [C].

[A] This statement suggests that Dawson did mention, as conjectured in the introduction to subsection 1.2, the coconut story in his presentation to the Geological Society.

[B] This is a reference to a 2 column story in the *Daily Chronicle* 19 December, under the title: "OLDEST HUMAN SKULL – Ape-Like Remains Found in Sussex – Missing Link ? – Excavators Describe Their Prize".

[C] See Edwin Ray Lankester's article on "The new fossil man from Sussex", which appeared in his regular column "Science From an Easy Chair" in *The Daily Telegraph* (December 19). The one page (3 column) article was accompanied by a figure comparing the mandibulae of Heidelberg, modern human, the Sussex specimen and chimpanzee. From all indications Lankester had access to the Piltdown specimens on several occasions prior to the meeting of the 18th (see 1.2.15).

1.3.2 DF 116/9 Barrow 19 December 1912

(a) George Barrow (Geological Survey of England); (b) handwritten letter to Woodward on plain stationery: "12 Jermyn Street, [London] S.W."; (c) annotated by Woodward: "4th Retd."

This letter accompanied a collection of flint tools sent for Woodward to examine; which were returned to Barrow on 4 January 1913.

I congratulate you on the delivery of your paper which was so totally free from the newspaper style of the "armchair" [A]. I am not capable of judging the merits of the skull, but was greatly interested in the deposit and especially the flints. If you should have an excursion there I would very much like to go with you [B] . . . [C].

If you have the "stones" at the Museum later on I would much like to see them if it would not be troubling you [D].

[A] Evidently a snide reference to Ray Lankester and his popular column "Science from an Easy Chair" in *The Daily Telegraph*, see Note C: 1.3.1.

[B] Later, in the summer of 1913, Woodward organized under the auspices of the Geologists' Association an excursion to the Piltdown pit, see Note A: 2.3.8.

[C] At this junction Barrow briefly describes his "flint collection."

[D] Contrary to popular mythology Woodward did not make it difficult for legitimate investigators to view the original specimens. Indeed, Woodward's correspondence (1913-23) is peppered with such requests, which from all indications were invariably approved. For example, the anatomist Wilfrid Le Gros Clark (1895-1971), who later played a role in the debunking of Piltdown in 1953, viewed the specimens while a graduate student at St. Thomas' Hospital, London, see 4.2.20, and the letter from the Rev Henry Kidner (2.3.11), who notes: "I thank you for the trouble which you so kindly took in showing me the Piltdown fossils, of such great interest. You made the points so clear."

1.3.3 DF 100/32 Irving 20 December 1912

(a) Rev. A. Irving; (b) handwritten letter to Woodward on printed stationery: "Hockerill Vicerage, Bishop's Stortford, Hertfordshire; (c) annotated by Woodward: "21st". Underlining in original by Irving.

Irving was an amateur geologist, with evident connections to William Boyd Dawkins (see DF 100/32 Irving 9 September 1912). Irving had evidently become interested in the claims of Reid Moir (see 1.2.21), particularly after the discovery of the Ipswich skeleton in 1911, and was, as his letter suggests, critical of both Keith and Moir. As Keith later noted in his book *The Antiquity of Man* (1915): "The Rev. A. Irving has paid close attention to the more recent deposits of Essex . . . [and has] formed the opinion . . . [that stratum which lay over the Ipswich skeleton did] not represent an extension of the chalky boulder clay, but is a much more recent deposit . . ." (p 218). See Irving (1912) for an example of his critique of Moir. As for his opinion on Piltdown, he believed the specimen was "pre-Chalky boulder clay" (1914:393).

We are all much indebted to you and Mr. Dawson for the splendid work of which the results were given on Wednesday at the G[eological]. Society. I am glad to find that you think the Post report as good [A]: I thought it the best I have seen, better even than the Times report. Nature gives the whole thing in – I suppose as correct a form as you might have written it yourself. In the years that are long past, I was more or less familiar with that part of the country, and can recall some of its features, which give a living reality to your work. How completely you have given the Ipswich people the "Go=by"! I thought Dr. Keith's little bit "feud" feeble [sic]. Why will he persist in falling back upon Schoetensack's conclusion as to age of the Heidelberg, [B] after (as I know) Werth's article in Globus of 2 years ago has been more than once forced upon his attention [C].

There is just one point in the Nature article of this week on which I should like to be a little clearer. When you say "Lower Pleistocene" would you draw the line (say with Penck) at the Riss period, or with Boule at the "Würm"? Or do you – admitting Werth's conclusions as to H. heidelbergensis – take the Mindel-Riss Interglacial period for the time of the Eoanthropus? [D]

[A] Refers to a detailed 2 column article in *Morning Post* (London), 19 December.

[B] See Note D: 1.2.1. Schoetensack (1908) referred the Mauer jaw to the Lower Pleistocene based on his detailed geological study of the site. What is important here is that Schoetensack believed that the basal Mauer sands in which the jaw had been found corresponded "to the preglacial forest beds of Norfolk." Hence Keith's intense interest in Moir's discovery of stone artifacts (1910) and then a human skeleton (1911) in deposits that lie under the chalky boulder clay of East Anglia (see Moir & Keith 1912).

[C] Emil Werth (b 1869), a German anthropologist. See Werth (1909). For his subsequent views on Piltdown and the question of Tertiary Man, see Werth (1916, 1918, 1928).

[D] Unfortunately Woodward's response to this question has not been preserved.

1.3.4 DF 116/9 Cole 20 December 1912

Arthur Grenville Cole (1859-1924); (b) handwritten letter to Woodward on printed stationery: "Royal College of Science for Ireland [Dublin]; (c) annotated by Woodward: "21st./ Yes- if asked will do". See Letter 1.3.8.

I wish I could have heard you and Mr. Dawson at the great meeting on Wednesday. I understand that Praeger was there [A], and he well bring us a good report. Who owns the skull? [B] I write, because I think that the Royal Dublin Society would do its very best to arrange for a special evening meeting during the winter, if you could possibly bring the remains over and give us a discourse on them and on the present position with regard to Moir's find and other modern discoveries, and the Neanderthal race [C]. We saw Dubois' Pithecanthropus remains thus some years ago, when we had a far inferior theatre for meetings than that now available. [D]

[A] Listed among the visitors to Burlington House on Wednesday December 18th is a "RL Praeger". It is conjectured that this is Robert Lloyd Praeger (1865-1953), a botanist at The Queen's University of Belfast.

[B] See Section 2.1 for further details on this question.

[C] See Letter 1.3.8.

[D] Dubois visited Dublin in 1896, see *Trans Roy Soc (Dublin) VI* (Pt I): 1-26, 1896.

1.3.5 DF 100/32 Boule 20 December 1912

(a) Marcellin Boule (1861-1942); (b) handwritten note to Woodward on a postcard bearing printed title: Muséum National d'Histoire Naturelle, Laboratoire de Paléontologie, 3 Place Valhubert, Paris"; (c) –.

Boule (1.2.11) had written Woodward earlier in the year about his La Chapelle specimen (see DF 100/32 Boule 1 February 1912) and again at the beginning of December (DF 100/32 Boule 5 December 1912). In this latter communication he had made brief reference to the Piltdown specimen and suggested an exchange. Woodward's annotation to this letter indicates a promise of "eventual full value in exchange" when the Piltdown casts became available. But judging by the above postcard requesting further information on " votre Homme fossile", Woodward did not divulge any details regarding the discovery to Boule.

1.3.6 DF 116/9 Thompson 21 December 1912

(a) Percy G. Thompson; (b) handwritten letter to Woodward on printed stationery: "The Essex Field Club, Derwent House, Loughton, Essex; (c) –.

Thompson was "Honorary Secretary" of The Essex Field Club, and is believed to have been a friend of Woodward. In this short letter, he notes, "with regret", not hearing Woodward's presentation at Burlington House, and requested a reprint of the paper when published.

1.3.7 DF 116/9 Clotten 23 December 1912

(a) F.E. Clotten; (b) handwritten letter on printed stationery: "F.E. CLOTTEN, 9 Drakefield Road, Balham, London S.W.; (c) annotated by Woodward: "24th. Still private property. Probably Damon will sell casts in Feb."

An enquiry from a prospective distributor of the Piltdown casts when available. As indicated by Woodward's annotations the question of ownership needed to be decided before casts could be made and sold, and that with this question resolved it was already decided that the R.F. Damon Company would handle the making and distribution of casts. As indicated in Note B: 1.2.23, Barlow was a partner in this company.

1.3.8 DF 116/9 Cole 25 December 1912

(a) Arthur Grenville Cole (1859-1924); (b) handwritten letter on printed stationery: "10 Winton Road, Leeson Park, Dublin" [Cole's home address]; (c) –.

A reply to Woodward's letter (sent December 21), see Letter 1.3.4. Cole notes that the Royal Dublin Society will meet in January to discuss the question of inviting Woodward to Ireland to give a lecture. In due course Woodward received an invitation. For details of his Dublin lecture, see notes to 2.3.4.

1.3.9 DF 116/9 Lankester [25] December 1912

(a) Edwin Ray Lankester (1847-1929); (b) handwritten letter [undated, see (c)] to Woodward on printed stationery: "29 Thurloe Place, South Kensington." This address is crossed-out, and beneath Lankester has written an address in Bournemouth; (c) annotated by Woodward: "26th promised. Sent 26th."

That was a great evening last Wednesday at the Geological; and you may well be proud of it.
I want you to let me be one of the early ones to get a cast of the jaw – I should like to have it whilst I am down here [at Bournemouth], and have time to look at it. I had not appreciated the great feature – the long flattened symphysis and its backwardly continued flange – till you showed it to me on Tuesday.
Will you send me the two flints I lent you down here [A]. The good one is to go back to you for the Museum ultimately, but I should like to have it here for a time before then. It was picked up by Edgar Willett when with me, and he told Dawson it should ultimately go to the Museum [B]. The Heildelberg jaw might be sent to my house [in Kensington] . . . with directions . . . Not to be forwarded [C].
It seems to me quite possible that the jaw and the skull do not belong to the same individual – though more probably that they do – But if they don't then they might well be Upper Pliocene. That must remain uncertain till further bits of Eoanthropus dawsoni are found in the neighbouring field – not yet dug over [D].

[A] See Letter 1.2.19.

[B] Later (see Woodward 1917) material of a second *Eoanthropus* was found.

[C] See 1.2.29.

[D] See Note A: 1.2.19.

1.3.10 DF 116/9 MacCurdy 26 December 1912

(a) George Grant MacCurdy (1863-1949); (b) Typewritten letter to Woodward on printed stationery: "Yale University, Peabody Museum of Natural History, Anthropology Section"; (c) annotated by Woodward: "7th. Damon, after paper is published."

MacCurdy was an American physical anthropologist stationed at Yale. In this letter, MacCurdy requests two sets of casts. One is for the Yale Museum, and the other for the American Museum of Natural History in New York City. The reason for the latter request coming through MacCurdy, was as he explained: "I am at present installing a hall of European prehistoric archaeology for the American Museum . . . "In his reply, Woodward indicated that the Damon Co. would be making the casts (1.3.7) and that they would not be distributed until after the appearance of his paper with Dawson in the *Quart J Geol Soc Lond*.

1.3.11 DF 116/9 Duckworth 27 December 1912

(a) Wynfrid Laurence Duckworth (1870–1956); (b) Handwritten letter to Woodward on printed stationery: "East House, Jesus College, Cambridge"; (c) annotated by Woodward: "28th"

In this brief note Duckworth indicates the desire of the "Cambridge Anatomical Department" to purchase casts of the "new skull" when they become available (see 1.3.7). He makes no mention of the meeting on the 18th at Burlington House. Duckworth, however, was keenly interested in the subject of human origins and Woodward's *Eoanthropus* (see 2.2.16). His views on human evolution are not dissimilar to those of Keith, see Duckworth (1912).

1.3.12 DF 100/32 Abbott 27 December 1912

(a) William James Lewis Abbott (1853-1933); (b) typewritten letter to Woodward on plain stationery: "8 Grand Parade, St. Leonard's O/S"; (c) annotated by Woodward: "28th". Underlining in original by Abbott.

This letter was evidently in response to Woodward's reply to Letter 1.2.30.

. . . *The "silly nonsense" as you so aptly call it continues: It is bad enough when writers take the responsibility themselves, but it is altogether worse when reporters put words into one's mouth. As an example of the former one might cite some of Ray Lancaster's [sic] nonsense [A], about the [Piltdown] skull being in general characters closely similar to the inhabitants of that part of Sussex 1000 years ago; or his remark about the Weald being a great valley bordered N. EAST, S. & W. by a chalk ring which chalk once extended over the whole area . . . [B]*

The whole subject [of Piltdown] turns upon three points. The morphology of the skull; the stratigraphy; and the lithoclaziology [sic]. With reference to the first I do not claim to be in it, compared with many men who have given their lives to the study; but I should not be so mad as to "father" that big-chinned, beetle-browed, receding [sic]–foreheaded, Roman-footed athlete of the Illustrated London News! [C] When, however, it comes to the other two, I think I can with all modesty assert a claim. It is absolutely certain that the prevalent ideas of Wealden denudation, leave no place for a bed of Pliocene age, so that new facts must be made to fit the old theories, and it will not be until the geology is revised that the Piltdown deposit will find its true position.

. . . With reference to the Chellean age of the flints, who is the authority for this classification? Pycroft's [sic] man is shown with a coup-de-poing in his hand [D]; was anything like this found? [Y]ou know that with most people Chellean means the oldest known. Would it be too much to ask if you have any photos you could let me see either of the bones or the flints? My broad flat pointed implement from

the Cromer Forest Bed [E] would be classified even as Acheulean by many . . . So far as I can hear it is the idea of the imp[lement]s. being of Chellean character that is proving the stumbling block to many. I should like to see these. I shall be very much surprised if there is any anachronism in them. There are over a dozen patches of gravel, within half as many miles of Piltdown that require working out. I hope that now the pressure of Xmas is over that I shall be able to give a little more time to them. I should very much like to know the evidence upon which this gravel is claimed to belong to the Ouse, I shall be very surprised to find it to be of Pleistocene age, or anything to do with the Ouse [F]. . .

[A] A reference to Ray Lankester's article in *The Daily Telegraph* (19 December). For a similar view expressed of Lankester's column, see Note A: 1.3.2.

[B] At this juncture, Abbott proceeds to elaborate further on his revisionist theory of Wealden geology, see his earlier Letter 1.2.30 for further details.

[C] A reference to Pycraft's article in *The Illustrated London News* (28 December), see introduction to subsection 1.3 for further details.

[D] See Pycraft's *Illustrated London News* article in which appears a full-page picture showing an impressionistic reconstruction of *Eoanthropus* hunting on the banks of the River Ouse. The caption to the illustration reads: "A discovery of supreme importance to all interested in the history of the human race."

[E] See Abbott (1897, 1911).

[F] See introductory notes to Section 1.2; and Abbott (1915). See also 4.1.19.

1.3.13 DF 116/9 Underwood 30 December 1912

(a) Arthur Swayne Underwood (1854-1916); (b) handwritten letter to Woodward on printed stationery: "26 Wimpole Street [London]; (c) –.

Many thanks for the canine I will attack him at once. If the rascal has thin enamel I shall think all the big beasts are rather impostors and their enamel a make believe. My little private meeting is on Tuesday 14th January so I shall pop down and see you after you return." [A]

    P.S. No I didn't do the B.M.J. [B] By the way I see some of them are shaking their heads over the teeth ! I am quite certain our model is right and they are wrong [B].

[A] Details of this meeting on the 14th are not known. It may, however, have had something to do with Underwood's planned description of the Piltdown mandible. This work was published in the *British Journal of Dental Science* (1913) and is illustrated with a number of x-ray photographs of the mandible (Note C: 2.3.66). This paper was later attacked by Waterston (1913; see also Table 1.2) who had criticized Woodward's attempt to weld a pongid jaw to hominid braincase. Although subscribing to the monistic interpretation of the Piltdown remains, it should be noted that Underwood nevertheless was impressed by the similarity of the jaw to that of a chimpanzee.

[B] A reference to an anonymous article entitled "A new type of fossil man" in *Brit Med J* (21 Dec 1912) pp 1719-1720.

2 New Discoveries and The Mounting Controversy Over Woodward's Reconstruction and Other Issues

2.1 A Question of Ownership and Security

During the first weeks of 1913, Woodward and Dawson were faced with two important problems. The first involved the question of security. Although precautions had been taken not to reveal the exact location of the site, it was evident that any enterprising reporter or fossil hunter would have had little difficulty in discovering where it was located. In due course this fear materialised in the form of an anonymous article published on 18 January 1913 in the London based magazine *The Sphere*, which described in striking detail not only the site but also gave precise directions on how to get there! While Woodward's reaction to this article went unrecorded, it must have undoubtedly caused him considerable concern. The other issue, which Dawson aptly characterized as a "storm in a tea-cup," concerned the ownership of the materials recovered from the gravel pit. The owner of Barkham Manor, George Maryon-Wilson contended that the remains had been removed from the estate without his approval, and that they legally belonged to him. In due course, however, with Dawson acting as mediator, this issue was rapidly settled.

CORRESPONDENCE

2.1.1 DF 116/12 Dawson 1 January 191[3]

(a) Charles Dawson (1864-1916); (b) handwritten letter to Woodward on printed stationery: "Town Hall Chambers, Uckfield". This letter is dated "1 January 1912." However, from the context of the letter, the date should almost certainly be 1 January 1913; (c) underlining in original by Dawson.

An "Express" correspondent from Hastings asked me for a photo of the place where the skull was found as he intends writing a laudatory article which I expect will be awful! [A]

I forgot to ask you about the Illustrated London News who sent me a two page telegram asking for a photograph to publish along with your portrait and Elliot Smith's. This was just before Xmas, and I sent the open air photo -- but nothing so far has appeared nor have they returned anything, so perhaps something may appear next Friday. The telegram led me to suppose that you and E. Smith had sent portraits, but I forgot to ask you if that was so [B].

I hear that some of the youth about here are preparing all sorts of prehistoric surprises for future diggings! Also that a deformed hare's skull is being pickled for presentation to me. My clerks have warned me of these "goings on." I have no doubt the young Kenwards are in it [C].

The old Kenward is very much impressed [? by it] all and has been spending his time in hoofing off enthusiasts from his farm, and the Miss K's [sic] are especially pugnacious against intruders! [D].

[A] See *Daily Express*, 4 January 1913. This two column article is entitled: "Wizard of Sussex" and is illustrated with a photograph showing Dawson and Woodward digging at the site (see Fig 1.3b with "Cyril Woodward" obliterated) and an inset on the left depicting Dawson's discovery of natural gas at Heathfield, see Note C: 1.1.1. The article deals exclusively with Dawson and his career as an amateur palaeontologist and antiquarian. Woodward's name is not mentioned.

[B] Most probably William P. Pycraft's article, in *The London Illustrated News*, published on Saturday, December 28th. This article contains a photograph of Dawson and Woodward digging at Piltdown, with their portraits inset in the lower left and upper right corners respectively (Fig 1.3c). This article makes no mention of Grafton Elliot Smith. Letter 2.1.2 suggests that Woodward had "approved" this article.

[C] For further details on the Kenward family, see 4.2.13.

[D] See 2.1.2.

2.1.2 DF 116/15 Kenward 3 January 1913

(a) Mabel Kenward (1885-1978); (b) handwritten letter to Woodward on plain stationery: "Barkham Manor, Piltdown"; (c) –.

Letter from the daughter of Robert Kenward, Chief Tennant at Barkham Manor.

It is very good of you to have sent us "The London Illustrated" [News] with the picture of the "Piltdown Man" in it [A]. We have been very interested in reading it, and hope to have the large picture [A] framed. We are all very much looking forward to seeing the skull and shall be very glad to accept your kind offer to show it to us – when next we are in London. We shall hope to see you and Mr. Dawson again if you continue your search next spring – at present the "tomb" of the "Prehistoric Lady" or Man (!) is under water [B]. In spite of the actual spot not being mentioned we have had several visitors – and one local shopkeeper is doing a great trade in postcards [C] . . .

[A] Reference to the Pycraft article, see Note B: 2.1.1.

[B] See Note D: 1.3.12.

[C] Possibly Frisby of Uckfield, (see Note B: 1.2.20), or Warner of Uckfield (2.2.43).

2.1.3 DF 100/35 Maryon-Wilson 4 February 1913

(a) George Maryon-Wilson (1861-1941); (b) handwritten letter on printed stationery: "Searles, Fletching, Sussex". The letter is addressed to "The Secretary, Natural History Museum, South Kensington"; (c) –.

With reference to the "Piltdown Skull" etc., recently found by Mr. Charles Dawson on Barkham Manor farm – in the occupation of my tenant, Mr. Robert Kenward, and which I understand has been taken by him and deposited with the Nat. History Museum, I find myself obliged to point out that as the owner of this farm which belongs to the Searle's Estate the skull etc. is unquestionably my property (as there can be no question of "treasure trove" in the matter) and I must formally claim the ownership of it and the other fossils which were found at the same time and further request you to kindly take care that they are not removed by Mr. Dawson or any other person, without my permission. Mr. Dawson who is the steward of the Manor of Barkham – of which Piltdown Common, adjoining the farm, forms a part – and of which I am the Lord of the Manor – has omitted to consult or refer to me throughout – his zeal as an antiquarian may have caused him to overlook this nescessity. I was obliged to write to him yesterday and point out the position – and my only knowledge of the discovery and dealings with the skull etc. was derived from the daily press. In these circumstances I shall be glad to allow the skull to remain for the present in the custody of the Museum. and as it represents a valuable addition to previous discoveries of the same character, if the Trustees will apply to me to formally present it to the Museum as a gift, it will give me much pleasure to consider their request . . .

An attached Museum memorandum, dated 6 February, informed Woodward that Maryon-Wilson's letter of 4 February had been acknowledged, and that he should communicate directly with him, applying of behalf of the Trustees for the gift of the Piltdown specimens.

2.1.4 DF 116/11 Dawson 4 February 191[3]

(a) Charles Dawson (1864-1916); (b) handwritten letter to Woodward on stationery embossed: "The Castle Lodge, Lewes". The letter is marked "PRIVATE." Although dated "4 Feby. 1912" this is clearly incorrect and should be 1913. It is conjectured that the date February 4th might also be wrong; (c) –.

This letter was evidently in response to one from Woodward regarding Maryon-Wilson's position on the ownership of the Piltdown remains, see Letter 2.1.3.

Yes, I have had a characteristic letter. I am coming up tomorrow (Wednesday) and will call at the Museum but I fear I shall not be there very early in the afternoon. If the neighbourhood of Burlington House will suit you better to meet me please send a wire early in the morning to "Dawson Uckfield" where to meet. I have promised to dine out that night. It is a well-established rule of law that there is no property in human remains [A]!

It is not known if this letter was written before or after the scheduled meeting in London.

[A] This "rule" he repeated to Maryon-Wilson, see 2.1.5.

2.1.5 DF 100/35 Dawson to Maryon-Wilson 5 February 1913

(a) Charles Dawson (1864-1916); (b) Carbon-copy of typed letter on printed stationery: "Town Hall Chambers, Uckfield". The vast majority of Dawson's surviving correspondence is handwritten. This letter was originally enclosed with 2.1.7; (c) –.

I very much regret that you should conceive the slightest cause for complaint respecting the "Piltdown Skull" which I hoped might have been rather a subject of congratulation.

If I had realized before that you would have taken any interest in the field I should have been only too pleased to have given you full particulars, and I have not seen you since the pieces of skull have been put together. I have nothing to do with the newspaper accounts but the official account (illustrated) will be published in March, when I shall be pleased to send you copies, should you wish it? You will then find that I have followed the usual cause [sic] in acknowledging your kindness in granting me permission [A], last summer, to search for fossils in the gravel. So far, I have not mentioned the ownership of the land or the exact spot because I did not wish Mr. R[obert]. Kenward [tenant] to be troubled by trespassers.

In accordance with my practice for nearly 30 years past I have given the pieces of skull to the British Museum where they will be properly guarded and treated. If I had [not] gone to the trouble and expense of making this exploration the specimen might have fallen into other hands and been utterly lost to Science or the Nation, for it is well established law that no right of property exists in human remains . . .

[A] It appears from 2.1.7, that while Dawson had received approval to search the gravels in a general way, he had not indicated to Maryon-Wilson precisely what this "search" would entail (see 2.1.11).

2.1.6 DF 100/35 Maryon-Wilson 6 February 1913

(a) George Maryon-Wilson (1861-1941); (b) typed carbon-copy of letter to Dawson. This letter was originally enclosed with 2.1.7; (c) –.

A reply to Dawson's letter 2.1.5.

I must thank you for your letter this morning with [an] explanation as to why you did not communicate with me with reference to the discovery of the skull etc. which of course I quite accept although you must allow me to point out that even were I not interested in scientific discoveries or antiquarian research generally such a discovery as this, on which I most certainly congratulate you, in conjunction with the fact that it was made on my property, was practically bound to secure my interest. As regards the actual ownership of the skull, I find that the Museum authorities certainly take the view that it belongs to me as the owner of the soil in which it was found and I have formally claimed it as such so as to present it in due course to the Trustees on behalf of the Museum.

I hope you may be successful in making further valuable discoveries, and I shall be glad of an official account when published next month, if you will kindly send me one.

2.1.7 DF 100/34 Dawson 7 February 1913

(a) Charles Dawson (1864-1916); (b) handwritten letter to Woodward on printed stationery: "Town Hall Chambers, Uckfield"; (c) annotated by Woodward: "8th." Underlining in original by Dawson.

I enclose a copy of a letter which I sent to Mr. Maryon-Wilson [2.1.5] and he has written to me in answer that he accepts the explanation [2.1.6] and makes no reference whatever to my having dug at Barkham without his consent. Then he congratulates me and hopes I may find more but it is clear that he very much desires to present it, as the owner of the soil. As to this (although it may not be a strict legal view) it is quite understandable, and I suggest that the entry and label should be made as:

"Presented by the Discoverer Mr. Charles Dawson, F.S.A., F.G.S. and Mr. George Marion-Wilson [sic] the owner of the soil."

At the same time I think the usual formal thanks should be sent us individually.

In writing to him I suggest that you should thank him for his letter containing an offer to present the specimen, for which the Trustees thank him etc. and herewith enclose their formal thanks.

I think you should state that "Mr. Dawson has already made over to the Trustees any interest he possessed in the specimens. I think if you do this all will go well.

There is just one point I wish you to guard against and that is he mentions he intended to present it "in due course" [2.1.6] to the Trustees. These words might be deemed to include a certain amount of time when the skull etc. might be taken out of your hands for a while! I very much object to this course, because of any damage that might accrue and also because, as I have already pointed out, that there is no legal property in human remains except as, perhaps, Museum specimens under the Museums Act . . .

I send you a copy of the two letters [A] as I think in justice to me you should clear up any suspicion, with the Trustees, that Mr. Wilson's letter might have evoked, that I had no authority to make the excavations.

I trust this storm in a tea-cup may now end!

P.S. I find that my manager distinctly recollects my obtaining Mr. Wilson's consent to the excavations.

[A] See Letters 2.1.5 and 2.1.6.

2.1.8 DF 100/35 Maryon-Wilson 8 February 1913

(a) George Maryon-Wilson (1861-1941); (b) handwritten letter on printed stationery: "Searles, Fletching, Sussex", addressed to Charles E. Fagan (1855-1921), British Museum's (Natural History) Assistant Secretary; (c) an attached note reveals that Maryon-Wilson's letter was referred by Fagan to Woodward.

I thank you for your letter of the 6th – for which I am much obliged. I have noted its contents and will wait until I hear further from you. I regret the misunderstanding as to the ownership of the skull for which so far as I can judge, the Museum authorities were in no way responsible.

See Letter 2.1.9.

2.1.9 DF 100/35 Woodward 10 February 1913

(a) Arthur Smith Woodward (1864-1944); (b) handwritten letter on plain stationery. ? Draft or copy of letter from Woodward to Maryon-Wilson, in response to 2.1.8.; (c) –.

I have received from the Assistant-Secretary your kind letter of Feb. 4th in reference to the remains of the Piltdown skull and associated fossil discovered by Mr. Charles Dawson. For the past 30 years our friend Mr. Dawson has sent all his numerous discoveries to the Museum, so I have now the whole of the Piltdown collection and, in accordance with your expressed wish, I will continue to take care of it [A]. I have shown the specimens to several of the Trustees who are most interested in the discovery, and they are all anxious to be allowed to add it to the great collection under their charge. On their behalf, I venture to express the hope that you will be so kind as to present the collection to them, and if you will authorise me to hand it to the Trustees at their next meeting, I am sure they will acknowledge the valuable gift with gratitude.

As indicated by Letter 2.1.10, the above letter or a version of it was sent to Maryon-Wilson.

[A] See Note A: 2.3.5.

2.1.10 DF 100/35 Maryon-Wilson 11 February 1913

(a) George Maryon-Wilson (1861-1941); (b) handwritten letter to Woodward on printed stationery: "Searles, Fletching, Sussex"; (c) annotated by Woodward: "14th"

I have to thank you for your letter of yesterday's date and have much pleasure in acceding to your suggestion that I should authorize you to offer to the Trustees of the Museum at their next meeting the Piltdown skull and other fossils found by Mr. Dawson . . . I shall be glad if you will kindly do this and express the pleasure it will give me to present this collection to the Trustees on behalf of the British Museum.

See Note B: 2.1.11.

2.1.11 DF 116/11 Dawson 27 February 1913

(a) Charles Dawson (1864-1916); (b) handwritten letter to Woodward on printed stationery: "Town Hall Chambers, Uckfield"; (c) annotated by Woodward: "27th." Beneath his own signature Dawson has written, "To: 4 Scarsdale Villas, Kensington W." This is Woodward's London address. In light of Woodward's annotation and the context of the letter it is believed that it was written before the 27th (probably the 25th or 26th) and that it was sent from Uckfield.

Maryon-Wilson came to the Bench today and I invited him and some other magistrates to inspect the cast of the skull in which they were all greatly interested [A]. Afterwards I had it out fairly with Mr. W. and cleared up all difficulties. He tells me that he had quite forgotten that he gave me leave and now fully accepted matters as he now remembered it.

He also has given me full authority to go and dig when I like but wishes me not to give more publicity to the fact than is absolutely necessary as he has strong objections to anyone going there unauthorized or digging on a large scale by anyone. He wishes me to throw the public off the track, by all means, as to the situation of the gravel. As he has a particular opposition to people wandering about his estate and being bothered with applications for leave to dig. He says he will probably send me any future applications to deal with! So all is well.

I am sorry that I caused you trouble [by] giving some particulars to the press about Sat[urda]ys meeting [B] but it was not part of the Trustees Meeting and I take it a mere act of courtesy to me on a noteable occasion which will probably not occur again in our lifetime.

[A] As this suggests work was essentially complete on the making of casts of Woodward's reconstruction of the Piltdown skull. See 2.3.4 and subsection 2.2 for details on the availability and distribution of the casts.

[B] A reference to the formal presentation of the remains to the Trustees of the Museum, which occurred on the morning of Saturday, 22 February 1913. The event was reported in 4 major London newspapers; *The Times* (25 Dec), *Daily Express* (24 Dec), *The Globe* (24 Dec 24),and *Westminster Gazette* (24 Dec) [see DF 116/1 (1)]. Among those present were the Archibishop of Canterbury, Sir Edward Gray, the Duke of Bedford, Sir Thomas Barlow (President, Royal College of Physicians), Dr [later Sir] Lazarus Fletcher (Director, British Museum of Natural History), Lord Avebury [John Lubbock], Lord Dillon, Frederick Ducane Godman, Captain Morley Knight, and Sir H.H. Cozens-Hardy (the Master of the Rolls). In *The Times* it was noted: "The specimen will now shortly be placed on public view in the large hall of the Natural History Museum at South Kensington." It is unclear why Dawson thought these reports would cause Woodward "trouble" – unless perhaps some of the Trustees later objected to their names appearing in the newspapers (?)

2.2   Reprints, Casts and Enquiries

During the first half of 1913 Woodward received a mounting number of requests for both reprints and casts of his restored model of *Eoanthropus dawsoni*, as well as some requests for further information. A number of these requests came from European and American scientists, some of whom later figured in the debate over the association of the apelike jaw with the palpably modern human braincase. In February, a circular (prepared by the Damon Company) was issued giving information on the price and availability of the Piltdown casts (Table 2.1). As indicated by a number of letters in the following collection (see particularly those from Boyd Dawkins), the distribution of casts was slow. "Separates" [i.e. reprints] of the Dawson & Woodward (1913a) paper became available a month or so after its appearance in the March issue of the *Quarterly Journal of the Geological Society of London*.

CORRESPONDENCE

2.2.1. DF 100/34 Dawkins 16 January 1913

(a) William Boyd Dawkins (1837-1929); (b) handwritten letter to Woodward on printed stationery: "The Athenaeum, Pall Mall [London], S.W."; (c) annotated by Woodward: "17th. Mastodon teeth Retd."

Boyd Dawkins' letter, entitled "Re: Sussex Skull," (written from his London club), indicates that he had intended to visit Woodward at the Museum, and is rather anxious to receive a set of Barlow's casts for the "Manchester Museum. "[W]ithout them Elliot Smith can't finish his paper", Dawkins declared. See Letter 2.2.2. Regarding Woodward's annotation, the "Mastodon teeth" apparently were fragments of a Pliocene specimen found at Doveholes Cave in Derbyshire, and on loan from Manchester University Museum. These specimens were exhibited by Dawkins, along with the Piltdown materials, at the Geological Society on 18 December 1912, see *Quart J Geol Soc* (1912-13) 69: iv.

2.2.2 DF 100/34 Dawkins 19 January 1913

(a) William Boyd Dawkins (1837-1929); (b) handwritten letter to Woodward on stationery embossed: "Fallowfield House, Fallowfield, Manchester"; (c) –.

Further reminder from Dawkins (2.2.1) regarding the need for a set of Barlow's casts.

2.2.3 DF 116/15 Peake 24 January 1913

(a) Harold J.E. Peake (1867-1946); (b) handwritten letter to Woodward on printed stationery: "Westbrook House, Newbury, Berkshire"; (c) annotated by Woodward: "24th. Promised to write later."

Brief letter from the anthropologist Harold Peake requesting further information, along with photographs of the celebrated skull.

2.2.4 DF 116/15 MacCurdy 27 January 1913

(a) George Grant MacCurdy (1863-1949); (b) typed-written letter to Woodward on printed stationery: "Yale University, Peabody Museum of Natural History, Anthropology Section"; (c) –.

See 1.3.10 for background information on MacCurdy. In this communication MacCurdy requests further information on the Piltdown casts and possible access to photographs to illustrate a scheduled lecture [? at Yale University], and a planned article for *American Anthropologist* (see MacCurdy 1913, 1914).

2.2.5 DF 100/34 Lankester 31 January 1913

(a) Edwin Ray Lankester (1847-1929); (b) handwritten letter on printed stationery: "29 Thurloe Place, South Kensington"; (c) –.

Enquiry about the availability of casts.

2.2.6 DF 116/15 Hughes 2 February 1913

(a) Thomas Cann Hughes (1860-1948); (b) handwritten letter to Woodward on printed stationery: "78 Church Street, Lancaster"; (c) annotated by Woodward: "3rd. Ref. to Damon."

Hughes was Town Clerk of Lancaster and an amateur antiquarian, who introduced himself to Woodward as being "well-known to Dr. Boyd Dawkins." His letter sought information on the availability and costs of purchasing casts of the Piltdown specimens.

2.2.7 DF 116/15 Teppner 15 February 1913

(a) Wilfried Teppner; (b) handwritten letter [in German] to Woodward on printed stationery: "Geologisches Institut der Universität Graz [Austria]"; (c) in bottom left hand corner is a brief summary of letter – presumably made by a later archivist.

This letter from Teppner, an Austrian palaeontologist [author of *Fossilium Catalogus Animalium*, Berlin 1914], requested further information on "Eoanthropus".

2.2.8 DF 116/15 Orrego 1 March 1913

(a) Alfredo Escuti Orrego; (b) type-written letter (in Spanish) to Woodward on plain stationery: "Arica, Chile"; (c) –.

A request for information on the Piltdown remains and photographs.

2.2.9 DF 116/15 Lubbock 1 March 1913

(a) Sir John Lubbock [Lord Avebury] (1834-1913); (b) handwritten letter to Woodward on printed stationery: "Kingsgate Castle, Kingsgate, Isle of Thanet [Kent]; (c) annotated by Woodward: "3rd"

A letter from the archaeologist and influential Liberal-Unionist politician John Lubbock, requesting Woodward "look over" an enclosed manuscript (not preserved). Based on Lubbock's reply (DF 116/15 Lubbock 4 March 1913) to Woodward's letter of March 3rd. The "manuscript" was evidently a passage from Lubbock's book *Prehistoric Times*, related to Piltdown. (see Lubbock [Avebury] 1913: 337).

2.2.10 DF 116/15 Swanton 31 March 1913:

(a) E. W. Swanton; (b) handwritten letter to Woodward on stationery embossed: "Hutchinson Museum, Surrey"; (c) annotated by Woodward: "4th. Damon"

A letter from E.W. Swanton, Curator of the Hutchinson Museum, Surrey, seeking information about Piltdown casts for display. This privately owned museum was founded by the surgeon and pathologist, Sir Jonathan Hutchinson (1828-1913).

TABLE 2.1. The "Damon" Piltdown casts * (1913).

		Price	
Cast(s)	Cat No	coloured	uncoloured
Cranial fragments (4)	428	£2.2.0	£1.10.0
Right ramus of mandible	429	1.10.0	12.0
Restoration of whole skull	430	5.0.0	3.10.0
Endocranial cast	431	1.5.0	15.0
Flint implements (6)**	432	2.10.0	1.0.0

* In 1914 the right "lower" canine was added to the collection, Catalogue number 429A. The cost of a coloured canine was 3 shillings, and 1 shilling and sixpence for an uncoloured one.

** 3 palaeoliths and 3 eoliths.

2.2.11 DF 116/15 Puccioni 1 April 1913

(a) Nello Puccioni (1881-1937); (b) handwritten letter (in Italian) to Woodward on printed stationery: "Museo Nazionale d'Antropologia e Etnologia, Firenze"; (c) annotated by Woodward: "7th. Promised not to forget."

Evidently Puccioni had written earlier (not preserved) about securing reprints of the Dawson & Woodward paper. As indicated by the above annotation, Woodward promised not to forget. Puccioni subsequently published two articles (1913, 1914) on the Piltdown remains in which he argued that the jaw and skull were not from a single individual. He believed the jaw was more reminiscent of a Neanderthal than a chimpanzee (1913), a view he reaffirmed in his second article (1914).

2.2.12 DF 116/15 Tomes 4 April 1913

(a) Sir Charles S[issmore] Tomes (1846-1928); (b) handwritten letter to Woodward on printed stationery: "Mannington Hall, Aylsham, Norfolk"; (c) annotated by Woodward: "April 5th"

Brief note from the odontologist Charles Tomes [see his book (1914)], accompanying 3 rather poor photographic views of the Piltdown mandible sitting on top of what looks like a cigar box. The circumstance(s) surrounding this curious communication are not known.

2.2.13 DF 116/15 Combes 23 April 1913

(a) Paul Combes (b. 1889); (b) postcard to Woodward from Paris; (c) annotated by Woodward: "promised"

A brief note from the French geologist Paul Combes requesting a reprint of the Dawson & Woodward (1913a) article.

2.2.14 DF 116/15 Allsear 25 April 1913

(a) Thomas S. Allsear; (b) handwritten letter to Woodward on printed stationery: "Garmondsway House, Coxhoe, S.O."; (c) annotated by Woodward: "27th. Promised info. later"

A letter from an amateur prehistorian requesting reprints and information on Woodward's two lectures at the Royal Institution. The first of which was held on Tuesday, 1 April 1913 [see report in *The Globe* 2 April, *The Standard* 2 April; *Daily Telegraph* 2 April] and focussed on the Neanderthal question, with specific reference to the recently discovered La Chapelle-aux-Saints specimen. The second lecture held on 8 April [see reports *Manchester Guardian* 9 April; *The Star* 9 April; *Edinburgh Evening News* 8 April] dealt with the discoveries at Piltdown. The text of these lectures was not published by the Royal Institution.

2.2.15 DF 116/15 Dawkins 5 May 1913

William Boyd Dawkins (1837-1929); (b) handwritten letter to Woodward on stationery embossed: "Fallowfield House, Fallowfield, Manchester"; (c) –.

Another reminder (see 2.2.2) from Boyd Dawkins about his need to secure a set of Barlow's casts.

2.2.16 DF 116/15 Duckworth 5 June 1913

(a) Wynfrid L. H. Duckworth (1870-1956); (b) handwritten letter to Woodward on plain stationery: "Jesus College, Cambridge"; (c) annotated by Woodward: "6th"

Duckworth (see his earlier communication 1.3.11) asks Woodward to forward a reprint of his paper to the German anatomist Gustav Schwalbe (1844-1916) in Strassburg, see letter DF 116/15 Schwalbe 11 June 1913 (in German), annotated by Woodward: "20th". It is interesting to note that Schwalbe (1914) was not willing to accept the proposition that the Piltdown jaw and skull belonged to a single individual. Like Hrdlička (1914), he too considered the facts too uncertain for a positive opinion on the signficance of the Sussex remains. For further details on Duckworth's letter of 5 June, see 2.3.17.

2.2.17 DF 116/15 Hiersemann 17 June 1913

(a) Karl W. Hiersemann; (b) typewritten letter (in English) to Woodward on printed stationery: "KARL W. HIERSEMANN, Buchhandler und Antiquar, Konigstrasse 29, Leipzig"; (c) annotated by Woodward: "20th replied, also to Damon."

A brief letter requesting information on the company responsible for distribution of the Piltdown casts.

2.2.18 DF 116/15 Puccioni 23 June 1913

(a) Nello Puccioni (1881-1937); (b) handwritten letter (in Italian) to Woodward on printed stationery: Museo Nationale d'Antroplogia e Etnologia, Firenze"; (c) annotated by Woodward: "Wrote to Damon 27th"

See 2.2.11, Puccioni again requests reprints and further details on the Piltdown specimen.

2.2.19 DF 116/15 Hrdlička 3 July 1913

(a) Aleš Hrdlička (1869-1943); (b) type-written letter to Woodward on printed stationery: "Smithsonian Institution, United States National Museum, Washington D.C."; (c) –.

A request from Hrdlička [1.2.16] for information about casts. See Letter 2.2.32.

2.2.20 DF 116/15 Munro 13 July 1913

(a) Robert Munro (1835-1920); (b) handwritten letter to Woodward on stationery embossed: "Elmbank, Largs, Ayrshire"; (c) annotated by Woodward: "14th"

A brief communication from the author-anthropologist, Robert Munro, who notes that he is preparing a new book for Norgate & Williams of London [*Prehistoric Britain* (1914)] and requests permission to examine and draw the Piltdown skull. As indicated by Munro's published text, he accepted without reservation Woodward's interpretation of the Piltdown remains. See 2.2.25.

2.2.21 DF 100/35 Moir 25 July 1913

(a) James Reid Moir (1879-1944); (b) handwritten letter to Woodward on printed stationery: "12 St. Edmund's Road, Ipswich [Suffolk]"; (c) –.

Moir (see 1.2.21) requests a reprint of the Dawson & Woodward (1913a) paper. For further details on this communication, see 2.3.13. Moir (1912) had gone on record as being an avid supporter of Woodward's interpretation of the Piltdown remains.

2.2.22 DF 116/15 Smith 26 July 1913

(a) Reginald A[llender] Smith (1873-1940); (b) handwritten letter to Woodward on printed stationery: "Department of British and Mediaeval Antiquities and Ethnography, British Museum, London W.C."; (c) annotated by Woodward: "28th"

A short note thanking Woodward for reprint. See Table 1.2 for a summary of Smith's views on Piltdown.

2.2.23 DF 116/15 Hinton 26 July 1913

(a) Martin Alister Campbell Hinton (1883-1961); (b) handwritten letter to Woodward on printed stationery: "2 Garden Court, Temple [London W.C.]"; (c) –.

Hinton's letter thanks for the reprint, and notes: "I do not think that I (nor any one else who was privileged to be present) will ever forget the occasion on which it was read." For further information on Hinton, see 4.2.2 and 6.3.18.

2.2.24 DF 116/15 Haward 28 July 1913

(a) Fred N[airn] Haward (1871-1953); (b) handwritten letter to Woodward on printed stationery: "F.N. HAWARD, A.M.I.E.E., 49 Queen Victoria Street, London E.C. Beneath this printed address, Haward has written "44 Gunnersbury Lane, Acton", presumably his home; (c) –.

Fred N. Haward was a professional electrical and mechanical engineer and a well-known amateur geologist. In fact he had just published a paper on "The chipping of flint by natural agencies" in the *Proc Prehist Soc East Anglia* I (Part 2): 185, 1912, which had attracted considerable interest particularly in the eolithophile community. Haward's letter thanks Woodward for the reprint of the Dawson & Woodward paper (1913a), and notes with regret having missed the Geologists' Association excursion to Piltdown in July.

2.2.25 DF 116/15 Munro 29 July 1913

(a) Robert Munro (1835-1920); (b) handwritten letter to Woodward on stationery embossed: "Elmbanks, Largs, Ayrshire"; (c) underlining in original by Munro.

See Letter 2.2.20. After thanking Woodward for a reprint of the Dawson & Woodward (1913a) paper, Munro writes:

. . . *So far as I can judge taking all the collateral circumstances into account* <u>Eoanthropus dawsoni</u> *is not older than the Chellian [sic] period for reasons which I will give in my forthcoming little volume on Prehistoric Britain [A] . . .*"

[A] See Letter 2.2.20.

2.2.26 DF 116/15 Seligman 30 July 1913

(a) Charles Gabriel Seligman (1873–1940); (b) typewritten note to Woodward on printed stationery: "36 Finchley Road, London N.W."; (c) –.

A brief note thanking Woodward for reprint. Seligman was well-known in anthropological circles, see Note I: 1.2.11.

2.2.27 DF 116/15 Willett 30 July 1913

(a) Edgar [William] Willett (1856-1928); (b) handwritten letter to Woodward on printed stationery: "Farmleigh, Worth Park, Crawley [Sussex]; (c) –.

A note of thanks for reprint of the Dawson & Woodward paper. For further details on Willett, see Note B: 1.2.2.

2.2.28 DF 116/15 Thane July 1913

(a) George Dancer Thane (1850-1930); (b) handwritten letter to Woodward on printed stationery: "University of London, University College, Gower Street, London W.C."; (c) –.

In this note of thanks for the Dawson & Woodward reprint, Thane wrote in reference to the latter: "However we may agree to differ as to interpretation, I value the work highly." See 2.3.54.

2.2.29 DF 116 Fraipont July 1913

Calling card of Charles Fraipont, son of the Belgian anatomist Julien Fraipont (1837-1910), requesting an opportunity to view the Piltdown specimens. The Museum's visitor book confirms Fraipont's visit.

2.2.30 DF 116/15 Dollo August 1913

(a) Louis Dollo (1857-1931); (b) handwritten note (in French) to Woodward on a printed postcard: "Musée Royal d'Histoire Naturelle, Bruxelles"; (c)–

A note thanking Woodward for reprint.

2.2.31 DF 116/15 [I]oled 2 August 1913

(a) C. [?I/T] Ioled; (b) handwritten letter (in German) to Woodward on plain stationery: "Vahrn (Tirol)"; (c) –.

The identity of this individual is unknown. After thanking Woodward for reprint of the Dawson & Woodward (1913) paper, he goes on to note that the discovery is of "singular" interest and "perhaps it will oblige us to alter considerably our present ideas of primitive man."

2.2.32 DF 116/15 Hrdlička 2 August 1913

(a) Aleš Hrdlička (1869-1943); (b) type-written letter on printed stationery: "Smithsonian Instution, United States National Museum, Washington D.C."; (c) –.

This letter is addressed to Alfred Cort Haddon (1855-1940) at Cambridge requesting his assistance in getting further details on the Piltdown specimens for an article he was preparing for the *Annual Report of the Smithsonian Institution* and noting that recent articles in America, such as MacCurdy's in the *American Anthropologist* (1913) were unsatisfactory. In Haddon's covering letter to Woodward (dated August 15th: DF 116/15 (63)) he asks that Hrdlička be sent a reprint. From Hrdlička's piece on Piltdown (published in 1914) it is evident that Woodward did send him a number of photographs. Also Hrdlička's Library at the US National Museum contains Dawson & Woodward's 1913 paper and subsequent reprints on Piltdown. As for Hrdlička's views on the Sussex remains, he wrote in his (1913) 1914 report: ". . . the last word has not yet been said as to its date and especially as to the physical characteristics of the being it stands for" (p 509).

2.2.33 DF 116/15 Valderrama 4 August 1913

(a) José Valderrama; (b) handwritten letter (in English) to Woodward on plain stationery. The address is simply "Madrid"; (c) –.

Valderrama's letter requests further information on the Piltdown remains. He goes on to note that he wants to "formulate some laws and principles stating the geometrical basis upon which improving crania is modified [sic]."

2.2.34 DF 116/15 Puccioni August 1913

(a) Nello Puccioni (1881-1937); (b) handwritten (in Italian) postcard to Woodward. Postmark: "Firenze"; (c) –.

A further inquiry about promised reprints and casts. See Letters 2.2.11 and 2.2.18.

2.2.35 DF 116/15 Sergi 9 August 1913

(a) Giuseppe Sergi (1841-1936); (b) handwritten note (in English) to Woodward on plain stationery; (c) –.

Sergi was a well-known Italian anthropologist, based in Rome. His brief note acknowledges receipt of the Dawson & Woodward reprint. In 1914, Sergi published an article on the Piltdown remains in *Revista di Antropologia* (Roma), in which he accepted without reservation Woodward's reconstruction.

2.2.36 DF 116/15 Dawkins 9 August 1913

(a) William Boyd Dawkins (1837-1929); (b) handwritten note Woodward on plain stationery; (c) underlining in original by Dawkins.

A short note asking: "Can you <u>hurry up</u> the casts?" See Dawkins' early requests: 2.2.1, 2.2.2, and 2.2.15.

2.2.37 DF 116/15 Rehlin 13 [August] 1913

(a) W. Rehlin; (b) handwritten letter (in German) to Woodward on printed stationery: "Nürnberg, Sulzbacherstrasse 22"; (c) annotated by Woodward "15th".

I still await your kind reply . . . about the price of casts . . . Prof. Keith wrote me yesterday that the braincase, mandible and canine tooth probably derive from 3 individuals [A].

In these circumstances I withdraw for the present my request for casts of the cranium, canine and mandible. It would interest me to hear from you whether you are of the same opinion as Prof. Keith.

This letter is listed in the Museum archive-index as being written in August 1913, but this is considered to be wrong. Rehlin has written "Inz", which is the old-fashioned German script for "Dez." or "Dezember". This being the case, then this would explain what otherwise would be a premature reference to the Piltdown canine found by Teilhard de Chardin on 30 August, see Note A: 2.3.35.

[A] Rehlin uses the term "Individuen" which could also mean "separate species of 3 animals".

2.2.38 DF 116/15 Deichmuller 19 August 1913

(a) Johannes Victor Deichmuller; (b) handwritten (in German) postcard to Woodward, postmarked: "Dresden"; (c) –.

Deichmuller was a well-known German mineralogist. His brief note thanks Woodward for reprints and notes that Piltdown had sparked a "lively discussion" at a recent gathering of the German Anthropological Institutes at Nuremburg. For further details on the Nuremburg meeting, see Letter 2.3.31.

2.2.39 DF 116/15 Kendall 20 August 1913

(a) Rev E.O. Kendall; (b) handwritten letter to Woodward on printed stationery: "The Rectory, Winterbourne Bassett, Swindon"; (c) –.

After thanking Woodward for the Dawson & Woodward (1913) reprint, he notes that his special interest is flint implements and is unquestionably an eolithophile, and thinks the Piltdown eoliths should be called "Kent Plateau type tools" – evidently in deference to Harrison (2.2.40) and Prestwich's earlier work (see introductory notes to Section 1.2).

2.2.40 DF 116/15 Harrison 22 August 1913

(a) Benjamin Harrison (1837-1921); (b) type-written letter to Woodward on ruled notepaper: "Ightham"; (c) annotated by Woodward: "25th. Should go to Bloomsbury if kept"

In the mid 1890s Harrison achieved national prominence through his work with Joseph Prestwich that endeavoured to establish the authenticity of an eolithic industry in the high Plateau gravels of Kent. Having thanked Woodward for the Piltdown reprint, Harrison then went on to describe flint tools he had found near Penshurst, Kent. As indicated by Woodward's annotation these "implements" accompanied this letter.

2.2.41 DF 116/15 Boule 27 August 1913

(a) Marcellin Boule (1861-1942); (b) handwritten postcard to Woodward, bearing printed title: "L'ANTHROPOLOGIE, Muséum National d'Histoire Naturelle, 1 Place Valhubert, Paris" (c).

See 1.2.11, for background information on Boule. In his brief note Boule confines himself exclusively to thanking Woodward for reprint. For his developing views on Piltdown, see Letter 4.1.10.

2.2.42 DF 116/15 Firth 27 August 1913

(a) R. Firth; (b) handwritten note (in German) to Woodward on a postcard marked: "Innsbruck, Austria"; (c) annotated by Woodward: "Damon"

A request for information about purchasing a set of casts of the Piltdown remains.

2.2.43 DF 116/15 Warner 7 September 1913

(a) [Rev] John A. Warner; (b) handwritten letter on printed stationery: "The Vicarage, Hadlow Down, Uckfield, Sussex"; (c) annotated by Woodward: "Paid for by stamps enclosed in postage book."

Warner's letter and 5 enclosed postcards were originally sent to the 'Secretary' at the Museum. One card bears a printed rhyme about the Piltdown "woman", across the top of which someone has written: "from our lunatic contributor." The other postcards depict drawings (made by Warner) of the restored Piltdown skull.

2.2.44 DF 116/15 Woodward 8 September 1913

(a) Henry Woodward (1832-1921); (b) handwritten letter to Woodward on stationery embossed: "Geological Magazine"; (c) annotated by Woodward: "9th".

Henry Woodward was the former Keeper of Palaeontology at the Museum (1880-1901). As editor of the *Geological Magazine* (1864-1920), H Woodward requested "some copy" on Piltdown for the October issue of his magazine. Later, Smith Woodward sent him a two page abridgement of his upcoming address in Birmingham to the British Association for the Advancement of Science, see *Geol Mag* 10: 433-434, 1913.

2.2.45 DF 116/15 Wright 9 September 1913

(a) William Wright (1874-1937); (b) handwritten letter on printed stationery: "The London Hospital Medical College (University of London), Turner Street, Mile End, London"; (c) –.

William Wright was Dean of London Hospital Medical College. After thanking Woodward for reprint, Wright sent "best wishes for Birmingham". The latter refers to Woodward's scheduled presentation on Piltdown before the British Association for the Advancement of Science in Birmingham, see 2.3.36.

2.2.46 DF 116/15 Derry 15 September 1913

(a) Douglas E[rith] Derry (b 1874); (b) handwritten letter on printed stationery: "Windspoint, Higher Drive, Purley"; (c) –.

In this letter, Derry, an anatomist, apologized for the delay in conveying thanks for the Piltdown reprint. Derry had just returned from America. For further information on Derry, see 2.3.56 and introductory notes to Section 4.1.

2.2.47 DF 116/15 Gregory 20 September 1913

(a) William King Gregory (1876-1970); (b) handwritten note to Woodward on postcard: "American Museum of Natural History"; (c) –.

Gregory was a vertebrate palaeontologist, based at the American Museum in New York

City. In this note Gregory thanks Woodward for the "kindness and courtesies" extended to him during his recent visit to London (see Teilhard de Chardin's Letter No 30 (dated 10 September 1913) cited in Note A: 2.3.35), and asks for a copy of the Piltdown paper.

2.2.48 DF 116/15 Wright 30 September 1913

(a) George Frederick Wright (1838-1921); (b) type-written letter to Woodward on printed stationery: "Bibliotheca Sacra Company, Publishers, Oberlin, Ohio"; (c) –.

Wright was editor of the *Bibliotheca Sacra*, a religious and sociological quarterly. In addition to these duties and teaching at the Oberlin Theological Seminary, Wright also had a self-taught interest in geology. In the early 1890s he had published two controversial books: *The Ice Age in North America* (1889) and *Man and the Glacial Period* (1892). Wright had contended, contrary to the views of the American scientific establishment that the Glacial period had been a single rather than a multiple event. Wright's letter thanked Woodward for the reprint of the Dawson & Woodward (1913a) paper and asked for further information concerning the age of the Ouse deposits.

2.3 Piltdown Under Attack

In July 1913, coinciding with the distribution (at least in England) of the Barlow-Damon casts of the Piltdown remains, Woodward's reconstruction was vigorously attacked by Arthur Keith, Conservator at the Royal College of Surgeons. Keith used the forum of the International Medical Congress, which convened in London during the middle of August, to present his criticisms and to promote an alternative restoration of the Piltdown cranium [1].

Following in the wake of Keith's onslaught, a canine tooth was recovered from the Piltdown site on 30 August by Teilhard de Chardin, which essentially vindicated Woodward's restoration. Although this fortuitous "discovery" rescued Woodward's reputation it did not dampen Keith's critique of the controversial remains. Throughout October and on into November he and Grafton Elliot Smith clashed in the pages of *Nature* over specific points relating to the cranial and neuroanatomy of *Eoanthropus*, which did much to obscure Waterston's argument (see Table 1.2) regarding the association of the jaw and skullcap, that was also published in *Nature* (1913).

Although a few workers had registered, along with Waterston, some reservations about the taxonomic status of the jaw and its association with the skullcap (Hrdlička (1913) 1914; Lankester 1913; Puccioni 1913), by the year's end, scientific opinion was, by and large, favorably inclined to Woodward's monistic interpretation of the remains (Anthony 1913; Boule 1913; Elliot (1913) 1914; Giuffrida-Ruggeri 1913; Haddon 1913; MacCurdy 1913; Munro 1913; Shattock (1913); Elliot Smith 1913a, 1913b, 1913c, 1913d; Thacker 1913; Underwood 1913; Vram 1913; Walkhoff 1913) [2].

In addition to the important discovery of the canine tooth, several other remains were also recovered at the Piltdown site during the summer of 1913, see subsection 2.4 for a summary. Furthermore, from all indications it was during this season that Dawson reported finding "the frontal part of a human skull" at a site situated "a long way from Piltdown" (2.3.21). While the provenance of this specimen remains uncertain, it appears that this might well have been the frontal bone later attributed to the so-called Barcombe Mills assemblage, later described by Montagu (1951b).

NOTES

[1] See article in the *Illustrated London News* 16 August 1913: "Ape-Man or Modern Man? The Two Piltdown Skull Reconstructions."

[2] Dates with parentheses indicate year paper was read, while those without indicate date of publication. In 1913 Boule's assessment of the Piltdown remains while reserved is sympathetic, and essentially a review of Dawson & Woodward 1913a. A more definitive statement was issued in 1915. As indicated by this latter work Boule remained favourably disposed to Woodward's reconstruction, and was openly critical of Waterston's view that the jaw did not belong with the skull. But this position subsequently changed. As for Giuffrida-Ruggeri, while supporting the monistic viewpoint, like Boule he did register some doubts about the distinctness of the genus *Eoanthropus* from *Homo*.

CORRESPONDENCE

2.3.1 DF 116/15 Elliot n.d. January 1913

(a) George Francis Scott Elliot (1862-1934); (b) handwritten letter to Woodward on printed stationery: "Drumwhill, Mosdale, Scotland"; (c) –.

In this otherwise general letter, Elliot (author of *Prehistoric Man and His Story* (1915) writes:

I think I am right in . . . that James Geikie [the Scottish geologist 1839-1915] said in one of his Monro Lectures that the Heidelberg jaw belonged to the Günz-Mindel interglacial. I have tried hard to make the Piltdown woman Mindel-Riss, but really Günz-Mindel seems by far the most satisfactory age for her.

For further discussion of this, see Elliot's paper delivered to the Royal Philosophical Society of Glasgow on 3 December, 1913 (Elliot 1914). As indicated by this paper and his book (1915), Elliot was supportive of Woodward's reconstruction:

The jaw in some respects resembles that of a young chimpanzee . . . [but is] . . . representative . . . of one of the very earliest strains of mankind, perhaps the very first of one the very earliest strains of mankind, perhaps the very first known of the original "generalized world-ranging type" from which all other varieties were derived (1915:128-129).

2.3.2 DF 116/5 Elliot Smith 7 January 1913

(a) Grafton Elliot Smith (1871-1937); (b) handwritten note to Woodward on a printed postcard: "4 Willow Bank, Fallowfield, Manchester; (c) annotated by Woodward: "17.1.13. Asked for return of cast."

A response to a telegram Woodward sent on January 7th enquiring about his report on the cranial cast for the *Quarterly Journal of the Geological Society*. Elliot Smith notes (with apologies) that the report had been sent.

2.3.3 DF 116/15 Johnson 30 January 1913

(a) Arthur Johnson; (b) handwritten letter on printed stationery: "University of Edinburgh"; (c) annotated by Woodward: "31st"

In this curt note Johnson writes:

In the mandible of an adult chimpanzee in our Museum the labial cusps of one molar are worn quite flat, but the flattening only affects half the surface, the labial half.

2.3.4 100/34 Dawson 31 January 1913

(a) Charles Dawson (1864-1916); (b) handwritten letter to Woodward on stationery embossed: "The Castle Lodge, Lewes"; (c) –.

Thank you for the newspapers from Ireland [A].

Clement Reid [B] had an idea that the thrust which raised the Goodwood Beach and the [?Brighton] Raised Beach also brought up the Piltdown gravels. The former are marine and the latter freshwater and apparently there exists no connection between the raised beach and any known marine deposits underlying the Weald. I have always had an idea that the lift which brought up the marine deposits was more confined to the coastal region between the Downs and the sea. Perhaps after the Geologists Association has been over the country there may be some fresh ideas on the subject [C].

When we discussed the subject of taking the original specimens to Ireland I quite thought you had abandoned the idea of doing so. However, I am glad that they are back safely.

I have got my casts on view at my office and people are flocking in to look at them [D]. I am hearing all sorts of rumours of new gravels and teeth and bones high up in the Weald . . . Two men in Lewes have gone perfectly mad over our Eolithic finds and are accumulating large collections and I am a little disliked for venturing an opinion as to the possibilities of some of them.

[A] For details of Woodward's trip to Ireland, see Grenville Cole correspondence Letters 1.3.4 and 1.3.8 and report in *Irish Times* January 29 and *Daily Express Dublin* January 29. Commenting on the meeting Cole is reported as having said: "This was one of the greatest scientific meetings ever held in Dublin. . . . It was a great privilege for the Royal Dublin Society to be able to see the actual skull and specimens of what may prove to be the beginning of a series of still more brilliant discoveries . . ." (*Irish Times*, 29 January 1912).

[B] Clement Reid (1853-1916) of the Geological Survey, see Note C (below). This subject was raised at the Dublin meeting, see *Daily Express Dublin* 29 January 1913.

[C] Indeed, Reid had stressed a similar argument in the discussions that followed Woodward & Dawson's presentation at the Geological Society on 18 December 1912:

. . . [N]o detailed 'drift survey' has yet been made of this particular area [Weald], but perhaps the survey of the Sussex coastal plain might throw light on the age of the deposit at Piltdown . . . It seems, however, that the low Plateau of the Weald, on which the Piltdown deposit probably lies, must belong to a period later than that of maximum depression, for otherwise these lowlands of the Weald would be covered by marine deposits, as is the coastal plain . . . The deposits are not preglacial or even early Pleistocene – they belong to an epoch long after the first cold period had passed away; but they occur at the very base of the great implement-bearing succession of Palaeolithic deposits in the South-East of England (Dawson & Woodward 1913a: 150).

Picking up on this a Professor Joly of Dublin said that if the "raised beach" in which the Piltdown skull was found "was younger than the ice age, and that if that were so the skull was [therefore] later than the glacial period" (*Irish Times*, 29 January 1912). This individual is believed to be John Joly (1857-1933), an Irish geo-physicist.

[D] See Letter 2.1.11.

2.3.5 DF 116/12 Dawson 23 February 1913

(a) Charles Dawson (1864-1916); (b) handwritten letter to Woodward on stationery embossed: "Uckfield, Sussex"; (c) annotated by Woodward: "28th". Clipped to this letter is a sepia-toned photograph of the Piltdown mandible (superior view) and labelled. Underlining in original by Dawson.

Following my observation about the depressions caused by the roots of the canine tooth and premolars in the <u>Eoanthropus</u> jaw, I took a photograph yesterday and send you a print [A]. I think it clearly shows *the position of the bottom of the root of the canine and the 1st premolar on the floor of each socket? The walls seem to bulge outwards as if the teeth projected beyond the outer line.*

I should think Barlow's mould would show, in negative form, the position of the base of the roots. They should appear as tubercles on the mould of this part of the ramus.

[A] This suggests that Dawson possessed a camera as well as the capability of developing prints. It is not clear from the photograph if the specimen is the original or a cast – however, in the light of Letter 2.3.4, it would appear to be the latter rather than the former. See also 2.1.11.

2.3.6 DF 116/12 Dawson 1 [March] 1913

(a) Charles Dawson (1864-1916); (b) handwritten letter to Woodward on printed stationery: "Town Hall Chambers, Uckfield". Originally Dawson had dated this letter "1st February", and then corrected it to "1st March". In the top left hand corner some later archivist has incorrectly dated this letter as "14 March". In the left margin (page 1) of this letter is a sketch of a mandible, illustrating text; (c) annotated by Woodward: "3rd". Underlining in original by Dawson.

Thanks for your letter. I have some amusing things to tell you when we meet.

Yesterday Banbury [A] (one fair J.P!) and I went out in his motor elephant hunting! We ran down two; a mastodon and an Elephas of sorts. The Mastodon specimen is one tooth and a half and a piece of jaw [according to Dawson's sketch the fragment was 16 inches in length] in which they are fixed which was brought by a man for 8d and reposes in a pub at present, but I am doubtful as to its origin . . . . It has an old label on it [B] . . . The jaw is much mineralized, a sort of iron/sandstone. The tooth is a yellowish white iron stained. Perhaps you can throw some light on it from the label?.

If we can buy it I [will] bring it up or try and borrow it any how? If you do not want it Banbury would like it for himself. The other tooth was found in a deposit dug into for the foundation of a house and so far as I can judge overlaid the Hastings Beds. It is true elephas type . . . we are going to inspect the deposit, and the tooth, as soon as we can get hold of the builder . . . . The Mastodon specimen is rather fine (?) Mastodon arvernensis type, but large.

[A] Believed to be Capt. Cecil E. Banbury, who is listed as a member of the Sussex Archaeological Society, and residing in Uckfield. Banbury was evidently a local magistrate and Justice of the Peace. In 2.3.10, Dawson refers to him as "Capt. Banbury."

[B] Here Dawson endeavors to duplicate the information on the label.

2.3.7 DF 100/34 Abbott 3 March 1913

(a) William James Lewis Abbott (1853-1933); (b) typewritten letter to Woodward on printed stationery: "W.J. LEWIS ABBOTT, Jeweller, Gem Importer . . . etc 8 Grand Parade, St. Leonard's-on-Sea"; (c) annotated by Woodward: "5th Retd., probably Gibraltar Macaque ASW"

Accompanying this letter was a nonhuman primate skull, which Abbott said had been found in 1907 at Braintree, Essex [see Note C: 2.3.10]. *"As you have your attention now on the Anthropoidea I am sure you will be interested with the enclosed specimen,"* Abbott explained. To which he added: *"I shall be glad to hear your identification of it, as it may prove an opportunity for going into other monkey remains that have been found."* As Abbott subsequently admitted in Letter 2.3.8, this skull belonged to a friend who had himself submitted the specimen to Woodward for identification circa 1908.

2.3.8 DF 100/34 Abbott 5 March 1913

(a) William James Lewis Abbott (1853-1933); (b) typewritten letter to Woodward on printed stationery: "W.J. LEWIS ABBOTT, Jeweller, Gem Importer . . . 8 Grand Parade, St. Leonard's-on-Sea"; (c) –.

Following further explanation of the specimen mentioned in 2.3.7, Abbott noted that Dawson had been to see him recently. Elaborating on this, he said:

. . . [Dawson] was most surprised to find that an excursion had been fixed by the G[eologists']. A[ssociation]. I intended to have offered to have taken them to see some of those flint gravels, with a view to a realization of the antiquity of the Piltdown gravels; but my time is so occupied with business . . . that I did not."

To this curious note the following postscript, handwritten, is added in the left margin:

He [Dawson] brought me what I suppose he would consider his best implement. It owed its shape to natural fissure. Along the front edge there was some percussion flaking, which might have been any age, but certainly no one would say 'Chellean'!

[A] A reference to the Geologists' Association excursion to Piltdown which took place on Saturday, 12 July. From all indications no definite plans for this trip had been made at this time. In fact another six weeks were to pass before provisional dates were released, see "Geologists at Piltdown" in *Sussex Daily News* 22 April 1913. For further details on this excursion, see Weiner (1955) and Spencer (1990).

2.3.9 DF 116/5 Elliot Smith 5 March 1913

(a) Grafton Elliot Smith (1881-1937); (b) handwritten letter to Woodward on printed stationery: "The University, Manchester"; (c) annotated by Woodward: "6th".

In this letter Elliot Smith notes his return from Ireland where on 18 February he gave a lecture on the Piltdown skull to the Royal Dublin Society. This lecture was illustrated by slides supplied by Woodward. [See DF 116/5 Elliot Smith 10 February 1913 and 12 February 1913. As indicated by the latter, Woodward gave him a cast of the Piltdown mandible and 3 lantern slides; and "ordered 7 more slides" for him]. Elliot Smith goes on to note that he managed, with "much difficulty" to silence the "newspaper people":

I . . . told them [in Dublin] that the Sussex man's brain was quite as extraordinary as his jaw and that it was quite inconceivable that two such remarkable individuals should have left their remains side by side in the same patch of gravel. I heard little in the way of argument against this view."

Elliot Smith also noted that as per Woodward's directive he had loaned his Piltdown slides and casts to Mr [W.H.] Sutcliffe, [F.G.S.] and "who has sent in a paper to the Manch. Lit. & Phil. on the antiquity of man, in which there are free references to *Eoanthropus*." Sutcliffe's paper was read at the Manchester Society on 18 March 1913, and published in June 1913 under the title: "A criticism of some modern tendencies in prehistoric archaeology."

2.3.10 DF 116/11 Dawson 10 March 1913

(a) Charles Dawson (1864-1916); (b) handwritten letter to Woodward on stationery embossed: "The Castle Lodge, Lewes"; (c) annotated by Woodward: "11th. Underlining in original by Dawson."

I have come to the conclusion that our friend at St. Leonard's is a dangerous person! He wrote to Keith the other day and told him some yarn about my having said something about the Ipswich skeleton which shocked poor K. considerably [A].

   Abbott thinks our Chellean or Pre-Ch[ellea]n implements are Pliocene. This idea is founded on Moir's _best_ specimens [B].

I told Abbott his skull was a comparatively modern Barbary Ape (Macacus inuus) but you will see from his letter enclosed he has no idea of being taught! [C]

I don't believe in this galaxy of monkeys in this country. In either Roman or in the Boulder-Clay, a most unlikely deposit!

Mr W [D] seems to be quite stirred about the Eoanthropus and quite furious when somebody told him that it was about the same age as the Heidelberg jaw. He said he knew better and it was far older.

I am told that at the Royal Societies Club, someone is going to give a lecture shortly on our discoveries at Piltdown. A man told me this this morning who is a member of the Club, and said it was "some well known man" but could not remember the name [E]. I have written to the Secretary of the Club to enquire.

[A] It is believed that Dawson was commenting not only on Abbott's recent communication to Woodward (2.3.8) but also on Abbott's recent article "On Prehistoric Man" published in the *Hastings & St. Leonard's Observer* Saturday, 1 February 1913. The substance of Abbott's communication to Arthur Keith is not known.

[B] See 2.3.8.

[C] It is conjectured that this specimen is represented in the Abbott Collection [now in the Wellcome Historical Medical Museum] which is labelled: "261558 Skull of Macaca. 'The only fossil monkey skull found in England' complete with lower jaw. Braintree D.2." (see DF 116/18 Abbott File.

[D] Maryon-Wilson, see Section 2.1.

[E] The Royal Societies Club was located in Pall Mall. Dawson subsequently discovered that the speaker was Woodward, see Letter 2.3.12.

2.3.11 DF 116/15 Kidner 18 March 1913

(a) Rev. H[enry] Kidner; (b) handwritten letter on printed stationery: "194 Shelbourne Road, Bournemouth"; (c) annotated by Woodward: "19th. Promised to inform him when Guide book ready."

In this brief letter, Kidner (a Fellow of the Geological Society of London), thanked Woodward for showing him the Piltdown specimens. Evidently Kidner's visit was prompted by his on-going exchange with F.A. Jones of Ilford in the pages of *The Baptist Times and Freeman* over the question of human antiquity. And in a postscript, Kidner added:

Dr Keith allowed me on Thursday to see the Ipswich skeleton [see 2.3.13]. I doubt whether it can be accepted as evidence in regard to early man.

2.3.12 DF 116/12 Dawson 20 March 1913:

(a) Charles Dawson (1864-1916); (b) handwritten letter to Woodward on printed stationery: "Town Hall Chambers, Uckfield"; (c) underlining in original by Dawson.

I have heard from the Secretary of the Royal Societies Club that they contemplated asking you to dine before your lecture [A] so I have arranged with him that the Committee ask you and I shall waive the honour of entertaining you that night, pro-forma [?] but I shall be present. The Bishop of [?] Barking to take the Chair. Why all these Bishops! We shall have to create a See of Piltdown with shrine.

Boyd Dawkins was over there with Willett and seemed disappointed that the "gravel pit" was not more imposing in appearance [B]. . . . I shall be at the B[ritish]. Museum tomorrow with Capt. Banbury [C] and the Elephant's tooth at 11.30 p.m. [sic].

[?] word unclear.

[A] See Letter 2.3.10.

[B] The circumstances of this meeting are unknown. The implication is that Dawkins had been visiting Willett at Crawley. For information on Willett, see 1.2.9. Boyd Dawkins visited the Piltdown site again in March 1915 (see Note A: 4.2.21).

[C] See 2.3.6.

2.3.13 DF 110/35 Moir 11 April 1913

(a) James Reid Moir (1879-1944); (b) handwritten letter to Woodward on printed stationery: "12 St. Edmund's Road, Ipswich"; (c) annotated by Woodward: "12th." Underlining in original by Reid Moir.

During the opening months of 1913, Woodward and Moir had exchanged letters regarding the Ipswich skeleton and other sites in Suffolk with which Moir was associated. In January he sent Woodward a collection of animal bones for identification, see DF 100/35 Moir 13 January 1913. This task was given to Charles William Andrews (1866-1924). Later in March, Moir wrote about some sub-Crag specimens which he had given to Frank Corner (1862-1939), a London physician and known member of the Ightham Circle, for identification. Woodward was familiar with Corner. In fact it had been Corner who had secured the Galley Hill skull (see Note B below) which ultimately went to the British Museum, see DF 100/30 Keith 6 July 1911. According to Moir's letter (DF 100/35 Moir 1 March 1913) it was Corner's considered opinion that the bones represented a "new kind of elephant." Knowing nothing about bones, Moir confessed: "I thought if I wrote to you, you might feel inclined to examine these sub-Coralline things if Corner brought them up to you. I have written him advising him to do this, but if you could drop him a card it would have a great effect and induce the doctor to hurry up a bit!" From all indications Woodward obliged but it appears as if Corner was reluctant to comply with Moir's wishes, see DF 100/35 Moir 13 April 1913 and DF 100/35 Moir 25 July 1913. It was in this general context that the following letter was written.

I am sending you Keith's and my account of the Ipswich Man [A] which I hope you will be interested in. I see that you are reported as saying that this and the Galley Hill skeletons must be burials.

I know nothing of the Galley Hill affair [B] but I know more than anyone else about this Ipswich Man, and I unhesitatingly say that there is no possibility of these having been buried in a grave cut through the clay which was above them!

It is for expert geologists to say what this clay is – Whitaker states that it is undisturbed Boulder Clay [C]. Mind you I quite realize your position – you say that this Piltdown creature made Chelles implements, and as it is almost impossible to conceive of a more primitive type of being, then there could not have been any earlier and therefore all flaked flints earlier than Chelles must be natural.

I, on the other hand, say that I believe your Piltdown person made the Harrisonian eoliths with which the bones were definitely associated – and further that such a creature could not have made Chelles implements. I also consider that there is unassailable evidence that man goes back for a far greater period behind the Chelles implements than that separating us from the Chellean man. The old objections which were raised against the palaeoliths are now brought up against the pre-palaeoliths, and will certainly be defeated and I am glad to think that I shall have taken some little part in attacking these ancient ideas.

On May 7th we shall all have an opportunity of telling each other what we think when the sub-Crag flints are described by Lankester at University College. I hope there will be no "wigs upon the green"!

[A] See Moir & Keith (1912), and Keith (1915).

[B] The Galley Hill remains were found near Northfleet, Kent, in 1888, and later described by Edwin T. Newton (1840-1930) in 1895. Newton contended that their discovery on the brow of the 100-ft terrace of the Thames river valley was indicative of the specimen's great antiquity. This proposition, however, failed to gather any support at the time (Spencer 1990). Later in 1908, Frank Corner secured the remains, and shortly thereafter Keith embraced the specimens to support his developing thesis on the antiquity of the anatomically modern human skeleton (see Keith 1911 and particularly 1915).

[C] The geologist, William Whitaker (1836-1925).

2.3.14 DF 100/34 Dawson 23 April 1913

(a) Charles Dawson (1864-1916); (b) handwritten letter to Woodward on stationery embossed: "The Castle Lodge, Lewes"; (c) annotated by Woodward: "24th. No"

Many thanks for the casts [sic] safely received and will see that it does not get injured. I have been trying an experiment with it by duplicating the parts of the skull and jaw on each side in a slightly different shade of brown. I have done this in water-colour which rubs off easily [A].

I like it better this way because it helps the uninitiated. I have got three different shades for the real, the restored, and the hypothetical. It does not look as if it had been ever restored. Please drop me a line if we are to visit the Sherstone gravel pits [B] on Sunday.

[A] See Note B: 2.3.21.

[B] Inserted here, and in slightly bolder handwriting (? Dawson) is: "at Barcombe." See Letter 2.3.21 which refers to the site where Dawson reported finding a human frontal bone.

2.3.15 DF 116/15 Woodward 7 May 1913

(a) Horace Bolingbroke Woodward (1848-1914); (b) handwritten note to Woodward on printed letter card: "85 Coombe Road, Croydon"; (c) –.

In this letter, Horace Woodward, comments on Smith Woodward's recent Royal Institution lectures:

I was bothered by an account . . . printed in the Morning Post, in which you were reported [contrary to what you concluded in the Geological Society paper] that the skull was Pliocene, but even the Morning Post is not infallible . . ."

From all indications Horace Woodward was referring to the *Morning Post* April 9, 1913: "He [Woodward] described it as belonging to the early part of the Pliocene period. . . [and] must have been almost contemporaneous with the Heidelberg mandible."

2.3.16 DF 116/5 Elliot Smith 3 June 1913

(a) Grafton Elliot Smith (1871-1937); (b) handwritten letter to Woodward on printed stationery: "The University, Manchester"; (c) –.

. . . University administrative work has monopolized all my time of late so that I have done very little work on the Piltdown casts, but I am now settling down to the job and do not think it will take long to get it ready for the Royal Society.

As indicated by Letter DF 116/5 Elliot Smith 17 June 1913, Smith intended to prepare an exhibit-demonstration for a Soirée at the Royal Society [during the weeks of June], but was prevented from doing so by his duties at Manchester.

2.3.17 DF 116/15 Duckworth 5 June 1913

(a) Wynfrid L. H. Duckworth (1870-1956); (b) handwritten letter to Woodward on printed stationery: "East House, Jesus College, Cambridge"; (c) annotated by Woodward: "6th".

In an earlier letter (1.3.11), Duckworth had noted his intention of making a comparative study of the Piltdown mandible – with particular reference to the variation in the mylo-hyoid ridge. Referring to this study, he wrote: "I am still unable to match the Piltdown mandible in regard to the symphysial (or para-symphysial) region!" His letter also indicated that Gustav Schwalbe was rather anxious to receive a reprint, see Letter 2.2.16.

2.3.18 DF 114 Woodward 28 June 1913

(a) Arthur Smith Woodward (1864-1944); (b) handwritten memo to W.P. Pycraft on a printed slip: "British Museum (Natural History), addressed to "Dear Pycraft" [A]; (c) underlining in original by Woodward.

Do you think you could extract upper molars 2 and 3 from the skull of a large chimpanzee? If you think this is possible, Dr Leon Williams [B] would be glad to come and study them with the corresponding teeth of Pithecanthropus of which he has casts."

[A] William Plane Pycraft (1868-1942), a mammalian osteologist in the Department of Zoology, British Museum (Natural History).

[B] Leon Williams (1852-1932), an American dentist, living in London. From all indications Williams was working on the Piltdown problem with Keith, see 2.3.24 and 2.3.37.

2.3.19 DF 100/34 Dawson 29 June 1913

(a) Charles Dawson (1864-1916); (b) handwritten letter to Woodward on stationery embossed: "The Castle Lodge, Lewes"; (c) annotated by Woodward: "30th"

This letter is devoted primarily to a box of specimens sent from a Hasting's quarry, samples of which he promised to bring Woodward on Wednesday morning [2 July]. Following this, he writes: "I hear that Keith is to be one of our party on July 12th [scheduled excursion of the Geologists' Association to Piltdown]. He seems to be spreading his new views about the skull." For more specific details, see Letter 2.3.22 and 2.3.28. And in a postscript, Dawson adds: "Can you send me a photo of the brain-cast if one is to be had ready printed? C.D."

2.3.20 DF 114 Nayler 1 July 1913

(a) John Nayler; (b) handwritten letter to Woodward on printed stationery: "Chudleigh Vale, 5 Dudley Road, Wimbledon"; (c) appended to this letter is a memorandum from Woodward to William Pycraft, dated 2 July: "Will Mr Pycraft be here on Saturday and does he care to meet these people [A]? I shall be away at Piltdown" [DF 116 (5)].

John Nayler was President of the British Phrenological Society Inc.

I have been in communication with Prof. Keith and he has mentioned your name. I have arranged with a party of friends – ladies and gentlemen – all interested in crania to visit S[outh]. Ken[sington]. Museum of Sat[urda]y. next. We meet at the entrance at 3 o'clock. I asked Prof. Keith if he or an assistant could attend and tell us something about the Sussex skull. Unfortunately Prof. Keith cannot – but he says we shall find two very able anthropologists at the Museum – yourself and Mr. Pycraft.

If it will not cause any inconvenience I would be glad if yourself or someone acquainted with the subject could give us a little guidance . . .

[A] As indicated by 2.3.34 Pycraft stood in for Woodward.

2.3.21 DF 116/11 Dawson 3 July 1913

(a) Charles Dawson (1864-1916); (b) handwritten letter to Woodward on stationery embossed: "The Castle Lodge, Lewes"; (c) underlining in original by Dawson.

I have picked up the frontal part of a human skull this evening on a ploughed field covered with flint gravel. It [sic] a new place, a long way from Piltdown, and the gravel lies 50 feet below level of Piltdown, and about 40 to 50 feet above the present river Ouse. It is not a thick skull but it may be a descendant of Eoanthropus. The brow ridge is slight at the edge, but full and prominent over the nose. It was coming on dark and raining when I left the place but I have marked the spot [A]. The base of the nose is very rotten so I have put some of Barlow's mixture [? on that part]. Will you get Barlow to give us the recipe for gelatinizing, as the bone looks in a bad way and may go wrong in drying. I have got a saucepan and gas stove at Uckfield [B]. Or would it be a good opportunity to give Barlow a day off on Friday or Saturday to see Piltdown?

I will look out for you at the quarter to one train Uckfield tomorrow Friday [4 July] and will have the bit of skull at my office, but don't expect anything sensational [C]!

Farrant is sending a man with tubs and sieves over for Friday and Saturday.

I have not heard from Banbury about Saturday, but one of our magistrates (Baxendale-Pickford) is going to send us a motor with lunch as an advance guard on the day of the Geological Excursion so that we can show the way for the Charabancs! [D] If Banbury can't come I will try and get hold of Conan Doyle for Sat[urda]y.

[?/] Words unclear.

[A] It is conjectured that this specimen is represented in the assemblage known as the Barcombe Mills remains (Note A: 1.2.19), and that the site described above might be the one Dawson mentioned in Letter 2.3.14. See also Letter 4.2.22.

[B] This passage is of interest since it throws some light on the charge later made by Captain Guy St. Barbe who lived at Coombe Place, near Lewes, that Dawson might have been the perpetrator of the Piltdown forgery. His reasons for suspecting Dawson were based largely on an encounter he had with Dawson early in the summer of 1913. According to St. Barbe, in an interview with Weiner, he had paid Dawson an unexpected visit and on entering his office noticed a peculiar smell "like a chemist's shop." He recollected that Dawson looked very perturbed. On the table were porcelain dishes, some containing different brown liquids and some with bones soaking in liquids (see 6.3.21, and Weiner 1955: 165-166). St. Barbe relayed a similar story to Kenneth Oakley at an interview on 27 January 1954 (DF 116/ 29, see 6.3.31).

[C] A memorandum from Woodward Pycraft, dated 2 July 1913 [2.3.20], confirms that Woodward did in fact spend the weekend of the 4th and 5th at Piltdown. This was followed by an another session on the 11th and 12th, see 2.3.24.

[D] An account of the excursion printed in the *Sussex Daily News* (Monday, 14 July) identifies this individual as Mr. F. Hugh Baxendale, J.P.

2.3.22 DF 116/5 Elliot Smith 4 July 1913

(a) Grafton Elliot Smith (1871-1937); (b) handwritten letter to Woodward on printed stationery: "4 Willow Bank, Fallowfield, Manchester"; (c) annotated by Woodward: "8th". Underlining in original by Elliot Smith.

Now that our summer term is virtually ended I am getting a little more time than I had hitherto to examine the Piltdown braincast and to work at the problems which arise from the study of it. I took advantage of my journey to London for the Royal Society Council yesterday to look up a number of points at the R[oyal]. C[ollege]. Surgeons Museum. While there I saw Keith and he showed me his restoration of the Piltdown skull, at which he has been working ever since the Piltdown casts were acquired by the R.C.S. Museum a month ago [A]. As the matter of putting together of the fragments vitally affects my part of the work I carefully examined all the points raised by him; and as a result I am quite convinced that we shall have to modify the restoration in some respects. I was never quite happy about the right parietal and occipital regions in the braincast and spoke to Barlow about it on the night of the Geological Society's meeting in November [sic]: but he assured me that all the pieces fitted quite accurately [B]. Since I have received the models of the bone fragments I have not had time to investigate the matter for myself: but in the light of Keith's work I see quite clearly what has happened. The brain (both cerebral and cerebellar hemispheres) is markedly assymetrical and the ridges of separation of the cerebral and cerebellar depression on the occipital bone are <u>not</u> *in the mesial plane, the positions of which is shown by the crest on the inferior surface of the occipital. This means that the occipital in your reconstruction must be rotated to the right. This will throw out the right parietal and broaden the skull.*

I have not yet had time to go further into the examination of the temporal region, but according to K[eith]. the temporal bone has been inclined at an angle with the parietal. His third point is that the mandibular fragment includes the symphysial region: so that normal sized human teeth will completely fill up the space allowed by the alveolar process. I have convinced myself that the occipital and right parietal regions in your reconstruction need some modification: into the other two points I have not gone in detail yet, but there seems a strong prima facie case for a reexamination of them also.

I think as the casts are now in the hands of a good many people (who no doubt will ultimately be led to such conclusions) that some statement should be made as soon as possible with regard to the matter. Perhaps you would look into the evidence Keith has collected and see what you think of it? Or would you prefer me to reexamine the whole matter at issue and send a note to "Nature"? What I fear may happen is that Schwalbe or some other continental authority may arrive at these conclusions before any British statement has been made. Hence the need of a note published as soon as possible after we are all convinced of the need of modification.

In the meantime I am making an independent reconstruction for the purposes of my own part of the work: and by the time you have had time to reply [I] will have come to some decision on the other points raised here. I should like to know what you think should be done, once you are convinced of the need of altering the occipital region.

[postscript] From further communications I gather that Schwalbe is working at the Piltdown specimens."

Shortly after receiving this letter, Woodward contacted Keith at the Royal College of Surgeons and a meeting was scheduled to discuss the Piltdown reconstruction, see 2.3.23. Exactly what transpired at this meeting is not known. However, contrary to Elliot Smith's expectations Woodward made no revisions to his reconstruction. As a consequence this led to the eventual public confrontation between Woodward and Keith on 11 August at the International Medical Congress in London. For further details see 2.3.25.

[A] See Letter 2.3.29.

[B] This does not tally with 1.2.25 in which Woodward told Boyd Dawkins: "We are having much trouble putting the skull together."

2.3.23 DF 100/34 Keith 8 July 1913

(a) Arthur Keith (1866-1955); (b) handwritten letter to Woodward on printed stationery: "Royal College of Surgeons of England, Lincoln's Inn Fields, London W.C."; (c) annotated by Woodward: "8th. Yes 2.0"

For background to this letter, see notes appended to Letter 2.3.22.

I shall keep the whole of Thursday afternoon free. But try and come early – as soon after 2 as you can make convenient as the Council of the College meets at 4 and usually several of them come a little before 4 to see what is being done in the Museum. I sent the braincast I took out of the reconstructed skull to Elliot Smith but I'll try and get another made by Thursday. The cubic capacity is more than I told you at first – it is about 1450-1500 c.c.

According to Keith's day-diary (1913), Woodward went to the Royal College, in the company of Ray Lankester, on Thursday afternoon, 10 July.

2.3.24 DF 116/12 Dawson 9 July 1913

(a) Charles Dawson (1864-1916); (b) handwritten letter to Woodward on stationery embossed: "Uckfield, Sussex"; (c) –.

I have booked your room for Friday and Saturday and left Sunday open as it is doubtful if I can get to Piltdown on Sunday this week [A].

It will be very awkward if a considerable error has been made about the capacity of the skull. Of course if the space on either side of the median line is extended in an unlimited way the capacity will be increased accordingly. I should have thought the very thickness of the cranial walls could have prevented the capacity being so high as 1500 cc. I suppose Keith's idea is to try and make out that the capacity was normal to fit in with some of his former determinations such as in the case of the Ipswich skeleton?

I shall be glad to hear from you on Thursday after you have had your meeting [B]?

I was talking to E. T. Newton [C] about it at the G[eological]. S[ociety]. Soirée and he said that when he pieced together the Galley H[ill] skull he was very much puzzled because such a very slight alteration in the pitch of two fragments of bone in the middle of the skull made such a difference to the whole form of the cranium [D]. It is a pity that you were not present when E[lliot]. Smith was there.

I shall look forward to see the films another day, when in town [E].

P.S. Will you bring the casts for exhibition and some of the odds and ends I left with you.

[A] From all indications when they did work at Piltdown it was generally for three days, see 2.3.32.

[B] See Letters 2.3.22 and 2.3.23.

[C] Edwin Tulley Newton (1840-1930), who was responsible for bringing the Galley Hill skeleton to the attention of the British scientific community in the mid 1890s. For further details, see Note B: 2.3.13.

[D] See Newton's descriptive account of the Galley Hill specimen in *Quart J Geol Soc Lond* in 1895.

[E] It is not known if by "films" Dawson is implying merely a roll of film, or a motion-picture film. The possibility of it being the latter is supported by evidence in the American Museum of Natural History. In their photographic archives they have a negative of a photograph showing Woodward and Dawson screening gravel at the Piltdown pit; to their right a workman stands on the spot of the original discoveries. According to the notation accompanying this negative [No 327-937], it was "Enlarged from a film made in the year 1912 under the direction of Dr. J. Leon Williams, who presented it to the American Museum the Williams Collection of prehistoric crania." This photograph was later used to illustrate Henry Fairfield Osborn's Piltdown monograph (1922). During the early 1970s, Mr Nicolas Noxon, an M.G.M. producer investigated this question but was unable to locate the alleged film, see DF 116/34 Williams (1-26). For further references to Williams, see Letters 2.3.18 and 2.3.37.

2.3.25 DF 116/15 Thomson [?13] July 1913

(a) [John] Arthur Thomson (1861-1933); (b) handwritten letter to Woodward on printed stationery: "Department of Human Anatomy, University Museum, Oxford"; (c) annotated by Woodward: "14th Yes"

In this letter, Thomson indicated that at a recent meeting of the Anatomical Section of the International Congress of Medicine he was "authorized" to invite Woodward to demonstrate the Piltdown remains on Monday, 11 August at 3.00 pm in the "Organic Chemistry Lecture Room," Imperial College of Science, London. As indicated by

Woodward's annotation he agreed to the date suggested. It was subsequently arranged, however, to demonstrate the remains in Woodward's department at the Natural History Museum. This was followed (on the same day) by a devastating counter demonstration by Keith at the Royal College of Surgeons. For further details, see Note C and Teilhard's Letter (No.29) in Note A: 2.3.35.

2.3.26 DF 116/12 Dawson 15 July 1913

(a) Charles Dawson (1864-1916); (b) handwritten letter to Woodward on stationery embossed: "The Castle Lodge, Lewes"; (c) annotated by Woodward: "16th"

I am sorry I shall not be able to go to Piltdown this weekend. . . . I shall have to go slow till more money comes in [A]. I will walk over and dig out that crevice as soon as I can, but the weather is very bad and I expect it is full of water. I have told Venus [Hargreaves] to take the things back to Farrant.

This is the first and only mention made by Dawson to a shortage of money. As indicated earlier Woodward and Dawson shared the costs of the excavations at Piltdown.

2.3.27 DF 100/35 Moir 28 July 1913

(a) James Reid Moir (1879-1944); (b) handwritten letter to Woodward on printed stationery: "12 St. Edmund's Road, Ipswich" (c) annotated by Woodward: "Aug 1st. [?] Acton"

I am sending off per rail tomorrow the sub-Crag bones I wrote about [A]. I hope some may be of interest but I don't think they are anuthing great and if none of them are any good do hesitate to throw them away. These sub-Crag bones remind me very much of your old friend Piltdown. I mean as regard colour and mineral condition. Never remember seeing a Pleistocene bone in the same condition as your man, and I fully believe you have found ___Homo___ of the Pliocene!

[?] Word unclear. The mention of "Acton" in Woodward's annotation is clearly a reference to an area of London, now a part of Ealing, and quite possibly a reference to Fred Haward (2.2.24).

[A] See DF 100/35 Moir 25 July 1913, and Letter 2.3.13.

2.3.28 DF 116/15 Abbott 28 July 1913:

(a) William James Lewis Abbott (1853-1933); (b) typewritten letter to Woodward on plain stationery: "8 Grand Parade, St. Leonard's o/s"; (c) annotated by Woodward: "29th." later annotated by Kenneth P. Oakley: "Seen for the first time – shown to J[oseph]. W[einer] today. 1.VIII.57.KPO"

I am exceedingly obliged to you for the superb edition of the most important paper now before the world [A]. No one will appreciate it more than I shall. . . It is a great credit to you both. I am quite certain that the excursion was a grand success, but I need not remark it was no ordinary excursion to emphasize this that or the other well known fact or a new detail of one, it was bran [sic] new ground that with none of the older ideas. I have been quite busy over questions that have arisen. If you and he do not mind me saying it, it was a pity Mr. Dawson did not work with someone else who had paid closer all round attention to the subject of flint and flint working. I overheard two very prominent and old members of the [Geologists'] Association talking, one said to the other "Well what do you think of it?" "Well what can you think of anything a chap does that don't know what a bit of tabular flint is?" How is it that people do not rise to the superlative importance of lithocaieology? "I did not see a single piece of tabular flint" is the remark I have heard from everyone that visited the place, and to build a theory on a thing that is not there is sure to bring down critism [sic] on the whole thing and it makes it very hard for one like myself who feels it impossible to overate [sic] the importance of the discovery, but I tell you it is not all ease [sic] defending the young lady. To me it is crowning jewell [sic] of my life's work, especially of the last 25 years! I am like a man in love "I cannot do without her"!

I am not sure if sent you this reprint [B]. I made out a list of those to whom I intended sending them [*/amongst which yours occurs] but the time went on and I sent them out spasmotically [sic], without checking the list. I hope you find a suggestion here and there that may pay you wading through it.

[*/] Words added in Abbott's hand.

[A] A reference to Dawson & Woodward (1913a).

[B] See DF 116/1 (between pages 58 and 59): A reprint from the *Hastings and St. Leonard's Observer* (1 February 1913), a 3 column article by Abbott entitled: "PREHISTORIC MAN: The Newly Discovered Link in His Evolution."

2.3.29 DF 116/25 Keith 29 July 1913

(a) Arthur Keith (1866-1955); (b) handwritten letter to A.S. Kennard on printed stationery: "Royal College of Surgeons of England, Lincoln's Inn Fields, London W.C."; (c) –.

This letter was addressed to Alfred S. Kennard (1870-1948), an amateur malacologist, a close friend of Martin Hinton (2.2.23) and Frank Corner (2.3.13). It is presumed that Keith was replying to an inquiry from Kennard, whose letter is not preserved in Keith's papers at the Royal College of Surgeons.

Two months ago I got the casts of the Piltdown fragments and it was easy to see at once that a grave blunder had been made. When the bones are articulated in the manner we put human skull bones together – the Piltdown comes out a huge head – with a capacity of about 1500 c[ubic]. c[entimetres]. a little above the average of today and the size of the jaw, the type of joint for the jaw – the size of the muscles of mastication absolutely exclude the possibility of a large canine tooth. In Piltdown we have a cousin of the great headed [?] race but whereas in that race or species – the eyebrows have retained the simian form – the mandible and chin has assumed the modern shape. In Piltdown the opposite has occurred: the eyebrows are modern and the chin simian. The mandible and other Pliocene remains, came as you know from the deepest Piltdown stratum – the Chellean flints were not there. Now is it possible that the Weald was cut from the level of Lenham to the level of Piltdown in the Pliocene! How do you fit the Piltdown gravel into the Thames Valley deposits? – with those Dewlish [A] or at Selsey [B]?

The most remarkable thing is that the skull which Wm. Newton found in his gravel pit at Dartford – a pipe [sic] he says 7 feet below the surface [C] – is a modern counterpart of Piltdown – so much so that it gave me at once the key to Piltdown. I had the gravest doubts of Newton's skull but I begin to think the old man was nearer the truth than I was.

You can see the importance of a late Pliocene or early Pleistocene person with a brain of modern size – the estimate of size is not opinion: it is elementary anatomical fact.

[?] word unclear.

[A] This refers to a Pliocene deposit that occurs near Dewlish, a small town on the Dorset coast (between Exmouth and Torquay) and about 100 miles west of Piltdown. In 1910 eoliths were found in the Dewlish neighbourhood which were said to resemble those found by Prestwich and Harrison in Kent, see Grist (1910); Keith (1915: 314-315).

[B] A small coastal town in West Sussex, situated between Portsmouth (west) and Bognor Regis (east).

[C] Keith is referring to the discovery of the so-called Dartford skull in 1902, which its discoverer William M. Newton presented to the Royal College of Surgeons in 1911. For details on this specimen and Keith's views on it, see Keith (1915: 165-170; 375).

2.3.30 DF 116/12 Dawson 4 August 1913

(a) Charles Dawson (1864-1916); (b) handwritten letter to Woodward on stationery embossed: "The Castle Lodge, Lewes"; (c) annotated by Woodward: "5th".

Yes, I shall be very pleased to come on the 11th Monday. It ought to be amusing and interesting [A]. I hope Elliot Smith and Dawkins may be present. The latter is sure to be amusing with Keith.

Friday afternoon, Sat[urda]y., and Sunday aft[ernoo]n. will suit for digging. I will get Venus to come over [B].

Teilhard is in England and may be able to come, but it is not probable till later on [C]. So far as I know the following week also will suit . . .

Will you please bring some of Barlows's hardening solution. I think it is made of spirit and shellac, but I am quite out of it, and want some for that bit of grinder (Elephas) in the matrix. I hope that we may have better luck and we must follow that fissure, both sides.

Tomorrow I am off to Hastings to judge in an "historical pagent" [sic] and expect to meet Lewis Abbott and will ask him about his "Wealden glaciers. . ."

[A] The planned meeting of the Anatomical Section of the International Congress of Medicine to review the Piltdown remains at the British Museum (Natural History), see notes to 2.3.25 and 2.3.32.

[B] Venus Hargreaves, the farm labourer employed to do the digging, see 2.3.50.

[C] For details of Teilhard's visit (3 days) to Piltdown in 1913, see notes to 2.3.35.

2.3.31 DF 116/5 Elliot Smith 8 August 1913

(a) Grafton Elliot Smith (1871-1937); (b) handwritten letter to Woodward on printed stationery: "4 Willow Bank, Fallowfield, Manchester"; (c) –.

This letter was a reply to an earlier inquiry (date unknown) from Woodward.

I owe you a thousand apologies for not having answered your letter sooner, but I have been waiting in the hope that I might find time to work at the Piltdown casts. But now I have reached the day when I have to go to the Intern[ational]. Med[ical]. Congress. As soon as I returned here after seeing you last in London I had to take up the duties of the Deanship of the Medical Faculty and since then have not had a moment free for the Piltdown work. It is a matter of intense regret that I have not been free: for I see by today's paper that the German band has begun to play [A]!

[A] This is a reference to the meeting of the German anthropologists [Deutsche Anthropologische Gesellschaft] in Nuremburg [3-10 August] at which British anatomists were openly censured for giving their approval to the manner in which the Piltdown skull had been reconstructed (see F. Birkner. *Archiv für Anthropologie* XLIV: 102-103, 1913-14). Thus many observers were anxiously awaiting the meeting of the anatomical section of the International Congress of Medicine in London to see if the German viewpoint would be rejected or endorsed.

2.3.32 DF 116/11 Dawson 13 August 1913

(a) Charles Dawson (1864-1916); (b) handwritten letter to Woodward on printed stationery "Town Hall Chambers, Uckfield"; (c) underlining in original by Dawson.

It is presumed that this letter was in response to one from Woodward following the meeting at the Royal College of Surgeons on 11 August 1913.

I am very glad to have your letter and to see that you have got your men together once more [A].

Keith was most unfair in the way he tried to saddle you with [the] dummy base of the skull after your explanation. When I saw him in the morning I gathered he had got an idea that you were sneering at his efforts. I did all I could to disabuse his mind but evidently without success. I don't think he would have been so wild if he had not been nettled with the cautious way in which his observations were received by the meeting [B]. From his Times *article I gather he expected the meeting would decide definitely in his favour. [C]*

I was surprised to find that it was Leon Williams [D] that had been working with him but I didn't think our dentists shone much in the discussion. The Daily Express *wired me to Lewes that night for 500 words, but I did not return in time to do much and telephoned a letter which they published on Tuesday [E]. The local paper[s] (*Sussex Daily *and* Southern Weekly*) have been at me today, and I have given them a few generalities.*

The idea of a man with a brain of 1500-1600 cc in the Pliocene age! How we have all been mistaken!

I will make arrangements for Friday aft[ernoo]n. and Sat[urda]y. I think we had better leave Sunday out this week. My partner is just off for his holiday so that my presence may be curtailed but I cannot tell, till the time comes.

[A] Referring presumably to Edwin Ray Lankester, Grafton Elliot Smith, William Pycraft and Arthur Underwood who had rallied behind Woodward at the meeting of the Anatomical Section of the International Congress of Medicine in London. For a contemporary report of this incident, see *The Times* [London], 12 August 1913; (Note C below).

[B] Dawson's grasp of the situation can be gleaned from a long statement he made to the *Sussex Daily News* just prior to the meeting (printed on 11 August 1913) in which he endeavoured to explain the present controversy. His statement is of particular interest since he notes: "It is early days to commence speculating as to the exact conformation of the Piltdown skull. Only on Saturday last [9 August] I found another fragment of this extremely interesting fossil, and when we have done with the pick and shovel it will be quite time enough to call in the doctors." It is believed Dawson is referring here to the recovery of nasal bones from the pit. This event was recorded by Teilhard in a letter he wrote to his parents on 15 August, see Teilhard, 2.3.35 for further details.

[C] According to *The Times*, during the discussion that followed Keith's presentation at the Royal College of Surgeons:

Woodward interposed with the observation that the parts of the skull as represented by him in the base of the skull were not meant to be representations of the actual parts . . . To this Professor Keith replied: "Then, why represent them?" Professor Keith said the impossibility of Dr. Smith Woodward's reconstruction was the result of a misconception as to the nature of the teeth and jaws of this fossil man. A chimpanzee palate and jaw had been fitted on a skull that could not carry them. All the evidence was against a big canine tooth. There was no room for a great anthropoid eye-tooth. . . [Keith then went on to demonstrate that Woodward's reconstruction] was wrong; and he put to them – one which gave us a massive and well-shaped symmetrical head – the only possible reconstruction.

The now famous oil painting by the Chelsea artist John Cooke: "A Discussion on the Piltdown Skull," is supposed to represent the discussion which took place at the Royal College of Surgeons on the afternoon of 11 August 1913 (Fig 3.1). Represented in the painting are portraits of Sir Ray Lankester, Dr Grafton Elliot Smith, Mr Charles Dawson, Dr Smith Woodward, Mr William Pycraft, Mr Frank Barlow, Dr Arthur Keith, and Mr Arthur S. Underwood. In reality the discussion group also included Dr Wynfrid Duckworth, Dr Raoul Anthony of the Muséum d'Histoire Naturelle, Paris (Note C: 2.3.45), Dr. Arthur Thomson, Chairman of the anatomical section of the Congress, and Mr. Leon Williams (an American dentist who assisted Keith in his reconstruction). Although Teilhard (Note A: 2.3.35) attended Woodward's presentation at the Natural History Museum, he did not go to the Royal College. For further details on this painting see Note E: 3.1.32.

[D] See 2.3.18, 2.3.24, 2.3.37.

[E] Dawson's (anonymous) letter, printed in the *Daily Express* Friday, 15 August reads: "I am told that Dr. Arthur Keith and Dr. Bather [F] are disputing in *The Times* as to what is my right name. Permit me to say that I have not the slightest objection to Dr. Keith naming his plaster reconstruction Homo Keithii, if he will only leave me at rest, but I do not think it right he should discuss a lady's age."

[F] Francis Arthur Bather (1864-1934) was Assistant Keeper in Woodward's department at the British Museum (Natural History). Bather became embroiled in the controversy when he challenged Keith's proposal to change the name of "Eoanthropus" to "Homo", see *The Times* 13 August 1913. For Keith's response, see *The Times* 14 August 1913.

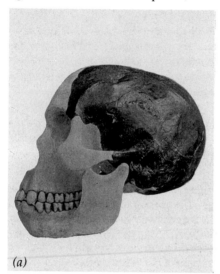
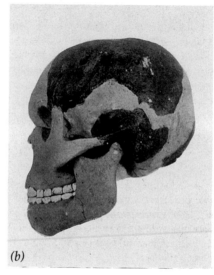

(a)   *(b)*

Fig. 2.1 Piltdown gets a face-lift (1913). (a) Woodward's reconstruction. Note the overall prognathic appearance of the face, and in particular the receding chin and large projecting lower canine. (b) Keith' reconstruction. In addition to making the braincase more voluminous, Keith also made the jaw less apelike. Note the absence of a large projecting canine. Courtesy of the Trustees of the British Museum (Natural History).

2.3.33 DF 116/15 Sollas 14 August 1913

(a) William Johnson Sollas (1849-1936); handwritten letter to Woodward on printed stationery: "173 Woodstock Road, Oxford"; (c) annotated by Woodward: "15th"

   . . . *I am astonished at the bad form displayed by Keith.*

   Even supposing you did get the bones out of the middle line (I know nothing about this) what of it? We all make mistakes. But that is no reason why the first man who thinks he has found one out should spread his wings and crow in this shameless fashion.

   It doesn't seem to me to matter two straws whether the cranial capacity is close on 1100 c.c. or 1500 c.c. Your point is the combination of a human brain and an ape's jaw and the more human the former the more interesting the combination becomes.

   Both 1100 and 1500 c.c. are actual human capacities at the present day: so why all the fuss? And now like a child crying for the moon he wants to be allowed to name your fossil! Cock-a-doodle-doo! Just see what a monstrous egg I have laid!

   I hope to be passing thru London on my way to Paris in a few days. Shall you be at the Museum?

This letter from Sollas, then Professor of Geology at Oxford (1897-1936), is of interest since it provides some insight into Sollas' relationship with Woodward. According to James Archibald Douglas (1884-1978), who had succeded Sollas at Oxford, the two men were bitter rivals. In fact it was this rivalry which, so Douglas claimed (just prior to his death), motivated Sollas to perpetrate the Piltdown forgery (see Halstead 1978) and thereby humilate Woodward. The general argument against Sollas, however, is not compelling. See Blinderman (1986) and Spencer (1990) for a discussion of this case.

2.3.34 DF 114 Nayler 28 August 1913

(a) John Nayler [2.3.20]; (b) handwritten letter to William Pycraft on printed stationery: "Chudleigh Vale, 5 Dudley Road, Wimbledon"; (c) annotated by Pycraft: "Answd /15.11.13.

I notice that since I and my friends visited S[outh]. Kensington there has been quite a controversy on the Piltdown Skull. It occurs to me that our people would be very glad if you would attend a meeting of our Society on Tuesday evening September 23 – 7.45 pm. . . You have, I think, promised to attend one of our meetings, and this would be a good opportunity of doing so. . .

2.3.35 DF 116/11 Dawson 2 September 1913

(a) Charles Dawson (1864-1916); (b) handwritten letter to Woodward on printed stationery: "Town Hall Chambers, Uckfield"; (c) originally Dawson had written "August". This is crossed-out and "Sepr" is written above in his handwriting. Underlining in original by Dawson.

Many thanks for your letter. I sent you a wire this morning as I am sure you will be disgusted as I am that someone has let out about the tooth to the "Express" The worst of it is that I have no doubt it was done by someone here who ought to have known better. It is a great pity and undermines things in more ways than one and I am very annoyed about it. [A] The Sussex Daily News people have just rung me up and I have referred them to you as I do not know which course you wish to adopt. Perhaps no more better be said till the [British] Assoc[iation]. [for the Advancement of Science] Meeting [B] but you will know best.

I expect to be at the Museum with my brother either tomorrow or Thursday [C].

[A] The "leak" Dawson is referring to concerns the discovery of the canine tooth by Teilhard de Chardin on 30 August. This story appeared in the *Daily Express* on 2 September.

As indicated in Letter 2.3.30, Teilhard returned to England in August, where he remained until the beginning of September. His itinerary is revealed in a letter to his parents, dated 27 July 1913:

. . .I leave Paris on August 1. Friday night I'll be in Canterbury (Hales Place, Canterbury, Kent) where I think I'll be until the 8th and from there I go on to Hastings. I will make my retreat at Ore Place from the 15th to the 24th; in the beginning of September I'll be going to Jersey to do a little excavating. I'll be back at Vieux-Colombier by the 1st of October (Letter No.27, in Teilhard (1965) 1967:93)

Prior to his planned retreat, Teilhard apparently spent a few days with Dawson in Lewes, see Letter No 28, Teilhard 6 August 1913 (Canterbury), in Teilhard (1965) 1967:97). Following his return to Hastings he wrote (Friday, 15 August) his parents:

. . . I arrived here Monday night after an excellent stay in Lewes with my friend Dawson. I told you once before that he lives in a very pretty villa, covered with ivy and surrounded with flowers [the Castle Lodge] and located within the very walls of the old castle of Lewes. I was received in true English fashion like an old friend; they took care of my every whim and for three days I lived in the purest comfort of this most enjoyable of homes. Most of the time we spent digging in Uckfield in the gravel pits of Piltdown; I went on Friday afternoon [8 August], all day Saturday [9 August], and Sunday afternoon

[10 August]. This type of research is completely "exciting"; unfortunately, we did not find too much this time: just a small fragment of a nose(?) [1]. At least the weather was beautiful, Piltdown is a very beautiful corner of Sussex, with many trees, near a "golf course," and it has a very beautiful park which you have to go through to get to Uckfield. During the three days, Dr. Woodward, from the British Museum, worked with us. . . Monday I went to London with Mr. Dawson and Dr. Woodward to attend an exhibition of the remains from Piltdown, held by the Congress of medical anatomists (among them I found many I had known from the Museum). At the second session, which I could not attend, having taken the train for Hastings, Dr. Woodward was very much criticized by a certain Professor Keith who wants (and rightly so I believe) to have the skull reassembled in a new way. . . (Letter No.29, in Teilhard (1965) 1967; 98-99).

[1] Believed to be a reference to the turbinal bones described in Dawson & Woodward (1914a). In fact it is conjectured that it was to this particular discovery that Dawson was referring to in the interview published in the *Sussex Daily News* on August 11, 1913 (see Note B: 2.3.32).

Later, in a letter dated August 29th, Teilhard noted his intention to visit Dawson again, (see Letter No 30, in Teilhard (1965) 1967:102). The details of this visit can be found in Letter No 32 [from Jersey], dated September 10th (in Teilhard (1965) 1967:104-105). Here Teilhard told his parents:

. . . I went to Lewes to have breakfast at Castle Lodge. Afterwards Mr. Dawson and I left to go digging in Uckfield along with Dr. Woodward; among the workers I'll have to include a 'pet goose' [1] who never left us alone while we were digging . . . This time we were lucky: in the earth dug up from previous excavations and now washed by rain I found the canine tooth from the jaw of the famous Piltdown Man, – an important piece of evidence for Dr. Woodward's reconstruction plan: it was a very exciting experience! Imagine, it was the last excavation of the season! [2] . . . [Following this Teilhard apparently spent Sunday in Hastings before going to London] . . . I arrived in London on Tuesday morning (Sept. 25) [3] and had the honor of staying with Dr. Woodward who was most hospitable. . . He had me write my name on a piece of cloth covered with the signatures of many geological celebrities [4], and spent an enjoyable evening téte-à-tête with Woodward, a certain Gregory (from the New York Museum [4], an important contact), and an ornithologist from the British Museum, [William Plane] Pycraft . . .
*   I did some useful work at the British Museum and then left for Ipswich (Suffolk) where I was anxious to see some ground that was very important to me. I was met by Mr. Reid Moir and stayed at his home. During the two-day stay he drove me around to all the noteworthy spots. I met a very charming man, Colonel Underwood (who was crazy about silex and had them lying about all over his house) . . .*

[1] This goose, named "Chipper" is pictured in a number of the Frisby photographs of the Piltdown site.

[2] As indicated by Letters 2.3.49 and 2.3.50, 30 August was not the last dig of the season.

[3] Clearly this date is an error, and should be the 2nd. The same mistake also appears (without editorial comment) in the French edition. (Letter No. 132, Teilhard 1965:408).

[4] William King Gregory, see 2.2.47.

[B] As this passage suggests it had originally been decided that the news of the discovery would be released at the meeting of the British Association in Birmingham later in September. On the same day the *Daily Express* printed its exclusive story on the discovery of the canine, Woodward told a reporter from this newspaper:

I cannot possibly make any authoritative statement yet . . . but I was present when the tooth was found, and it is undoubtedly a discovery of tremendous importance. Its importance lies in the fact that it may serve to clear up the question whether its owner was of simian shape or not . . . I have been digging with Mr. Dawson most energetically all the summer, and the fact that the fossilized tooth was picked out from among the gravel shows how carefully such searches have to be conducted.

The tooth is quite perfect, but I cannot discuss it further till the matter has been thoroughly dealt with by the scientists interested" (in *Daily Express* 3 September 1913).

A similar statement was also made to a reporter of the *Sussex Daily News* and printed on 3 September. For further information on the British Association meetings, see Notes to 2.3.36.

[C] Dawson had two brothers: One was the Rev. H. L. Dawson, vicar of Clandon, Bath (see 1.1.37), and the other was [Sir] Trevor Dawson (1866-1931). It is conjectured that his visiting brother was the former, rather than the latter.

2.3.36 DF 116/11 Memorandum 4 September 1913

(a) Managing Editor of the *Sussex Daily News* [Brighton]; (b) carbon copy of handwritten memorandum to Mr. Strevens, Lewes, on printed stationery: "The Southern Publishing Company Limited."; (c) –.

Please see Mr. Dawson and say that our London Representative saw Dr. Woodward about the Pilt Down [sic] tooth and he said he would let Mr. Dawson have an advance copy of the paper he is to deliver to the M[ee]t[in]g of the British Ass[ociatio]n., with a view to the "S[ussex]. D[aily]. N[ews]." getting a good account of it ready for publication on the day after its delivery. Will Mr. Dawson kindly let you see the paper as soon as he receives it, so that we may have all that is material to the subject and get it in type ready for publication the day after Woodward delivers it.

Woodward delivered his paper at British Association meetings in the Central Hall, Birmingham on the evening of 15 September with Sir Oliver Lodge (1851-1940), principal of the University of Birmingham, presiding over the proceedings. The story appeared in a number of the national dailies, as well as the *Sussex Daily News*. The tooth essentially vindicated Woodward's original reconstruction.

2.3.37 DF 100/34 Keith 6 September 1913

(a) Arthur Keith (1866-1955); (b) handwritten letter to Woodward on printed stationery: "Royal College of Surgeons of England, Lincoln's Inn Fields, London W.C."; (c) annotated by Woodward: "9th".

It is conjectured that Woodward had requested an opportunity to examine Keith's reconstruction of the Piltdown skull before going to the British Association meetings in Birmingham. See 2.3.38

Leon Williams has [x/had] all my casts at his workshop in Hampstead [A]. I have written to him asking him to have [them] here if possible on Tuesday by 3 o'clock – but . . [B] . . . to write to you on receipt of my casts – as I am going out of town over the weekend but will be back on Thursday.

[x/] word written and crossed-out by Keith.

[A] See 2.3.18 and Note E: 2.3.24.

[B] The transition here is abrupt, and suggests that there is a missing page between "but . . . to write".

2.3.38 DF 116/5 Elliot Smith 6 September 1913

(a) Grafton Elliot Smith (1871-1937); (b) handwritten note to Woodward on printed postcard: "4 Willow Bank, Fallowfield, Manchester"; (c) annotated by Woodward: "8th"

I am keenly interested in the latest news and congratulate you on the new find. On Monday morning I am going seriously to tackle an independent reconstruction of the skull fragments. I shall be at this address [A] until Thursday morning and will do anything I can to help you. If you have not sent (with the Neanderthal cast and the occipital) my other brain casts. . . would you have it sent to this address.

As indicated by this letter and 2.3.37, Woodward was busily mustering his counterattack against Keith, which he planned to deliver at the meetings of the British Association in Birmingham.

2.3.39 DF 116/11 Dawson 8 September 1913

(a) Charles Dawson (1864-1916); (b) handwritten letter to Woodward on printed stationery: "Airds, Parton N.B."; (c) annotated by Woodward: "10th/11th." Underlining in original by Dawson.

As indicated by 2.3.41 Dawson was away on business and not on holiday.

I am here till the 13th Sept[ember]., and go that day to <u>Ford Castle</u>, <u>Ford</u>, <u>Northumberland</u>, where I shall be till about the 23rd Sept[ember] when I return home.

I have had a letter [A] from the Editor of the <u>Sussex Daily News</u> in which he says you are sending me an advanced paragraph about the Piltdown Skull to be passed on to him for the 17th Sept[ember]. If you will do this fairly early, you will know where to find me, but it takes a long while to get here and we only get letters at 9 am, once in a day.

I have read Keith's article in the Sphere [B] and Pocock's in the Outlook [C], neither very illuminating. I am afraid you had bad weather last Saturday. It has been fine and dry here for some time and they got more of the wet in the South.

Will you ask Barlow to send me a cast of the tooth as soon as he can spare one. I have got the casts of the rest up here.

[A] See 2.3.35 and 2.3.36.

[B] Keith's article, entitled "Our most ancient relation" was published on 6 September in *The Sphere*.

[C] Reginald Innes Pocock (1863-1947), was an entomologist at the British Museum (Natural History) from 1885 until his appointment as Superintendent of the Zoological Gardens at Regent's Park in 1904. It is interesting to note that Pocock was a former student of Sollas. His article in *The Outlook* also appeared on September 6th.

2.3.40 DF 116/5 Elliot Smith 10 September 1913

(a) Grafton Elliot Smith (1871-1937); (b) handwritten letter to Woodward on printed stationery: "4 Willow Bank, Fallowfield, Manchester"; (c) annotated by Woodward: "11th". Underlining in original by Elliot Smith.

For the first time since the casts of the bone fragments came into my possession I [x/have] had time yesterday to sit down for an hour and puzzle them out, so that when your restoration came today I was able to telegraph at once. Keith has been led astray by opposing the "articular" surface of the temporal squama to that of the parietal and everything in that region depends upon the true fit which the real specimens in your possession give. I think your reconstruction [is] a close approximation to the truth. In my work yesterday I put the right parietal further back than you have done so as to bring it almost to touch the small fragment linking it to the occipital. I think your right parietal boss is further forward than the left: in modern brains with the type of occipital asymmetry shown in this cast the par[ietal]. protuberance is usually a trifle further <u>back</u> than the left. I also made the median line cut the frontal tongue of bone about 4 to 5 mm. further to the right than you have done.

None of these things however materially affect my published statement. A bit of the temporal boss comes on to the big bone fragment so that it is a real thing and I am convinced the temporal pole is genuine.

So that I think it correct to say that while. the brain shows a remarkably poor development of these regions which modern research leads us to associate with the power to remembering words to fit [x/on] to ideas the remarkable [x/boss] temporal boss shows signs of active expansion in that area. This does not mean that the creature hadn't the power of speech. The chimpanzee [x/it] is unable to speak not by reason [x/because] of the shape of his jaw or the development of his tongue musculature, but because his brain development has not advanced sufficiently for natural selection to have [?] anything in the nature [?] of sound production [x/sufficiently] which is of vital importance to seize hold of and make essential to the creature's existence. We have nothing to show [x/that] whether or not Eoanthropus [x/did] had the power of speech: but the balance of probability is strongly in favour of his possessing some limited power of [?] communicating with his fellows. [x/This] The great temporal boss shows that [x/further of the] the area concerned with the appreciation and the meaning of sounds is expanding. Analogous changes are evident in the [x/other] two other great areas – parietal and frontal – most intimately related to mental phenomena. While both are distinctly human and not simian still they are relatively small and in the parietal area (especially the right) there is a well marked boss showing how this area is expanding.

What traces of sulci are recognisable conform to a very primitive pattern.

Perhaps it would be well not to put my conclusions quite so baldly as I did in the printed Q[uarterly]. J[ournal]. G[eological]. S[ociety].: but no great harm would be done if you do so. I would use the term "most primitive" in preference to simian. . .

I do not think I shall be at Birmingham: but if I can be of any service to you there I can run over [A].

[x/] Words were written and deleted by G.E.S; [?]: indistinct word deleted by G.E.S.

[A] Elliot Smith attended the meeting and participated in the discussion following Woodward's paper.

2.3.41 DF 116/12 Dawson 11 September 1913

(a) Charles Dawson (18641-1916); (b) handwritten letter to Woodward on printed stationery: "Airds, Parton, N.B."; (c) –.

See Letter 2.3.39.

Many thanks for your letter of yesterday [A]. I am sorry you had such bad luck on Saturday [B]. I do not know what Godwin-Austen [C] is doing with a theodolite etc. at Piltdown, but I shall look forward to hear of his news on the geological location and shall hope to join in the digging on my return. If he [? Godwin-Austen] means to do it this year we ought to begin quickly.

I should like to hear what Elliot Smith has to say. If you have time drop me a line to Ford Castle, Ford, Northumberland. I have dropped a line to the Sussex Daily News people about Monday and told them to call you Monday morning.

We have been very hard worked here and I think harder than at Piltdown! Such energy is worthy of a better cause, but I hope it will do me good and set me up for the winter.

I very much wish I could be at Birmingham on the 16th Sept[ember].

[A] See Letter 2.3.39.

[B] This seems to indicate that Woodward continued working at Piltdown in Dawson's absence.

[C] Henry Haversham Godwin-Austen (1834-1923), the geologist and explorer. It is unclear if Godwin-Austen's presence at Piltdown was unsolicited or not. But the implication that he was perhaps intending to survey the site is not without significance. Later, in 1916 he assisted Woodward at Piltdown, see 4.2.16 and 4.2.17.

2.3.42 DF 116/12 Dawson 12 September 1913

(a) Charles Dawson (1864-1916); (b) handwritten letter to Woodard on printed stationery: "Airds, Parton, N.B." This address has been crossed-out, and above Dawson has written: "at Ford Castle, Ford. Telegrams: Ford Castle, Crookham"; (c) – .

As this letter indicates Dawson is still in the north of England, and has relocated to Crookham, Northumberland.

I am very glad to have your letter as to Elliot Smith's report. I think it is rather important that you should get a good report into the Times so hope you will succeed in capturing their man, in good time [A]. I shall look forward to reading the news on Wednesday evening when the papers arrive at Ford. No doubt Pycraft will blossom again in the Illustrated London News or perhaps Lankester in the Telegraph [B]?

[A] See report in *The Times* entitled: "Dr Smith Woodward's rejoinder" (17 September).

[B] In fact, Pycraft did "blossom" in the *Illustrated London News*, 20 September 1913.

2.3.43 DF 116/5 Elliot Smith 13 September 1913

(a) Grafton Elliot Smith (1871-1937); (b) Post Office Telegram from Elliot Smith from his home at Fallowfield, Manchester; (c) –.

Writing tonight criticism only of details. My published statements stand.

2.3.44 DF 116/15 Gregory 16 September 1913

(a) John Walter Gregory (1864-1932); (b) handwritten letter to Woodward on printed stationery: "Maple Bank, Church Road, Edgbaston"; (c) annotated by Woodward: "17th"

Gregory was professor of geology at the University of Glasgow.

Heartiest congratulations on your great triumph, fine lecture and dignified treatment of Keith.
  I hope we shall [?hear] no more objections to Eoanthropus as a genus. I felt sincerely grieved at your worries at the Med[ical]. Congress . . . and the very unfair, as it obviously was, representation of the question in the Times. I draughted a letter of protest to it in reference to K[eith]'s proposed name, but I could not frame a letter which did not seem open to the retort by Keith that the name is a detail and as objection was taken to that, Keith's view on the main issue appeared to pass unchallenged. So I did not send it and was glad to see Bather had done so [A].
  I am sure your success last night was as popular as it was complete. . .[B]

[A] See Note E and F: 2.3.32.

[B] Reference to Woodward's presentation to the British Association meeting in Birmingham, see 2.3.36.

2.3.45 DF 116/5 Elliot Smith 26 September 1913

(a) Grafton Elliot Smith (1871-1937); (b) handwritten letter to Woodward on printed stationery: "The University, Manchester"; (c) annotated by Francis Arthur Bather (see Note F: 2.3.32): "p.c. 27 Sept. 1913 F.a.B."; and Woodward: "Oct 8th" [A].

Would it be convenient to you if I were to go to the Museum next Saturday (Oct. 4th) morning to examine the actual Piltdown fragments before making my drawings [B]. I have now worked over all the material for my report and have received the La Quina cast from Anthony [C].

I have no doubt how the things go but want to confirm several points of detail on the actual fragments.

The more I study the material the more surprised I am that there ever was any difference of opinion. The grooves for the sinuses and the meningeal vessels on the inside and obelion (or the obelic flattening) on the parietal leave no doubt as to the situation of the median plane; and I have collected a lot of most instructive specimens for comparison during the last week which make the whole interpretation quite clear and definite.

Wood Jones [D] returned to me last Saturday the brain-casts I had collected in May for comparison and I was surprised to find [?] (for I had forgotten how much work I had done on these locked-up specimens) how closely [x/many] some of the primitive Negro, Australian and Tasmanian brains simulate the curious temporal formation in <u>Eoanthropus</u>.

To put myself right with local people [E] and the anatomists generally – some of whom are only too ready to make reckless statements concerning me – I have sent a note to "Nature," [F] which I think you will approve. Without treading on anyone's toes I have made quite clear my own opinions; and I hope it may have some influence in checking the malicious gossip now current.

[x/] Word(s) written and deleted by G.E.S. [?] Word[s] unclear, written and deleted by G.E.S.

[A] As indicated by the annotations to this letter Woodward was not at the Museum when Elliot Smith's letter arrived. From all indications, after the British Association meeting in Birmingham, Woodward went to Holland on Museum business.

[B] As indicated by Woodward's annotation, the date was inconvenient (see 2.3.58).

[C] The French neuroanatomist Raoul Anthony (1874-1941), see 2.3.32 and 1.2.27.

[D] Frederick Wood Jones (1879-1954), the anatomist and anthropologist; a former student of Keith's at the London Hospital medical school.

[E] A probable reference not only to Boyd Dawkins' circle but also that of Arthur Keith's.

[F] This note was published in *Nature* on 2 October, which sparked an immediate response from Keith (1913b). This exchange continued on through into November, see Elliot Smith (1913b).

2.3.46 DF 100/35 Mitchell 27 September 1913

(a) Peter Chalmers Mitchell (1864-1945); (b) handwritten letter to Woodward on printed stationery: "Zoological Society of London"; (c) Letter marked "PRIVATE". Annotated by Woodward: "Oct 25th. <u>Request not yet</u>".

Mitchell was Secretary of the London Zoological Society.

Have you considered the question of fully publishing the matter relating to Piltsdown [sic] skull? It occurs to me that it would be very interesting if each bone were figured life size from both aspects, and if very careful figures and descriptions of the various suggested restorations were also published. I should think that a large part of our "Transactions" might very well be devoted to so special an object as this. . . Perhaps you could turn this over in your mind and let me know if possible before October 15th, if you could contemplate posposing [sic] this to the Society.

As indicated by the above annotation, Woodward did not pursue this invitation.

2.3.47 DF 100/35 Teilhard de Chardin 1 October 1913

(a) Pierre Teilhard de Chardin (1881-1955); (b) handwritten letter to Woodward on plain stationery: "13 rue du Vieux-Colombier, Paris"; (c) annotated by Woodward: "23rd. Probably C[ervus]. etueriarum. Photo in Geol. Lib."

When coming back to the Museum, two days ago, I found the photographs of Carnivora you allowed me to get from your collections, and that reminded me I ought to have thanked you much sooner for your so friendly hospitality: you must be sure I felt very deeply your kindness with me.

I have been very glad to see, in many newspapers sent to me by Mr. Dawson, that your lecture at Birmingham has been attended with great favour [A]. Prof. Boule is not yet back to Paris, nor Dr. Obermaier, so I could not get their opinion about the Prof. Keith's trial [B].

I send you herewith, in case it would interest you or Mr. Andrews (please give him my best regards), a photograph of the antlers we recently dug out in a raised beach at Jersey. Do you think possible to put a name on that deer?

As indicated by Woodward's annotation, he believed the deer specimen Teilhard had found in Jersey was *C. etueriarum*.

[A] For further details, see 2.3.36.

[B] For further details on Boule and Obermaier, see notes appended to Letter 1.2.11.

2.3.48 DF 116/15 Bennett 2 October 1913

(a) George F. Bennett; (b) handwritten letter on plain stationery: "Kulgori, Northgate, Near Brisbane, Queensland, Australia"; (c) –.

The individual's connection with Woodward is unclear; possibly a collector.

. . . I see you had a pretty hot meeting at the Congress of Medicine in London on August 15th [sic] but I expect you will outlive that. I was very pleased to see by the papers that you are probably going to visit us which I believe to be in August next . . .

Woodward's plan to visit Australia was not realized.

2.3.49 DF 116/11 Dawson 5 October 1913

(a) Charles Dawson (1864-1916); (b) handwritten letter to Woodward on stationery embossed: "The Castle Lodge, Lewes"; (c) –. The conclusion to this letter has quite obviously been removed, with scissors [? censored]. Underlining in original by Dawson.

I think next Friday and Sat[urda]y will be about the last opportunity at Piltdown as the water begins to collect.

The pieces of bone we found last time are without doubt <u>sheep</u>. Portions of the <u>tibia</u> are just like one Barlow has from Jersey.

Yesterday [Samuel] Woodhead and I went to the pit and searched the gravel which had been washed and Woodhead found a tooth which I think may be badger, probably modern [A]. We spread the gravel out and about again for next time.

I saw Keith last week. He is rather chastened but is still looking for trouble. He says the canine was worn by the incisor and not by the upper canine and showed me a <u>female</u> Gorilla jaw which showed this rather well [B]. The upper incisor seemed to be out of use except perhaps for defence.

I send you a few scraps of literature which you may have missed abroad.

I look forward to hear[ing] more about <u>Pithecanthropus</u> [C]. I hope [?] have had a good time . . . .

[?] Word unclear.

[A] Samuel Allinson Woodhead (1862-1943), a chemistry instructor at Uckfield Agricultural College and County Analyst. It was Woodhead who had analysed for Dawson and Woodward a fragment of the Piltdown skullcap, see 1.2.22. Dawson's mention of Woodhead's discovery of a "badger's tooth" on October 4th is not without interest. Years later, Woodhead's eldest son, Leslie, in a letter to Kenneth Oakley (1954) wrote: ". . .the tooth was found within a day or so of the jaw – on a Saturday as a matter of fact", see 6.3.29. In this instant Leslie Woodhead was referring to the celebrated canine tooth, which he contended was found just prior to the jaw! While not doubting for one moment this informant's sincerity, it is quite likely that his memory of his Father recounting of how he had assisted Dawson at Piltdown from time to time (Dawson 1913; 75-76) had become compressed into a series of closely related events. As a consequence, it appears that the memory of finding the "badger's tooth" (later identified as a beaver) had become compressed and confused with other events that had unfolded at Piltdown. Weiner (1955:194) arrived at a similar conclusion. While this, of course, must remain merely conjecture, it is nevertheless most interesting to note that 4 October, in 1913, fell on a Saturday! Furthermore, shortly thereafter the broken ramus of a beaver was recovered (see Dawson & Woodward 1914a:82-85).

[B] See Letter 2.3.63.

[C] This statement suggests that while in Holland he had visited Dubois in Haarlem and viewed the remains of *Pithecanthropus erectus*. If this is so then this casts a somewhat different light on Hrdlička's depiction of the Dutch anatomist as an eccentric recluse. According to Hrdlička (who incidentally had tried to view the remains of Java Man in 1912), Dubois had since the turn of the century ceased publishing in palaeoanthropology, and kept the famous Pithecanthropine remains hidden under the floor of his home in Haarlem, and had refused scientific access to them until after World War I. See Spencer (1979,II:415-421) for further details on Hrdlička's visit to Haarlem.

2.3.50 DF 116/11 Dawson 14 October 1913

(a) Charles Dawson (1864-1916); (b) handwritten letter to Woodward on printed stationery: "Town Hall Chambers, Uckfield"; (c) annotated by Woodward: "15th". Underlining in original by Dawson.

Thank you for your letter. I am afraid I did not realize that you were badly hurt as you evidently were [A]. I hope you are mending all right. My rheumatics are subsiding owing to the extra case last Sat[urda]y.

Venus was waiting for his pay on the bridge when I arrived on Monday [B]. He says that he uncovered the piece we told him to do and the gravel awaits search in situ. I am sorry that I can not put you up this weekend if you come nor shall I be able to come on Sunday, but Friday afternoon and Sat[urda]y. I shall be free and I expect Willett on Saturday [C].

Shall I book you a room at Bellinghams? [D] The weather was fine all Sunday and Monday – a bit cloudy today – and tomorrow is our agricultural root show, when it always rains!

I felt sure the fragment of Rhino would turn out Pliocene from its mineralized appearance [E]. I have received Elliot-Smith's splendid manifesto in Nature. Also Keith's Birmingham address, in the B.M.J. in which all his old theories are trotted out once more [F].

I have no objection to the Xmas night [G] being put down as our supplementary reading, but I think R[eid].Moir sho[ul]d be curbed as to his exhibits or there will be no room for a large attendance. How would it be to have the specimens in the Library except such as are needed for actual reference when reading the papers.

These "Eolithic" people never seem to know when to stop with their exhibits and spoil their show by introducing loads of "road metal" [H]. Personally I think such exhibits ought to be reserved for the R[oyal]. Anthrop[ological]. Ass[ociatio]n. [sic] where more latitude of discussion would be allowed and the Geol[ogical]. Society does not seem the right place.

[A] Evidently Woodward had sustained an injury while digging at Piltdown during the weekend of 10-12 October. The nature of the injury is not known.

[B] Venus Hargreaves, a local farm labourer who was regularly employed to do the manual work at the Piltdown site, see 1.2.9.

[C] In contrast to a year earlier, Edgar Willett is now a member of the inner circle (Note B: 1.2.2). From all indications Woodward did not go to Piltdown that weekend; instead Dawson was assisted by Willett and Lankester. It was on this occasion that Lankester recovered a "remarkable flint implement" (see Lankester 1921:60).

[D] At the Geologists' Association Excursion which had been held on July 12 1913, tea was served at Uckfield Town Hall by a Mr Bellingham, owner of a local cafe ("Mocketts") [Denton: personal communication].

[E] See subsection 2.4, Table 2.2.

[F] See Note F: 2.3.45 for details on Elliot Smith's paper. On 7 October Keith delivered the opening address for the beginning of the Winter Session in Medicine at the University of Birmingham. The title of his paper was "Present problems relating to the origin of modern races." (Keith 1913a).

[G] This is a reference to their planned joint paper summarizing the results of the 1913 season at Piltdown. The paper, entitled "Supplementary note on the discovery of a Palaeolithic human skull and mandible at Piltdown (Sussex) [with an Appendix by G. Elliot Smith]," was read on the evening of December 17th at Burlington House, see Section 2.4 for details.

[H] See Note B: 3.1.35.

2.3.51 DF 116/15 Duckworth 15 October 1913

(a) Wynfrid L.H. Duckworth (1870-1956); (b) handwritten letter to Woodward on printed stationery: "East House, Jesus College, Oxford"; (c) annotated by Woodward: "20th"

See Letter 2.2.16.

. . . The discovery of the tooth comes with extraordinary appropriateness, and I shall be most interested in your revised reconstruction of the cranium. In a few days I hope to return to my own efforts at reconstruction which resulted in the production of a cranium of a capacity between the figure given by you and that proposed by Keith. I had got as far as this in August when we last met, and this result will have little or no interest for you now. But I feel that even if I am shown to be in error, the mere fact of having attacked the problem may make me a better judge of such matters.

2.3.52 DF 116/15 Balfour 17 October 1913

(a) Henry Balfour (1863-1939); (b) handwritten letter to Woodward on printed stationery: "Langley Lodge, Headington Hill, Oxford"; (c) annotated by Woodward: "20th". Underlining in the original by Balfour.

Balfour belonged to Exeter College and was Curator of the Pitt-Rivers Museum, Oxford.

. . . I must congratulate you and Mr. Dawson on the discovery of the canine. It was most important. When I first saw your interesting reconstruction, the only criticism which I felt able to make was that I thought the introduction of so large a canine was not quite justified and that the prognathism was somewhat exaggerated. Now, while I feel relieved by the actual canine being somewhat smaller, I can nonetheless congratulate you on having vindicated your belief that it must have been a large one and of distinctly simian type. Keith's diagnosis will require modification in several respects. I hope that by good luck the central portion at any rate of the brow ridges may be found and some of the incisors. Sometime I should like to have a good look at the flint impl[ements] found associated with the remains.

2.3.53 DF 116/5 Elliot Smith 18 October 1913:

(a) Grafton Elliot Smith (1871-1937); (b) handwritten note to Woodward on printed postcard: "4 Willow Bank, Fallowfield, Manchester"; (c) annotated by Woodward: "20th. Yes"

See Letter 2.3.45.

. . .Is there any trace of the lambdoid suture on the outer face of the small fragment on the [x/lef] right side of the main occipital piece? In the cast there seems to be some evidence of this. If so it is very important."

[x/] word incomplete. Written and deleted by G.E.S.

2.3.54 DF 116/15 Thane 20 October 1913

(a) George Dancer Thane (1850-1930); (b) handwritten note to Woodward on printed postcard: "University College [University of London], Gower Street, London W.C."; (c) –.

See 2.2.28.

. . . The "canine" is a most formidable weapon, and must have the greatest influence on doubters.

2.3.55 DF 116/11 Dawson 21 October 1913

(a) Charles Dawson (1864-1916); (b) handwritten letter to Woodward on stationery embossed: "The Castle Lodge, Lewes"; (c) annotated by Woodward: "22nd" Underlining in original by Dawson.

Reg[inal]d Smith was rather jocular on the subject of Piltdown [A]. He said he believed that the flint which Venus [B] picked up was an implement, but that it was too rough to be certain about, and they had got nothing to match it at Bloomsbury.

Your implement [C] he thinks is pre-Chellean and of similar age to the worked flints from the bottom of the 100 foot terrace at Swanscombe, near Galley Hill. The workmanship on the one face is like that of Chellei [sic], but Chelles are always <u>implements</u> made from the "<u>core</u>" and ours are implements made from flakes, one side being otherwise unworked. They have got nothing exactly like ours at Bloomsbury. I will go to Piltdown as soon as possible.

P.S. 22nd Oct[ober] I motored over to Piltdown with the two clerks and searched but found nothing but Eoliths [D].

[A] Reginald Smith (1873-1940), a antiquarian and prehistorian, at the Bloomsbury branch of the British Museum. For Smith's views on the Piltdown assemblage, see Table 1.2

[B] See Note B: 2.3.50.

[C] See Dawson and Woodward (1914a: 84-85, and particularly Plate XIV figs 1a-1c & 2a-2c).

[D] During the period 1911-1916, Dawson had 3 clerks working for him: Albert Victor Eade, H.H. Wakeford, and Clifton G. Turner. It is not known which of these 3 clerks accompanied Dawson to Piltdown. For further information on them, see transcript of Kenneth Oakley's interview with Eade on 16 August 1969 (DF 116/17). This interview, however, provides no insights on either Wakeford or Turner. Likewise, Wakeford's reply to Weiner's enquiries in 1954, yielded no information on either Eade or Turner, and only minimal details of his relationship with Dawson (see MSS WEI 3.7 Wakeford 19 February 1954). For some details on Turner, see 4.2.24.

2.3.56 DF 116/15 Derry 23 October 1913

(a) Douglas E[rith] Derry (b 1874); (b) handwritten letter on printed stationery: "University College [Univeristy of London], Gower Street, London W.C."; (c) –.

See Letter 2.2.46.

. . . The discovery of the canine tooth was most fortunate and timely. I hope to be out at South Kensington shortly and if I may will ask for you, as there are still one or two points in the reconstruction which according to my view are not quite right. I have a notice from Damon of a new reconstruction and I am ordering the model of the tooth.

2.3.57 DF 100/35 Teilhard de Chardin 24 October 1913

(a) Pierre Teilhard de Chardin (1881-1955); (b) handwritten letter to Woodward on printed stationery: "Muséum National d'Histoire Naturelle, Laboratoire de Paléontologie, 3 Place Valhubert, Paris"; (c) –.

See letter 2.3.47.

I have been so pleased to secure your letter and the news about Piltdown! When speaking of it with Prof. Boule, today, he told me that he was anxious to get, before long, the plaster casts of the Eoanthropus skull and jaw, in order to set down an article on them in "L'Anthropologie" [A].

He wished to write to you that, if you could send to him the Piltdown's cast (separate, I understood), he would in turn, and immediately, send back to you a cast of the Chapelle-aux-Saints skull [B]; but as he is extremely busy, now, he asked me to write it to you, in his name.

[A] Boule was editor of the French journal *L'Anthropologie* (Paris). During the next few years Boule published a number of critical articles on the Piltdown remains, see Boule (1915, 1917a, 1920). See also Letter 2.3.60.

[B] An important French Neanderthal skeleton found in 1908, see Boule (1909, 1911-1913). For further details, see Day (1986:31-36) and Hammond (1982).

2.3.58 DF 116/5 Elliot Smith 24 October 1913

(a) Grafton Elliot Smith (1871-1937); (b) handwritten letter to Woodward on printed stationery: "The University, Manchester"; (c) –.

For background to this letter, see G.E.S's earlier communication: Letter 2.3.45.

Many thanks for your postcard. I shall go to the Museum on Friday next at about 10.30, and if you can induce him to come, will bring Prof. Wilson of Sydney [A] as a perfectly sane and unbiased witness. I think you have probably got the reconstruction right now, but there are a number of small points that I want to examine for [x/my] the purpose of my brain paper. The brain part is working out beautifully.

During the last few days I have heard of so many scientific people who have been hypnotized by Keith's letter in Nature in to the belief that he has a real case that I have written a letter frankly and clearly pointing out the fallacies in his statements of facts and arguments and breaking the fall by pointing out the great difficulties presented by the [x/sub–] reconstruction. I wrote the letter originally a week ago but recalled it as being too brutally frank and have now toned it down [B].

[x/] indicates word written and deleted by G.E.S.

[A] John T. Wilson (1863-1945), who on Alexander Macalister's death in 1916, became professor of anatomy at Cambridge [see 2.3.61]. From all indications Wilson did accompany Elliot Smith to the Museum and viewed the original specimens. In fact, according to Elliot Smith (Dawson & Woodward 1914a:97), Wilson had "pointed out that the inclination of the floor of the anterior cranial fossa" which provided evidence to support his own observations on the determination of the skull's median plane.

[B] See Note F: Letter 2.3.45 and 3.1.13 for further details on the developing animus with Keith.

2.3.59 HP/NAA Marett 27 October 1913

(a) Robert Ranulph Marett (1866-1943); (b) handwritten letter to Aleš Hrdlička [1.2.16] on printed stationery: "Exeter College, Oxford"; (c) underlining in original by Marett.

This letter was in response to an inquiry from Hrdlička, dated 16 October 1913 [carbon-copy HP/NAA].

. . . Now to turn to quite a different matter [A] – the Piltdown fossil. I presume that you already possess Smith Woodward's paper (Quart. J. Geol. Soc. 1913) and his note [in] Geol. Mag. Oct. 13, admitting a previous error, and announcing the confirmatory evidence of the canine tooth found by Father Teilhard.

As to the value of the find – its <u>supreme</u> value, I might say – there can, I think, be no doubt.

<u>Horizon</u>: The <u>mammalian remains</u> yield a Pleistocene horizon; if you admit that <u>Cervus elaphus</u> is never found in the Pliocene. <u>Hippopotamus</u> and <u>Castor</u> are consistent with this allocation, while <u>Mastodon</u> and <u>Stegodon</u> are so much rolled and battered that they are certainly derived from earlier formations. The implememts, apart from "Kent-plateau" eoliths which may or may not be human are very rough but, as far as I could judge from handling them for a moment or two, certainly human. They <u>might</u> be Mousterian at latest . . .[?] . . . I don't think one would be far out in assigning one and the same to the Piltdown and Mauer fossils.

<u>Reconstruction</u> Here I trespass on a province not my [?] at all, while it is emphatically yours – so forgive vagueness and hesitation on my part.

The <u>mandible</u>, if it existed by itself, is in my opinion, a find of the greatest importance – as interesting as the Mauer specimen or even more so. The ramus is not to [?] as that of the Mauer jaw, but the space occupied by the anterior teeth (about 60 mm) is enormous. Woodward, as you know, boldly postulated an immense canine, while Keith went on Mauer lines. The discovery of the missing canine (I have not actually seen it, but I suppose its authenticity is certain) triumphantly vindicates Woodward. The calotte on the other hand is in four pieces which cannot be fitted directly together; so that there is much scope for discussion. As you know, Keith accused Woodward of making the skull too small and ape-like by neglecting to identify the middle line of the roof as indicated by the internal groove of the longitudinal blood sinuses . . . [B].

Arthur Thomson [C] thinks that the groove is correctly identified by Keith in the posterior, but not in the anterior part of the fragment A [referring to Marett's crude diagram] so that forwards the skull [?/nearer] to something like Woodward's estimate. Also he thinks both have got the base too broad – it is broader than any skull in his collection. – So there is plenty for you experts to settle. But the find is a grand one all the same [D].

[?] word unclear.

[A] The first part of Marett's letter discusses his plans to attend the XIXth Congress of Americanists scheduled for 1915 in Washington.

[B] A rough sketch comparing Woodward's and Keith's arrangement of the 4 cranial fragments.

[C] See 2.3.25.

[D] See Marett's invited letter to the *Daily Express* (19 August 1913) commenting on the Woodward-Keith controversy.

2.3.60 DF 100/34 Teilhard de Chardin 27 October 1913

(a) Pierre Teilhard de Chardin (1881-1955); (b) handwritten letter to Woodward on plain stationery: "13 rue du Vieux- Colombier [Paris]"; (c) underlining in original by Teilhard.

I was very wrong in my last letter when I told you that Prof. Boule wished to have <u>only</u> the separate plaster casts of the Piltdown skull. He would like to get <u>also</u> your restored model. I hope you will be able *to give him satisfaction. . . [A].*

See Letter 2.3.57.

2.3.61 DF 116/15 Macalister 27 October 1913

(a) Alexander Macalister (1844-1916); (b) handwritten letter to Woodward on printed stationery: "New Museums, Cambridge"; (c) –.

Macalister was professor of anatomy at Cambridge.

Thanks for your paper on the Piltdown Skull which throws fresh light on that elusive and vexatious "find". I do not know if you are sufficiently acquainted with Duckworth's papers to sign the enclosed. If you can do so I will be very much obliged." [A]

[A] It is not known what he wanted Woodward to sign. It is interesting to note, however, that Duckworth was Macalister's protégé at Cambridge, whose chair did not go, as expected, to Duckworth but to the Australian anatomist John Wilson, see 2.3.58.

2.3.62 DF 116/15 Corner 29 October 1913

(a) Frank Corner (1862-1939); (b) handritten letter to Woodward on printed stationery: "The Manor House, Poplar E."; (c) an earlier archivist has misread Corner's signature as "Frank Snell".

Many thanks for your paper. I was delighted at the finding of the tooth. It will set a lot at rest. You will have no doubt found more remains by now – and more yet to come I trust! I think your "man" [?] . . . not likely to make finely shaped and delicately tapering flint implements. His brain must have been very small indeed. It seems almost incredible that Pliocene man should have been found by such a tiny stream and in an absurdly small a section.

It was most lucky that Dawson was about, what a loss we should have had. . .

Corner was a general practitioner in the East End of London and known associate of the Ightham Circle. For further details on Corner, see notes to Letter 2.3.13 and Spencer (1990).

2.3.63 DF 100/34 Dawson 31 October 1913

(a) Charles Dawson (1864-1913); (b) handwritten letter to Woodward on printed stationery: "Station Hotel, Heathfield. F.W. Reed, Proprietor"; (c) annotated by Woodward: "Nov 1st & sent Evening Discourse"

I am sorry I did not see you to thank you for a pleasant evening last night.

The female Gorilla tooth at Keith's [sic] is curiously like ours but larger [A]. The incisor comes right above it as shown in the rough drawing [B]. I put the reference to the specimen on the drawing. The tooth (canine) when in position in the jaw does not show the worn surface. There is no wear shown by the upper incisor. The portion of the tooth below the worn part is polished but little worn if at all. The wear goes right down on the upper end of the pulp cavity rather more than ours and the upper canine projects free of the lower and was almost useless. The bone has been stripped to show the fang on each side of the mandible. The wear has given the tooth a lancet shape like ours.

[A] See Letter 2.3.49.

[B] Dawson's sketches are drawn at the end of his letter. The first is of a right anterior portion of Gorilla mandible and maxilla depicting the arrangement and fit between upper and lower incisors. Below and to the right of this is a smaller sketch of a Gorilla incisor, above which is written: "Female Gorilla G.416 (best) and A.63.3." These numbers apparently are the Royal College of Surgeons' accession numbers. Beneath these sketches at the foot of the page, Dawson has written: "C. Dawson. 30 Oct. 1913". For further details, see 2.3.66.

2.3.64 DF 116/5 Elliot Smith 19 November 1913

(a) Grafton Elliot Smith (1871-1937); (b) handwritten letter to Woodward on printed stationery: "The University, Manchester"; (c) annotated by Woodward: "20th"

I expect to spend the greater part of next week in London as the representative [of] Manchester on the General Medical Council and hope to get a few hours free at odd times. I should like to spend this time working at the Piltdown problem so as to clear up certain points that have cropped up in the course of my work. I should like to get some photographs of the fragments to show certain points in the texture of the bones.

Yesterday I gave an address to the Literary and Philosophical Society here summing up the whole controversy.

My duties as Dean have prevented me from doing any continuous work since I was last in London, but I have devoted a good many odd moments to the work.

See Letter 2.3.45, and particularly Note F.

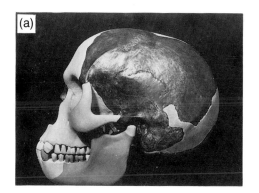
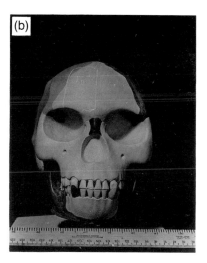
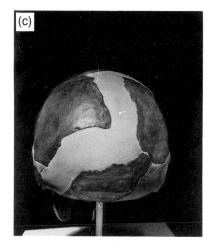
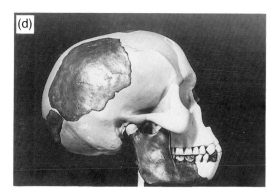

Fig. 2.2 Woodward's revised version of the Piltdown skull (1914). White areas reconstructed. Dark areas indicate original bone. (a) Left lateral view; (b) frontal view [note nasal bones]; (c) occipital view; (d) right lateral view [note canine]. Courtesy of the Trustees of the British Museum (Natural History).

2.3.65 DF 116/5 Elliot Smith 22 November 1913

(a) Grafton Elliot Smith (1871-1937); (b) handwritten letter to Woodward on printed stationery: "The University, Manchester"; (c) annotated by Woodward: "23rd"

All this week I have been immersed in teaching and administrative work incidental to the Deanship of the Medical School and have had no time to do more than glance at the beautiful cast you have sent me. It seems to me satisfactory: but [x/if] there are a number of points I should like to see again on the originals before Barlow starts making replicas [A].

I have to lecture in London at the Royal Society of Medicine tomorrow week and shall be free all day on Friday (31st inst.) to work at the bones at South Kensington.

If you have a spare copy of the literature (Q.J.G.S.) relating to the Piltdown things I should be glad if you would send copies to Dr Eugéne [sic] Pittard, 72 Florissant [B]. He is an excellent man and tells me he has to deliver a discourse at his University on primitive man and wants to get reliable first hand information.

[x/] word written and deleted by G.E.S.

[A] This new version was not completed and ready for distribution until the Spring of 1914.

[B] Written in the right-hand margin of this letter, beside Pittard's name, Woodward has written: "25th". Eugène Pittard (b. 1867) was a Swiss anatomist and anthropologist.

2.3.66 DF 100/34 Dawson 26 November 1913

(a) Charles Dawson (1864-1916); (b) handwritten letter to Woodward on plain stationery: "The Castle Lodge, Lewes"; (c) annotated by Woodward: "28th" Underlining in original by Dawson.

As time is getting short I called at the College of Surgeons and took a squeeze of the side of the female Gorilla jaw where the right upper lateral incisor works on the lower canine [A]. I send you my two squeezes and a small one of the inner worn surface of the canine. If you have a plaster cast made of these squeezes you will almost have as good a specimen as the actual thing. The cast may be useful to photograph. I also send a rough sketch of the canine tooth in 4 positions and the jaws closed. I hope these may be helpful to Barlow and Pycraft [B].

Afterwards Keith invited me into his room to discuss a new subject about the mandible. He points out that the 3rd molar so far as he can judge from Woodrough's skiagrams was not quite "up" [C]. And therefore the animal was young (as the sutures also show). Then, that the canine and the 3rd molar in Anthropoids always grow their permanent 3rd molars and their canines at the same time. Ergo. As the canine is so worn it could not have belonged to the same individual. I reminded him that supposing that this was a rule with the apes, we were dealing with an intermediate form and as the times for appearance of the 3rd molars in the human jaw were most variable and quite unconnected with the growth of the canines – that his new theory was not a very safe one. I also reminded him that the 3rd molars have already showed rudimentary characters both in the human jaws as well as certain of the anthropoids. The 3rd molar is often placed at such an angle as to look inward and is almost useless for mastication and the fangs are often not fully developed. Besides all this we have two molar teeth worn quite as much as the canine! We both remained unconvinced it seems! He points out that the cancellous tissue of the bones of the mandible is apelike, the holes of the network being squarer in man,[?/] the squares in apes being dragged laterally. However he still believes the mandible belongs to the skull and evidently does not think Waterson [sic] counts at all [D]. He mourns the goings on of E. Smith [E]!

I will look in on Monday to see what Barlow has been able to do with my squeezes.

P.S. Keith thinks that there was never a tubercle at the base of the crown of the Eoanthropus tooth.

[?/] Two unclear words written and deleted by Dawson.

Attached to this letter is a folded piece of paper: One half has a sketch similar to the one appearing in Letter 2.3.63 (details of anterior portion of right side of Gorilla mandible and maxilla). This sketch is annotated: "G.251 [boxed]; "Portion from which squeezes have been made"; "modelling wax used, C.D." On the other half of the page are 5 labelled sketches [various views] of a female Gorilla incisor.

[A] See Letter 2.3.63.

[B] These two workers were engaged in the prepartion of a new model which was ready for distribution in the spring of 1914.

[C] "Woodrough" may have been the name of the technician Underwood employed. But while this is uncertain, it is clear that the reference is to the X-ray photographs in Underwood's article, see Note D (below) and Note A: 1.3.13. For further details on this issue, see introduction to subsection 2.4. A "skiagram" is an X-ray photograph. This term, along with "roentgenogram" and "radiogram" were commonly used during the first decades of the twentieth century.

[D] This is a reference to a letter published in *Nature* on 13 November, 1913 by David Waterston, then professor of anatomy at King's College, London, in which he attacked Underwood's X-ray pictures and interpretations published earlier in the *British J Dental Sci* (see notes to 1.3.13). As for Keith's noted conviction that the mandible and cranium were associated, contrast this statement with that relayed to Woodward by Rehlin in Germany (2.2.37).

[E] See Note F: 2.3.45.

2.3.67 DF 100/35 Teilhard de Chardin [1] December 1913

(a) Pierre Teilhard de Chardin (1881-1955); (b) handwritten letter to Charles W Andrews (1866-1924) on plain stationery: "Laboratoire de Paléontologie, 3 Place Valhubert, Paris"; (c) letter undated and appended to 2.3.68. Annotated by [?] Andrews: "Ans.1-12-13".

This letter was an inquiry directed to Charles Andrews regarding Tertiary (Fayum) Carnivora. Andrews was specialist in Fayum mammals (1906) at the British Museum (Natural History).

2.3.68 DF 100/34 Teilhard de Chardin 14 December 1913

(a) Pierre Teilhard de Chardin (1881–1955); (b) handwritten note to Woodward on a printed postcard: "Muséum National d'Histoire Naturelle, Paris"; (c) annotated by [?] Andrews: "Ansd. 15/12/13".

Further enquiry about Fayum specimens, see Letter 2.3.67. No mention is made of Piltdown. As indicated by the above annotation the letter was subsequently passed to Andrews.

2.3.69 DF 116/15 Dawkins 15 December 1913

(a) William Boyd Dawkins (1837-1929); (b) handwritten letter to Woodward on plain stationery; (c) –.

I thank you for your kind gift of papers relating to Eoanthropus of singular value to my study of the subject.

If possible I will call on Wednesday morning – I propose to dine at the [Athanaeum] Club and to attend meeting afterwards [A]

[A] Reference to the scheduled meeting on December 17th of the Geological Society of

London, at which Dawson, Woodward, and Grafton Elliot Smith presented their respective "supplementary note[s] on the discovery of a Palaeolithic skull at Piltdown (Sussex)." For further details on this meeting see subsection 2.4.

2.3.70 DF 116/11 Dawson 20 December 1913

(a) Charles Dawson (1864-1916); (b) handwritten letter to Woodward on stationery embossed: "Uckfield, Sussex"; (c) annotated by Woodward: "19th/23rd". Underlining in original by Dawson. Attached to the letter, by a brass pin, are two unidentified newspaper cuttings relating to the discovery of mammoth remains at Whitstable, Kent. [A].

In case you have not seen enclosed cuttings, I send them to you. In one cutting it is referred to as a "MAN" and in the other a "Mammoth." It might be worth your while to enquire.

I have offered the Geol[ogical] Survey a selection of the specimens now at Burlington House for their "Rock Specimen Series."

I have received a [sic] invitation from the <u>Morning Post</u> "News Editor" to answer Keith's two articles of the 17th and 18th Dec[embe]r. and I have referred them to Pycraft who I hope may be able to make a bit on it [B].

I leave home on <u>Sunday</u> (21st inst.) for Bath, Somersetshire, <u>The Lansdown Grove Hotel</u> till the (Friday) morning of Boxing Day (26th December) when I return home. I expect to visit Cheddar and may take a photo of the skull there if they let me [C]. My parson brother is well known there and much interested in a child-like way [D] !

I caught an awful cold on the meeting night and feel very bad. Very many thanks for the Geol[logical] Society]. dinner with its <u>"Piltdown Mince Pies."</u> I must send the Barkham people a souvenir this Xmas of some sort from Bath.

[A] Cutting 1 entitled: "Mammoth Man. Workmen find at Whitstable Today." Cutting 2 entitled: "Mammoth Find At Whitstable."

[B] For further details on the Keith articles, see Spencer (1990). From all indications Pycraft did not accept Dawson's invitation. However, on the 23rd the *Morning Post* printed two long letters one from William Boyd Dawkins and the other from Douglas E. Derry dealing with the Piltdown issue.

[C] See Note I: 1.2.11.

[D] See 1.1.37 and Note C: 2.3.35.

2.3.71 LP/WBD Colbeck 27 December 1913

(a) Thomas W. Colbeck; (b) handwritten letter to William Boyd Dawkins (1837-1929) on plain stationery: "7 [?] De Cham Avenue, St. Leonards-on-Sea". (c) Original not examined. Following based on photocopy found in Langham Papers.

... I have little or no acquaintance with geology or Palaeontology and all that I know about the Piltdown Skull is derived from newspaper paragraphs, which the late Mr. Justice [?] pronounced to be "mostly lies." One statement I saw was that the skull could not be that of an adult because the old fart had not cut one or more of her (?) wisdom teeth. In the course of 40 years practice I met with one man who did not cut a lower wisdom tooth until he was 43; this was confirmed by a dentist in Brighton who, some weeks afterwards, extracted the tooth which had then come through and was practically in a useless condition . . . I do not know whether these facts have a bearing upon this particular case, but an old friend who knows a great deal about flint implements etc., [A] wanted me to write to the Morning Post, but I had no desire to rush into print being an ignoramus in geology. However, seeing your letter in the M[orning]. P[ost]. [B]. I thought I would write you . . .

Judging from the opening and closing of this letter Colbeck was not unknown to Dawkins.

It would appear, however, that this letter was unsolicited. From all indications Colbeck was either a general practitioner or a dentist.

[?] Word unclear.

[A] Given Colbeck's address in St Leonard's, Abbott's name springs immediately to mind, but there is no evidence linking Colbeck with Abbott.

[B] As indicated in Note B: 2.3.70, the *Morning Post* had published several anonymous articles relating to the meeting at the Geological Society on December 17th [see 2.3.70]. One was published on the 17th and the other the day after. It was this latter article which triggered Dawkins' long letter to the Editor, published on December 23rd.

2.4   Burlington House December 1913

Following a dinner at which "Piltdown mince pies" were served, the highlight of the Geological Society's meeting on 17 December 1913 was a report by Dawson, Woodward, and Elliot Smith on the progress made at Piltdown during the past year. Although the Society's visitor book indicates that there were comparatively fewer guests at this meeting than had been present at the "unveiling" a year earlier, it nevertheless managed to attract a crowd that far exceeded normal attendance figures for the Society, particularly for a session so close to the Christmas holidays.

Dawson began by noting that where previously they had thought the surface soil consisted of only 2 layers, their summer excavations had demonstrated a third layer that consisted of "reconstructed material from the underlying Wealden rock (Hastings Series)." He stressed, however, that this "third bed" had yielded no artifacts or bones. Following an account of the method employed in their excavations, Dawson then, with reference to an exhibit, quickly surveyed the various new finds that had been made (Dawson & Woodward (1914a; 82-85) and Table 2.2). These included the nasal bones (Note B: 2.3.32), a canine tooth (see 2.3.35 and annotations), and the molar fragments of *Stegodon* and *Rhinoceros* (Note E: 2.3.50), plus an incisor and broken ramus of beaver (*Castor fiber*) (Note A: 2.3.49), and two palaeolithic implements. At this juncture, Dawson yielded to Woodward, who proceeded to review the significance of the nasal bones and lower canine tooth, and associated mammalian fauna (Dawson & Woodward 1914a:86-92). The former, he attributed without reservation to *Eoanthropus dawsoni*, which, he said confirmed, with only slight modification, the conformation he had originally given the skull. As for the mammalian fauna, he claimed that the new finds supported the earlier contention that the Pliocene forms at Piltdown were essentially derived. Picking up on Woodward's reference to the original reconstruction, Elliot Smith (1913a, 1913b; 1914:93-97) brought the presentation to a close with a brief discourse on the reconstruction issue, in which he noted that careful study of the fragments in November (see 2.3.58, 2.3.64 and 2.3.65), particularly the left parietal, had provided evidence which allowed for the determination of the exact median plane of the skull. The results of this study he said confirmed Woodward's reconstruction (exhibited to the Society in December 1912) and that it was a much closer approximation to the truth than any of the various models so far exhibited. He also noted that he was in the midst of preparing a full report on the brain of *Eoanthropus* for presentation to the Royal Society of London[1]

In the discussion that followed Arthur Keith congratulated Dawson and Woodward on the progress that had been made in the last 12 months. He then went on to register his continuing dissatisfaction with the reconstruction. He believed the occipital and temporal bones were still oriented incorrectly, and was convinced that "when these defects were removed, and the two sides of the skull were made approximately symmetrical, it would be found that the brain capacity was about 1500 c.c." (Dawson & Woodward 1914a:98). Keith also noted that while there were some other lingering problems, namely with the jaw and canine tooth, he nevertheless agreed with the view that the jaw, skull, and canine tooth belonged to *Eoanthropus* – though not necessarily the same individual (see 2.2.37 and 2.3.66) One of the features that troubled Keith was that the canine tooth displayed considerable wear, and this did not equate with X-ray picture of the mandible which showed quite clearly that the third molar was not completely erupted (see 2.3.66). Addressing this issue, Arthur Underwood argued that the first and second molars in the Piltdown mandible showed considerable wear, and that his "radiograms" (Note A: 1.3.13) plainly revealed that the sockets of this molar were "not those of an erupting tooth, the roots had been quite completed and the tooth was in its final position at death" (Dawson & Woodward 1914a:99).

The next discussant was William Sollas who endorsed without reservation the conclusions arrived at by Dawson and Woodward (1914a:98). At the same time as concurring with this latter view, Boyd Dawkins also registered his patent disapproval of the various points raised by Keith. In particular he rejected the opinion that the age of the Piltdown deposit was Pliocene. All of the evidence, he contended, pointed to "an early stage of the Pleistocene Epoch" (Dawson & Woodward 1914a:98). Indeed, in a number of newspaper arcticles and several lectures he gave during the coming weeks, Dawkins shifted the emphasis of the debate away from strictly anatomical considerations to those of geology and palaeontology, namely to the question of dating.

NOTES

[1]   Communicated to the Royal Society at their meeting on 19 February 1914, see Letter 3.1.33.

TABLE 2.2: Material recovered from Piltdown (Barkham Manor) during 1913.

Material	Finder
"Human Remains"	
nasal bones (2)	Dawson[1]
turbinals	Dawson[1,2]
canine	Teilhard[1,2]
Mammalian Fauna	
Castor fiber lower jaw (fragment)	Dawson & Woodhead[3]
C. fiber incisor	Dawson & Woodhead[3]
Rhinoceros etruscus molar	Woodward[1,4]
Stegodon sp. molar (fragment)	Dawson[1]
Implements	
Flaked flint E 603	Dawson[5]
Eolith, triangular flake E 614	Dawson[6]
Worked flint	Woodward[4,7]

1: Dawson & Woodward (1914); 2: see Notes to Letter 2.3.35; 3: see Letter 2.3.49; 4: Woodward (1948); 5: from notes prepared by Woodward for Henry Fairfield Osborn, September 1933 (DF 116/46); 6: "C.D." written on specimen; 7: see Letter 2.3.55.

3 1914: A Thickening Plot at Piltdown

3.1 New Finds & Old Doubts

Sometime during the early summer of 1914, the gravel pit at Piltdown yielded the major find of the season, a bone implement that had evidently been carved from the limb of some extinct elephant (see subsection 3.2 for a discussion of this and other remains discovered during the 1914 season). The implement was some forty centimetres in length and shaped, as someone later remarked, rather like a cricket bat! To the supporters of eolithic theory and the notion that the human lineage had its origins in the Pliocene, this discovery was considered highly significant. Although the age and utility of this specimen provoked considerable discussion, it did not by any means silence the continuing debate surrounding Woodward's reconstruction of the Piltdown skull. In particular Keith remained convinced that it was fundamentally incorrect. It was against the backdrop of this debate that Keith was challenged in January (1914) by two of his anatomical colleagues, namely Frederick Gymet Parsons (1863–1943) of St Thomas' Hospital and Douglas Derry (2.3.56) of University College, to accurately reconstruct a human cranium they had deliberately broken. In the space of two weeks Keith succeeded in "reproducing the essential features" of this skull, and thereby, in the eyes of many, restored confidence in his anatomical expertise[1]. At the same time the rift between Keith and Elliot Smith widened.

Although, as noted earlier, some opposition to the monistic interpretation of the Piltdown had been voiced, this movement was of little consequence, at least until 1915. In the meantime, while scientific opinion remained polarized on some other issues, such as dating, there emerges from both the published literature (popular and otherwise) and the correspondence of 1914, a pervasive feeling that the controversy was almost exhausted and that a consensus was imminent in British scientific circles. The large oil painting by John Cooke entitled: "A Discussion of the Piltdown Skull" (based on the much publicized meeting of 11 August 1913 at the Royal College of Surgeons), is somewhat indicative of this mood (Fig 3.1). At the picture's centre is Keith (wearing a laboratory coat), seated at a table examining the Piltdown skull. To his left, also seated are Pycraft and Lankester, while to his right (standing) is Underwood. Behind, and looking on (from left to right) stand Barlow, Elliot Smith, Dawson and Woodward (for further details, see Note E: 3.1.32). Indeed, the only note of dissatisfaction to surface from the following collection of letters is from Dawson, who became convinced that he had not received sufficient recognition for his discovery (see Letter 3.1.6).

NOTES

[1]   This incident formed the basis of Keith's presidential address to the Annual General Meeting of the Royal Anthropological Institute on 20 January 1914. This address, entitled "The reconstruction of fossil human skulls" was subsequently published in the Institute's journal (Keith 1914a).

Fig. 3.1. The Cooke painting: "A discussion of the Piltdown skull", see Section 3.1 and Note E: 3.1.32. (Courtesy Geological Society of London).

CORRESPONDENCE

3.1.1 RP/IRSNB Abbott [4] January 1914

(a) William James Lewis Abbott (1853-1933); (b) typewritten letter on plain stationery: "8 Grand Parade, St. Leonard's o/s" addressed to the Belgian prehistorian Louis Aimé Rutot (1847-1933) in Brussels. (c) The date is unclear, it is either the 4th or 9th. The letter was subsequently edited in Abbott's handwriting.

I do not think I have written to you since I received the delightful photos of you[r] reproductions of the busts forming part of the series of the evolution of the hominidae [A] . . . We are still in the thick of the controversy over the Piltdown man. You will see that I have given Boyd Dawkins what some people have called his "eternal quietus" [B].

    Dawson behaved very badly to me over the whole affair, for as my principal assistant said when he saw no reference to me in the report:- "[I]t is very certain no Lewis Abbott, no Piltdown man" [C]. The whole material ought to have been put into the hands of the very best authority. I think I have told you that I have worked out the whole geological succession from the transgression of the Lenham Deistan Seat to recent man, and the gravels I have called the Meridionalis gravels are the ones in which Piltdown was found. The way Boyd Dawkins has hypnotized his old student Smith Woodward is a quite a psychological study. That distortion of the age into Chellian [sic] is as dishonourable as it is perposterous and disgraceful to science. The way this B[oyd]. D[awkins]. sweeps away as beneath his notice the splendid life work of my friend and example Rutot is disgraceful. A well-known authority wrote me: "[W]hat we want in the scientific world is something akin to the power possessed by the

Royal College of Surgeons, the Pharmaceutical Society, and the Lew [sic] Courts. When a man outrages everything as this man does, he ought to be struck off the Rolls." But I suppose he will go on making his oracular pronouncements of no prepa[leo]lithic man, and the oldest one post glacial, as long as he lives now [sic]. One of his friends wrote me today "if he makes no attempt now to retrieve his honour it will be forever lost, and no one can look upon him as a man, let alone a scientist.

Abbott maintained an episodic correspondence with Rutot, spanning the years from 1907 through 1915. The only letter remaining in the Rutot collection dating from 1913 was written in September and makes no mention of receiving photographs, which suggests Abbott wrote again between September 1913 and January 1914.

[A] Presumed to be photographs similar to those illustrating Rutot's book: *Un Essai de Reconstitution Plastique des Races Humaines Primitives* (1919).

[B] Reference evidently to Abbott's letter printed in the *Morning Post* 1 January 1914, written in response to Dawkins' earlier letter printed on 23 December, see Note B: 2.3.71. This long and critical letter (aimed primarily at Boyd Dawkins) followed a shorter one from A.Irving (1.3.3). As indicated in another letter to Rutot in September 1913, Abbott's animosity toward Dawkin clearly preceded the 23 December letter to the *Morning Post:*

It is a long time since I worried you with anything about what I have been doing. I have been at work, s[t]ill unravelling the true history of the Weald, which places our Later Tertiary Deposits in their right order and age, and gives a sequence of events correlatable [sic] with those of the continent. I am sending you something about the Piltdown from which you will see th[a]t I have [been] closely associated with it all through. Your colleague knows my colleague Dawson, from his being a collector of Wealden fossils: but it was I that urged upon him the necessity of working the gravels near his place at Uckfield. Unfortunately Wealden geology is in the worst state of any branch of the science (by "wealden" I mean the denudation of the weald). . . . I expect to be publishing some full details shortly as all the societies are at me about so doing. We have still a large number in this country who think perfect Pleistocene man dropped from the clouds, such people look up to Boyd Dawkins, and are very sore to think that neither they nor their leader can return a blow. No one can write about pre-Chillian [sic] man, or rule him out if they cannot read the geology of the weald, and of this – strange as it may seem nobody knows anything, they have all left it alone, accepting the "plane of marine denudation" theory or the "subaerial" and as neither of these would hold water Lancaster [sic] recently propounded something (if possible) even worse making some 2000 feet chemically dissolved away . . . But what became of the hundreds or square miles of land, thousands of feet thick, he does not tell anymore than the others! (RP/ IRSNB Abbott 1 September 1913).

[C] See Abbott's letters 1.2.24 and 2.3.8, as well as Dawson's: 2.3.10.

3.1.2 DF 116/13 Cartailhac 13 January 1914

Emile Cartailhac (1845-1921); (b) handwritten letter to Woodward on printed stationery: "Musée d'Histoire Naturelle et Jardin Zoologique, Toulouse"; (c) –.

This is a brief note from the well-known French prehistorian (and early mentor of Marcellin Boule), thanking Woodward for the reprint of Dawson & Woodward (1913a).

3.1.3 DF 116/5 Elliot Smith 31 January 1914

(a) Grafton Elliot Smith (1871-1937); (b) handwritten letter to Woodward on printed stationery: "The University, Manchester"; (c) annotated by Woodward: "Feb 6th"

I finished my appendix [A] and sent it to Belinfante [B] last night.

I shall be very glad to have Pycraft's results to add to my Royal Society memoir [C]. If it is possible I should very much like to have copies of his models of skull and brain before the end of next week; or failing the models, full-sized photographs of the things from different points of view.

If you have any photographs showing the texture of the diploe of the cranial bones, and any displaying the details of the mandible, especially the area just above the shelf in front, I should be very glad to have prints (I want the latter for reference in the discussion of the speech problem) [D].

I am very glad to have the abstract [E]. Belinfante sent me 12 of them, but there have been so many urgent requests for it that I let them all go.

[A] Dawson & Woodward (1914a).

[B] Louis Belinfante, see Note B:1.2.28

[C] Elliot Smith read his paper to the Royal Society on 19 February 1914. During the discussion period that followed, he and Keith clashed, see 3.1.13.

[D] The newspaper reports on Elliot Smith's lecture at the Royal Society made much of his contention that the "creature possessed the power of speech." See for example reports in *Manchester Courier* 20 March; *Times* 20 March; *Daily Express* 20 March; *Medical Times* 28 March and *British Medical Journal* 28 March.

[E] Most probably the abstract published in the *Proc Geol Soc Lond* (1913c), see also Dawson & Woodward (1914b).

3.1.4 DF 116/13 Todd 2 February 1914

(a) T. Wingate Todd (1885-1935); (b) handwritten letter to Woodward on printed stationery: "Anatomical Laboratory, School of Medicine, [Case] Western Reserve University, Cleveland, Ohio; (c) – .

Prior to his move to Cleveland in 1912, Todd had been Chief of Staff in the Anatomy Department at Manchester when Elliot Smith was appointed Professor of Anatomy in 1909.

I received your reprints two days ago. Very many thanks. I have read them with the greatest interest and exceedingly glad to know just exactly what has been said and done in this very vexed question. Thanks to your kindness, and that of Andrews [A], Hrdlička [B] and one or two others, I am gradually awakening a wider interest in this school in anatomy . . .

[A] See 2.3.67.

[B] See 1.2.16.

3.1.5 DF 100/37 Matthew 7 February 1914

(a) William Diller Matthew (1871-1930); (b) typewritten letter to Woodward on printed stationery: "American Museum of Natural History, Department of Vertebrate Paleontology [New York City]"; (c) annotated by Woodward: "28th. Thanks".

Matthew was Curator of the Department of Vertebrate Paleontology. The first part of this letter concerns an earlier enquiry made by Woodward regarding a collector in Calgary. In the last paragraph, however, Matthew writes:

The Piltdown skull was the storm-centre of a lively discussion at the last meeting of the Ecological Section of the N[ew]. Y[ork]. Academy of Sciences, and we have all examined and studied the casts which Dr. Williams [A] brought with the greatest interest.

From all indications this was Leon Williams, see Note D: 2.3.18, who interestingly enough published an article on the remains in the December (1913) issue of *Scientific American*. It is also interesting to note that shortly after this meeting William King Gregory, a member of the Department of Vertebrate Palaeontology at the American Museum, published a detailed critique of the Piltdown remains. This article is of particular interest since it relates an aspect of the controversy not previously mentioned in the published literature, namely that a rumour was already circulating that the remains were forgeries:

It has been suspected by some that geologically they [the Piltdown remains] are not old at all; that they may even represent a deliberate hoax, a negro or Australian skull and a broken ape jaw, artificially fossilized and 'planted' in the gravel-bed, to fool the scientists ... [However] None of the experts who have scrutinized the specimens and the gravel pit and its surroundings has doubted the genuineness of the discovery" (Gregory 1914: 190-191).

It is unclear if Gregory had heard these rumours while in London in 1913 (see 2.2.47), or whether they had come from Williams (see Spencer 1990).

3.1.6 DF 100/36 Dawson 8 February 1914

(a) Charles Dawson (1864-1916); (b) handwritten letter to Woodward on printed stationery: "The Castle Lodge, Lewes"; (c) annotated by Woodward: "9th"

Many thanks for your letter. I enclose a rough section which was used for drawing the diagram at the meeting.
   I shall look forward with interest to Elliot Smith's paper on the 19th inst., thank you for the invitation [A]. I will join you at ten. I hoped to have joined the banquet on the 20th but have a feeling the G[eological]. S[ociety]. are treating me rather shabbily [B]. However I wish you all good things in your year of Presidency [C].

[A] Elliot Smith delivered his paper to the Royal Society on the 19 February, see Note C: 3.1.3.

[B] The Geological Society held its annual General Meeting on 20 February, when a number of Medals and Funds were awarded – but none to Dawson. Furthermore it appears that Dawson was actively campaigning to become a Fellow of the Royal Society – an ambition that was never realized. Dawson's candidacy certificate for election to the Royal Society was filed on 19 December, 1913. According to this certificate, he was proposed by Henry Woodward, seconded by Edwin Ray Lankester, and supported by Smith Woodward, Edwin Tulley Newton, William Carruthers, Clement Reid, Lazarus Fletcher, George William Lamplugh, Horace Bolingbroke Woodward, William Whitaker, and Peter Chalmers Mitchell. According to the records of The Royal Society, Dawsons candidature was renewed until his death in 1916. During this period it is worth noting that Smith Woodward was a member of The Royal Society Council (1913-1915). Regarding the apparent drop in the number of letters from Dawson during the next 12 months, there is no reason to suggest that this was directly related to Dawson's failure to receive a Fellowship of the Royal Society and any award from the Geological Society. There is no evidence to suggest that this had caused a rift in the Dawson-Woodward relationship.

[C] At this meeting on the 20th, the presidency of the Geological Society was formally handed over to Woodward; an office he retained for two years. Prior to this Woodward had served as Vice-President from 1908-1909, and Secretary from 1909-1914. Following his stint as President, Woodward served again as Vice-President for the Society on two further occasions: 1916-1918 and 1924-1927.

3.1.7 DF 116/5 Elliot Smith 10 February 1914

(a) Grafton Elliot Smith (1871-1937); (b) handwritten letter to Woodward on plain stationery; (c) annotated by Woodward: "11th". Underlining in original by Elliot Smith.

Many thanks for your letter and Pycraft's brain model, the criticisms of which I sent to P[ycraft].
   During the last few days I have become very sceptical of the inclination of the occipital in <u>all</u>

reconstructions.

Comparison of the under surface of the occipital in a large series of skulls of various sizes has convinced me that the spot marked a (in this rough sketch [A]) cannot be more than 2 or 3 millimetres from the margin of the occipital.

But in all the reconstructions a very wide gap has been left between the point a and the mastoid temporal.

Today by making a rough plasticene model I convinced myself that it was possible to correct this and still preserve the proper relations of the occipital to the right parietal fragment. It means a very material reduction in the cranial capacity. My rough model (measured by Gooding) worked out at 1140 c.c. which is precisely the figure Gooding obtains from your original [B].

Tomorrow one of my demonstrators will make a careful reconstruction, as I shall be tied up with Council work in the University here.

The enclosed sketch (which is only a very rough drawing and doesn't pretend to be exact) gives an idea of how my model works out. You might hand this on to Pycraft as I am too busy to acknowledge his letter received today, beyond this comment.

[A] Small, labelled sketch, drawn in centre of page.

[B] Gooding's identity is not known.

3.1.8 DF 116/5 Elliot Smith 12 February 1914

(a) Grafton Elliot Smith (1871-1937); (b) handwritten letter to Woodward on printed stationery: "4 Willow Bank, Fallowfield, Manchester"; (c) – .

Very many thanks for your letter.

I sent a telegram asking you not to take up Barlow's time until I have puzzled matters out. I shall be able to present my case next week and can exhibit plasticine models or possibly casts from them. When we have finally decided how things should go, perhaps Barlow can use them to work, but in the meantime I hardly think it profitable for him to spend his time on the job.

My demonstrator failed to make anything of it and I am now tackling the job myself.

It is very disconcerting to become critical at the eleventh hour: but the point cropped up in the course of my work and as it affected the question of using Pycraft's model as it stands I thought it best to voice my doubts to you. The problem of [x/?] modifying the orientation of the occipital [x/?] is an extremely difficult one but I am wrestling with it.

However it does not materially affect anything in our reports. With kind regards and abject apologies for again being a disturbing agent.

[x/?]: word (unclear) written and deleted by GES.

3.1.9 DF 100/37 Matthew 4 March 1914

(a) William Diller Matthew (1871-1930); (b) type-written letter to Woodward on printed stationery: "Department of Vertebrate Paleontology, American Museum of Natural History"; (c) annotated by Woodward: "17th /28th. Ackn. ? casts.

This is one of two letters received from Matthew in March (the other being dated 28 March), but both make no further mention of the Piltdown controversy (see Matthew's earlier communication: 3.1.5). Matthew's letter of the 28th, however, does mention Elliot Smith's pending trip to America and suggests that he might be interested to know that the American Museum had a series of natural and artificial brain casts of Tertiary mammals.

3.1.10 DF 100/36 Lyne 12 March 1914

(a) W. Courtney Lyne (d. 1949); (b) handwritten letter to Woodward on printed stationery: "Dunheved, Maple Road, Bournville [Birmingham]"; (c) annotated by Woodward: "17th" and in margin where Lyne asks for the measurement between the bicuspids he has written: "7.5 or 8.0 cm."

Lyne, a dentist by profession, subsequently wrote a highly critical paper on Piltdown dental anatomy which was communicated to the Royal Society of Medicine in January 1916. For further details on this communication, see 4.2.5.

I expect you will recall my calling at Christmas [A]. I am still very interested in Piltdown, and very respectfully I should be glad to know if any further light has been discovered on Piltdown. I have been able to compare Chimpanzee and Human structure (bone) since seeing you, and there is [a] distinct specific difference. I wrote Gerrards [B] as you suggested, but I can only try whole skulls, and it is too expensive. I am exceedingly anxious to get hold of a fossil (Tertiary) horses or dogs tooth – not petrified, and I don't know where to get one. Would it be troubling you to let me know the measurement from the posterior margin of ascending ramus of Piltdown to the imaginary dental foramen (between bicuspids) the measurement running at level of [?/mental] foramen?

I was very grateful to you for your courtesy at Christmas.

[?] Word unclear.

[A] According the Museum's Visitor Book, Lynn visited Woodward on Tuesday, 30 December 1913.

[B] Gerrards' identity is not known.

3.1.11 DF 100/36 Lyne 18 March 1914

(a) W. Courtney Lyne (d 1949); (b) handwritten note to Woodward on printed stationery: "Dunheved, Maple Road, Bournville [Birmingham]"; (c) – .

Thank you for your courteous and kindly note. I was a little afraid of the state of the teeth of Tertiary horse – however it is very good of you to suggest as you do. Many thanks for your measurement of Piltdown.

See annotation to Letter 3.1.10.

3.1.12 DF 116/13 Assheton 24 March 1914

(a) R[ichard] Assheton (1863-1915); (b) handwritten letter to Woodward on printed stationery: "Grantchester, Cambridge"; (c) from the context of this letter it is presumed that it was hand-delivered.

Assheton was an anatomist at Cambridge.

May I introduce <u>Professor O. Grosser</u> of the K.K. Deutsche Karl Ferdinand Universität in Prague [A].
   Prof. Grosser has been in Cambridge for a few days for a meeting [B] and is very anxious to see the Piltdown skull [C].
   May I also take this opportunity of thanking you for the kind congratulations you sent me through Mrs Smith Underwood and my wife. Needless to say I am extremely satisfied and pleased by my election for recommendation for the Fellowship of the Royal Society and I was especially pleased to receive congratulations from you.

Otto Grosser (1873-1951), human embryologist.

[B] Grosser was attending a meeting of the "L'Institut International d'Embryologie."

[C] This is further evidence of Woodward's willingness to show the original specimens to scientific visitors.

3.1.13 LP/AHP Elliot Smith 8 April 1914

(a) Grafton Elliot Smith (1971-1937); (b) photocopy of handwritten letter to Haddon on printed stationery: "4 Willow Bank, Fallowfield"; (c) Original not examined, but underlining appears to have been executed by G.E.S.

Letter addressed to Alfred Cort Haddon (1855-1940), the Cambridge physical anthropologist. From the context of the letter it appears that Elliot Smith was responding to an earlier letter from Haddon.

The criticism was meant to be hard on A[rthur]. K[eith]. His wobbling has produced the utmost confusion both at home and abroad and I am getting an embarrassing stream of queries from foreign anthropologists to know what it all means. I had to speak straight because so many British anatomists have been content to dance to Keith's rag-time, without attempting to think for themselves; and foreign anthropologists think therefore that all the anatomists are supporting him. Even so I would not have taken upon myself the unpleasant task of unmasking Keith's game of deliberately fouling the pitch – and incidentally acquiring a little notoriety and hard cash – if he had not dragged in the asymmetry question [A]. After his last letter in "Nature" I replied to it pointing out the error of A.K.'s statements. The editor apparently intended to publish it; for he sent it to Keith to reply to, and the result was that the editor was persuaded not to publish my correction. I saw Keith and discussed the whole matter with him (early in November) and pointed out that the whole of [x/the] facts and inferences in [x/the] his last letter to "Nature" were false. Yet he trots all these errors out again in the January "Bedrock"! [B]. I don't mind a man making mistakes or changing his mind: but to publish stuff which he knows to be false is I think unpardonable. He and Duckworth *richly earned all they got.*

For years I have stood up for Keith, at times at the peril of my own reputation [? and] sanity, in the hope of restraining him from too wild excesses. I hoped the F.R.S. would have made him regard his utterances more seriously [C]. But this disgusting mess is the result [D]!

[?] word unclear; [x/] word written and deleted by G.E.S.

[A] Tension between Elliot Smith and Keith increased as a result of the confrontation between Keith and Woodward at the Royal College of Surgeons in August 1913. G.E.S.'s first paper to *Nature* was published on 2 October. This paper reveals the relation between his 1912 Presidential Address to the British Association (Section H: Anthropology) and his belief that Piltdown was genuine. Keith's response, printed in *Nature* on 16 October brings in the question of symmetry. Each of them published two further letters, the last being Keith on 20 November (see Note F: 2.3.45).

[B] Article on "Significance of the discovery at Piltdown" published in *Bedrock* (see Keith 1914b).

[C] Keith was not elected a Fellow of the Royal Society until the spring of 1913. On receiving this honor, Keith noted in his diary: "Thus one of the goals I expected to reach ten years ago comes now" (KP/RCS; also in Keith 1950:363).

[D] By this it is believed that Elliot Smith is referring not only to the exchanges in *Nature* but also to his interaction with Keith at the Royal Society in February (1914). At this meeting they had a heated exchange. Recalling the incident in his autobiography, Keith wrote:

I did not mince my words in pointing out the glaring errors in the reconstructed brain-cast he exhibited to the meeting. It was a crowded meeting, and so it happened that he and I filed out side by side. I shall never forget the angry look he gave me. Such was the end of a long friendship.

To which Keith added:

He must have felt I was in the right, for he never published the paper he read to the Royal Society. (Keith 1950:327).

3.1.14 DF 116/5 Elliot Smith 23 April 1914

(a) Grafton Elliot Smith (1871-1937); (b) handwritten letter to Woodward on printed stationery: "The University, Manchester"; (c) annotated by Woodward: "25th"

I am very glad to hear from Pycraft that you will allow Barlow to make a model of his reconstruction of the Piltdown skull and hope that it will be possible to make use of Barlow's work before I send in my M.S.S. to the Royal Society [A].

The arrangement of the sutures at the fronto-sphenoidal junction is extremely interesting affording new evidence of striking simian [x/ features] resemblances.

[x/] Word written and deleted by G.E.S.

[A] As indicated in Note D: 3.1.13, this paper was never published.

3.1.15 DF 116/5 Elliot Smith 20 May 1914

(a) Grafton Elliot Smith (1871-1937); (b) handwritten letter to Woodward on printed stationery: "The University, Manchester"; (c) –.

. . . As I may see you tomorrow and in any case on Saturday, when I hope to be able to spend the morning checking my R[oyal]. S[ociety]. manuscript from the actual fragments, I can postpone the discussion of names of people to whom to send copies of the paper. Lest I forget, however, Prof. E. Fischer (University of Freiburg) [A] and Prof. Huntington, Columbia University, New York [B] are people I should not like to be overlooked.

Tomorrow we leave Manchester and I expect to spend a week in London, trying to finish off the Piltdown job, before departing for Australia [C]. It is quite possible that I may not be able to get away in time for the R[oyal]. S[ociety]. Council: but I hope to be there.

[A] Eugen Fischer (1874-1964), the German anatomist and physical anthropologist.

[B] George Sumner Huntington (1851-1916), the American neuro-anatomist.

[C] While in Australia, Elliot Smith attended the British Association meetings that were held that year in Sydney. At these meetings Smith drew attention to the importance of the Talgai skull and its relevance to the Piltdown specimen. This skull was discovered in 1884 at "Talgai" on the Darling Downs in south-east Queensland. Prior to Elliot Smith's reference to it in 1914, the skull had languished in the Australian Museum. Later, Keith (1915:45) referred to it as a representative of "Australian Pleistocene man." On returning to Britain, Elliot Smith gave an illustrated lecture on the Talgai skull and its relevance to the Piltdown issue in February of 1915 to the Manchester Literary and Philosophical Society. For further details on this episode and its significance, see Langham (1978).

3.1.16 DF 116/13 Marett 20 May 1914

(a) Robert Ranulph Marett (1866-1943); (b) handwritten letter to Woodward on printed stationery: "Exeter College, Oxford"; (c) –.

See Letter 2.3.59.

Very many thanks for your interesting and important addendum [A] to my knowledge about the Piltdown lady. My poor Mousterian fellow from Jersey [A] cannot stand up to her at all!

[A] Reprint of Dawson & Woodward (1914a). This article appeared on 25 April in the *Quart J Geol Soc Lond.*

[B] This is a reference to Marett's excavations of La Cotte de St. Brelade, Jersey, Channel Islands. Marett worked at this site from 1910 until the outbreak of war in 1914. During this time 12 hominid teeth were recovered which were studied by Keith and Knowles (1911). See also Hrdlička (1914) for a summary of work at this site.

3.1.17 DF 116/13 Jones 20 May 1914

(a) Frederick Wood Jones (1879-1954); (b) handwritten note to Woodward on a printed postcard: London (Royal Free Hospital) School of Medicine for Women (University of London)"; (c) –.

Please accept my best thanks for the reprint [A] concerning the gentleman who has been so [?] to put friendships asunder [B]."

[?] word unclear.

[A] See Note A: 3.1.16.

[B] Evidently a tangential reference to the break-up of Keith's long-standing friendship with Elliot Smith (3.1.13).

3.1.18 DF 116/13 Munro 23 May 1914

(a) Robert Munro (1835-1920); (b) handwritten letter to Woodward on stationery embossed: "Elmbank, Largs, Ayrshire"; (c) –.

See 2.2.20 and 2.2.25.

Many thanks for the supplementary note on the Piltdown remains which considerably defines the facts of the discovery [A].

I however still stick to my opinion that this fossil man (or woman) is not older than the Chellean age. I can only regard the opinion of Dr. Arthur Keith as a negation of the [sic] evolution theory and all its evidences so far as they have hitherto come before us.

[A] See Note A: 3.1.16.

3.1.19 DF 100/37 Lankester 16 June 1914

(a) Edwin Ray Lankester (1847-1929); (b) handwritten letter to Woodward on printed stationery: "The Briar Gate, 331 Upper Richmond Road, Putney, [London] S.W."; (c) annotated by Woodward: "17th".

I am correcting and illustrating – more or less rewriting my D[aily]. T[elegraph]. articles on your great discovery – the chimpanzee-like nature of the Piltdown jaw [A] – for a volume of reprints – and explaining your argument – with warm tribute to your insight [B] – May I copy (not actually borrowing the blocks, but re-drawing them) some of the text figures in your two Geol[ogical] Soc[iety]. papers on the subject – of course with fullest acknowledgment. They are the side views of lower jaws of man, chimp and Piltdown, and the small completed figure of the restored Piltdown skull with nasal bones and canine.

I should be very much obliged if you would give your consent to my making these copies . . .

[A] Lankester's "Piltdown" articles in the *Daily Telegraph* include: "Facts and Theories About Primeval Man -I" Monday, 6 January 1913; "From Ape to Man - II", Monday, 27 January 1913; "From Ape to Man – III", Monday, 3 February 1913; "From Ape to Man – IV", Wednesday, 12 February 1913; "A Tooth Which was Lost And Is Found" December 1913.

[B] Here Woodward has written in the left margin: "Like Science from An Easy Chair" – the title of Lankester's column in the *Daily Telegraph*.

Council) and want to spend the morning finishing off my long delayed M.S.S. of the Piltdown Skull for the Royal Society [D].

I have heard nothing of the picture to which you refer in your letter but if you arrange for me to meet the "Chelsea artist" [E], I can fall in with your arrangements. [F] The Medical Council will I expect sit on the 24th, 25th and 26th inst. and I shall be free each day until eleven o'clock.

[A] For contemporary reports of Elliot Smith's sojourn in Australia, see interview printed in the *Sydney Morning Herald* 3 July and reports of the B.A.A.S. meetings in Sydney: *Sydney Morning Herald* 22 August (1914); *Scientific Australian* September (1914); see also Langham (1978).

[B] Johnson Symington (1851-1924), who held the Chair of Anatomy at Queen's College, Belfast. Exactly what transpired between Symington and Elliot Smith in Adelaide is not clear. However, Elliot Smith was wrong to think Symington had been silenced. Later, in 1916 the two clashed again, this time at the summer meetings of the Anatomical Society of Great Britain and Ireland held in Edinburgh.

[C] A reference to the Talgai skull, see 3.1.15 and 4.1.34. His reference to "Piltdown" is incorrect. It should be "Pilton". For a complete description of the site and skull, see Oakley *et al* (1975:203-204). See also Langham (1978) for a discussion of GES' views on Talgai and its relationship to Piltdown.

[D] See Note D: 3.1.13.

[E] The "Chelsea artist" was John Cooke (d. *circa* 1930) who was responsible for the large oil painting entitled: "A Discussion on the Piltdown Skull" – based on the much publicized meeting of 11 August 1913 at the Royal College of Surgeons (see 2.3.32, and 4.1.17). The painting, containing portraits of Lankester, Elliot Smith, Charles Dawson, Smith Woodward, Pycraft, Barlow, Keith and Underwood was not a commissioned work, but produced for the annual (May) exhibition of the Royal Academy for 1915 (Fig 3.1). From all accounts the picture attracted considerable attention, so much so that a "reproduction in photogravure of the picture" (18" X 13") was made by the engraver Emery Walker, and a limited edition (signed by the artist) was published. The cost of this reproduction was three guineas. The original oil painting was purchased from the artist for £25 by Dr. C.T. Trechmann F.G.S. [MSS WEI 3.18 Trechmann 24 May 1984] who presented it to the Geological Society where it was hung in the "Society's rooms on the staircase wall over the entresol landing" (see *Abst Proc Geol Soc Lond* No 1251, 1932). Although it appears that Woodward had planned to sit for Cooke on 12 December it is not known if Elliot Smith joined him. As indicated by Letter 4.1.17, the various portraits of those depicted were painted separately by Cooke and not as a group.

[F] In margin, Woodward has written: "To Cooke 12th", see Note E (above).

3.1.33 DF 100/37 Osborn 16 November 1914

(a) Henry Fairfield Osborn (1857-1935); (b) type-written letter to Woodward on printed stationery: "American Museum of Natural History, New York"; (c) annotated by Woodward: "Jan 25th 1915"

Osborn, an American palaeontologist was then President of the American Museum.

I am very much interested to see in __Nature__ a report of your revised restoration of the Piltdown skull, and I trust you will be good enough to send us a copy. In the meantime a former student of mine, Professor J. Howard McGregor [A], has made a model, using the cast which you kindly sent us, and placing the canine in the upper jaw [B]. The result is remarkably interesting. We are having copies made and will send you one as soon as it is completed. I shall be interested to see how it compares with your new model . . .

[A] James Howard McGregor (1872-1954). Pictures of McGregor's reconstruction were used to illustrate (Figs 71-72, pp 142-43) Osborn's book *Men of the Old Stone Age*, published in 1915. The technique used by McGregor is similar to that employed by Rutot, see 3.1.27. In his book Osborn posited the view that the Piltdown remains constituted an extinct offshoot of the human lineage; a view similar to that expressed by Keith (1915). For further details on the developing views of Osborn and his circle at the American Museum, see 4.1.2 and 4.1.7.

[B] This is of interest since Woodward considered it to be a right lower canine, whereas Osborn, following the conclusions of his protégé, William K. Gregory (1914: 196), considered it to be a left upper canine; see also 4.1.27.

3.1.34 DF 100/36 Dawson 21 November 1914

(a) Charles Dawson (1864-1916); (b) handwritten letter to Woodward on stationery embossed: "The Castle Lodge, Lewes"; (c) annotated by Woodward: "23rd". Underlining in original by Dawson.

Many thanks for your letter and kind invitation to dine at the Geol[ogical]. Club on the 2nd Dec[ember]. which I am very pleased to accept.

Not having seen your draft I do not know whether you have included any reference to the microscopic structure of the bone implements [A]?

Sometime ago you spoke of comparing this with remains of other fossil elephants to see if it were possible to assign the fragment to any particular group of Elephas, Pleistocene or Pliocene. It is worth trying, though the hope may be small [B].

Another point would be interesting [and] that is – to point out the most probable region of the femur from which the fragment was derived, making a diagram of a femur with the outline of the implement dotted upon the surface for demonstration [C].

The mode of exhibition of the specimen will have to be studied so as to secure it from damage, while showing every available feature.

I cannot think of any other points at present.

P.S. It is intensely cold here and good for walking the ploughed fields.

[A] A reference to the "bone implement", the primary object found during the 1914 season. According to Woodward (1948), he found one piece, and Dawson found the remainder. See subsection 3.2 for further details on this and other finds made during the summer season (see also 3.1.23).

[B] See introduction to subsection 3.2.

[C] Woodward employed this idea, see Fig 3.2b, and Dawson & Woodward (1915a:146). As indicated by the diagram in this paper, it was Woodward's considered view that the "bone implement" had been carved from the mid-part of the third trochanter of *Elephas meridionalis*, see Note B: 4.1.25 and Spencer (1990).

3.1.35 DF 100/37 Moir 11 November 1914

(a) James Reid Moir (1879-1944); (b) handwritten letter to Woodward on printed stationery: "12 St. Edmund's Road, Ipswich"; (c) – .

I am very glad you found my paper on the striations of flints interesting [A]. This was read more than a year ago and at that time I was a Fellow of the Geological Society. When the proof was sent to me I overlooked the fact that F.G.S. was printed after my name and suppose that as my subscription has now run out I am not entitled to this distinction. But I will see that the mistake is not made in future. As you perhaps know, I did not consider the Geological Soc[iety]. people treated me quite fairly in the arrangements made for showing my flints before them last year [B]. I would never have thought of doing so had I known beforehand I would only have a few minutes given to me to describe the specimens, and before the day of the meeting I wrote and also wired to try and find out if I would have the opportunity of explaining my exhibit – and yet barely got five minutes or so!

I don't mind any opposition I meet, but I must have fairplay, and as I considered I had not had it, I fore-with resigned my Fellowship. Perhaps I acted hastily – but there it is [C]!

[A] This paper, entitled: "The striation of flint surfaces" was published in *MAN* **XIV** (November): 177-181.

[B] From all indications this refers to a meeting arranged by Aubrey Strahan at the Geological Society on 19 November 1913 (*Proc Geol Soc Lond* **70**:ii–xiii, 1914) devoted to the eolith controversy. In addition to Moir, other exhibitors included several notable proeolithic and antieolithic workers. Each contributor was invited to demonstrate their respective artifacts and to "explain briefly the nature and object of his exhibits". Despite Woodward's attempts to smooth things over, Moir continued to believe that he had been unfairly treated, see Moir (1935:25). It is interesting to note that Dawson was opposed to the Strahan meeting, see Letter 2.3.50.

[C] Following this communication, Moir visited Woodward at the Museum on Friday, 20 November – which prompted Letters 3.1.36 and 3.1.37.

3.1.36 DF 100/37 Moir 22 November 1914

(a) James Reid Moir (1879-1944); (b) handwritten letter to Woodward on printed stationery: "12 St. Edmund's Road, Ipswich"; (c) annotated by Woodward: "27th". Underlining in original by Moir.

I would like to express to you my thanks for your kindness in showing me those precious specimens from Piltdown last Friday. [I]t was a very great pleasure to me to be able to handle and examine them [A]. This morning I have been going over some of my sub-Crag bones and am sending you a small selection. I am doing this because I would like you to see the difference in condition which exists in various specimens from this horizon and while the large majority are very heavily mineralized there are a few which are in quite a different condition.

There can be no doubt that (as has been pointed out by Lankester) these specimens, though all occurring in one bed, are of very different degrees of antiquity – the heavily mineralised examples being much older than the "Crag" epoch. While the others are probably contemporaneous with this period.

Now I think the opinion is very general that <u>all</u> sub-Crag bones are necessarily heavily mineralised – but this is not really the case among the [Piltdown] specimens I saw at South Kensington the other day – the fragment of mastodon tooth etc. Some were quite as mineralised as the majority of the sub-Crag specimens but the worked piece of elephant bone was not [B]. This, however, does not to my mind preclude the possibility of its being of Pliocene date, because, as I have shewn, a good few of the undoubted Pliocene sub-Crag bones exhibit a somewhat analagous mineral condition. The skull fragment appeared to me to be more mineralised than the elephant bone and to show distinct signs of "smoothing" by water-action – but I think you will be quite justified in suggesting they are both of the same age.

Though the elephant bone was not actually found <u>in situ</u> I don't think anyone could possibly dispute its age which is to my mind amply demonstrated by the yellowish clayey deposit which is to be seen in its crevices and cracks.

The question of mineralisation of bone, like the patination of flint is at present rather an unknown and understudied subject – but from experience – such as it is, I would be inclined to regard the condition of <u>all</u> the Piltdown bones as <u>pointing</u> to a Pliocene date.

But perhaps I am not on very safe ground in doing so. I can, however, speak with more confidence as to the condition of that elephant bone when it was fashioned by man as I have lately conducted a series of experiments with modern and fossil bones, and it is clear that the latter are not amenable to any cutting or hacking. So that the elephant that supplied the bone and the man who fashioned it were contemporaneous. You have found portions of the man, is it possible to identify the elephant? Do you think that sections of the bones say of E[lephas]. Meridionalis and E. Primigenius would show any difference in structure? But perhaps this has been tried. The deeper staining of the "worked" parts of the bone I attribute to the exposed structure being more absorbent than the other more "natural" surface. . . The flint implements found at Piltdown are very peculiar, and those found in the "human stratum" apparently undatable – but I must say that I think – on reviewing all the evidence and being anxious naturally to be on the safe side – you are justified in assuming the man found to be early Pleistocene. On the other hand I think there are many indications *that he is Pliocene, but further digging and discoveries will no doubt clear up this important point.*

I hope you won't think this long letter an interference on my part in a matter which does not really concern me – but you know how interested I am – and offer this as my excuse.

[A] As indicated by earlier letters Woodward had been quite open in showing interested individuals the materials recovered at Piltdown.

[B] A reference to the "bone implement" found at Piltdown during the early summer of 1914. For other views on the bone implement, prior to December meeting of the Geological Society where they were formally discussed, see Haward's letter (3.1.23), as well as that of Dawson (3.1.34) and Moir (3.1.37).

3.1.37 DF 100/37 Moir 28 November 1914

(a) James Reid Moir (1879-1944); (b) handwritten letter to Woodward on printed stationery: "12 St. Edmund's Road, Ipswich"; (c) underlining in original by Moir.

In my opinion there is every probability *that the worked bone and the human bones found at Piltdown are of the same age.*

The difference in their mineral condition does not weigh with me at all especially as your evidence goes to show that our specimen was derived from yellow sand and the other from dark brown gravel. These differing matrices are in every way [x/different] sufficient to account for the different degrees of mineralization.

The reason I say this is because for some months past I have been working here at a "floor" containing many bones and worked flints which is sometimes covered by clay and sometimes by sand.

There can not be any doubt at all that every find on this floor is of the same age – yet those specimens of bones under the sand are in a totally different condition to those occuring under the clay. *And the same applies to the flint implements. I shall hope to publish this later on, but you are at perfect liberty, if you wish, to make use of any part or all of this or my former letter, or not to use them at all. My wife has just reminded me that we have accepted an invitation to dine out next Wednesday and so much to my regret I shall be unable to be present at your meeting. I only wish I could be present [A].*

I don't feel able to arrive at any definite decision as to the Piltdown remains, but it is wise to be on the safe side and you are in my opinion, perfectly justified in leaning towards a Pleistocene date. Surely no one will dispute the age of that worked bone. The material in its crevices satisfied me as to its antiquity. Also its condition precludes a modern date.

[x/] Word written and deleted by JRM.

[A] Reference to the meeting at which Dawson and Woodward read their paper "On a bone implement from Piltdown, Sussex" held on Wednesday, 2 December. For details of this meeting see subsection 3.2, and Dawson & Woodward (1915a).

3.1.38 KP/RCS Moir 14 December 1914

(a) James Reid Moir (1879-1944); (b) handwritten letter to Arthur Keith (Royal College of Surgeons) on printed stationery: "12 St. Edmund's Road, Ipswich"; (c) –.

I was pleased to read your excellent letter in <u>Nature</u> in which you referred to the work of our mutual friend Collins [A]. . .

Your note on Wookey Hole too is very clear and good [B]. Fancy old [Boyd] Dawkins still believing the Cheddar Man is Neolithic [C] – but I suppose he stated this many years ago and being infallible what he said is true for all time!

Shall we ever get into that state of mind? I hope not, and for myself would much prefer to be dead. . .

[A] Reference to Keith's letter to the Editor concerning "Soldiers as Anthropologists" *Nature* **94**:391-392 (1914c). The "mutual friend" was a "Major E. R. Collins D.S.O." who was responsible for collecting artifacts while engaged in trenching operations in the Boer War. It is interesting to note that when the United States entered the war, Hrdlička (1917) reiterated Keith's sentiments.

[B] A review by Keith (1914d) of a book by H.E. Balch on *Wookey Hole* , published by Oxford University Press, 1914. This site had first been explored by Dawkins in 1859, who supplied an introductory chapter to the book. Dawkins' work was later followed up by the author, Henry Balch. Keith's review is politely critical of the work, and as Moir implies, especially of the views of Boyd Dawkins.

[C] For details on this cranium, see Note I: 1.2.11.

3.2   Burlington House 1914

On the evening of 2 December Dawson and Woodward read their paper "On a bone implement from Piltdown, Sussex" (published in the September 1915 issue of the Society's *Quarterly Journal* (1915a), see also Dawson & Woodward 1914c, 1915b, 1915c).

The proceedings began with Dawson, who reviewed the progress made at Piltdown during the summer of 1914, followed by a brief description of the various finds that had been made (Table 3.1). This was followed by Woodward's demonstration and discussion of the bone implement found sometime during June (see 3.1.23, 3.1.34 and 3.1.36). This implement (Fig 3.2) is a stout, and almost straight blade of bone, measuring 41 cm. long and varying from 9 to 10 cm. in width. One end (the thicker end) of this object is pointed (carved) while the other is rounded (also carved). Woodward contended that the object had been modelled from the upper part of a third trochanter belonging to an extinct species of *Elephas* that had once roamed Western Europe at the end of the Pliocene and beginning of the Pleistocene. As for the probable use of the implement Woodward said: "Its shape is unique, and an instrument with a point would be serviceable for many purposes" (Dawson & Woodward 1915a: 147).

The paper was then discussed by G. F. Lawrence, W. Dale, Reginald Smith, E. A. Martin, Arthur S. Kennard, F. P. Mennell, and S. Hazzledine Warren.

Dale opened with the comment: "The tool-marks appeared to have been made, not with a flint flake, but with some stronger cutting or chopping implement" (Dawson & Woodward 1915a: 148). This opinion was also echoed by Smith, who went on to say that he could not imagine any use for an implement that looked like part of a cricket-bat (Dawson & Woodward 1915a:148). Martin, however, thought it had probably been used as a club. Returning to the question raised by Dale, Kennard believed the object had not be fashioned from fresh bone, and suggested that experiments on fresh bone might shed some light on the question of how the visible cut marks on the implement had been made (Dawson & Woodward 1915a: 149). Mennell, however, was surprised that "so primitive a being as *Eoanthropus* should be capable of making and using implements at all" (Dawson & Woodward 1915a: 149). This latter speaker also had some doubts that elephant bone would have been a satisfactory material for making serviceable tools. This viewpoint, however, was countered by Warren who said: "wood and bone must have been used before flint and the evidence from Piltdown seemed to confirm this opinion" (Dawson & Woodward 1915a: 149).

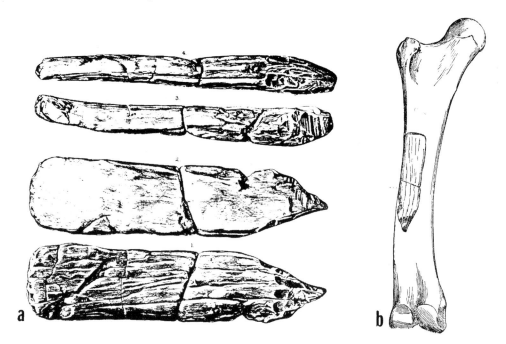

Fig. 3.2 The bone implement from Piltdown. (a) Various views of the implement: (1) Original outer surface of the bone; (2) inner (medullary) surface; (3) outer edge of the bone; (4) inner flaked edge. From Dawson & Woodward (1915a: Plate XIV). (b) Outline of a left femur of Elephas meridionalis, showing the part of the bone represented by the Piltdown implement. From Dawson & Woodward (1915a:146).

TABLE 3.1: Material recovered from Piltdown (Barkham Manor) in 1914.

Material	Finder
Mammalian Fauna	
Rhinoceros etruscus	Black[1,2]
Mastodon arvernensis	Woodward[1]
Implements	
Bone implement	Woodward & Dawson[2*]

1: Dawson & Woodward (1915a); 2: Woodward (1948); *: Woodward (1948) says that he found the first half and Dawson the remainder.

4 1915-1917: Piltdown Under Siege

4.1 1915: Undeclared Discoveries

At the beginning of January, Dawson informed Woodward that he had discovered a cranial fragment of what appeared to be a second *Eoanthropus* (see 4.1.1). Later in the year, Dawson reported finding "a new molar tooth" (4.1.21), which he claimed belonged to *Eoanthropus*. This latter find subsequently became known as Piltdown II (Woodward 1917, 1948) – but for reasons which Woodward never made clear, he chose to hold back on announcing it until 1917.

In the meantime, however, Woodward's reconstruction came under increasing fire from a number of American workers. The first shots came from Henry Fairfield Osborn's group at the American Museum in New York City (see 4.1.16, 4.1.27 and 4.1.35). They claimed, in particular, that the canine tooth, discovered by Teilhard, belonged in the upper and not the lower jaw as Woodward's reconstruction demanded. Woodward, however, remained unperturbed by these criticisms. Of greater concern, however, was the broadside delivered at the end of the year in the form of Gerrit Miller's paper (4.1.36), which struck at the very heart of Woodward's monistic model.

CORRESPONDENCE

4.1.1 DF 100/38 Dawson 9 January 1915

(a) Charles Dawson (1864-1916); (b) handwritten letter to Woodward on stationery embossed: "The Castle Lodge, Lewes"; (c) annotated by Woodward: "12th". Attached to this letter is a pen drawing showing two views (labelled) of the cranial fragment discussed in letter. Underlining in original by Dawson.

I believe we are in luck again! I have got a fragment of the left side of a frontal bone with portion of the orbit and root of nose. Its outline is [x/?] [*? nearly] the same as your original restoration and being another individual the difference is very slight.

There is no sura [sic] orbital foramen and hardly any superciliary ridge. The orbital border ends abruptly in the centre with a sort of tubercle, and between it and the nose is a groove or depression ¾ inch in length. The section is just like Pycraft's model section and there are indications of a frontal suture. The wall of the left sinus shows as a shallow depression in the [?] section. The tables are thin and the diploe very thick. The general thickness seems to me to correspond to the right parietal of Eoanthropus *[A].*

The weather has been awful but I shall have another search before the plough comes along. I enclose rough sketches made from pencil outlines. When is Elliot Smith likely to be in town? I will bring it up as soon as I can get away.

P.S. The outer surface is very rough, but the general colour and condition much the same as Eoanthropus. *The forehead is quite angelic!*

[?] word unclear; [x/?] unclear word deleted; and [*/] word added by C.D.

[A] It is uncertain when Woodward came into possession of this and related specimens (see 4.2.22). Judging from the Lankester's letter 4.1.39, it would appear that Dawson had not only retained the specimens but also had shown them round. The next find in the (*Eoanthropus*) "new series" was made sometime in July, see 4.1.21. While it is conceivable that Woodward took possession of these remains at this time, this is far from being certain (see Note B: 4.2.22).

4.1.2 DF 100/39 Osborn 12 January 1915

(a) Henry Fairfield Osborn (1857-1935); (b) typewritten letter to Woodward on printed stationery: "American Museum of Natural History, New York City"; (c) –.

I am preparing for you especially three recent models made by Professor J. Howard McGregor partly under my direction which I know will interest you:
    The Piltdown skull and jaw
    The Piltdown brain from the interior of the reconstructed skull
    The Piltdown head showing Professor McGregor's method of modeling
    The Piltdown head complete.
This work affords a somewhat different interpretation from that reached by the modelers and your direction. I have enjoyed in Professor McGregor the advantage of the work of a man who combines I think exceptional artistic skill with what may be called strong imagination in comparative anatomy. Before the modeling was begun we held a long series of conferences, Dr. McGregor, Dr. Gregory and myself, on the fragments you so kindly sent over and you will observe that we have taken advantage of the latest information afforded in your papers as regards the median line of the skull. [A]
    I am using these results in my forthcoming book "Man of the Old Stone Age" a copy of which I will send you immediately on publication [B].
    Your attitude in this matter has been so different from that of Marcellin Boule [C], who not only did not allow his assistants to show me the La Chapelle skull while I was passing through Paris but has managed to keep away from us even a cast of the same; but we have just come into possession of an excellent cast by a round-about route. I trust you will not feel that we have taken any unfair advantage of your generous action. . .

[A] See Elliot Smith, cited in Dawson & Woodward (1914a).

[B] This work was based on Osborn's "Hitchcock Lectures" given at the University of California, Berkeley, 1914. The book was published by Scribner in November 1915.

[C] A similar story is told by Hrdlička who visited Boule in the summer of 1912, see Spencer (1979, II: 407).

4.1.3 DF 116/14 Postlethwaite 26 January 1915

(a) J. Postlethwaite; (b) handwritten letter to Woodward on printed stationery: "18 Erskine Street, Keswick"; (c) –.

A letter thanking Woodward for a copy of his *Guide to the Fossil Remains of Man* (1915). Aside from noting the publication of this work, Postlethwaite's letter is of interest since it is conjectured that he might be a relative of Dawson's wife, whose former husband had been a Postlethwaite. Also it appears that before moving to Keswick, J. Postlethwaite had lived at 7 St. Johns Terrace in Lewes, a short distance from Christopher Gaster, see 4.1.30.

4.1.4 DF 116/14 Dixon 3 February 1915

(a) A[ndrew]. Francis Dixon (d 1936); (b) handwritten letter to Woodward on printed stationery: "73 Grosvenor Road, Dublin"; (c) –.

Letter thanks Woodward for a copy of his *Guide*, see 4.1.3. This letter is of particular interest since the bottom part of the letter [containing a ? postscript] has been carefully removed!

4.1.5 DF 116/14 Kenward 5 February 1915

(a) Mabel Kenward (1885-1978); (b) handwritten letter to Woodward on stationery embossed: "Barkham Manor, Piltdown, Uckfield"; (c) –.

In this letter from Mabel Kenward, daughter of Robert Kenward the Chief Tenant of Barkham Manor, thanking Woodward for sending a copy of Henry Woodward's biographical of Arthur Smith Woodward (1915), she notes: "The pit is at present a "Lake", but we shall look forward to seeing you and Mr. Dawson, find[ing] other wonderful things, – when the summer comes again."

4.1.6 DF 116/14 Jones 11 February 1915

(a) Frederic Wood Jones (1879-1954); (b) handwritten letter to Woodward on printed stationery: "London (Royal Free Hospital) School of Medicine for Women (University of London); (c) –.

I was very glad to get the guide [A] and the Dryopithecus paper [B]. I have read both already. The interrelation of these types is a most interesting problem. As for the guide it strikes me that without a thorough desire to split hairs it would be quite beside the mark to take exception to the passages you mention – I see no other way of putting the case to those who visit museums.

I hope that when Elliot Smith's paper appears the points which constitute his trumps will be put out very clearly. Piltdown man will not be incomplete for want of criticism anyhow.

[A] Woodward (1915).

[B] Woodward (1914b).

4.1.7 DF 100/39 Osborn 25 February 1915

(a) Henry Fairfield Osborn (1857-1935); (b) typewritten letter to Woodward on printed stationery: "American Museum of Natural History, New York City"; (c) underlining in original by Osborn.

I was very glad to get your letter of January 25th and was extremely interested in the papers, namely your recent description of the Piltdown material in the Catalogue [A], your account of <u>Dryopithecus</u>, and the admirable biographic notice of your work [B].

I am going to present to the British Museum the series of models which have been prepared by Professor J. Howard McGregor [C]. . . They include the reconstructed head and jaws, the restoration of the head in flesh, and the intracranial cast which was made by the ingenius [sic] method of setting the pieces of bone within the skull cast, filling up the interspaces and then securing an intra-cranial mould. It is interesting to observe that the brain displacement is exactly that estimated in the Catalogue, namely 1300 cc. . . . He has also done the <u>Pithecanthropus</u> head, both the skull and the head proper, and the same with the Neanderthal head, and is now doing the Cro-Magnon, Upper Palaeolithic Man. . . McGregor is prepared to dispose of reproductions. I think he takes $100 for the whole set, which is a very modest amount. . . [D]

[A] See Note A: 4.1.6.

[B] Woodward (1914b). The biographic notice is a reference to Henry Woodward's paper on Arthur Smith Woodward published in the *Geological Magazine* (1915).

[C] James H McGregor (1872-1954). These reconstructions are to be found in the collections of the Department of Palaeontology: No E 632 and E 636.

[D] See Osborn (1915): Pithecanthropus (pp 81-82), Eoanthropus (pp 142-143); Neanderthal [La Chapelle-aux-Saints] (p 201); and Cro-Magnon (pp 300-301).

4.1.8 DF 1003 Dawson 25 February 1915

(a) Charles Dawson (1864-1916); (b) handwritten letter to Woodward on stationery embossed: "The Castle Lodge, Lewes"; (c) annotated by Woodward: "27th". Underlining in original by Dawson.

Many thanks for sending your man to clear my boxes off on Wednesday. I had a busy two hours packing. I sent you my little case of starch fractures and my type series of Flint "prismatics" and "columnars." I have an idea that some flints are sometimes more prismatic than conchoidal in fracture and vice versa, and that the Crag ones are perhaps more conchoidal in their fracture but it only <u>predominates</u> *the prismatic influence. Starch is only slightly conchoidal in fracture and mainly columnar or prismatic [A]. There is a blending of these factors. I dipped all the specimens of starch fractures in Barlow's spirit and shellac solution [B] to harden them, as they are very crumbly and seemed ready to split up into other prismatic fragments or perhaps "micro-eoliths". It is all very curious.*

[A] A reference to the subject of Dawson's paper "Sussex Ouse Valley Culture" read at a joint meeting of the Prehistoric Society of East Anglia and the Royal Anthropological Institute, held at the Institute (50 Great Russell Street, London), on Tuesday evening of 23 February 1915. For the text of Dawson's unpublished paper, see DF 116/16. See also Weiner (1955:103) and note in the *J Royal Anthropol Inst* (1915:364). Dawson's paper was essentially an attack on eolithic theory. For a discussion of this paper and its implications, see Spencer 1990.

[B] An asterisk has been inserted here, and evidently not by Dawson. The asterisk refers to a footnote written by neither Dawson nor Woodward, that reads: "Beeswax, resin, carnauba – see Plenderlith, 1934 p.29". As this indicates the "hardening" solution Dawson is referring to here is not Barlow's bichromate solution, see Note D: 1.1.10 and 1.1.24.

4.1.9 DF 100/38 Lyne 25 February 1915

(a) W. Courtney Lyne (d.1949); (b) handwritten letter to Woodward on printed stationery: "Dunheved, Maple Road, Bournville [Birmingham]; (c) –.

When I saw you at Christmas 1914 [A], and you were kind enough to allow me to inspect the Piltdown remains, I understand you to say that when replicas of the canine found at Piltdown were made public property, you would try and let me have one. Is it possible for you to spare me a cast? or else can you tell me where I can obtain one – I see Mr. Humphry has a cast in his Museum at our University [B].

 By the way, X-ray pictures have been taken of the mandible and molars of Piltdown – has any X-ray of the canine ever been taken?

[A] Lyne's visit is not recorded in the Department's visitors book covering the period from December 1914 through to the end of January 1915.

[B] In contrast to Lyne's earlier correspondence, see 3.1.10-3.1.11, Woodward now appears somewhat reluctant to assist the dentist in his research. The identity of Humphry is not known.

4.1.10 DF 110/36 Boule 6 March 1915

(a) Marcellin Boule (1861-1942); (b) handwritten letter (in French) to Woodward on printed stationery: "Muséum National d'Histoire Naturelle, Laboratoire de Paléontologie, 3 Place Valhubert, Paris"; (c) annotated by Woodward: "8th".

I was about to lose hope and was dreading a disaster at sea because of the German submarines when, a few minutes ago they delivered your parcel.

 I hasten to acknowledge its receipt and thank you. The casts [A] arrived in perfect condition. I also thank you for the pamphlets that you included in your February 16th letter and I found your "little guide" especially interesting [B].

I will now be able to continue and finish writing my article on human palaeontology in England which will appear in the first issue of the anthropological journal of 1915 [C]. The last issue of 1914 having been delayed because of the war, is now being printed. . .

It goes without saying that I find this latest and important discovery extraordinary and that I agree with most of your ideas except for some points of detail [D].

I have reiterated to Keith what I thought of your geological, anatomical, and palaeotological aptitudes. I am, however, surprised that in your "Guide" you give the cranial capacity of [Piltdown] 1300 c.c. instead of 1180 c.c. that you had previously attributed to it. Do we have to understand from this that you are acknowledging the basis of Keith's criticism?

. . . Professor Teilhard left me a few days ago after the general mobilization. He was first sent to an infirmary in Clermont-Ferrand. I received a letter he wrote to me from a little village on the front at the Oise [E]. He is a stretcher-bearer attached to an artillery regiment and therefore in a vulnerable position . . . and I worry about him.

[A] See 3.1.20.

[B] See Woodward (1914b) and (1915). See also Note D [below].

[C] See Boule (1915) which was published in April 1915.

[D] It is presumed that Boule is referring to the discovery of the bone implement. Since, as indicated by 4.1.20, Dawson & Woodward's article (1915a) did not appear until sometime during the early autumn, in all probability this opinion was based on the published abstract (Dawson & Woodward 1914c).

[E] See 4.1.11.

4.1.11 DF 100/38 Dawson 9 March 1915

(a) Charles Dawson (1864-1916); (b) handwritten letter to Woodward on printed stationery: "Town Hall Chambers, Uckfield"; (c) annotated by Woodward: "12th". Underlining in original by Dawson.

I enclose a P[ost]. C[ard]. from Teilhard at the French front [A]. He no doubt, would be glad of any little bits of literature which you can send him.

I have been receiving abusive letters about "Starch" [B], especially from Lewis Abbott who seems specially annoyed! Reid Moir sent me a lot of specimens of non-prismatic forms to which the old washtub theory would more nearly apply.

I cannot find the literature of that "120 degree" pressure or fracture which a <u>Mr. Barnes</u> raised at the meeting. Do you know of any reference? I cannot find it referred to in the Civil Engineering text books, but I once read a newspaper article upon it. It does not so much effect the issue as the <u>cause</u> of columnar structure. Your mineral people would probably know? It is common to all colloids but starch is a hardy material to investigate. In a number of cases these prismatic or sub-prismatic cleavages have been mistaken for "flaking" of the ordinary form and the conchoidal flakes sometimes mask the cleavages or fissures [C].

I hear Keith has gone to the U.S.A. whence we shall probably hear from him [D].

[A] This postcard is not preserved. This correlates with information relayed by Boule, see 4.1.10. For further references to Teilhard in Dawson's 1915 correspondence, see Letters 4.1.17 and 4.1.21.

[B] Weiner (1955:103) gives the impression that these "abusive" letters were exclusively from Abbott, but this does not appear to have been the case. What connection, if any, there is between this and the blackmail rumour mentioned in the Barbe interview (see 6.3.21) is largely a matter of conjecture.

[C] See Note A: 4.1.8 for further details on Dawson's starch paper.

[D] For details on Keith's American tour, see Note B: 4.1.14.

4.1.12 DF 116/14 Lucas 10 March 1915

(a) Frederic Augustus Lucas (1852-1929); (b) handwritten letter to Woodward on printed stationery: "American Museum of Natural History, New York"; (c) –.

Lucas was an American osteologist at the American Museum. After thanking Woodward for a copy of his *Guide* (1915), he writes: "I have great admiration for the manner in which scientific work and publication is being carried on by you under the stress of the bitter war and sometimes wonder how you have the heart for it."

4.1.13 DF 116/14 Black 26 March 1915

(a) Davidson Black (1884-1934); (b) handwritten note to Woodward on a plain postcard: "Anatomical Department, [Case] Western Reserve University, Cleveland, Ohio"; (c) –.

Black thanks Woodward for his *Guide* (1915) and reprint of his *Dryopithecus* paper (1914b).

4.1.14 DF 116/14 Todd 27 March 1915

(a) T. Wingate Todd (1885-1938); (b) typewritten letter to Woodward on printed stationery: "Anatomical Laboratory, School of Medicine, [Case] Western Reserve University, Cleveland, Ohio"; (c) –.

Very many thanks for the reprints [A] which I have read with great pleasure. It is not necessary to agree in every detail over Eoanthropus *of course! But at present Keith and I spend our spare moments (he is living with us just now) each trying to convince the other on points of mutual disagreement over that much tried specimen. It is necessary to add that no result is obtained.*

[A] Presumed to be reprints of Woodward's *Guide* (1915) and *Dryopithecus* (1914) papers.

[B] Todd had invited Keith to give a course of 5 lectures at the Medical School in Cleveland. Keith left England with his wife, Celia, on Sunday, 7 March 1915, arriving in New York on the 15th. From 9 March until 30 March they were house guests of Todd in Cleveland, Ohio. Following a whirlwind tour of various American institutions in the northeast, plus Toronto and Montreal, Keith returned to Britain via Liverpool on 24 April.

4.1.15 DF 116/14 Todd 30 March 1915

(a) T. Wingate Todd (1885-1938); (b) handwritten letter to Woodward on printed stationery: "Anatomical Laboratory, School of Medicine, [Case] Western Reserve University, Cleveland, Ohio"; (c) –.

Many thanks for your note of March 16. I had hoped to have your reconstruction here in time of Keith's lectures [A]. Damon promised it for last January but has been delayed. Apparently he never grasped the urgency of the situation. Personally I plead guilty to being unconverted in many points [B]. Black came here just as strongly convinced. But we have both moderated during the winter. Your comparison with the child's tooth and skull is of great interest and I should be glad indeed to have a copy of the supplement on the canine tooth.

[A] 4.1.14.

[B] See Todd (1914) for a review of his position on human phylogeny.

4.1.16 DF 100/39 Osborn 5 April 1915

(a) Henry Fairfield Osborn (1857-1935); (b) typewritten letter to Woodward on printed stationery: "American Museum of Natural History, New York"; (c) annotated by Woodward: "29th"

On my return from the South [A] I was interested and delighted to find your revised model of the head of Eoanthropus, and I shall have an opportunity this afternoon of placing it side by side with the model made by Professor McGregor in cooperation with me. Will you not kindly give the date of your revised model, which I believe antedates that of Professor McGregor [B]. I am intensely interested in it. The cranium is substantially similar in form to that in our restoration, but the face and the dental series is somewhat different. I venture the opinion that your model demonstrates that the canine tooth is not inferior but superior; you will observe how aptly it fits above in McGregor's restoration.

. . . My book "Men of the Old Stone Age" is now well advanced in the press at Scribners, and again I have been obliged to differ from you in placing the Piltdown man relatively late in the Pleistocene because of the undoubted association of his remains with flints of pre-Chellean time; not a single trace of pre-Chellean flints have been found in Europe in deposits earlier than the Third Interglacial Stage. . . [C]

[A] In an earlier letter (4.1.7), Osborn noted that his wife had been unwell and that he was taking a months leave. His destination was not disclosed.

[B] See Note C: 4.1.7.

[C] See Note B: 4.1.2; and pages 137, 142-143 of Osborn's *Men of the Old Stone Age* (1915).

4.1.17 DF 100/38 Dawson 30 April 1915

(a) Charles Dawson (1864-1916); (b) handwritten letter to Woodward on stationery embossed: "Uckfield, Sussex"; (c) –.

Thank you very much for the tickets for the [Royal] Academy [of Art] private view which I have given to Mrs. Dawson who is in Town today and will be able to use them [A]. I have been in London the last few days at Marylebone about a pearl robbery so cannot spare time to go again so soon. I must go and see the picture some day as I have not seen it since Elliot Smith was painted in [B]. I did not think that the Moir bone "implements" [C] would turn out right. It is rather too much to expect! Lewis Abbott has been lecturing at Hastings on new strata he has discovered – "Pliocene". I went and had a look on my own but there is no doubt that the so-called Pliocene deposit is only a recent surface soil affair with modern beach stones such as you see on the cultivated areas around the coast. The beach is put on the roads and farm yards and gets scraped up and put on the lands as "road-scrappings" for [?manorial] purposes! A section alongside of a road there is obviously only a remnant of the road when it was situated at a higher level in the road cutting.

I am afraid we old stagers are getting out of date with the "modern school" of thought and sadly interfere with its scope [D].

We shall soon hear of – prehistoric – bombs [E] discovered at Ipswich and laid at the feet of the East Anglian Scientific Society [F].

P.S. Teilhard has now been moved to near the back of the English line in Flanders. He says he is all right "Body and mind". [G]

[?] Word unclear.

[A] Prior to being hung at the Royal Academy, John Cooke's "Piltdown" painting had a private showing at his studio [2 Trafalgar Studios, Manresa Road] in Chelsea on 23, 24 and 25 March 1915.

[B] See Note E: 3.1.32.

[C] See Moir (1915). It is interesting to note the similarity between Moir's "Group II" specimens [Plate XXVII] and the Piltdown bone implement (Dawson & Woodward 1915a).

[D] For more of Dawson on the "new school", see *Sussex Daily News* 11 August 1913.

[E] J. Weiner (1955: 184) has transcribed this as "balls".

[F] Presumably Dawson meant to write the "Prehistoric Society of East Anglia".

[G] See Note A: 4.1.11.

4.1.18 DF 116/14 Turner 1 May 1915

(a) William Turner; (b) handwritten letter to Woodward on printed stationery: "Euston Hotel, London, N.W."; (c) –.

The identity of this individual is not known. The brief letter indicates Turner's intention of calling at the Museum on Monday, 3 May to view the Piltdown skull. The Museum's visitors book confirms that the appointment was kept.

4.1.19 DF 100/38 Dawson 22 May 1915

(a) Charles Dawson (1864-1916); (b) handwritten letter to Woodward on printed stationery: "Town Hall Chambers, Uckfield"; (c) annotated by Woodward: "24th. Proposed Piltdown 28th & 29th". Underlining in original by Dawson.

Thank you for the cutting. I have seen the <u>Illustrated [London News]</u> print [A] which seems rather poor and fuzzy owing to the paper being inferior to what it was before the war.

I do not know what the Geo[logists']. Association will say as to Lewis Abbott's <u>Pliocene</u> river-beds and deposits. I have been over all the ground and can only see beach stones from the shore mixed with surface soil, derived from farm-yards and road-scrapings put on the land for manure. A small line of beach flints 3 inches thick adjoining an old hollow road and shown in a section of this bank is the remains of old road mending when the road ran at a higher level some years ago. J.W.L.A. [B] calls this a <u>Pliocene</u> river bed [B]!

It is all most astonishing and I hope some of the Association people give L.A. the benefit of their experience, but I should think that some will be rather furious to be brought down over such nonsense.

I enclose a notice of our four yearly meeting at Piltdown which led years ago to the discovery of the gravel bed at Piltdown [C].

[A] A probable reference to a story relating to the Cooke painting, see "Scientists Discussing Piltdown Skull," *Illustrated London News* CXLVI:672.

[B] Reference to W.J. Lewis Abbott. For a review of Abbott's thinking at that time, see his article on "The Pliocene deposits of the southeast of England" in *Prehistoric Society of East Anglia* (1915).

[C] This notice is attached to the inside cover of Woodward's "Piltdown Scrapbook" (DF 104), and reads: " A GENERAL COURT BARON and CUSTOMARY COURT of George Maryon-Wilson, Esquire, Lord of the said Manors will be held in and for the above Manors [Barkham, Tarring Camois and Netherhall], at BARKHAM MANOR HOUSE, PILTDOWN, FLETCHING, SUSSEX, on THURSDAY, the 10th day of JUNE, 1915 at 12 NOON, at which all Copyhold and Freehold Tenants, having business in either of the said Manors, are requested to attend." The printed notice is dated 20 May, and signed by Dawson.

4.1.20 DF 100/38 Dawson 11 June 1915

(a) Charles Dawson (1864-1916); (b) handwritten letter to Woodward on printed stationery: "Town Hall Chambers, Uckfield"; (c) Woodward has not annotated this letter, but it has been stamped: "British Museum (Natural History), Cromwell Road, London". Underlining in original by Dawson.

I have returned the proof to Belinfaunt [sic] approved [A]. I think however you have not given the full reference to the Fayum Elephas in the Brit[ish]. Mus[eum]. which stands in the proof as (No M) [B] with a query in the margin.

Sml[?] Laing in his "Problems of the Future" Chapter V [C], quotes cut bones of Elephas meridionalis etc., mentioned by Quatrefages in Histoire des Races Humaines 1887 [D]. I think at St. Prest, see also his Homes fossiles [sic]. [E]. These references seem to have been overlooked but I cannot find them at the Geol[ogical] Soc[iet]y. or [Society of] Antiquaries. I have heard from Nature and the editor of Man that Reid Moir is trying to get at me over the Starch etc. He does not seem to know how to contain himself about it all, and is trying to get an unfair advantage by premature publication [F]. I do not think however that his sub-Crag things owe much to the starch fracture. They all were of the "wash tub" variety. I have great difficulty in completing my paper owing to lack of opportunity of proper references at present [G].

You should go and see Dewlish when in Dorsetshire: the flints look very much like Piltdown [H].

P.S. I return the Application form [of the] R[oyal]. S[ociety]. Many thanks – but it is not what I want [I]

[?] Word unclear. See Note C.

[A] Louis Belinfante, Secretary of the Geological Society of London. See Note B: 1.2.28

[B] Reference to proofs of Dawson & Woodward (1915a): "On a bone implement from Piltdown", page 145. The relevant portion of the published text reads: ". . . resembling those in a subfossil femur of *Elephas* from a lake-deposit in Egypt, now in the British Museum (No M8526)."

[C] This is believed to be a reference to *Problems of the Future and Essays* (London: Chapman & Hall, 1890) by Samuel Laing (1812-1897).

[D] This reference to Armand Quatrefages' (1810-1892) book (published in Paris: Hennuyer) is correct.

[E] This is probably Quatrefages' *L'Hommes fossiles et hommes sauvages* (published in Paris: Baillière 1884).

[F] A reference to Moir's (1915) paper on "bone implements" in Suffolk, see Note C: 4.1.17.

[G] Dawson never completed the paper, see Note A: Letter 4.1.8 for further details.

[H] For details on the Dewlish find, see Keith's *Bedrock* article (1914:444), and Note A: 2.3.29.

[I] As indicated in Note B: 3.1.6 the Fellowship of the Royal Society had been one of Dawson's ambitions. But this statement (viewed in the light of Letter 4.1.22) suggests that Dawson was now disenchanted with this idea.

4.1.21 DF 100/38 Dawson 30 July 1915

(a) Charles Dawson (1864-1916); (b) handwritten postcard to Woodward [dated by Dawson 30th July 1915]; postmarked: "Uckfield", date and time are smudged; the card was addressed to Woodward's home: "4 Scarsdale Villas, Kensington"; (c) annotated by Woodward in 1933: "This is Charles Dawson's handwriting and refers to his discovery of the tooth with the second Piltdown skull". On the address side of the postcard (bottom left hand corner) there is the annotation: "E 646" made by a later archivist, see explanation below [A].

I am sorry I shall not be able to come to Keith's demonstration [B]. I wonder if he has seen the new paper on Pleistocene and Pliocene Primates in the Indian Gov[ernment]. Geol[ogical]. publication. The writer sent me a separate but I forget his name [C].

Boule has been writing to me about Starch Eoliths and I have sent him a sample of them. He has promised to send me a separate of some new paper he has written about Eoanthropus [D].

Teilhard wrote yesterday – he is quite well and in a quiet spot at present. I have got a new molar tooth (Eoanthropus) with the new series [E]. But it is just the same as the others as to wear. It is a first or second right m[olar]. The roots broken. At Piltdown the road is falling in at the edge where we got too close and Kenward has put up a fence.

[A] In 1926 Hrdlička wrote to Francis Bather (Woodward's succesor at the Museum) about the circumstances relating to the discovery of the second molar, together with the two cranial fragments that constituted the remains of a second "Eoanthropus", see 5.1.24, and 5.1.25. Bather's reply was vague, and did little to dispel Hrdlička's scepticism that these specimens represented a second individual. As a consequence of Hrdlička's critical note in his book *Skeletal Remains of Early Man* (1930: 87), Woodward made a more careful review of his correspondence with Dawson and "discovered" the above postcard. This he transmitted to William Dickson Lang (1878-1966), then Keeper of Palaeontology, noting:

. . . I think that this should be carefully preserved, and that a reference to it should be added to the number of the specimen in the Register. Hrdlička (Smithson. Miscell. Coll. Vol. 83, p.87) has already doubted my statement about Dawson's discovery, and there may be other doubters for whom Dawson's own record is needed" (DF 100/38 Woodward to Lang 16 January 1933).

Lang did as Woodward requested (DF 100/38 Lang 17 January 1933). The number E 646 is the accession number given to this material. At the same time Woodward drew attention to this matter in a letter published on 18 February in *Nature* (1933). Later, in October 1972, Dawson's postcard was transferred to the Department of Palaeontology, [DF 100] Bound Correspondence. The only other known demonstration at the Royal College is the one staged by the eolithophile Harry Morris of Lewes — but this occurred in March (see *Lancet*, 13 March, pp 561-562).

[B] This reference is curious, since Keith's papers at the Royal College of Surgeons do not indicate that he put on any kind of a "demonstration" either in July or August of 1915. His demonstration on "skull reconstruction" at the Royal Anthropological Institute was given on 20 January 1915.

[C] Probably referring to Guy Ellock Pilgrim's (1875-1943) paper on Siwalik primates, which was published in February 1915.

[D] See Boule (1915).

[E] In the left and right margins of this letter, a vertical line has been scored (presumably by Woodward) to highlight the first two sentences of this paragraph. Also the latter sentence, beginning: "I have got a new molar . . ." has been underlined.

4.1.22 DF 100/39 Osborn 20 September 1915

(a) Henry Fairfield Osborn (1857-1935); (b) typewritten letter to Woodward on printed stationery: "American Museum of Natural History, New York"; (c) annotated by Woodward: "Oct. 5th"

I have received your letter of September 3rd [A] and hasten to say that I shall be very glad indeed to have you give Dawson a copy [B]. . . I will try to secure one for you and send it to you immediately . . . I deeply regret to learn that Dawson feels he has not received enough honour and credit because I think you have gone out of your way and have treated him most magnanimously in every respect, in fact, you could not possibly have done more than you have both in describing and naming the specimens [C].

[A] Acknowledgment of receipt of an earlier letter written on 9 July (DF 100/39) that reiterates Osborn's intentions to donate McGregor's Piltdown reconstructions to the British Museum. Osborn did not receive confirmation of their safe arrival until receiving

Woodward's letter dated 5 October.

[B] Reference to McGregor's model, see Letter 4.1.27.

[C] See Letter 3.1.6.

4.1.23 DF 100/38 Dawson 27 September 1915

(a) Charles Dawson (1864-1916); (b) handwritten letter to Woodward on printed stationery: "Town Hall Chambers, Uckfield"; (c) annotated by Woodward: "28th"

I hear that there has been a wash out by the sea just above Pagham Harbour near Selsea, Sussex and that bones and an elephant tusk (5ft) has been found. The way to get there is by train from Chichester on the Selsea Railway. I have just got home from the north.

4.1.24 DF 116/14 Nathorst 6 October 1915

(a) Alfred Gabriel Nathorst (1850-1921); (b) handwritten letter (in English) to Woodward on printed stationery: "Naturhistoriska Riksmuseets (Stockholm); (c) underlining in original by Nathorst.

Nathorst was a Swedish geologist and palaeobotanist, and then Director of the Riks-Museum of Natural History in Stockholm.

I have just received No 281 of the Q.J.G.S. and I read with great pleasure the paper of Mr. Dawson and yourself on the curious bone implement from Piltdown. But I was at once struck by the likeness which exists between the workings on the pointed end of the implement and those made by beavers when they are cutting through a stem or a branch. We have many such examples from our great masses and I have figured one on p. 305 of Svenges Geologi *– the first one described. The figure is a copy from my paper in* Ofnessikt *of Vet. Akad. Forth. 1892, p.439.*

What is characteristic for the markings produced by the incisors of the beaver are the two parallel furrows separated by a ridge – the latter corresponding to the interspace between the two teeth. Now it is curious that the markings on your implement in several places also seem to consist of two parallel furrows separated by a ridge, even seen where the markings are more isolated e.g. Figs 2 and 4. [A]

Now, your implement being of bone and not of wood I naturally don't mean that the markings could have been produced by a beaver. *But may they not have been made by another animal when the bone was still soft? Or is the likeness only accidental? It is consequently not my meaning that the implements should not be human work. But regarding the importance of the find itself I thought it not inconvenient to draw your attention to the matter.*

[A] Reference to Plate XIV, fig 1: "Original outer surface of bone [implement]", fig 2: "Original inner (medullary) surface of bone [implement]" in Dawson & Woodward (1915a), see introduction to Section 3.2 and Fig 3.2.

4.1.25 DF 100/38 Dawson 8 October 1915

(a) Charles Dawson (1864-1916); (b) handwritten letter to Woodward on printed stationery: "Town Hall Chambers, Uckfield"; (c) –.

Andrews [A] very kindly attended to me the other day and I was very much interested in the Chatham elephant [B]. The photo[graph]s of the Okapi head turned out very well [C]. I have learnt a great deal more about starch and columnar structure but the subject is very complicated and what with worries we are going through with the war and its effect on business I have not felt able to set it all down clearly. My clerks are gradually disappearing into "Kaki" [sic] which is of course quite right but you can imagine the trouble it causes in routine work and accountancy.

I think you better register the things as you suggest and no more need be said about it. The labelling can stand as it is. I was very disappointed with the Eo[anthropus]. bust, as Andrews may have told you! It represents a common type among the Sussex agricultural labouring class in by no means the lowest stage [D].

The Americans are evidently not used to seeing the type and imagine it to be a very savage appearance. Rutot's busts are not any better and all represent a Herbert Spencer-like being in various moods [E]! I think there is yet scope for further artistic efforts. Perhaps an india-rubber balloon stretched over the plaster cast might inspire a sculptor. With such a thick skull Eo[anthropus]. might well have done without such a head of hair. Beards were evidently a secondary acquisition in apes no doubt resulting from sexual selection! . . .

P.S. I hear that some bones are coming from Hastings, but not much I fear [F].

[A] Charles William Andrews (1866-1924), palaeontologist in Department of Geology.

[B] This is a reference to the skeleton of *Elephas antiquus* found at Upnor, near Chatham circa 1911-12. Largely through the efforts of a local enthusiast, Sidney Turner (see his correspondence with Woodward, DF 100/35 and DF 100/41), the skeleton (almost complete) was recovered. The specimen, subsequently aroused considerable interest because it was the first specimen of *E. antiquus* recovered in Britain "found in association". For further details on this specimen, see Andrews (1915) and Andrews & Cooper (1928).

[C] Nothing is known about these photographs, nor Dawson's interest in the "Okapi head". ? connected with Okapi skull mentioned by Black, see 3.1.28.

[D] This refers to McGregor's (see 4.1.2) restored model of Eoanthropus which had recently arrived at the Museum. This bust is reproduced in Osborn's text *Men of the Old Stone Age* (1915), Figs 71 and 72 (pp 142-143).

[E] See 3.1.27.

[F] See 4.1.26.

4.1.26 DF 100/38 Dawson 15 October 1915

(a) Charles Dawson (1864-1916); (b) handwritten letter to Woodward on stationery embossed: "The Castle Lodge, Lewes"; (c) –.

C. Taylor, the foreman of the gang at Old Roar Quarry (Buckhole) Silverhill, St. Leonards [A], writes today that he has gone to Erith. I suppose as a war job. I think as so little stone is being used on the roads they have closed the quarry. He has sent me a box full of odds and ends which he has been saving and must now get rid of. . . . [B]. I shall have to send Taylor something for them, but I expect to see you shortly and will decide then what they are worth . . . I may be up Wed[nesda]y. or Thursday next. I trust Cyril goes on well [C].

[A] See Letter 1.1.2.

[B] The remaining mid section of the letter is devoted to a general desciption of the Roar Quarry collection.

[C] "Cyril" is Woodward's son who was recovering from appendicitis that had been complicated by post-operative thrombosis.

4.1.27 DF 100/39 Osborn 21 October 1915

(a) Henry Fairfield Osborn (1857-1935); (b) typewritten letter to Woodward on printed stationery: "American Museum of Natural History, New York"; (c) –

In reply to your letter of October 5th, we shall send you the bust of <u>Eoanthropus</u> as soon as Professor McGregor returns, which I fear will not be before the early part of January next. . . [A] I shall investigate the matter of the placing of the canine tooth further although we made a most exhaustive comparative study before we reached the conclusion that it belonged to the upper jaw. Naturally the *original specimen is far better material for study than even the most excellent cast which you sent [B].*

[A] See 4.1.22.

[B] Early in November, Woodward received a short, handwritten note from Osborn, (dated "October 27th": DF 100/39) in which he states that William K. Gregory was studying the question of the canine: "I send you his very frank report, in response to my request, stated in his characteristically cautious way". This communication bears annotation by Woodward: "Nov 6th. Promised upper human milk canine". Unfortunately, Gregory's report has not survived. Much later, the New Zealand dentist R.M.S. Taylor, at a meeting of the Australian and New Zealand Association for the Advancement of Science in Auckland, 1937, confirmed the argument that the Piltdown canine was an upper, rather than a lower tooth as Woodward demanded. This worker also demonstrated that the dentition as represented in Woodward's restoration could not have existed in life. But contrary to expectation Taylor's Auckland presentation went unnoticed until after the forgery was detected (see Taylor 1937, 1978).

4.1.28 DF 116/5 Elliot Smith 1 November 1915

(a) Grafton Elliot Smith (1871-1937); (b) handwritten letter to Woodward on printed stationery: "The University, Manchester"; (c) –.

Very many thanks for your interesting reprint, which I am very glad to have [A].

After eighteen months of perpetual interruptions to my work I am now fairly sure of getting the Piltdown paper completed. The last two years have been most exasperating for I have never had a single day free from interruptions in which to sit down calmly and put the finishing touches on the work. [B]

I go to London today for the Gen[era]l. Med[ical]. Council and hope to see you this week. As you are going off the R[oyal] S[ociety] Council I wonder whether you would propose W. D. Matthew (who is a British subject and proud of it) [C] and D.S.M. [sic] Watson for the R[oyal]. S[ociety] [D].

[A] Reference to Dawson & Woodward (1915a).

[B] See Note D: 3.1.13.

[C] William Diller Matthew (1871-1930), a palaeontologist at the American Museum in New York City, see Letter 3.1.5. Matthew's was elected FRS in 1919.

[D] David Meredith Seares Watson (1886-1973). Between 1912 and 1921 Watson was lecturer in vertebrate palaeontology at the University of Manchester. See also Letter 4.2.17.

4.1.29 DF 116/14 Haddon 2 November 1915

(a) Alfred Cort Haddon (1855-1940); (b) handwritten note to Woodward on printed postcard: "3 Cranmer Road, Cambridge"; (c) –.

See 3.1.13. A brief note thanking Woodward for a reprint of the "bone implement" paper.

4.1.30 DF 100/38 Dawson 2 November 1915

(a) Charles Dawson (1864-1916); (b) handwritten letter to Woodward on stationery embossed: "The Castle Lodge, Lewes"; (c) annotated by Woodward: "6th"

I met Jenner Wright [A] who tells me that Gaster is a young man who lives in Lewes (probably a clerk) and that he has studied chalk [? word] of which he has made a collection. Jenner does not think that Gaster has any general collection from the Chalk. [B] I saw a long review of Keith's book in last Sunday's Observer [C]. He has not sent me a copy of his book. . .

P.S. I enclose some small fish teeth which Teilhard gave me some years ago. I do not think they are anything much." [D]

[A] Jenner C. Wright is listed as a member of the Sussex Archaeological Society (1914), and as living in Eastbourne, Sussex.

[B] From the Bound Correspondence [DF 100] of the Department of Palaeontology, Gaster's full name was Christopher T. A. Gaster, who in 1915 lived at 23 St. Johns Terrace, Lewes. He is not listed as member of the Sussex Archaeological Society in 1914. Later, in 1929, Gaster published a paper on the "Chalk zones" in the neighbourhood of Brighton, Sussex.

[C] Keith's book, *The Antiquity of Man* was published by Williams and Norgate on Friday, 8 October 1915.

[D] Dawson's postcript is written in pencil.

4.1.31 DF 116/14 Munro 5 November 1915

(a) Robert Munro (1835-1920); (b) handwritten letter to Woodward on plain stationery; (c) Underlining in original by Munro.

See Letter 2.2.20.

Thanks very much for your paper on the discovery of a bone implement at Piltdown which in my opinion lessens the enormous antiquity assigned by some anthropologists to Eoanthropus. I have not seen Keith's Antiquity of Man [A] but if he holds to the large cranial capacity of the Piltdown man and yet puts it at the beginning of the evolution of humanity he is making a scale of life inconsistent with the gradual evolution of humanity. In my opinion big brain had high thinking power and produced tools of an advanced order. All we can say at present about the Piltdown man is that he was a toolmaker both of flint and bone. I have no doubt he was a maker of wooden clubs but of course these have all decayed. Your discovery may at any time be supplemented but at present it can only be suggestive.

[A] See Note C: 4.1.30.

4.1.32 DF 100/38 Lankester 9 November 1915

(a) Edwin Ray Lankester (1847-1929); (b) handwritten letter to Woodward on printed stationery: "29 Thurloe Place, South Kensington"; (c) annotated by Woodward: " 13th. Try Gregory or Bather [A]. Borrow Implements from F. Corner [B]."

I am going to give three lectures after Easter at the Royal Institution on "Flints and Flint implements" and I am just now trying to find specimens of cut and polished flints which I can exhibit . . . There used to be many people who collected all sorts of flints and have them cut and polished . . . Can you tell me who has such collections (private) now? Have you anything important of the kind at the Museum?

[A] John Walter Gregory, see 2.3.44; and Francis Arthur Bather, see 4.1.21.

[B] Frank Corner, see 2.3.62.

4.1.33 DF 116/5 Elliot Smith 23 November 1915

(a) Grafton Elliot Smith (1871-1937); (b) handwritten note to Woodward on a printed postcard: "From The Dean of the Faculty of Medicine, The University, Manchester"; (c) –.

I shall have the slides sent off tomorrow – they consist of a map of Queensland to show the spot where the [Talgai] skull was found, and views of the skull from every aspect. They were taken before the skull was cleaned. I am sending herewith some newspaper cuttings which give further information about the skull. There is no hurry about returning them, so long as I get them.

See 4.1.34.

there is a number of Pliocene students [A]. I am sorry to say this town is especially hard hit over the war, and the strenuous times are enough to knock the science out of anybody [B]! Still one must keep an eye open for things that crop up, or they are forever lost . . .

[A] see Abbott (1915), Note B: 4.1.19.

[B] After the war Abbott's financial position worsened, see 6.3.8.

4.2.7 DF 100/40 Merriam 27 January 1916

(a) John Campbell Merriam (1869-1945); (b) typewritten letter to Woodward on plain stationery: "Berkeley, California"; (c) –.

In this letter Merriam (a palaeontologist at the University of California) thanks Woodward for allowing David Prescott Barrows (b 1873), an ethnologist and later president of the University of California (1919-23) to view the Piltdown remains. He also draws attention to Miller's (1915) paper.

4.2.8 DF 100/40 Dawson 6 February 1916

(a) Charles Dawson (1864-1916); (b) handwritten letter to Woodward on stationery embossed: "The Castle Lodge, Lewes"; (c) annotated by Woodward: "7th". Underlining in original by Dawson.

Thank you for your letter and cutting. I have been very ill, and am to have injections of serum in London which will make me worse, temporarily. They begin next Tuesday. [A]

The pulp cavity of the "Eo[anthropus]" canine is certainly large [B]. It does not seem to have occurred to anyone that as one end is open the walls of the cavity may have been the subject of post-mortem decay, and that bacteria may have cleaned away the comparatively soft walls during a prolonged soakage in water and sand.

I think I have noticed this in fossil teeth and broken bones. You have plenty of material to decide this.

P.S. I hope your son is now quite well again [C].

[A] Dawson's condition did not improve, and on 10 August he died. See introduction to subsection 4.2 for further details on Dawson's illness.

[B] A reference to a point raised by Courtney Lyne in his paper to the Royal Society earlier in January, see Note A: 4.2.5.

[C] See Note C: 4.1.26.

4.2.9 GMP/SIA/B4.F2 Andersen 10 February 1916

(a) Knud Andersen; (c) handwritten letter to G.S. Miller on printed stationery: "British Museum (Natural History), Cromwell Road, London, S.W."; (c) –.

Andersen was a Danish mammalogist who worked as a private individual in the Department of Zoology (Mammal Section) from 1904 to 1918. He worked mainly on Chiroptera and produced a catalogue of the Megachiroptera. Andersen's letter is addressed to Gerrit S. Milller at the U.S. National Museum of Natural History in Washington, D.C., see 4.1.36.

. . . I read with more than usual pleasure your paper on the jaw of the Piltdown man, – for three reasons:- Because, in my humble opinion, it is a model of clear and logical reasoning; because it settles the matter; and, chiefly, because, I believe for the first time in history, I find, myself in agreement with you.

Your letter, though postdated Jan[uary]. 17th, only came a few days ago. It had passed through the Censor's Office. . .

See also Letter 4.2.2.

4.2.10 GMP/SIA/B4.F2 Mitchell 11 February 1916

(a) Peter Chalmers Mitchell (1864-1945); (b) typewritten letter to G.S. Miller on printed stationery: "Zoological Society of London, Regent's Park, London S.W."; (c) –.

In the December 30th issue of *Nature*, Mitchell (1915:480) had criticized Miller's proposal to rename the Piltdown mandible: *Pan vetus*. The following is Mitchell's reply to a letter from Miller (copy not preserved in GMP/SIA collections), in which the latter evidently had explained his position.

Thank you for your letter. I quite admit that there are two points of view. The importance or duty of giving names to every identified natural history specimen [sic]. Your naming of the Piltsdown [sic] specimens seemed to me an extreme example of this view. It appeared to me that there was no gain to Science in the matter, and on the other hand that it confused or obscured some very interesting collateral facts about the specimens. I thought moreover that however extreme a view you might take of the importance of naming things it would have been easily possible for you to refrain from applying the rules of nomenclature to a case in which you have never seen the specimen.

On the other hand I have no doubt you will appreciate that in my letter I did not dispute your determination on the correctness of your application of the law of priority but only the usefullness [sic] of applying it in this case.

4.2.11 DF 100/40 Etheridge 23 March 1916

(a) Robert Etheridge (1847-1920); (b) typewritten letter to Woodward on printed stationery: "The Australian Museum, Sydney"; (c) annotated by Woodward: "May 8th. Probably crocodilian".
This letter from Etheridge [A], a palaeontologist and Director of The Australian Museum in Sydney is devoted to a rather technical discussion regarding the identity of a reptilian fossil found in New South Wales. In concluding this inquiry, Etheridge notes: "Hope you are keeping well and not altogether killed by discussions on the Piltdown skull!"

[A] In 1891 Etheridge and Woodward had collaborated on a study of the "Occurrence of the genus *Belonostmus* in Central Queensland. Furthermore, as noted by Langham (1978), Etheridge had been involved in matters concerning the Talgai skull (see 3.1.15 and Note C: 3.1.32).

4.2.12 DF 100/40 Godwin-Austen 23 March 1916

(a) Henry Haversham Godwin-Austen (1834-1923); (b) handwritten letter to Woodward on stationery embossed: "Nore, Godalming"; (c) annotated by Woodward: "24th. Declined with thanks ASW."

A letter from Godwin-Austen, the well-known explorer and geologist, see Note C: 2.3.41. In this brief communication, Austen noted that he was reading Keith's *The Antiquity of Man* and offered to donate a watercolour of Kits Coty (prehistoric dolmen situated between Maidstone and Rochester, Kent) made circa 1860 to the Museum. Woodward declined the offer. See Letters 4.2.16 and 4.2.17.

4.2.13 DF 100/49 Kenward 19 May 1916

(a) Robert Kenward; (c) handwritten letter to Woodward on stationery embossed: "Barkham Manor, Piltdown, Uckfield"; (c) annotated by Woodward: "23rd. Arrive Sat. July 1st for about fortnight. I and Elliot Smith as paying guests if possible".

Robert Kenward was Chief Tenant at Barkham Manor.

I am very glad to hear from you again, and I shall be very pleased to see you at the pit any time you can come. I might be able to find a man in July, but we are very short of them now, but no doubt it might be managed for someone to dig in the early mornings or evenings so that you could look it over in your spare spare [sic] time. I am glad to say I am much better but unable to do much work. I am almost alone both my sons are away with their regiments, one in Essex, and the younger one has again gone to France, we had him home for a month after he was wounded, but he had to return last Wednesday week. . . My other son is a Lieut[enant] in the Beds. Yeomanry and my eldest daughter is doing Red Cross Nursing so I think we are doing our share of the war . . . I hope your son is getting strong again.

4.2.14 DF 100/40 Keith 9 June 1916

(a) Arthur Keith (1866-1955); (b) handwritten letter to Woodward on printed stationery: "Royal College of Surgeons of England, Lincoln's Inn Fields, London, W.C."; (c) – .

In this brief note Keith noted Woodward's intention to continuing working at Piltdown, see Woodward's annotation to 4.2.13: "I sincerely hope you may have good luck at Piltdown for there are lots of puzzles which have to be settled."

4.2.15 HP/NAA Symington 12 June 1916

(a) Johnson Symington (1851-1924); (b) typed letter to Hrdlička. The original is not in the Hrdlička collection; (c) –.

This letter was evidently in response to an enquiry from Hrdlička at the Smithsonian Institution. Unfortunately Hrdlička did not preserve a copy of his letter to Symington who held the Chair of Anatomy at the Medical School, Queen's University of Belfast.

. . . I was in London last month and found Dr. Pycraft of the Kensington Museum busy studying skulls of the chimpanzee and hoping to prove that the mandible found at Piltdown is human and that Mr Gerrit S. Miller is wrong in maintaining that it belonged to a chimpanzee [A].

The mandible is certainly very similar to that of a chimpanzee, but on the whole I am inclined to the view that the two molars are human rather than simian. I am very doubtful about the canine belonging to the same skull, mainly on account of the incomplete development of its root. You are doubtless aware of the fact that an English dentist – Mr. W.C. Lyne – has recently published a paper in the Proc[eedings]. of the Royal Society of Medicine (Feb. 1916) on this point [B].

I cannot pretend to have studied the question of the mandible and teeth sufficiently to justify my giving a definite opinion, but these are my general impressions from an examination of the very limited comparative material at my disposal. I believe that most of the anatomists in this country agree that there has been too much rash speculation regarding the significance of the Piltdown fragments. As you are aware, I have endeavoured to correct this tendency so far as the brain estimates are concerned [C]

[A] See Miller (1915), and 4.1.36.

[B] See Note A: 4.2.5.

[C] See Symington (1916). This paper is an elaboration of certain points raised in his Sir John Struthers Lecture for 1915: "On the relation of the inner surface of the cranium to the cranial aspect of the brain" published in the February issue of the *Edinburgh Medical Journal* (1915).

4.2.16 DF 100/40 Austen 17 June 1916

(a) Henry Haversham Godwin-Austen (1834-1923); (b) handwritten letter to Woodward on stationery embossed: "Nore, Godalming"; (c) annotated by Woodward: "19th"

Apparently during an earlier visit to the Museum (? May) Woodward had indicated to

Austen his intention to work at Piltdown during August, see 4.2.13. In this letter Austen asked if he might be of assistance.

4.2.17 DF 100/40 Austen 6 July 1916

(a) Henry Haversham Godwin-Austen (1834-1923); (b) handwritten letter on stationery embossed: "Nore, Godalming"; (c) annotated by Woodward: "9th"

From all indications Austen assisted Woodward during August, and that he lodged with Woodward and Elliot Smith at Barkham Manor. See 4.2.16 and Kenward's letter (4.2.13).

4.2.18 GMP/SIA/B4.F2 Pycraft 22 August 1916

(a) William Plane Pycraft (1868-1942); (b) handwritten letter to G.S. Miller on printed stationery: "British Museum (Natural History), Cromwell Road, London S.W."; (c) underlining in original by Pycraft

Very many thanks for your extremely kind offer to send me casts of any material used by you in your paper on the Piltdown jaw [A].

I should indeed like to see casts of the two jaws which seem to have such a close likeness to the Piltdown jaw, more especially in regard to the rear of the teeth.

I am just off for a much needed holiday so cannot comment at length on your paper. I can only say this, that it amazes me. I have taken your objections and contentions, one by one, and I venture to say you haven't a leg to stand on.

Smith Woodward, Elliot Smith, Keith, Prof. Broom, and Dr. Watson [B] have all read my M[anu]S[cript] and they agree with me absolutely [C].

I have had the advantage of closely studying at least three times as many (chimpanzee skulls) as you seem to have had, and a vastly larger collection of human skulls: with which, by the way, you do not seem to have either a large acquaintance, or a large collection to draw upon [D]. Finally, you have laboured under the disadvantage of never having seen the actual Piltdown remains. But all these reasons should have saved you from dogmatism – but they didn't. However, my reply will reach you soon.

[A] A reference to Miller's 1915 paper. Pycraft received Miller's chimpanzee cast [AMNH 84655] early in 1917, see 4.2.21.

[B] It is conjectured that Pycraft is referring to the South African palaeontologist Robert Broom (1866-1951) and David Meredith Seares Watson, see Note D: 4.1.28.

[C] Pycraft's manuscript, entitled: "The jaw of the Piltdown man: a reply to Mr. Gerrit S. Miller" was published in *Science Progress* in January 1917. Gregory (4.2.26) considered the article "impudent and bombastic". The article embodies a rather curious mixture of abuse of Miller and his work. Although clearly written for a largely lay audience, the text is peppered with anatomical jargon.

[D] Although by comparison, the USNM's nonhuman primate collections were modest, the same could not be said for human crania. Recognizing the limitations of the former category, Miller had supplemented his comparisons with material from the collections of the American Museum in New York.

4.2.19 DF 100/41 Parsons 21 September 1916

(a) Frederick G. Parsons (1863-1943); (b) handwritten letter to Woodward on printed stationery: "Anatomical Department, St Thomas's Hospital [London] S.E."; (c) annotated by Woodward: "22nd". Enclosed with Parsons' note was Letter 4.2.20.

In this brief note, Parsons (see introduction to Section 3), asked if his former student, namely

Le Gros Clark (4.2.20), could examine the Piltdown remains.

4.2.20 DF 100/40 Le Gros Clark 21 October 1916

(a) Wilfrid Edward Le Gros Clark (1895-1971); (b) handwritten letter to Woodward on printed stationery: "Students' Club, St. Thomas' Hospital [London] S.E." Le Gros' letter was enclosed with a note from F.G. Parsons (4.2.19); (c) annotated by Woodward "22nd"

In this letter Le Gros Clark noted that he had been following the literature on Piltdown and would like to examine the remains himself. Later in the early 1950s, Le Gros Clark collaborated with J. S. Weiner and K. P. Oakley in the investigations that uncovered the fraudulent nature of the Piltdown assemblage.

4.2.21 DF 116/5 Elliot Smith 27 November 1916

(a) Grafton Elliot Smith (1871-1937); (b) handwritten letter to Woodward on printed stationery: "4 Willow Bank, Fallowfield, Manchester"; (c) annotated by Woodward: "29th"

The enclosed certificate has only just reached me and as Boyd Dawkins is away (in Hastings) I return it at once [A].

I expect to go up to London on Feb[ruary] 22nd to give a demonstration at the R[oyal]. S[ociety]. of the Talgai skull of which I now have the cast [B].

I am very sorry that you had to submit to such a crude address as I inflicted upon you under the auspices of the British Academy. I made a mess of my theme by trying to do too much, but when written out in full and published it will I think be useful [C].

[A] It is not known what Dawkins was doing in Hastings. It should be noted that Dawkins did have a long standing interest in Wealden geology. In fact he had worked with Topley and others in the 1860s on a primary survey of the region. As indicated in Note B: 2.3.12 he is known to have visited the Piltdown site on only two occasions, in March of 1913 and 1915.

[B] For further details on the Talgai skull, see 3.1.15 and Note C: 3.1.32.

[C] The subject of Elliot Smith's address to the British Academy was "Primitive Man", subsequently published in 1917(b).

4.2.22 DF 100/42 Dawson 7 January 1917

(a) Hélène Dawson (1859-1917); (b) handwritten letter to Woodward on plain stationery: "The Castle Lodge [Lewes]; (c) annotated by Woodward: "15th. ackn. receipt & Dr Read".

Letter from Dawson's widow regarding specimens remaining in her husband's collection (see Note B).

. . . Now the fares have gone up I do not believe I shall ever get to London until I come for good so tomorrow I will send you very carefully packed the case of amulets – and the case of starch implements – wh[ich]. are too good to remain here unseen [A].

I have not yet come across pieces of skull answering to y[ou]r. description but as I am putting everything of that nature into a cupboard you will have a wide assortment from which to choose [B] . . .

[A] It would appear that Woodward's annotation above refers to this package and that some of this material may have gone to C.H. Read (Note D: 1.2.19).

[B] During January 1917, Frederick Du Cane Godman F.R.S (1834-1919) of Horsham "presented" the Barcombe Mills collection to Woodward. From all indications Godman did not own this collection but was merely delivering it for Mrs Dawson. In the Museum register (completed by Woodward) the cranial fragments are recorded as having been recovered from "Pleistocene gravel in field on top of hill above Barcombe Mills railway station." The single molar tooth is recorded as "probably from the same place (not certain)." The remains consist of: (1) a fragment of frontal bone [E.644a], (2) fragment of right parietal [E.644b], (3) pair of zygomatic bones, left [E.644c], right [E.644d]; and (4) a lower right second molar tooth [E.645]. For further details on the frontal bone, see 2.3.21 and 5.2.10. Whether Woodward retrieved the cranial material (later attributed to Piltdown II) at this time, or whether he was merely hopeful of finding additional undeclared material, is not at all clear. However, the above letter, correlated with 5.1.25, suggests that Woodward already had possession of the Piltdown II molar and was now seeking the cranial fragments Dawson had reportedly found in 1915 (see 4.1.1).

4.2.23 GMP/SIA/B4.F2 Pycraft 21 February 1917

(a) William Plane Pycraft (1868-1942); (b) handwritten letter to G.S. Miller on printed stationery: "British Museum (Natural History), Cromwell Road, London S.W." (c) underlining in original by Pycraft.

See 4.1.36.

The Chimpanzee jaw has arrived safely in spite *of German "frightfullness" – Damn them! Without question the molars are worn flat – BUT, the fact has no direct bearing on the Piltdown jaw since this flatness is not the result of normal wear, but is due to the abnormal position p[re]. m[olar]. 1 which stands high above the rest of the teeth, and shows an* unworn crown! *What was the other jaw like in this regard? I note that you very wisely retained that half for the chances of your specimen ever reaching me were certainly jeopardized. Had the half you sent me gone to the bottom you would have had its fellow. I propose to retain the jaw until I have your instructions to return it. It will be in safe keeping here: and if I may suggest it, here it had better remain until we have scooped up a few more of the Bosches submarines. He will no more succeed in this latest effort to escape his doom than in his attempt to frighten us with Zepplin raids and the bombardment of girls boarding schools, and other "fortified places." He is a swine.*

By now you will have read my reply to your paper on the jaw of the Piltdown man [A]. I am sending you a reprint, but this cannot reach you for some time, as I am not allowed to send papers out of England save through the regulation official channels – a perfectly proper and very salutory regulation: even if it slightly interferes with our convenience. . .

[A] See Pycraft (1917) and Note C: 4.2.18.

4.2.24 DF 100/42 Turner 27 February 1917

(a) Clifton G. Turner; (b) typewritten letter to Woodward on printed stationery: "Town Hall Chambers, Uckfield"; (c) – .

Turner was a clerk in the Dawson & Hart law firm (see Note D:2.3.55). His letter is in reponse to an enquiry from Woodward regarding where the remains attributed to Piltdown II were found. In addition to wanting to know where the cranial fragments had been found, Woodward was also anxious to know who gave Dawson a fragment of mineralized Rhinoceros tooth. Turner made enquiries but could not trace the source. He also relayed "particulars" from Miss Kenward as to where the fragments of the skull were found. These "particulars" have not been preserved. For further information, see Woodward (1917: 5).

4.2.25 DF 100/42 Miller 21 March 1917

(a) Gerrit Smith Miller (1869-1956); (b) typewritten letter to Woodward on printed stationery: "Smithsonian Institution, U.S. National Museum, Washington D.C." (c) annotated by Woodward: "May 14th". Underlining in original by Miller.

. . . I wish to ask you two questions about the Piltdown jaw, and trust that in doing so I shall not put you to any undue trouble.

Which do you consider the best representation of the molar teeth: the original wash drawings [A], the photographs in the Guide to Fossil Man [B], or the cast? Both Gregory and I have assumed that the photographs should be taken as the standards of comparison, but perhaps in doing so we have been wrong, and misunderstanding has resulted [C]. Between the photographs and the drawings the chief differences appear to lie in the relative length and breadth of the crowns as viewed from above and the degree of hypsodonty as viewed from the side. The cast most nearly resembles the photograph, but carries the narrowing a slight though readily perceptible degree further. I should be very grateful for a word from you on the subject. [X]

In Pycraft's recent article (Science Progress, January 1917) [D] there is a diagram on page 408 showing the relations of two lines in chimpanzee, Piltdown and modern man. The way these lines are drawn is explained on p.407. The part of this diagram that relates to Piltdown is shown in the attached tracing [see X]. I have added a broken line that shows approximately the correction that would be necessary to make the diagram represent the condition present in our cast. I do not pretend that the broken line is exactly placed; it is drawn by eye without photographing or projecting. But there is no doubt that it decidedly converges with the tooth line, not behind as the diagram has it, but in front. (I find, by the way, that the straight-edge is a very unsatisfactory instrument for locating the line through the ascending ramus. The line can be much more accurately established with two straight pieces of fine wire attached with a small lump of modeling wax to the anterior and posterior margins of the ramus at the right level [E]. By "sighting" they can be made to assume the positions of the two ends of the line in the diagram. Would you examine the original specimen and tell me whether or not our cast is faulty in this particular.

Professor Osborn [F] recently told me of your message to him about additional material which will forever demolish all heresies [G]. I am greatly pleased with this news, as it seems to offer a solution of all our difficulties.

[X] A drawing, showing a superior view (outline) of right side of (Piltdown) mandible, is pasted into the lower right margin, adjacent to the text of the second paragraph.

[A] Reference to Plate XX, Dawson & Woodward (1913a).

[B] Reference to Plate IV, Dawson & Woodward (1914a).

[C] See 4.2.26.

[D] See Note C: 4.2.18.

[E] See 5.1.12 for further discussion of this approach.

[F] Henry Fairfield Osborn, see 4.1.35. The date of Woodward's communication with Osborn is uncertain, and a search of his papers failed to recover the pertinent communication. It should be noted that Woodward officially announced the news of Piltdown II at Burlington House on Wednesday 28 February 1917. See also Note G (below).

[G] Given Lankester's mention of this discovery in his book in 1915 (4.1.39), Woodward's apparent reluctance to share this information with Miller is curious.

4.2.26 WKG/AMNH Gregory 30 March 1917

(a) William King Gregory (1876-1970); (b) typewritten letter to G.S. Miller on printed stationery: "American Museum of Natural History, Department of Vertebrate Palaeontology"; (c) the letter is edited in Gregory's handwriting.

. . .I have only just succeeded in reading Pycraft's paper with sufficient care to be able to answer your last letter [A]. As I wrote you before [B] I am disgusted with the lawyer-like, hectoring tactics which he adopts. He is perpetually begging the question and asserting that you have sadly misinterpreted the

evidence.

I feel that his Figure 1 [C], comparison of Piltdown with chimpanzee and Kaffir jaws, would have been a fairer one if he had shown the whole jaw, because without doubt the Kaffir jaws all have a well developed chin, while the Piltdown jaw is undeniably chimpanzee-like in that region, as shown in [x/ his] Smith Woodward's diagrams of the symphyseal regions in men and apes.

His Figure 2 [D], I think, shows that the Piltdown jaw from the back view of the ascending ramus is on the whole more like the human types there figured than like the chimpanzee types. Where there is so much variation I don't think this [/fact] [x/figure] is very demonstrative.*

In his Figure 4 [E] I don't think the divergent lines amount to very much, especially as Anthony [F] has just shown me that Piltdown resembles the chimpanzee if you take the long axis of the ascending ramus according to your method. It is very curious to me that in [/my] [x/one] top view the Piltdown jaw approaches certain human jaws as shown in my Figure 5, 1914 [G], while in your top view, Plate II, fig 2, it certainly approaches the chimpanzee jaws 1 and 3. I am not convinced by his remarks about the highlights [*/indicating convexities] on the inner side of the chimpanzee jaws shown in your Plate I, figs 1 & 3. It may be a character or it may not be. I still feel that my figures of the crown teeth, 1916, Figs 27 C and D, show a remarkable resemblance to the chimpanzee teeth [H]. These figures were based on a purely impartial study of Smith Woodward's enlarged photograph. Every one around here who has seen them thinks that they indicate a nearer affinity with the chimpanzee than with the Heidelberg man or any other man.*

*Pycraft's remarks on the molar pattern are quite [*unconvincing. He gives us] [x/as] the well known characters of the human molar pattern but I don't see that he has shown that these characters are present in the Piltdown molars. With regard to the fact that in the inner side view the Piltdown molars have longer crowns and are more taurodont than human molars, I should [x/only] think of this as [*/possibly] a specific difference. The fact that in the Piltdown the worn surfaces are very flat and the enamel thick as in human teeth does not carry conviction to me, as you do not claim that this is a modern species of chimpanzee. I see no reason why the Pleistocene species should not be a step nearer in some characters to the common man-anthropoid stem.*

So far as I can see at present the Piltdown jaw is still structurally more chimpanzee-like than human in most characters, and I formerly agreed with you that this proves that is a chimpanzee. If, however, Woodward has new evidence tending to confirm the association of the jaw with the skull [I] I shall only recognize that my conception of what constitutes generic and genetic agreements must have been wrong. At present, however, I feel doubtful whether Smith Woodward's new evidence will be adequate to prove the original association. The new molar will have to be absolutely identical with one of the old molars and the new piece of occiput will have to be beyond question the same as the old occiput and unless they have a large piece this will be difficult to prove.

I have always felt uneasy about attacking the original association of skull and jaw, although I know very well what the arguments are to show the possibilities of the chance association.

Upon re-reading his criticisms of your paper I remain unconvinced. For instance when he attacks your statement "[/(a)], one type of jaw (associated) with another type of glenoid region" [JJ], I still feel that this is of great weight. My figure 7, 1914, showing the temporal bones of Piltdown, Negro and Ape, in combination with my Figures 3 and 4, showing the lower jaws, fully substantiates your statements [K].*

So far as the occiput is concerned the Piltdown skull was adjusted to the upright position, while as you say the lower jaw is of the type usually found associated with the stooping position and unretracted face. The "absence of mechanical unity" between the mandible and face is not a "purely imaginery absence." It is a surprising incongruity especially in association with the human character of the nasals.

*In conclusion I hope you will publish a searching criticism of Pycraft's impudent and bombastic paper, and I hope you will pardon me for suggesting that you should treat his arguments in a purely objective and impartial way and admit whatever weight there may be in his [*facts and] figures. I imagine you would be the first to admit it if they have real evidence for the opposite conclusion.*

[*/] Word(s) added, or [x/] deleted by W.K.G.

[A] Reference to Pycraft's reply to Miller's earlier paper (1915). Pycraft's paper was published in *Science Progress* in January 1917, see Note C: 4.2.18. Miller's earlier letter does not appear to have been preserved.

[B] Date unknown. Also unable to locate Miller's letter in Gregory's correspondence at the American Museum.

[C] See Pycraft (1917: 395). As Gregory notes, Pycraft has depicted only the ascending rami of 6 male, 3 female, and 1 ? chimpanzee, plus that of Piltdown and a Kaffir [African].

[D] See Pycraft (1917: 398). Pycraft claims in the legend of this figure "that the Piltdown jaw more nearly conforms to the human than to the chimpanzee type."

[E] See Pycraft (1917:408). In this figure Pycraft depicts (superior view) the right side of the jaws of a chimpanzee, Piltdown and a modern European. In each he has drawn lines along the molars and through the ascending ramus, the purpose of which is to show that in the chimpanzee these lines converge, whereas in Piltdown and the modern European these lines diverge.

[F] Harold Elmer Anthony (b. 1890), a palaeontologist at the American Museum of Natural History.

[G] See Gregory (1914: 194).

[H] See Gregory (1916b).

[I] Reference to Woodward's paper on Piltdown II, delivered on February 28th.

[J] See Pycraft (1917:392-397).

[K] Gregory (1914): Fig 7 (p 196); Fig 3 comparison (outside lateral view) of Piltdown, female orangutan, and modern human mandibulae (p 192); Fig 4 comparison (inside lateral view) of Piltdown, female orangutan, and modern human mandibulae (p 193).

4.2.27 GMP/SIA/B4.F2 Pycraft 7 May 1917

(a) William Plane Pycraft (1868-1942); (b) handwritten letter to G.S. Miller on printed stationery: "British Museum (Natural History), Cromwell Road, London S.W."; (c) underlining in original by Pycraft.

Many thanks for your letter just at hand – in spite of U-boats.I am not surprised to find that my reply to you in Science Progress [A] read somewhat harshly [B]. But I must confess to a feeling of irritation while I wrote; you <u>were</u> so dogmatic, and there was that in your attack which breathed not a little of contempt, which none of us took kindly. Thus, then, we have each sinned, but we must take care to guard against like outbursts of agressiveness [sic] in future. We are, after all, or should be, concerned with the matter of interpretation of the Piltdown skull, and we do but divert attention from this and spoil our own cause by seeming to strain rather at the achievements of ends which should be left to politicians. We are out for the advancement of science, and anything therefore which savours of mere squabbling is to be deplored. This is the standard I hope to work by in the future.

. . . Smith Woodward has shown me your letter to him [C]. It seems that the "camera which cannot lie" has played you false. That is to say you were misled at the very outset of your interpretations by what <u>seemed</u> most trustworthy <u>evidence</u>!

Your proposal to substitute a line driven through the ramus at the <u>level</u> of the tooth-row seems surely to evade the issue at stake. I wanted, in using the line of the sigmoid notch, to show that the torsion of the ramus at this level, in the Piltdown skull, was the same as that of all other human skulls, and different from all Simian skulls, or at any rate Chimpanzee skulls. There may be exceptions to my rule, but so far it holds good. Your line, as Smith-Woodward has probably pointed out to you, cannot be *applied to the Piltdown skull, at any rate in terms of equating with a similar line in other skulls [D]. . .*

[A] Pycraft (1917).

[B] See concluding paragraph of Letter 4.2.26.

[C] See 4.2.25.

[D] See Letter 4.2.28.

4.2.28 GMP/SIA/B4.F2 Woodward 14 May 1917

(a) Arthur Smith Woodward (1864-1944); (a) handwritten letter to G.S. Miller on printed stationery: "British Museum (Natural History), Cromwell Road, London S.W."; (c) –.

I thank you for your letter of March 21st and should have replied long ago [A]. I think the drawings of the tooth of Eoanthropus are much better than the photographs, because the irregular arrangement of the brown stains rather confuse the latter. I have asked Pycraft about his lines on diagrams of the jaw, and he tells me that, on his scheme, the outer line should run along the top of the ascending portion. The specimens supplied by Damon are exact casts, not models: but he will shortly have ready an enlarged model of $\overline{M1}$ for comparison with similar models of $\overline{M1}$ of chimpanzee and Melanesian man.

[A] See Letter 4.2.25.

4.2.29 DF 100/42 Miller 7 June 1917

(a) Gerrit S. Miller (1869-1956); (b) handwritten letter to Woodward on plain stationery: "U.S. National Museum, Washington D.C."; (c) underlining in original by Miller.

Many thanks for your letter of May 14th [A] with its information about the illustrations of Piltdown teeth. My inquiry related to outlines rather than to surface markings, however, and the brown stains would not seem likely to confuse the former.

I should have been glad to know your personal opinion about the lines on Pycraft's diagram [B]. The outer one, as I take it, and as I understand that Pycraft intended it to be taken, seems at the highest possible level to remain within the bone under the lowest region of sigmoid notch. Thus taken, on our cast and on the one in the American Museum, it converges anteriorly with the tooth line.

[A] See 4.2.28.

[B] See Note E: 4.2.26.

4.2.30 GMP/SIA/B4.F2 Pycraft 7 August 1917

(a) William Plane Pycraft (1868-1942); (b) handwritten letter to G.S. Miller on printed stationery: "British Museum (Natural History), Cromwell Road, London S.W."; (c) underlining in original by Pycraft.

Your letter would have been answered earlier but for the fact that Smith Woodward was away on leave when it came – and the Piltdown [x/?] remains are in his charge – and before he came I went away for a few days [A].

I have taken the measurements you ask for: but must remark that I can not guarantee their absolute accuracy. I do not believe any two people measuring these teeth would arrive at exactly the same results, or even that exactly the same measurements would be given after any two attempts by the same person. However you will find that mine accord, within ½ mm. of those given by Tomes in his Dental Anatomy – last edition [B].

As to the height of the enamel I have [x/taken the] given the maximum.

These diagrams are of course not to scale, but are rough sketches [C].

Maximum width of crowns		M/1	*11 mm.*
		M/2	*11.5 mm.*
Height of crown:-	Outside	(M/1)	*9 mm.*
from fork of roots		(M/2)	*8 mm.*
	Inside	(M/1)	*7.5 mm.*
		(M/2)	*7 mm.*
Height from lower margin of enamel			
	Outside	M/1	7.5
		M/2	7.5
	Inside	M/1	5.5
		M/2	4.5

But before you can really do justice either to yourself, or the dear departed, in this matter, you must see the actual remains, and not only see but handle them. Presently the gentle Hun will have grown sick of U-boat warfare – and all other warfare – and you will be able to get across to us. You may even enjoy the spice of excitement in crossing now, if so, and you can get away come and see for yourself. You will then, I am sure, fall down on your knees and worship us, as great and sage interpreters, [? bursting] with "the Divine afflatus" – I think thats the right term, though someone said once it was "Êffluvium"! . . . .

[x/] Word written and deleted by Pycraft; [?] word unclear.

[A] It is not known if Woodward was at Piltdown.

[B] See Tomes (1914), and Letter 2.2.12.

[C] Inserted here are sketches of the two *in situ* Piltdown molars: "Outer" and "Inner" views.

4.3   Woodward's Trojan Horse

At Burlington House, on the evening of 28 February 1917, before a crowded meeting of the Geological Society, Woodward presented evidence supporting the existence of a second *Eoanthropus*. These remains (Table 4.1) were reportedly "discovered" by Dawson early in 1915 (see 4.1.1 and 4.1.21). While Dawson's illness and subsequent death might well have contributed to the delayed announcement of these discoveries, Woodward offered no explanation for his actions. Following a detailed description of the remains, Grafton Elliot Smith then gave a brief summary of his examination of the

TABLE 4.1: Remains recovered from Uckfield neighbourhood [Sheffield Park] attributed to Piltdown II.

Material	Cat No	Finder
Rt. frontal bone	E 646	Dawson[1,2]
Occipital bone	E 647	Dawson[1,2]
Molar		Dawson[1,2]
Rhinoceros lower molar		"friend"[1]

[1] : Woodward (1917); [2] : Letters 4.1.1 and 4.1.21; (3) 4.2.24.

frontal endocranial cast. He believed that this cranial fragment corroborated his earlier findings on the brain cast of Piltdown I, namely "that it presents features which are more distinctly primitive and ape-like than those of any other member of the human family at present available for examination (Woodward 1917:7-8).

At this juncture, Pycraft made a brief but critical review of Gerrit Miller's case against the monistic interpretation of Piltdown I (Woodward 1917:9).

In the discussion that followed both Keith and Lankester agreed that the new evidence made it impossible to regard Piltdown man as an isolated abnormal individual (Woodward 1917:10).

5 The Balance of Opinion

5.1 Between the Wars (1918-1939)

Although the announcement of Piltdown II did much to strengthen Woodward's position, it did not by any means lead to a scientific consensus. Throughout the inter-war years scientific opinion on the Piltdown issue remained pretty evenly divided between the monist interpretation (e.g. Broom 1918; Moir 1918, 1927, 1935; O'Donoghue 1918; Pycraft 1918; Burkitt 1921; Churchward 1922; Kleinschmidt 1922; Osborn 1921a; Osborn & Gregory 1923, Woodward 1923, 1933, Elliot Smith 1924, [& Hunter] 1924–25, 1931a; Keith 1925a, 1929, 1931, 1938–39; Gregory & Hellman 1926; Pilgrim 1927; Curwen 1929; Weinert 1933) and that of the dualist (e.g. Frassetto 1918, 1927; Giuffrida-Ruggeri 1918; Ramström 1919, 1921; Boule 1920; Teilhard de Chardin 1920; Mollison 1921, 1924; Hrdlička 1922, 1923, 1930; Miller 1929; Friedrichs 1932; Marston 1936b, 1937b; Sicher 1937; Weidenreich 1937).

In reviewing this situation in 1929, Gerrit S. Miller, who had been a major critic of Woodward's interpretation since 1915 (see Section 4.2), pointed to a major stumbling block in this debate. "Deliberate malice," he noted:

could hardly have been more successful than the hazards of deposition and recovery in so breaking the Piltdown fossils and losing the most essential parts of the original skull as to allow free scope to individual judgement in fitting the pieces together . . .

According to the different reconstructions the form of the cranium may be completely human in striking contrast to the apelike jaw, or it may have partially simian features which cause this contrast to become less . . . (Miller 1929:441).

But an even greater impediment, according to Miller, was the prevailing confusion in palaeontological circles regarding the question of the human pedigree and its origins (1929:416-423). While most workers from this period subscribed to the Darwinian thesis that modern human anatomy represented the product of a "long and gradual process of development away from nonhuman ancestors," opinions diverged on the details of this process. According to some the development of the brain had been the primary factor in human evolution, while others claimed that the emergence of an upright gait had been the crucial element in the hominisation process[1]. The case for the latter scenario rested largely on the controversial remains of *Pithecanthropus erectus* [*Homo erectus*] found by Eugène Dubois in Java in the early 1890s[2]; whereas the former position was supported by a variety of specimens such as the Galley Hill skeleton and Piltdown, that seemingly attested to the great antiquity of modern human neurocranial morphology. In the light of this evidence, Miller saw little prospect for the reconciliation of these two divergent viewpoints (1929:421), and as such no immediate resolution of the Piltdown problem.

During the years between the two world wars, however, a number of important additions were made to the human fossil record which collectively served to isolate and eventually to undermine many of the theoretical assumptions that had spawned and nurtured the Sussex chimaera.

The first of these new finds came from South Africa in 1925, when Raymond Dart, then professor of anatomy at the University of the Witwatersrand in Johannesburg, announced the discovery of an apelike fossil which he named *Australopithecus africanus* (Fig 5.1a). Although there had been few workers at that time who were willing to endorse Dart's claim that this fossil was a "missing-link", eventually, pressed by accumulating evidence, this viewpoint was slowly adopted, during the next two decades.

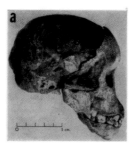 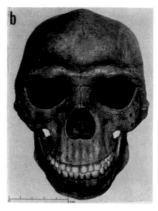 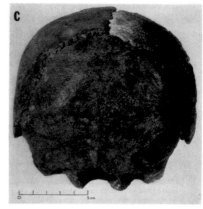

Fig 5.1.   Some important fossil hominid crania found during the period 1920-1940. (a) The Taung skull (right lateral view). Courtesy Professor P.V. Tobias; (b) Sinanthropus pekinensis (adult female) cast: frontal view, restored by F. Weidenreich. Courtesy of the Trustees of the British Museum (Natural History); (c) The Swanscombe skull (occipital view). Courtesy of the Trustees of the British Museum (Natural History).

While the remains from the South African sites were prompting workers to revamp their concept of the hominoid-hominid transition, so the discoveries in Asia during the late 1920s and early 1930s, first at Choukoutien (now Zhoukoudian) in China (Fig 5.1b), and then in Java, forced many palaeoanthropologists to rethink the earlier rejection of Dubois' *Pithecanthropus* as a specialised off-shoot from the mainline of human evolution. The European Neanderthals, which had suffered a similar fate, were likewise reconsidered in the light of these and other discoveries, particularly the ones made at Mount Carmel in Palestine between 1929 and 1934, Steinheim (Germany) in 1933, and then at Swanscombe (England) in 1935-36 (Fig 5.1c) [3].

However, in the meantime, Woodward remained resolute in his support of the Piltdown remains. Prior to his retirement from the Museum in 1923[4], he made almost annual excursions to the site. Thereafter, despite his failure to recover anything of significance, he continued to make, though with diminishing frequency, periodic visits to Piltdown to inspect the shallow pit. In 1938, he was instrumental in having a commemorative pillar erected at the site. After this event, however, the restrictions of war and a gradual failure of his eyesight robbed him of these outings. In his last remaining years he devoted himself exclusively to dictating a small book that summarized his work at Piltdown. This work, entitled *The Earliest Englishman* was completed just prior to his death in 1944 and published in 1947, with a Foreword by Arthur Keith.

NOTES

[1]   As might be expected, supporters of the monist interpretation of the Piltdown remains are seen to be advocates of the former viewpoint. The dualists on the other hand represent a high degree of theoretical heterogeneity. In some cases they are also seen to favour the notion of the pre-eminence of the brain in human evolution (e.g. Boule 1911-1913, 1921; Ramström 1921). There are other dualists, however, who despite a similarity in their arguments against the association of the Piltdown mandible and cranium, are clearly in opposition to the idea of the great antiquity of modern human neuroanatomy (e.g. Hrdlička 1930). Hence some caution should be exercised in evaluating the relative position of workers on these and related issues.

[2]   From the outset this fossil was embroiled in controversy. The remains consisted of a thick, undistorted calotte made up of the frontal, parietal and occipital bones, plus one complete femur and four femoral fragments. From all indications the femur was not found in direct association with the calotte. Likewise, as at Piltdown, the associated faunal assemblage appeared mixed indicating either an Upper Pliocene or Lower Pleistocene date for the site. Dubois (1895, 1899) believed the remains represented a transitional form, and fittingly dubbed them "Pithecanthropus erectus." In the light of doubts surrounding the provenience of the specimens, many workers argued that the calotte belonged to a fossil ape (e.g. Kollman 1895; Virchow 1895, Waldeyer 1895; Volz 1896; Branco 1898; Klaatsch 1899); while others who accepted the association tended to favour Dubois' diagnosis (e.g Cunningham 1895; Manouvrier 1895; Marsh 1895; Sollas 1895; Schwalbe 1899).

[3]   For a general overview of palaeoanthropological theory during this period, see Bowler (1986), Spencer (1984), and Hammond (1988). With specific reference to Australopithecine research between 1925 and 1953, see Tobias (1984, 1985), Lewin (1987), Reed (1983), and Boaz (1982). For developments in later hominid evolution, during the same time period, see Trinkaus (1982) and Smith & Spencer (1984). See also Day (1986) for descriptive and specific bibliographic details of the hominid remains.

[4]   During the years immediately preceding his retirement Woodward received a number of notable awards which included the coveted Royal Medal from the Royal Society of London (1917) and the Prix Cuvier from the French Academy (1918). On 10 July 1924 he received a knighthood. Three years earlier this same honour went to Keith (25 June 1921). Later, Elliot Smith was similarly honoured (27 June 1934).

CORRESPONDENCE

5.1.1 DF 100/43 Moir 28 January 1918

(a) James Reid Moir (1879-1944); (b) handwritten letter to Woodward, on printed stationery: "One House, Henley Road, Ipswich"; (c) underlining in original by Moir.

> . . . *I am naturally interested to find that the two specimens you have selected as being most like the Piltdown implements are both from beneath the Red Crag! [A].*
> *You are perfectly justified, from your standpoint, to qualify your remarks as to the resemblances . . . But I would point out, and with this I feel you will agree, that unless you can show that the characteristics of the flaking of the Piltdown specimens are only such as we know man to produce, while mine show characteristics pointing in the opposite direction, you must be equally doubtful about the Piltdown examples [B]. The finding of the human bones in the same gravel bed, of course, affords strong presumptive evidence that the Piltdown flints are human, but it does not and cannot prove it.*

[A] In 1916 Moir had announced that his researches showed that the human skeleton found at Ipswich in 1911 and attributed to a "pre-Boulder Clay" horizon, was in fact a "re-made" deposit and in all probability referable to the "late Palaeolithic epoch" (Moir 1916b). Although remaining committed to Eolithic theory (see 1916a, 1924, 1927) during the next decade Moir's position came under increasing attack (see Warren 1921). Hence Moir's interest in Woodward's comparative views on Ipswich versus Piltdown.

[B] A reference to the Piltdown eoliths, see Dawson & Woodward (1913a).

5.1.2 DF 100/43 Osborn 2 April 1918

(a) Henry Fairfield Osborn (1857-1935); (b) typewritten letter to Woodward, on printed stationery: "American Museum of Natural History, New York"; (c) –.

. . .I have written to Pycraft asking him not to put the personal element in his discussions [A]. I do not know whether Miller is right or wrong in this matter [B], but he is absolutely one of the most high-minded, conscientious investigators I know. His forthcoming second review of the Piltdown jaw is a masterpiece of fair statement, presented in a purely impersonal manner. . . I am keenly interested in your comparison of the newly found Piltdown tooth with the type and look forward to your paper [C].

[A] See Letter 4.2.26.

[B] Later in 1922, following an examination of the original remains at the British Museum, Osborn became a zealous supporter of Piltdown. For an account of this conversion, see Osborn (1922a); see also 5.1.22.

[C] See Miller's article published in the first number of the *American Journal of Physical Anthropology* (1918). This quarterly journal was founded by Aleš Hrdlička in 1918. Miller's article is essentially a reply to Woodward's paper (1917) and does not contain any reference to Eoanthropus II (Woodward 1917). From all indications Woodward's article was not published until 6 April 1918.

5.1.3 DF 100/43 Lyne 22 May 1918

(a) W. Courtney Lyne (d. 1947); (b) handwritten letter on printed stationery: "Dunheved, Maple Road, Bournville"; (c) annotated by Woodward: "June 27th".

I have been reading today in the Q.J.G.S. your further account of Piltdown finds [A], and [?] if you will kindly allow me to give you one or two impression that crossed my mind.

I have never doubted the humanity of the molars, since carefully examining them, and Mr. Pycraft's and also your remarks on this point I accept quite readily [B]. I can see no evidence of a tangible nature on behalf of G. Miller's view [C].

I think, however, that one cannot (perhaps this applies more particularly to Sir R. Lankester), assume any connection with this new molar and the previous mandible [D]. The type of wear is scarcely in conformity with the known tempero-mandibular joint of the previous specimen. Dr. Snow (of U.S.A.) [E] has clearly proved the relation of the "compensating curve" (curve of [?]) of the articulating teeth surfaces with a corresponding articular (joint) one, and we are necessarily led to the conclusion that this present style of wear (as depicted) has been associated with a flatter articular eminence (i.e. more apelike) or Neanderthaloid. Every week in our ordinary [?] of the natural teeth we have to work on this curve principle, otherwise we should constantly be having what are conflict "over bites". In this last find I think you will probably have to assume a deeper symphysis than the former. Here you got hold of a male this time and a female previously! [?/Also shape] of the pulp cavity should show some similarity to the other, if belonging to one creature. . .

[?] word(s) unclear.

[A] As indicated in Note C: Letter 5.1.2, Woodward's (1917) paper on Eoanthropus II did not appear until early April 1918.

[B] See Woodward (1917:5-6) and Pycraft, cited in Woodward (1917:9)

[C] See Miller (1915), and 4.2.25.

[D] In the discussion following Woodward's (1917) paper, Lankester had suggested that the Eoanthropus II fragments "belonged to the same individual as that represented by the imperfect skull and lower jaw already known" (p. 10).

[E] The identity of this individual is not known.

5.1.4 DF 100/43 Marriott 9 June 1918

(a) Major Reginald Adams Marriott (1857-1930); (b) hand-written letter on plain stationery: "J.D. Admiralty, [London] S.W."; (c) annotated by Woodward: "27th. Sent 2 reprints".

In this letter Marriott notes the similarity between some of the stone tools found at Lewes with those in the Piltdown assemblage. For further information on Marriott, see 6.3.21, 6.3.24 and 6.3.41; Weiner (1955) and Spencer (1990).

5.1.5 DF 100/43 Ashburnham 15 July 1918

(a) Major Ashburnham; (b) handwritten letter on printed stationery: "Melcombe Dingham, Dorchester"; (c) annotated by Woodward: "Aug 12th. Postponed until 29th".

The identity of this individual is not known. His letter deals with arrangements to assist Woodward and Godwin-Austen (see 4.2.16) in the continuing excavation of the Piltdown gravels, or as he put it: "looking for leg bones of Mrs. Eoanthropus [and] not to mention ancestors of the noble family of Proanthropi and Propithecanthropi." He also notes that rather than lodge with the Kenward's (4.2.13) he would prefer to "camp on the spot."

5.1.6 DF 100/44 Sutton 8 July 1919

(a) Arthur Warwick Sutton (1854-1925); (b) typewritten letter on printed stationery: "9 Upper Phillimore Gardens, Campden Hill, [London] W.8"; (c) –.

Sutton was a well known horticulturalist. Both Sutton and Woodward were members of the Linnean Society, and presumably it was in this context that the connection between the two was made. In this letter thanking Woodward for a copy of new edition of his "Fossil Guide" [A], Sutton writes:

You are right in thinking that I am interested in the ancestry of man, and I cannot understand how anyone can fail to be interested in a matter of such supreme moment to us all. It is most kind of you to offer to show me the Piltdown remains, and I shall hope to take an opportunity of doing so after your return to the Museum [B]. I hope you will have a very interesting time [C] at Piltdown, though doubtless you will be hard at work.

[A] The second edition of *Guide* was published in 1918, see Woodward (1915).

[B] Another example of Woodward's attitude to the Piltdown remains, which runs counter to the popular notion that he had blocked free-access to the specimens.

[C] Sutton had originally typed: "time", which he has crossed-out and written in hand: "holiday".

5.1.7 DF 100/44 Trevor 13 July 1919

(a) Captain Stephen L Trevor; (b) handwritten letter on plain stationery: "Piltdown"; (c) annotated by Woodward: "16th."

In this brief note Trevor mentions Woodward's recent visit to Piltdown:

I was sorry it was such rotten weather for you all during your stay and that I didn't have opportunities to see more of the family . . .

5.1.8 DF 100/44 Teilhard de Chardin 4 September 1919

(a) Pierre Teilhard de Chardin (1881-1955); (b) handwritten letter on printed stationery: "Maison Saint Louis, Jersey, C.I."; (c) annotated by Francis Arthur Bather (1863-1934): "recd. & ackd 8 Sept.1919, F.a.B."

A short letter from Teilhard in which he notes his recent demobilization from the army and that he is presently taking a short vacation in Jersey prior to resuming his studies in Paris. He asks about Piltdown, and adds: "The death of Mr. Dawson has been a real sorrow for me." As indicated by Bather's annotation, Woodward was absent from the Museum (for reasons unknown) when this letter arrived.

5.1.9 DF 100/45 Abbott 22 March 1920

(a) William James Lewis Abbott (1853-1933); (b) typewritten letter on printed stationery: "W.J. Lewis Abbott, 8 Grand Parade, St. Leonards"; (c) annotated by Woodward: "24th".

This is one of three letters Abbott wrote to Woodward during March 1920 concerning a collection of fossils he presented to the Museum. The 22 March letter is of particular interest since it mentions his earlier work on the Ightham fissures and his former connection with Martin Hinton and Edwin Tulley Newton.

5.1.10 DF 100/45 Keith 16 June 1920

(a) Arthur Keith (1866-1955); (b) handwritten letter on printed stationery: "Royal College of Surgeons of England, Lincoln's Inn Fields, London W.C.2."; (c) annotated by Woodward: "16th. ackd."

I send you the 4 bones which Reid Moir has sent here from time to time during the last two years – from Bramford and Foxhall [A]. I am very glad you are to work them over for I think they deserve to be rightly done [B].

[A] The Foxhall remains are of interest largely because it was at this site, a sandpit, located some 4 miles east of Ipswich, that a fossil human mandible was reportedly found and described by the craniologist R.H. Collyer in 1867. Collyer claimed a high antiquity for the specimen which was subsequently lost. During the early 1920s the Foxhall site attracted considerable interest, largely through the efforts of Henry Fairfield Osborn (1921b) and Moir (1924) to establish the validity of the idea of "Pliocene Man in East Anglia". This movement, however, was vigorously attacked by Hrdlička (1924, see also 1930:23–28).

[B] From all indications this work did not result in a publication.

5.1.11 DF 100/45 Teilhard de Chardin 4 August 1920

(a) Pierre Teilhard de Chardin (1881-1955); (b) handwritten note on printed postcard: "Ore Place, Hastings"; (c) annotated by Woodward: "5th".

I am at Hastings till the 15th of September (except from the 15th to the 25th August) and should be very glad to see you. Would you kindly let me know if I could meet you say, either at the South Kensington [Museum], or at Piltdown?

It is not known if this meeting took place, and is of interest since it coincided with the publication of Teilhard's paper on Piltdown. In this paper, published in the *Revue des questions scientifiques* (an organ of the Société Scientifique de Bruxelles in Louvain) Teilhard is explicitly in favour of the dissociation of the jaw.

5.1.12 WKG/AMNH Gregory 12 May 1922

(a) William King Gregory (1876-1970); (b) Carbon copy of typewritten letter from Gregory to Grafton Elliot Smith at University College [London University] [A]; (c) underlining in original by Gregory.

. . . I have studies of McGregor's stereoscopic views of the new and old lower molars side by side and I gladly admit they look very much alike and afford <u>nearly</u> convincing evidence for the association of jaw and skull [B]. But I do not regard it as especially important if <u>I was wrong</u>. I have had to "eat crow"

several times. It is not always pleasant but it is probably like the scroll of the prophet – bitter in the mouth but sweet in the belly.

It seems too bad that British authors speak so often of "American heresy" as if it were an international derision, rather than individual difference. Please look again at Miller's plates 2 and 5 of his first paper, and plates 1, 2, 3, 4 of his second paper and see if you do not think his evidence looks better than Pycraft's figs 1, 2, and 4 [C].

I have the greatest respect for your work and for Dr. Smith Woodward and I hope that neither of you feel that I have ever been led away by talking with either Keith or Miller. It never was a personal matter with me and the only thing I ever resented was Pycraft's remarks about Miller, which were most unfortunate [D]. Also it was "some nerve" to say the Dr. Gregory "accepts Miller's arguments without investigating the matter himself." If he only knew how much time I have wasted on the blessed business.

[A] In 1919 Elliot Smith succeeded George Dancer Thane as Professor of Anatomy at University College, London.

[B] In 1921, James H. McGregor [Note C: 4.1.7] of the American Museum in New York was allowed by Woodward to make a series of x-ray and "stereo-photographs" of the Piltdown teeth. These photographs, he told Osborn: "really show more than ordinary casts." To which he added: "Elliot Smith went over the original remains with me very carefully, and I am forced to admit that, like [W.D.] Matthew, the pro-Eoanthropus party has a pretty strong case" (HFO/AMNH McGregor 16 June 1921, cited in Spencer 1979, II:522).

[C] Miller (1915): Plate 2 compares the Piltdown mandible (superior and inferior view) with 3 chimpanzee mandibles from the US National Museum collections. Plate 5 depicts lateral views of 4 adult chimpanzee mandibles to show degree of individual variation. Miller (1918): Plate 1 shows a comparison of the Piltdown molars with those of *Pongo*, *Pan*, a modern human and a fossil hominid (Krapina). Plate 2 shows a comparative view (from lingual side) of Piltdown, *Pan*, and a modern human (Kaffir) jaws. Plate 3 compares (superior views) of the Piltdown, *Pan* and *Pongo* jaws. Plate 4: shows the skull of *Pan* sp. bearing cast of the reconstructed Piltdown jaw; Pycraft (1917): Fig.1: Compares the ascending ramus of Piltdown with the same region of 10 chimpanzee jaws and that of a Kaffir. Fig.2: Compares the contours of the posterior border of the ascending ramus, and of the condyle, in the jaws of chimpanzees, humans and Piltdown. Fig.4: This depicts the right side (superior view) of the jaws of a chimpanzee, Piltdown and a modern European. In each, Pycraft has drawn lines along the molars and through the ascending ramus. The purpose of these lines is to demonstrate that in the chimpanzee these lines converge, whereas in Piltdown and the modern European these lines diverge. See Letter 4.2.26 for Gregory's comments on these illustrations to Miller in 1917.

[D] See 4.2.26.

5.1.13 HFO/AMNH Woodward 31 May 1922

(a) Arthur Smith Woodward (1864-1944); (b) handwritten letter to Henry Fairfield Osborn, on printed stationery: "British Museum (Natural History), Cromwell Road, London S.W."; (c) –.

This communication introduces an incident in North American palaeontology involving Osborn and his co-workers at the American Museum in New York City. In 1922 Osborn announced the discovery of a fossil anthropoid tooth, claiming that it might even be ancestral to humankind. The tooth in question was later shown to be a tooth of an extinct species of pig. This incident is of interest since it clearly had in some quarters, a cautionary effect, see for example 5.1.30 and 5.1.43.

I thank you for your interesting note on Hesperopithecus [A] awaiting my return [B]. I have been studying it, and perhaps you have already learned that I am sceptical about it. I wrote the enclosed letter to the Times *when the discovery was announced there [C]. I hope before long there will be something more to decide whether or not my scepticism is justified. It will be splendid if you are right . . . I have very little time left this year for Piltdown. Still I hope to spend a few days there.*

[A] It is conjectured that Osborn may have sent Woodward either a reprint of his note on *Hesperopithecus* which appeared in the April issue of *Amer Mus Novit* (No 37, pp 1-5) or a copy of the *New York Times* report: "Nebraska fossil tooth proves man-ape existed in America" (27 April **19**:3). Later Osborn (1922) published a detailed account of the discovery in *Nature*. To a large extent, Osborn's enthusiasm for this specimen was fed by his mounting commitment to the idea of Central Asia having been the homeland of the human genus (see Osborn 1924, 1926). Although the tooth was subsequently shown to be a badly worn tooth of an extinct peccary, it did not dampen Osborn's ardour for the Asian hypothesis. For further details on this episode and its relation to the Piltdown problem, see Gregory & Hellman (1926); Gregory 1927a, 1927b, 1929a; and Letter 5.1.15.

[B] Woodward had been to France on an excursion arranged by the Geologists' Association to see the celebrated caves at Mentone and the Dordogne region. Apparently, while in the Dordogne the British group had been guided by the French prehistorian Denis Peyrony (1869-1954).

[C] Woodward's "Letter-to-the-Editor" appeared in the 22 May issue of the London *Times*. See also his note in *Nature* 109:750 entitled: "A Supposed Ancestral Man in North America." By contrast, Elliot Smith was far less sceptical, see his report published in *The Times*, 20 May 1922, p 17.

5.1.14 HP/NAA Hrdlička 23 June 1922

(a) Aleš Hrdlička (1869-1943); (b) carbon copy of typewritten letter addressed to William King Gregory at the American Museum in New York City; (c) –.

I would like very much to have your personal opinion of the "anthropoid tooth" from Nebraska [A]; there is no possibility of it being a bear's tooth? Somehow or other I find it difficult to accept it as that of a high class primate, but of course I have not seen the original [B]. Please regard this as between us two.

[A] See Notes A & C: 5.1.13.

[B] Contrary to Osborn (Note A: 5.1.13), Hrdlička was not a supporter of the Asiatic hypothesis, and was thus not only sceptical of this discovery but also critical of Davidson Black's latter claims for the remains found at Choukoutien (see Spencer 1979, II: 592-603). For a brief discussion of Hrdlička's developing viewpoint on human origins, see his paper "The Peopling of Asia" published in 1921.

5.1.15 HP/NAA Gregory 27 June 1922

(a) William King Gregory (1876-1970); (b) typewritten letter to Hrdlička at the Smithsonian Institution, Washington D.C., on printed stationery: "American Museum of Natural History, New York"; (c) –.

I am glad to give you my confidential opinion on the Hesperopithecus tooth [A]. We actually compared it with Carnivores before Professor Osborn published his description [B], and Dr. Matthew [C], who is perhaps the greatest living expert on carnivore teeth, made thorough comparisons and feels satisfied that it can be definitely excluded from Carnivora. Dr Gerrit S. Miller, after careful comparisons, decided that it was closest to the third upper molar of a certain chimpanzee, which we are figuring alongside of the type in all 6 views of the tooth [D]. Dr. Hellman [E] has a human tooth which on being ground down to the same level as the type shows a marked approach towards it. The characters of the roots and the form of the ruined surface are remarkably like those of the second upper molar referred to Pithecanthropus. There are numerous small points of resemblance to Pithecanthropus, gorilla and chimpanzee, and I do not see how the specimen can represent anything but one of man-anthropoid group, differing from chimpanzee especially in its heavier roots, in which respect it approaches Pithecanthropus. We are preparing illustrations. . .

[A] See Note A: Letter 5.1.13.

[B] See Osborn (1922b), and Note A: 5.1.13.

[C] William Diller Matthew see 3.1.5

[D] See Osborn's *Nature* article (1922).

[E] Milo Hellman (1872-1947), a dental specialist, who during the late 1930s collaborated with Gregory on the study of Australopithecine dentition.

5.1.16 HFO/AMNH Gregory 31 August 1922

(a) William King Gregory (1876-1970); (b) carbon copy of typewritten letter addressed to Henry Fairfield Osborn (Director of the American Museum); (c) –.

This letter was written, evidently, in response to a note from Elliot Smith to Osborn, that has not survived, regarding both the question of *Hesperopithecus* and Piltdown.

. . . It is curious how easily he [Elliot Smith] misinterprets and misquotes people [A]. For example, I have no recollection of expressing any opinion about the value or lack of value of X-rays [B]. Possibly Matthew may have said something of the kind. We have received the X-Ray photos and in Dr. Hellman's opinion they show that the pulp cavity and root canals of Hesperopithecus type more nearly resembles the M1 Indian molar than the chimp molars. . . . As to Eoanthropus, we must await Elliot Smith's evidence that the skull itself is "vastly more primitive than the Neanderthal [C] . . . I am sorry to have to differ with Elliot Smith in his low estimate of Keith. Of course Keith has made some sad mistakes, but his last two papers will be classics [D].

[A] It is conjectured that Gregory is referring to Elliot Smith's article on *Hesperopithecus* that appeared in *The Times* (London) on 20 May under the title "The Earliest Man? An American Discovery. Hitherto Unknown Genus. The Tale of a Tooth" (p 17). In replying to Gregory's letter, Osborn (HFO/AMNH: 7 September 1922) wrote: "I have come to the conclusion that he [Elliot Smith] is very brilliant, but that his judgement is unsound."

[B] See Note B: 5.1.12.

[C] In May 1922, Elliot Smith (with J.I. Hunter) presented a new reconstruction of the Piltdown skull to the Anatomical Society of London (see Elliot Smith & Hunter 1924-25), a revised version of the 1922 paper). Because of Hunter's death in December 1924, Elliott Smith was assisted by John Beattie [see Note B: 5.1.44] in revising the paper for publication. For Keith's response to this reconstruction, see his book *New Discoveries . . .* (1931:446-467) in which he deals with the relationship of Piltdown to the London [Lloyd's] skull discovered in 1925 (see 5.1.20).

[D] It is believed that Gregory is referring to Keith's book on human embryology (1921) and his paper (with G.C. Campion) on the growth of the human face (1922). Both papers are cited by Gregory in his book *Our Face: From Fish to Man* (1929b).

5.1.17 SPC Sollas 1 September 1922

(a) William Johnson Sollas (1849-1936); (b) handwritten letter to Woodward on stationery embossed: "University Museum, Oxford"; (c) annotated by Woodward: "2nd".

I cannot begin otherwise than by thanking you for your generous assistance yesterday. It helps me a good stretch on my way. . . [A]

[A] Sollas had been at the Museum comparing human fossil crania, in particular Piltdown and the Kabwe (Rhodesian) skull (discovered in 1921 and initially described by Woodward the same year). For further information on the latter specimen, see Day (1986:267-273). Sollas' work: "A method for the comparative study of the human skull" was communicated to the Royal Society, see Sollas (1922).

5.1.18 KP/RCS/Box KL1 Dart 26 February 1925

(a) Raymond Dart (1893–1988); (b) handwritten letter to Arthur Keith on printed stationery: "University of the Witwatersrand, Johannesburg"; (c) underlining in original by Dart.

"It was a great pleasure to receive your letter of congratulation today [A]. I especially appreciate too your kind suggestions with regard to the fuller publication. Naturally there were many things omitted in the first note – things too which are of very deep interest. The specimen came to me in the rock on Nov 28th and my paper went away on Jan 6th so you will judge that many things remain to be done [B].

But if any errors have been made they are all on the conservative (ape) side and it is certain that subsequent work will serve only to emphasise the <u>human</u> characters. Broom was here last week-end and we went over it very carefully together [C]. He places it in the direct line and if anything nearer to Piltdown man than I have cared to place it. He is going to write to Nature shortly and also to Natural History the popular publication of the American Museum. Two particular questions we were able to solve together – one is that the great wing of the sphenoid articulates with the parietal and the second that the premaxilla-maxillary suture is humanoid and not anthropoid. Further the first permanent molars, although large (14mm × 14mm) are remarkably human in their characters – cusps etc.

There seems therefore very little doubt that my Homo-Simiidae is a justifiable group and this Broom fully concurs in. The brain size and character along with these added points carry us right out of the living anthropoid series. I am most grateful to you for all the kindly things that you have said about me in the press [D] and trust that when the casts have been prepared and you visualise the remains there will be no difference of opinion amongst us.

[A] This is a reference to Dart's landmark publication on the Taung's fossil specimen which he had dubbed *Australopithecus africanus* (Dart 1925a). The initial response to the article was mixed. There were few willing to endorse Dart's view that the specimen represented a "missing-link" (e.g. Sollas 1925). By and large, most workers, though for varying reasons, tended adopted a more reserved interpretation of the find, arguing that at most it represented a fossil hominoid form (e.g. Keith 1925b; Woodward 1925; Duckworth 1925; Elliot Smith 1925a).

[B] See Dart (1925b; 1925c; 1926; 1929; 1934).

[C] For details of Broom's initial stance on *Australopithecus*, see Broom (1925a; 1925b).

[D] See Keith (1925c; 1925d, 1925e; see also Keith 1931:21-116).

5.1.19 HP/NAA Hrdlička 21 February 1925

(a) Aleš Hrdlička (1869-1943); (b) carbon copy of letter addressed to Raymond Dart, Anatomy Department, University of the Witwatersrand, Johannesburg"; (c) annotated by Hrdlička: "copy".

Permit me to congratulate you on your very interesting and evidently important find, the Australopithecus; and also to thank you for the very good cablegram which you sent in answer to the message sent to you at my suggestion by "Science Service" [A]. I have also just received and read "Nature" of February 7, in which you give your very good preliminary report, and I am asking "Nature" for the privilege of its republication in our journal [B].

In your article you mention that you are preparing a complete memoir on the subject. I presume that you will have no difficulty in its publication; but if there should be any then send it to me and I will be glad to give it prompt publication . . .

[A] As indicated by this letter, Hrdlička was enthusiastic about the Taung specimen. Morphologically he considered it to be an anthropoid ape, and did not attribute any hominid affinities to the specimen. "Just what relation this fossil form bears, on the one hand, to the human phylum, and on the other to the chimpanzee and gorilla, can only be properly determined after the specimen is well identified, for which we need additional and adult specimens", Hrdlička wrote at the time (1925: 390). Later that year Hrdlička became the first foreign anthropologist to visit the Taungs site (Spencer 1979; Tobias 1984).

[B] A reference to the *American Journal of Physical Anthropology* which Hrdlička had founded in 1918.

5.1.20 KP/RCS [Spec Coll I] Dawkins 23 October 1925

(a) William Boyd Dawkins (1837-1929); (b) handwritten letter addressed to Arthur Keith on plain stationery: "Fallowfield House, Fallowfield, Manchester"; (c) –.

I entirely share your doubts as to the [London] skull described by Elliot Smith. It appears to me (sketch in The Times) to be modern, and I am not satisfied that it was found in situ with Pleistocene remains. . ." [A]

[A] Keith's letter to Dawkins has not survived. Dawkins is referring to an account in *The Times* (Wednesday), 21 October 1925) of a preliminary report on the "London Skull" made by Elliot Smith to the London Zoological Society on 20 October. This skull was recovered from a building site situated at the intersection of Leadenhall and Lime Streets, owned by Lloyd's Corporation in central London. A more detailed report of the discovery was communicated to *The Times* on 28 October, page 15 by Warren R. Dawson (1888-1968). See Elliot Smith's Letter-to-the-Editor of *The Times* published 5 November and his piece in the *British Medical Journal* (1925b), and several notes published in *Nature* (1925c). Elliot Smith attributed the remains to an Aurignacian *Homo sapiens*, displaying Neanderthal affinities. Keith on the other hand believed the specimen was much older, probably Lower Pleistocene. He also dismissed Elliot Smith's view that it was Neanderthaloid. In his opinion it was anatomically modern with close affinities to Piltdown (Keith 1931:431-467). For further details on this find and how it was received in relation to Piltdown, see Hammond (1988) and Spencer (1990).

5.1.21 HFO/AMNH McGregor 30 October 1925

(a) James H. McGregor (1872-1954); (b) handwritten letter on plain stationery, addressed to Henry Fairfield Osborn at the American Museum in New York City; (c) –.

. . . I absolutely can't accept Keith's interpretation of certain depressions in the frontal bone as an attempt at trephining [A] . . . Had a delightful day at Piltdown site last Saturday as the guest of Sir Arthur and Lady Woodward [B]. Sir Arhur pointed out "the exact historic spot where Osborn recanted. . ." [C].

[A] McGregor worked at the American Museum of Natural History. The reason for his visit to Britain on this occasion is not known, though it appears he spent sometime in London where he met with both Keith at the Royal College of Surgeons and Elliot Smith at University College. The identity of the skull McGregor is referring to is not known. From all indications while visiting Elliot Smith he had an opportunity to examine the so-called London [Lloyd's] skull, see 5.1.20, and Elliot Smith (1925b, 1925c).

[B] Woodward received his knighthood in 1924, see the announcement in the *London Gazette* on 10 July 1924.

[C] 5.1.22 and Osborn 1921a.

5.1.22 HFO/AMNH Osborn 28 December 1925

(a) Henry Fairfield Osborn (1857-1935); (b) carbon copy of letter addressed to James H. McGregor in London; (c) –.

A reply to 5.1.21.

Without any disrespect to Sir Arthur Keith [A], I have a great deal more confidence in your anatomical insight and judgement than in him . . . You will find the British either extremely conservative or rather rash in their conclusions [B].

I am delighted that you visited the Piltdown site, including the exact historic site where Osborn recanted! At this spot I contributed £5 toward a monument to Piltdown man, but I have not heard of it being prepared and set-up [C].

[A] Keith received his knighthood in June 1921. See *London Gazette*, 25 June 1921.

[B] See Note A: 5.1.21.

[C] The Piltdown monument was finally commissioned (through private subscription) and erected in 1938, see 5.1.56.

5.1.23 DF 116/51 Hrdlička 6 October 1926

(a) Aleš Hrdlička (1869-1943); (b) typewritten letter to Francis Bather, on printed stationery: "U.S. National Museum of Natural History"; (c) –.

Among the Piltdown remains there is a loose molar tooth which looks as if it were a counterpart from the other side of the first molar of the Piltdown jaw. This tooth I was told by someone – or I read it somewhere, I cannot clearly recollect – was found after Mr. Dawson's death with some other objects among his possessions, but without any data as to the circumstances of its discovery [A]. Possibly you or your good assistant could tell me just what is what from the records in your possession or other knowledge [A].

[A] Hrdlička is referring to the molar of the so-called second *Eoanthropus*. As Hrdlička well knew, Woodward's (1917:3) paper left the provenience of these specimens very much in doubt. In fact in his 1922 paper Hrdlička had suggested that some mistake had been made regarding the isolated molar and that perhaps it had originally come from the first site – a suggestion Woodward flatly denied, see 5.1.25.

[B] See 5.1.24 for Bather's reply.

5.1.24 HP/NAA Bather 18 October 1926

(a) Francis Arthur Bather (1863-1934); (b) handwritten letter addressed to Aleš Hrdlička at the Smithsonian Institution, on printed stationery: "British Museum (Natural History), Cromwell Road, London S.W."; (c) –.

Thank you for your letter of Oct. 6th. I have looked up the Piltdown molar to which you refer. It is registered E 648. It was described and figured by A. Smith Woodward. Journ. Geol. Soc., LXXIII, p.3, pl.i, fig.4. We have no further information than is given in Woodward's paper which apparently you have overlooked [A].

From all indications Bather also relayed Hrdlička's inquiry to Woodward, see Letter 5.1.25.

[A] See 4.1.21.

5.1.25 HP/NAA Woodward 26 October 1926

(a) Arthur Smith Woodward (1864-1944); (b) handwritten letter to Hrdlička in Washington on printed stationery: "Hill Place, Haywards Heath, Sussex"; (c) –.

A reply to 5.1.23; see also 5.1.24.

. . . [T]he fragments of the second Piltdown skull and tooth were not "found" among Mr. Dawson's property after his death [A]. I knew they were there because he had told me of them at the time of his discovery; he also told me that he found them on the Sheffield Park Estate, but he would not tell me the exact place -- I can only infer from other information that I have.

Unfortunately, we have not worked at Piltdown this year because I have been away in Syria [B], but during the last five seasons we did not find anything . . . [C]

[A] See 4.2.22.

[B] See Note C: 5.1.32.

[C] Later, in 1930, Hrdlička published his book *The Skeletal Remains of Early Man* in which he presented a highly critical review of the Piltdown discoveries. For further details on this work, and in particular Woodward's response to it, see 4.1.21.

5.1.26 KP/RCS/Box KL2 Black 27 October 1926

(a) Davidson Black (1884-1934); (b) typewritten letter addressed to Arthur Keith at Royal College of Surgeons, on printed stationery: "Department of Anatomy, Peking Union Medical College, Peiping, China"; (c) –.

Black was Professor of Embryology and Neurology at Peking Union Medical College, see 3.1.28.

There is great news to tell you – actual fossil remains of a man-like being have at last been found in eastern Asia, in fact quite close to Peking. I enclose a copy of a note I have written on the subject and sent to "Nature" and "Man." [A] This discovery fits exactly with [x/my] the hypothesis as to the central Asiatic origin of the Hominidae which I reviewed in my paper "Asia and the dispersal of primates" [B]. I hope the copy of the latter paper I sent you last summer did not go astray . . .

[x/] word written and deleted by Black.

[A] The remains, found by the Swedish geologist Gunnar Andersson (1874-1960) at Choukoutien, consisted of two molars which Black considered belonged to an early hominid. In fact on the basis of these teeth (and their apparent geological antiquity) Black had established the taxon *Sinanthropus pekinensis* (Black 1926, 1927a), now known as *Homo erectus*. Further material, found in 1927 and 1928, confirmed Black's hominoid diagnosis (1927b). Between 1929 and 1932 the site at Choukouten yielded a spectacular series of early hominid skeletal material. For further details on these discoveries, see 5.1.30-5.1.32, 5.1.38 and 5.1.49.

[B] Black was an ardent supporter of the then popular view that Central Asia had been the cradle and nursery of the genus *Homo*, see Black (1925).

5.1.27 KP/RCS/Box KL2 Osborn 8 January 1927

(a) Henry Fairfield Osborn (1857-1935); (b) typewritten letter to Arthur Keith on printed stationery: "American Museum of Natural History, New York"; (c) annotated in Osborn's handwriting: "Sunday N.Y.Times Magazine Section. Jan. 10th." Underlining in original by Osborn [B].

In my opinion, the New and Old World monkeys separated early, but see Gregory's splendid memoirs for the last word on this subject [A], also my opinions [B]. Resemblances between New and Old monkeys, also between anthropoid apes and man are full of parallelism and homoplasy or convergence.

I am strongly advocating Dawn Man individual ancestry; see the New York Times, Magazine Section, on Sunday, January ninth" [C].

[A] See for example Gregory (1916a).

[B] Osborn has inserted an asterisk here referring to his handwritten footnote, see above annotation.

[C] See Osborn's annotation for the correct date.

5.1.28 HFO/AMNH Hopwood 4 June 1928

(a) Arthur Tindell Hopwood (1897-1969); (b) typed copy of letter to Osborn; original not found. The following extract is quoted in Osborn's monograph on *Proboscidea* (1942:965-966).

In this letter Hopwood claimed that the Piltdown skull should be associated with the older fauna and eoliths in the assemblage, on the grounds that the skull and older fauna are of the same chocolate colour, "whereas the younger fauna is represented by fragments of a lighter ochraceous colour." Hopwood then went on to explain that Dawson had soaked the first discovered fragments in a potassium dichromate solution to harden them. "This explains the very dark chocolate tone of parts of the brain-case with the lighter, slightly more greyish colour of the remainder", Hopwood wrote. For further details on Hopwood's work on the Piltdown assemblage, see his paper published in 1935. It is interesting to note that in 1925, and evidently in connection with the foregone work, Hopwood had checked the specific gravity of the Piltdown I mandible and occipital fragment, plus the frontal bone (E 646) of Piltdown II. The results were 2.06, 2.13 and 2.18, respectively. These results were later confirmed by Oakley in October 1953 (see DF 116/44).

5.1.29 KP/RCS/Box KL1 Black 5 December 1928

(a) Davidson Black (1884-1934); (b) typewritten letter addressed to Arthur Keith at the Royal College of Surgeons, on printed stationery: "Department of Anatomy, Peking Union Medical College, Peiping, China"; (c) –.

I have completed the formal arrangements with Barlow to have him manufacture for sale the cast and model of the molar tooth of Sinanthropus that I described last year [A]. As soon as I hear from him I shall make arrangements to present copies of both cast and model to you but I expect it will be six months or more before he will be ready for distribution [B].

[A] See Note A: Letter 5.1.26.

[B] According to an entry in Keith's desk-diary (KP/RCS), he received the Barlow casts on 4 April 1929.

5.1.30 KP/RCS/Box KL1 Black 12 February 1929

(a) Davidson Black (1884-1934); (b) typewritten letter addressed to Arthur Keith at the Royal

College of Surgeons, on printed stationery: "Department of Anatomy, Peking Union Medical College, Peiping, China"; (c) –.

It is delightful to know you too are excited over the Sinanthropus finds. I shall send you a copy of my Nature report as soon as it is ready [A]. . . I should get this ready by the middle of this summer. Would that be too late for you to use in your forthcoming additional volume of the Antiquity of Man? [B]. I would give a lot to be able to have our work, so far as it is, given such notice for there surely are a lot of unbelieving Devils in this world – especially since Hesperopithecus' fall from his high estate! . . .

. . . By the way who and what is "Arthur S. Underwood editor of the Brit. Journ. Dent. Sci"? [C] I have his so-called paper on the X-ray of the Piltdown jaw and I am far from being favourably impressed with the way he has used his opportunity to study the skiagrams. How does it come that he was able to publish them and why does he make no real acknowledgements, and why has not some more competent person done the work over again and thoroughly? His first skiagram is labelled "Mandible (Piltdown) seen from above" but his view is seen from below viz. with the occlusal surface next [sic] the X-ray film. This is obvious when one knows that it is the right side of the jaw that is preserved while his view if "from above" shows a left side. No detail is given of the orientation of the other skiagram shown but that can readily be guessed. His text is equally rotten for he does not discuss the skiagrams at all and merely pats himself on the back for having guessed as he thinks correctly about the canine. Can nothing be done to bring about an adequate and exhaustive X-ray study of this important specimen? . . .

[A] These new finds from Choukoutien consisted of several more teeth and mandibular fragments. For further details, see Black's note in *Science* (1929), Keith's report in the *Lancet* (28 September 1929, pp 683-684) and Elliot Smith's article in the *Illustrated London News* (19 October 1929, pp 672-673).

[B] It is presumed that Black is referring to the 7th impression of Keith's *The Antiquity of Man* which appeared in June 1929. Later, in 1931, Keith brought out another volume, entitled *New Discoveries* (see Note A: 5.1.37) which contains a long section on *Sinanthropus*.

[C] See 1.3.13.

5.1.31 KP/RCS/Box KL1 Black 20 March 1929

(a) Davidson Black (1884-1934); (b) typewritten letter addressed to Arthur Keith at the Royal College of Surgeons, on printed stationery: "Department of Anatomy, Peking Union Medical College, Peiping, China"; (c) –.

This new Sinanthropus material has provided just what was needed, for it makes it possible now to be a bit definite on some things, whereas when I wrote on the subject of dispersal in 1925, there was no early hominid material except Eoanthropus and Pithecanthropus.

Postscript: Thank you so much for your good letter of March 4th which reached me today after the above was written . . . I shall use Underwood's illustrations as you say. His qualifications match his text!"

As indicated by this and the preceding letter Black was still very much under the spell of Piltdown. The Choukoutien mandibles, like that of Piltdown, were chinless, which gave them a primitive, and apelike appearance, and as with *Eoanthropus* the teeth had a distinctly modern conformation. In his report Black stressed the differences between the Chinese *Sinanthropus* and the Javan *Pithecanthropus*. At this juncture Black was keen to portray his fossil as a more likely candidate for being an ancestral form of the modern human lineage.

5.1.32 DF 102 Teilhard de Chardin 14 June 1929

(a) Pierre Teilhard de Chardin (1881-1955); (b) typewritten letter addressed to Woodward, on printed stationery: "Musée Hoang Ho Pai Ho, Race Course Road, Tientsin, China"; (c) annotated by Woodward: "17.1.30. Probably Jurassic. Certainly not later than Cretaceous". Underlining in original by Teilhard.

In this letter Teilhard requested identification of an enclosed specimen of ganoid fish. Following this, Teilhard said:

. . . As you see I am back to China – just in time for supervising, with Dr. Black, the Chou-Kou-Tien excavations! Sinanthropus is in some way the Eoanthropus of the Far East [A]. But I think we want to know a little more about the real size of the brain [B] . . . I have received, here, your very kind letter of the November 13th. Many wishes for your excavations at Piltdown, and for a happy end of your work on the Lebanon fishes . . . [C].

[A] See notes to 5.1.31.

[B] This question was settled more definitely with the discovery on 2 December of an anatomically complete cranium (see Black 1929, 1934; Elliot Smith 1930c).

[C] In 1926 Woodward was invited by the American Museum in Beirut to study and arrange their collections of Cretaceous fish. With regard to Woodward's work at Piltdown it appears that between 1927 and 1928 he had made periodic visits (see DF 116/14 Edwards 18 August 1928). In this latter communication Wilfred Norman Edwards (1890-1956), a palaeobotanist and Assistant Keeper at the Natural History Museum, reported on wood fragments Woodward had recently (? date) extracted from the pit. Edwards likened these to charcoal from Neolithic hearths.

5.1.33 KP/RCS/Box KL1 Black 8 August 1929

(a) Davidson Black (1884-1934); (b) typewritten letter addressed to Arthur Keith at the Royal College of Surgeons, on printed stationery: "Department of Anatomy, Peking Union Medical College, Peiping, China"; (c) –.

We had a very interesting and worth while series of meetings in Java, as no doubt Elliot Smith will have told you [A]. His cordial backing after my presentation of the material at the Congress made all the difference in the world to its reception there. I tried to persuade him to come home via Peking and Siberia, but in view of the subsequent interruption of trans-Siberian traffic it is perhaps fortunate that he was unable to come north at this time [B].

[A] During April 1929 Elliot Smith had attended the Fourth Pacific Science Congress in Java.

[B] Later, in 1930, however, Elliot Smith was invited by the Trustees of the Rockefeller Foundation to visit the Peking Union Medical College which provided him with an opportunity to examine first-hand the Choukoutien site and the fossil hominid materials that had been recovered from this site, see Elliot Smith (1930a, 1930b, 1930c and 1930d).

5.1.34 WKG/AMNH Dart 28 February 1930

(a) Raymond Dart (1893-1988); (b) handwritten letter addressed to William King Gregory at the American Museum in New York City, on printed stationery: "University of the Witwatersrand, Johannesburg"; (c) –.

The dentition [of Australopithecus] is extravagantly human and is naturally a considerable support to the claims I originally made. The only thing I regret is that I am driven to conclusion of "non-Dryopithecine" origin, which run counter to your previously expressed opinions to some extent.

See Letter 5.1.35.

5.1.35 WKG/AMNH Gregory 3 May 1930

(a) William King Gregory (1876-1970); (b) carbon copy of letter addressed to Raymond Dart at the Anatomy Department of the University of the Witwatersrand, Johannesburg"; (c) –.

I appreciate also your friendly regret that you have not been able to agree with me as to the significance of the so-called "Dryopithecus pattern" of the molars of primitive man [A]. . . It is gratifying to realize, however, that sometimes even a radical difference in point of view and a lively criticism of opposing theories may coexist with sincere personal friendships and regard, as is the case with Professor Osborn and myself [B].

[A] See 5.1.36.

[B] See Gregory (1930a).

5.1.36 WKG/AMNH Gregory 3 May 1930

(a) William King Gregory (1876-1970); (b) carbon-copy of letter addressed to Davidson Black at the Peking Union Medical College; (c) –.

This brief note summarises the situation in human palaeontology at the beginning of the 1930s.

Dart has gone to the other extreme and tried to show that the Australopithecines are so far distinct from the modern anthropoids that the human-Australopithecine division must have branched off very far down, before the gibbon branch. Dart seems, in fact, to be blind to its other resemblances to the chimpanzees; just as the rest of the world were blind to its resemblances to man.

See 5.1.34 and 5.1.35.

5.1.37 KP/RCS/Box KL2 Osborn 11 May 1931

(a) Henry Fairfield Osborn (1857-1935); (b) typewritten letter addressed to Arthur Keith, on printed stationery: "American Museum of Natural History, New York"; (c) annotated by Osborn (Note E). Underlining in original by Osborn.

. . . I have been greatly enjoying your new volume on the antiquity of man [A], crowded as it is with your new splendid observations and comments and bringing us quite up to date among our ancestors.

Two points especially strike me. The first is that in your diagram you now take-off man and the anthropid apes from a common proto-anthropoid Oligocene stem [B]. This is most interesting to me and will be so to Dr. Gregory. This view of the separate descent of man and apes from proto-anthropoids is strongly supported in Schultz's recent monograph - a classic! [C].

I am assembling these phylogenies past and present for a brief popular article.

Second, you must allow much more time for the Pleistocene, namely, 1,000,000 years [D]. I now date the Piltdown man at 1,250,000 years from the very primitive <u>Archidiskon</u> [<u>Elephas</u>] <u>planifrons</u> with which he was found associated, certainly pro-Pleistocene [E] . . . [F]

[A] A reference to Keith's volume *New Discoveries Relating to the Antiquity of Man* which was published in April 1931.

[B] See diagram opposite frontispiece (Keith 1931), entitled "Diagrammatic synopsis of human evolution". Except for the addition of Australopithecus, this diagram is essentially the same as that published in *Antiquity of Man* (1925a).

[C] Adolph H Schultz (1891-1976), a Swiss anatomist at Johns Hopkins University, Baltimore. Schultz (1927a, 1927b), like Keith and Gregory (1927b, 1928a, 1930a, 1930b) favoured early divergence of the hominid lineage from a common hominoid stock. For further discussion of this viewpoint, see Bowler (1986), and Fleagle & Jungers (1982).

[D] In the first edition of *Antiquity of Man* (1915), Keith had adopted Sollas'estimate of 400-

500,000 years, but in the 1925 edition he reduced this by half. "Nothing has happened during the past five years to compel me to alter my later pronounced time chart," Keith wrote in 1931.

[E] Annotated (as a footnote) by Osborn: "See my new Ganometric (elephant molar enamel) time scale."

[F] See Osborn (1928b, 1930), and his posthumous monograph on the Proboscidea (1942).

5.1.38 DF 102 Teilhard de Chardin 17 May 1932

(a) Pierre Teilhard de Chardin (1881-1955); (b) typewritten letter addressed to Woodward, on printed stationery: "Musée Hoang Ho Pai Ho, Race Course Road, Tientsin, China"; (c) annotated by Woodward: "June 14th". Underlining in original by Teilhard.

. . . *As you know, perhaps, my last year has been almost entirely taken up by a journey in Chinese Turkestan with the "groupe Chine" of the Haardt-Citroen Expedition [A]. . .*

During my absence, the Choukoutien excavations went on successfully, and you know that, as a consequence of some observations made by Pei and myself before my departure, the Sinanthropus layers first supposed barren of industry, have yielded a rich series of stoney artifacts and burnt bones. Of course, I do not go so far as [to] recognize, with Breuil, a real bone industry [B]. . . but the stony implements are perfectly sure, and belong to a generalized Palaeolithic type. . . Black will give you the last pictures and the last views, in his lecture of December in London [C]. I shall perhaps be there also – my plan being to spend a few months in Paris, after September. I should be delighted to see you after such a long time. . . [D].

[A] For details see Cuénot (1965: 104–114) and Teilhard's summary in *La Géographie* (1932).

[B] L'Abbé Henri [Edouard Prosper] Breuil (1877-1961). See Breuil's article on the tool assemblages at Choukoutien (1931), and Teilhard de Chardin & WC Pei (1932).

[C] Black delivered the Croonian Lecture for 1932 in London (see Black 1934).

[D] Teilhard returned to Europe as planned where he remained until the end of 1933. According to Cuénot (1965: 139):
We know . . . that before Christmas (1932) he went to London, where he met Black. Of his English connections we know little. He had some friends at the British Museum and doubtless Oxford – old friends perhaps from his Hastings days, and new friends, assuredly, on account of his growing reputation, now, as a specialist in Far Eastern geology and palaeontology.

5.1.39 WKG/AMNH Gregory 21 January 1933

(a) William King Gregory (1876-1970); (b) carbon copy of letter addressed to Gerrit Smith Miller at the Smithsonian Institution ; (c) underlining in original by Gregory.

I welcome your note of January twenty eighth and confident that you will realize that I am not writing merely to "stir up the animals," but solely with the honest purpose of trying to change your point of view.
. . . I am not defending Elliot Smith, as I have not read his book [A]; I am merely pleading in general against your rulings about Pithecanthropus, Eoanthropus and Dryopithecus, and against the standards and criteria which you appear to be trying to establish [B]. For some years past I have held no opinions as to many of the ideas that you justly class as doubtful. For instance, the femur of Pithecanthropus may or may not belong with the skull top; the jaw referred to Eoanthropus may or may not belong with the skull. Nevertheless, when every concession has been made, the calvarium of Pithcecanthropus is a genuine fossil and its value and significance have been immensely heightened by the discovery of Sinanthropus.

Australopithecus is a superbly preserved fossil with nearly complete deciduous dentition and first permanent upper and lower molars of both sides. Possibly it would have grown up into an ape with almost chimpanzee-like jaws; but tooth by tooth, pattern by pattern, I think that you will see the many basic resemblances, on the one hand to Dryopithecus [sic] and the existing anthropoids, and on the other to man; also that *Australopithecus* as a whole strengthens the evidence from other sources that has sprung from an ancient anthropoid stock well above the level of the pronograde monkeys [C].

Let us leave all fossil anthropoids out of account for the moment and compare only the skeletons of recent man, anthropoids, lower primates, tree shrews etc. To me they present an array of evidence that man is a very highly specialized member of the Old World division, who has undergone many clearly visualized profound changes of function and structure. Point by point I regard Wood Jones's alleged "basal mammalian primitiveness of Man" as an (to him) "emotionally attractive hypothesis" which covers a lack of practical knowledge of the really primitive placental mammals of the Basal and Lower Eocene [D].

As to comparative anatomy of the brain, I do not claim expert knowledge but I do claim to be able to recognize significant similarities in patterns. In however many details one may criticize Elliot Smith or Tilney [E]. I take the resemblances between man and anthropoids figured in Tilney's Vol. II (e.g. pps. 1013, 1023, 1027, 670, and 816) as evidence that man and the anthropoids belong to a single superfamily [F].

Similarly, I take the resemblances in placentation recently pointed out in J.P. Hill's memoir as indicating a surprisingly close relationship between anthropoids and man [G].

As to the alleged resemblances in external genitalia between man and cebids, cited by Wilocki [sic], I may point to Pocock's quite different findings [H].

With thousands of such items of evidence for the reality of the superfamily bond between man and the anthropoid stock, I compare the diverse dentitions of the "*Dryopithecus*" lot and I homologize cusp by cusp and groove by groove [I]. Are not these also significant of common derivation, even though the foot of some *Dryopitheci* may well prove to be more simian than human?

Finally I come to the sacred doctrine of "Irreversibility". This is too vast a subject to be dealt with in a letter but I don't mind saying that my "thirty-odd years" study of fossil and recent vertebrates indicates to me that "evolutionary trends" are often merely "emotionally attractive hypotheses" for those who will not admit evidence for changes in the direction of evolution.

My general conclusion is that if we leave out hypothetical trends and take only positive characters in common, man and anthropoids are divergent derivatives of a stem anthropoid with a grasping hallux. To paraphrase Patrick Henry, "If this be emotionalism, make the most of it!" [J]

[A] A probable reference to Elliot Smith's then recent book: *The Search for Man's Ancestors* (1931b).

[B] For a review of Miller's views on human evolution, see his 1918 and 1929 papers.

[C] See Gregory (1922), (1927b), (1928a), (1934), (1938), and with Milo Hellman (1926), (1938) for an overview of his theoretical posture at this period in his career.

[D] Frederic Wood Jones (1879-1954). In contrast to Gregory, Jones believed humans were anatomically more primitive than any other Old World higher primate. He did not consider the tree shrews or lemurs to be primates. In his opinion the order Primates should be restricted to tarsiers and Anthropoidea, and had argued in his book *The Problem of Man's Ancestry* (1918) that the precursor of the human lineage had been a tarsoid creature (see 1919a, 1919b). His subsequent publications (e.g. 1923, 1928, 1929) had endeavoured to defend this position. Jones's views, however, met with considerable criticism, particularly from Gregory (1928b) and (1930b).

[E] Frederick Tilney (1875-1938).

[F] Tilney's 2 volume work is entitled *The Brain from Ape to Man* and was published in 1928. The book's Foreword was written by Henry Fairfield Osborn.

[G] James Peter Hill (1873-1954). See Hill's 1932 paper published in the *Transactions of the Royal Society*.

[H] George Bernays Wislocki (b 1892) and Reginald Innes Pocock (1863-1947). See Wislocki (1936) and Pocock (1920).

[I] See Gregory (1922), and Gregory & Hellman (1926).

[J] Patrick Henry (1736-1799), a Virginian lawyer and American revolutionary leader. In a speech at the Virginia Convention in May 1765, Henry said: "Caesar had his Brutus – Charles the First his Cromwell – and George the Third – ("Treason," cried the Speaker) . . . may profit by their example. If this be treason, make the most of it."

5.1.40 WKG/AMNH Miller 8 February 1933

(a) Gerrit Smith Miller (1869-1956); (b) handwritten letter addressed to William K. Gregory at the American Museum in New York on printed stationery: "Smithsonian Institution, U.S. National Museum, Washington, D.C.; (c) underlining in original by Miller.

After reading what you write I am impressed by the essential agreement of our reviews. I am fully in accord with your opinion that men and great apes are members of one superfamily, and that Wood Jones has failed to make a good case for his tarsian and primitive mammalian notions [A]. I also accept everything you say about all the structural resemblances that can be found when human teeth are compared with the teeth of great apes, living and fossil; and I admit that these resemblances, when combined with many others, point so conclusively to community of origin that the subject is no longer open to profitable argument.

It is only when we come to the nature of the relationship that we differ. I think that the members of a primate stock whose evolutionary progress has reached the very advanced stage represented by the great apes (from the living ones back to Dryopithecus) are related to man as cousins, and that a heavy burden of proof must be borne by him who would convincingly urge that there are direct human ancestors among them. You have declared that a direct line some 800,000 generations long connects Dryopithecus with the human remains found at Piltdown [B]. But, as I see it, your evidence (both published and in your letter) all favors cousinship instead of direct ancestry, and you have not successfully shouldered that burden of proof.

[A] See Note D: 5.1.39.

[B] See Gregory & Hellman (1926).

5.1.41 DF 102 Teilhard de Chardin 22 December 1933

(a) Pierre Teilhard de Chardin (1881-1955); (b) typewritten letter addressed to Woodward, on printed stationery: "The National Geological Survey of China, 9 Ping Ma SSU, West City, Peiping, China"; (c) underlining in original by Teilhard.

. . . You have received our short communication concerning the recent discoveries in the "upper cave" [A]. Since that time we have recovered a perfect skull, with its lower jaw and several limb bones . . . The cave . . . is now practically exhausted, and proves to be entirely independent from the much older looking Sinanthropus site. . .

I take this opportunity for telling you how much I have enjoyed this summer, to have such a long excursion with you and Lady Smith-Woodward [B].

[A] A probable reference to the collaborative report with W[en] C[hung] Pei (b 1904) published in 1933.

[B] In 1933 Woodward and his wife attended a meeting of the International Geological Congress in Washington. A highlight of the Congress was a post-meeting excursion to

California, Arizona, Dakota and Wyoming to visit geological sites. Teilhard apparently accompanied the Woodwards on this trip.

5.1.42 DF 116/36 Le Gros Clark 12 January 1934

(a) Wilfrid Edward Le Gros Clark (1895-1971); (b) handwritten letter addressed to Woodward, on printed stationery: "Department of Human Anatomy, University Museum, Oxford"; (c) –.

. . .*Are you in need of a manual worker at your excavations of the Piltdown site? If so I should be very glad to give a hand during the vacation sometime.*

While it is not known if Le Gros did assist Woodward at Piltdown, it is evident that his fascination with the Sussex site continued, see 5.2.2.

5.1.43 DF 102 Teilhard de Chardin 9 March 1934

(a) Pierre Teilhard de Chardin (1881-1955); (b) typewritten letter addressed to Arthur Tindell Hopwood (1897-1969), on printed stationery: "The National Geological Survey of China, 9 Ping Ma SSU, West City, Peiping, China"; (c) underlining in original by Teilhard.

. . . *I have read with great interest your description of the new Anthropoids of Kenya [A]. The "weakest" point in your conclusions (because based on no palaeontological evidence) is the idea that Central Asia might have been the place of formation for the human type. So long no traces of higher primates will be reported from the Pliocene formations of this part of the world, I will stick to the idea that Man is originally a tropical form (the tooth described by Sc[h]losser [B] from Ertente [sic] seems to me just as doubtful as Hesperopithecus!) [C]. But, of course, we have to be careful in such matters. Ten years ago, I should have sworn, also that no very ancient Man would ever be found in the Peking area.*

[A] A reference to Hopwood's paper on African Miocene fossil primates, in which he described *Proconsul africanus* (1933).

[B] The German palaeontologist Max Schlosser (1854-1932).

[C] For further details on *Hesperopithecus*, see 5.1.13 and 5.1.15. In 1923, Schlosser (see Note B) had described a tooth from Ertempte, Mongolia, attributing it to the species *Pliopithecus posthumus*. Teilhard was not alone in doubting this specimen, see Hürzeler (1954) and Piveteau (1957).

5.1.44 KP/RCS/Box KL1 Black 16 March 1934

(a) Davidson Black (1884-1934); (b) typewritten letter to Arthur Keith at Buckston Browne Farm, Downe, Farnborough, Kent, on printed stationery: "Department of Anatomy, Peking Union Medical College, Peiping, China"; (c) see Note F.

I have had my first bit of tiredness since I came to the East 15 years ago but I expect all to be well and going strong by the summer . . . Lincoln's Inn Fields will be a terrible place without you [A]. I know Beattie [B] and he's a good chap but I don't know what the place will do without you. I am so glad Harris [C] and Le Gros Clark [D] have got Cambridge and Oxford. They are the real kind of anatomists to carry on the traditions. As for my own future I expect to spend it mostly in Asia for I have great hope that when the "depression" is past I can get more funds to work in Baluchistan and Persia. . . The real history of the rise of neanthropic man (Pontian in age !!) won't be in Africa but in S.W. Central Asia I believe. The work Leakey has been doing is simply splendid and I know he will go ahead on it but the finding of neanthropic man in Kenya [E] is what one should expect in view of the Late Pliocene and Early Pleistocene tectonics of the Iranian plateau etc. . . [F]

[A] Due to ill-health, Keith was obliged to resign from his post as Conservator at the Royal College of Surgeons on 26 March 1933, whereupon he was installed as Master of the newly established Buckston Browne Research Farm at Downe. This research institute of the Royal College is situated on a thirteen acre estate that adjoin the grounds of Charles Darwin's former home, Down House. As Master of Buckston Farm, he was supplied a house (called Homefield) on the adjoining Down House estate. For further details on Keith's resignation and subsequent years at Downe, see his autobiography (1950).

[B] John Beattie (1899-1976), was Conservator at the Royal College from 1933 until 1942. See Note C: 5.1.16

[C] Henry Albert Harris (1886-1968). Prior to this appointment Harris had been liason officer between University College and University College Hospital, working under Grafton Elliot Smith. Harris is best remembered for his work on bone growth.

[D] Wilfrid Le Gros Clark (1895-1971), see 4.2.19-20 and 5.2.2.

[E] Louis Seymour Bazett Leakey (1903-1972). In addition to his work at Olduvai Gorge (see Leakey 1927, 1928, and Leakey, Hopwood & Reck 1931), Leakey had discovered by this time the Kanam jaw and Kanjera crania (see Leakey 1933).

[F] At the bottom of this unsigned letter, Black's wife, Adena, has handwritten the following note:

March 17th, 1934: My dear husband wrote this in pencil the last night of his life and went to his office on the 15th to sign it but his heart gave out before it could be done. He loved you and treasured your beautiful letter which we read together again. Thank you. Adena B.

5.1.45 DF 116/36 Woodward 29 August 1935

Arthur Smith Woodward (1864-1944); (b) handwritten letter to Dorothea M.A. Bate, Department of Geology, British Museum (Natural History), on printed stationery: "Hill Place, Haywards Heath, Sussex"; (c) underlining in original by Woodward.

Following your kind letter, I took the car to London yesterday and spent the afternoon with Mr. Marston [A]. I found that he and I had met at the Battersea Field Club, of which I am still president. His house has flints and bones spread everywhere, as he is a great enthusiast and he is not likely to allow the gem of his collection to depart yet for any museum. He had already shown the bone to Sir Arthur Keith and Mr. McCown [B], so my visit with him to the College of Surgeons was the second he had made to the place. I did not find out that until Mr. McCown walked up to us. Unfortunately the bone is not enough: we can only say that it is neither Piltdown nor ordinary Neanderthal. The Keithian verdict is that it belongs to H.sapiens, but I think that is most unlikely in the Acheulian age. It indicates another form of human skull in the Lower Pleistocene.

Mr Marston has agreed to show the fossil to Section H at Norwich, so I hope to be able to arrange this [C]. I am doubtful if he can speak to be heard, and whether he is capable of writing a scientific paper. There seems to be very little hope of finding more of the skull, but Mr. Marston still pays regular visits to Swanscombe, so we must wait for possible results. . . [D]

[A] Alvan Theophilus Marston (1889-1971), a London dentist and amateur archaeologist and palaeontologist. On 29 June 1935, Marston found, *in situ*, an almost complete and fossilized human occipital bone in association with Acheulean stone implements at Barnfield (gravel) pit, situated half a mile southwest of All Saints Church, near Swanscombe in Kent. From all indications his meeting with Woodward had been suggested by Miss Bate at the Museum. At this juncture the discovery had not been made public. It was not until October that news of the discovery was communicated by Marston to *Nature* (1935). For further details, see Marston (1936a).

[B] Theodore D. McCown (1908-1969). In 1931, McCown who was then a graduate student (and later a professor) at the University of California, Berkeley, began assisting Dorothy Garrod (1892-1968) in the excavations of the caves of Tabūn and Skhūl at Mount Carmel by the American School of Prehistoric Research. During the next three years these two caves were to yield a spectacular series of human skeletons exhibiting Neanderthal affinities. These remains and associated archaeological artifacts were described by McCown and Keith (1939). For further details on McCown and the Mount Carmel assemblage, see 5.1.53 and Day (1986).

[C] From all indications Woodward was able to arrange for Marston to exhibit the Swanscombe specimen at the BAAS meeting in Norwich (see Marston 1937a: 374).

[D] Woodward was wrong on both counts. Not only did Marston prove to be a most able and energetic communicator, the following year (15 March) he found the left parietal bone (Marston 1936a). The right parietal was not found until 1955 (see Wymer 1955). For further details on Marston and his discoveries at Swanscombe, see Letters 5.1.46-48, 50, 51, 52.

5.1.46 MHP/ DM-BMNH Marston 14 October 1935

(a) Alvan Theophilus Marston (1889-1971); handwritten letter to Martin Hinton at Natural History Museum, on printed stationery: "74 South Side, Clapham Common, London S.W.4"; (c) underlining in original by Marston.

A few weeks ago Dr. Corner [A] introduced me to you at the Royal Society's Club [B], and you kindly promised that if I sent the bones to you from Swanscombe, you would give them your personal attention.

The manner in which the pit face is worked has not given me the opportunity of doing much work at a time on the layer, but I have endeavoured to save everything that I could get. The layer is very rich but I doubt whether you can place any of the fragments as being human.

The symphysis of the elephant and the two teeth (which I take to be <u>E.antiquus</u>), occurred at the same height as the bone. If when you have examined the bones you will favour me with a report of the fauna, which I may quote, I shall be indebted to you [C].

P.S. The bones have been packed and Carter Patterson's have been asked to collect them.

P.S.S. Since the pit people have been very kind to me in allowing me to visit the pit, it would be much appreciated by them if you could send them an acknowledgement that you have received a box of bones from me. Mr. Cornhill is the manager at Barnfield.

[A] Frank Corner (1862-1939), a London physician and well-known amateur archaeologist and palaeontologist.

[B] Evidently a reference to the Royal Societies Club, located in St. James's Street, London S.W.1.

[C] For further details on the Swanscombe faunas see Hinton *et al.*(1938) and Ovey (1964). Between 1968 and 1970 the Swanscombe site was re-excavated. In addition to finding more worked flints, mammalian bones were also recovered which supported the view that the site dated from the close of the Second Interglacial (Mindel-Riss). Thermoluminescence dating suggests an absolute age of about 225,000 years (Bridgland *et al.*1985).

5.1.47 MHP/DM-BMNH Marston 21 December 1935

(a) Alvan T. Marston (1889-1971); (b) handwritten letter on printed stationery: "74 South Side, Clapham Common, London S.W.4"; (c) –.

I have completed my report on the Swanscombe occipital bone and have sent it to Sir Grafton Elliot Smith who is arranging for its publication [A].

I do not know whether you would wish your report on the fauna to go in with the same publication. I think that such would be desirable, owing to the important bearing which the new fossil has on the Piltdown remains, might I suggest that a comparison of the Piltdown fauna and of the Swanscombe fauna would be of interest. In my paper I have said that the anatomical features, the endo-cranial cast and the geological horizons indicate that Swanscombe is not only a more primitive type, but an earlier type than Piltdown – which is later than the Middle gravels of the 100 foot terrace [B].

A note too on the fauna of the London skull would be of like interest. . . [C]

[A] Elliot Smith was knighted in June 1934. From all accounts, just prior to the BAAS meeting in Norwich, Elliot Smith had on the basis of a preliminary study of the Swanscombe specimen agreed to supply a detailed study. Elliot Smith (quoted in Marston 1937a: 374) said that: "The exceptional size and form of the visual territories upon the two hemispheres of the endocranial cast, even if they suggest left-handedness are definitely Simian and point to a much more primitive stage than Eoanthropus. The new Kent skull although suggestive of the Piltdown is definitely more primitive." Unfortunately, during the opening months of 1936, Elliot Smith's already impaired health suffered a serious setback from which he never recovered. He died New Year's Day 1937. As a consequence of Elliot Smith's ill-health and the discovery of the parietal bone at Swanscombe in March of 1936, Marston abandoned his original publication plans and began work on his own descriptive analysis of the Swanscombe cranial remains (see Marston 1937a).

[B] As Marston (1936a: 201) noted: "While the geological horizon of Swanscombe as the fossil of the middle gravels of the 100-ft. terrace is authenticated and recognized by the Geological Survey, the Piltdown horizon has been referred to the 80-ft. terrace, the 50-ft. terrace, and the 100-ft. terrace. The presence of the "eoliths" or of the "bone implement" is not reliable evidence of a Pliocene or Early Pleistocene status for Piltdown . . ." Originally Dawson had estimated the height of the Piltdown gravels to be approximately 80-ft. above the River Ouse. Later, Sollas (1924:183), accepting this figure equated the terrace with those of the 100-ft. terrace. However, in 1925, Edmunds (see Letters 5.2.11 and 6.3.7) in his survey of the region, indicated that the true elevation was below the 50-ft level! This alone, Marston believed, was sufficient reason to invite an inquiry into the geological status of the Piltdown remains; but much to his surprise the suggestion failed to gather any support. As indicated by letter 5.1.51, Marston was by this time not only an ardent dualist, but also an advocate of downgrading the age of the cranial fragments (see Marston 1936b and 1937b). In 1937, largely as a result of his continuing agitations, a Committee of the Royal Anthropological Institute was formed to prepare an independent report on the Swanscombe finds, see Hinton *et al* (1938). See Letters 5.1.51 and 5.1.52 for further details on Marston's interpretation of the Swanscombe cranium and corresponding views on the Piltdown remains.

[C] As indicated by Marston's (1937a) paper, this comparative study was not undertaken. Instead the paper focused on the comparative differences and similarities between Swanscombe and Piltdown. For further details on the London skull, see 5.1.20.

5.1.48 MHP/DM-BMNH Hinton 30 December 1935

(a) Martin Alister Campbell Hinton (1883-1961); (b) carbon copy of typed letter to Alvan T. Marston; (c) –.

. . .I hope to prepare my report soon, but you will understand I am very much pressed with official work [A]. It would be well to revise the whole Swanscombe Fauna while I am about it; but that means finishing off the first big collection from that area – a job which I began nearly 35 years ago [B].

Your specimens will probably make it much easier to deal with some of the things which have puzzled me for a very long time.

By the "London Skull" I suppose you mean the "Lady of Lloyds." I must think about that. Hitherto I have regarded that skull, which I saw before the fuss started, as an ordinary Thames Alluvian specimen. It may of course be older but did not look it. The Rhinoceros bones from the same excavation came I think from a much older station [C].

[A] Hinton's notes on the Swanscombe fauna can be found in the "Report of the Swanscombe Committee" published in 1938, see Hinton *et al.* 1938.

[B] The primary emphasis of Hinton's research had been Pleistocene mammals and their use in stratigraphy and palaeoecology. Since the age of 16 his interest had focused on mammalian palaeontology and the light they shed on the Pleistocene history of the Thames valley. For further details on Hinton's career and bibliography, see Savage (1963).

[C] For further details on the London [Lloyd's] Skull, see 5.1.20.

5.1.49 DF 102 Teilhard de Chardin 5 March 1936

(a) Pierre Teilhard de Chardin (1881-1955); (b) typewritten letter to Woodward on printed stationery: "The National Geological Survey of China, 9 Ping Ma SSU, West City, Peiping, China"; (c) –.

You will be surprised to receive this letter of me [sic]. The reason of [sic] it is that I wish to give you a short personal account of the trip I made in India and Java during the past months.

Concerning India, nothing substantial to add to the report of de Terra [A] which is going to appear in one of the next numbers of Nature . . . [B]

In Java, I had the great pleasure of to meet young Dr. von Koenigswald [C] (a pupil of Brioli and Schlosser [D], presently palaeontologist in the Geological Survey of Bandoeng) . . . I will tell you nothing about the eleven skulls of H. soloensis (to be described soon by Dr. Mijeberg of Batavia), but these two things: 1) they are amongst the most astonishing human fossils I have ever seen, and 2) I am fully satisfied by their stratigraphical location. [E]

. . .Here, I have found Peiping in a most unstable condition. Still, we stick to the place (the Cenozoic Laboratory, I mean, the head office of the Survey has been moved to Nanking) and the Choukoutien excavations will be resumed next month. Dr. Weidenreich [F] is doing marvelous work on the old and new specimens of Sinanthropus, and is more and more astonished himself by the number of "primitive" features still impressed on the skull, jaws, and teeth of Peking Man. Several of his new publications will soon be published. [G]

[A] Helmut de Terra [1900-1981], a Research Associate of the Carnegie Institution of Washington and Associate Curator of Geology and Paleontology, Academy of Natural Sciences of Philadelphia.

[B] See de Terra (1936, 1937) and de Terra *et al.* (1936).

[C] GH Ralph von Koenigswald (1902-1982), German anatomist and human palaeontologist.

[D] Ferdinand Brioli (b. 1874) and Max Schlosser (see Note B: 5.1.43).

[E] Believed to be a reference to the Ngandong remains found in central Java between 1931 and 1933. See Day (1986: 358-362) for a general description of these remains.

[F] Franz Weidenreich (1873-1948), a German anatomist, who succeeded Davidson Black at the Peking Union Medical College.

[G] Between 1936 and 1945, Weidenreich published a series of detailed monographs on the Choukoutien remains. For further details, see Gregory (1949:251-267).

5.1.50 MHP/DM-BMNH Hinton 24 March 1936

(a) Martin A.C. Hinton (1883-1961); (b) carbon copy of letter to Alvan T. Marston; (c) –.

. . . I must congratulate you on finding the human parietal--bit by bit you will build up something good [A].

. . . My report is progressing, but I cannot tell you how long it will take to finish. The work is very complicated indeed [B].

[A] Reference to the discovery of the Swanscombe parietal by Marston on Sunday, 15 March 1936. For further details on this discovery, see Marston (1936a and 1937a).

[B] See Note A: 5.1.48.

5.1.51 DF 116/14 Marston 1 April 1936

(a) Alvan T. Marston (1889-1971); (b) typewritten letter to Arthur Smith Woodward at his home in Sussex, on printed stationery: "74 South Side, Clapham Common, London S.W.7"; (c) –.

From all indications this communication was prompted by a letter from Woodward that has not been preserved.

Friday April 3rd at the time mentioned in your letter will be quite convenient to me if still convenient to yourself.

If you could bring with you the scale contour lines of your Piltdown reconstruction, you would then see for yourself the differences as well as the resemblances, between it [Eoanthropus] and Swanscombe. There can be little doubt that the status of Piltdown will have to be revised; including the question of the canine tooth.

Since I feel that I have established a case for the rejection of the canine, and the matter will have to be thrashed out, I will let you see my evidence to the point when you come, because I feel that it would be better for the change of view which is bound to come, to come rather as a matter of concurrence of opinion based on the new knowledge which the new discovery has offered to the elucidation of which after all, not a great deal of certainty existed before, – than as a matter of controversy.

Piltdown cannot be earlier than Swanscombe, nor earlier than the Middle gravels of the 100 foot terrace. My opinion is that Piltdown is later, and certainly that if Swanscombe had been found first, Piltdown would have been accepted without question as an advanced Swanscombe type.

Do not think I am speaking boastfully, because I know that any fresh discovery may necessitate the re-orientation of previously accepted views, and moreover, because I know the re-orientation although it may be suggested by me will not be effected except by the judgement of science in general.

For background to this communication, see 5.1.45-47, and Marston's 1936b paper. Woodward's immediate reaction to Marston's proposition is not known. However, judging from his statements on Swanscombe published in his posthumous text *The Earliest Englishman* (1948) they were probably not substantially different from those expressed earlier in 5.1.45. See also Keith's assessment (5.1.54).

5.1.52 DF 116/51 Marston November 1936

(a) Alvan T. Marston (1889-1971); (b) copy of circulated printed notice; (c) underlining presumably by Marston.

NOTICE OF OPERATION

Eoanthropus dawsoni is about to undergo a major dental operation on Monday, November 23, at the next meeting of the Odontological Section of the Royal Society of Medicine at 8 p.m.

The operation will involve the extraction of the right lower canine tooth and the excision of the

*mandible. The condition of this tooth and of the mandible which has long been a serious problem, has
at length been accurately diagnosed.*

*After excision, it is proposed to offer the removed parts to the British Museum (Natural History) to
be placed in the section of fossil anthropoids. Eoanthropus has been so heavily doped, that no anaesthetic
will be considered necessary. Assistance may be needed, however, in holding the victim down.
Eoanthropus is expected to make a speedy return to convalescence. The prognosis is good. His mental
outlook will be more human. He will be less anti-social without a mandible which has prevented him
from eating and speaking like a human being.*

   Dental Surgeon: A.T. Marston, L.D.S.
Assistants: You.

According to Marston (1954: 14-16) this "Notice" was widely circulated at the British
Museum (Natural History), the Royal College of Surgeons, and at a number of the London
teaching hospitals; and from all indications he did give the demonstration. Although the
text of his paper was not published, it is conjectured that the argument presented to the
Royal Society of Medicine was not dissimilar to the approach he had taken in his article
published in the June issue of the *British Dental Journal* (1936b).

5.1.53 HP/NAA Keith 11 October 1937

(a) Arthur Keith (1866-1955); (b) handwritten letter to Hrdlička at the Smithsonian
Institution, on printed stationery: "Buckston Browne Research Farm, Downe,
Farnborough, Kent"; (c) –.

*I would like to submit an article to your Journal [A]. This is its nature. It gives a description of the
Swanscombe skull (Acheulean) and the light that this skull throws on the Piltdown skull and problem
[sic]. I've reconstructed the Piltdown skull on Swanscombe lines and it comes out nearly the same as
the reconstruction made by Elliot Smith in 1924 [B] – with some important exceptions. Ted [C] is now
busy with the text of the Palestinians for the press [D], I having done my share about 2 weeks ago. It
was then I turned to the Swanscombe skull – because, when the occipital was shown to me by its
discoverer 2 years ago [E] – I was struck be certain traits which I consider Piltdown[ian].*

   *It was Ted that suggested that I should send an account of my present research to you – for I should
have to wait 2 years to get it out in the J[ournal]. R[oyal]. A[nthropological]. I[nstitute]. . . . [F]*

[A] *American Journal of Physical Anthropology*, founded by Hrdlička in 1918.

[B] This reconstruction (made in collaboration with J.I. Hunter) was presented to the
Anatomical Society, London in May 1922, and published in the Society's *Proceedings* 1924-5
(See Note C: 5.1.16).

[C] Theodore D McCown, see Note B: 5.1.45.

[D] *The Stone Age of Mount Carmel* (1939), a thorough description and analysis of the fossil
hominids from the caves of Tabūn and Skhūl located near the port of Haifa. Although found
in the early 1930s, the description and analysis of this material had been delayed by the fact
that the skeletal material had first to be painstakingly extracted in the laboratory from the
hard limestone breccia in which they had been found. This extraction and cleaning process
took McCown several years. For a preliminary overview of this material, see the paper given
by Keith & McCown (1937) at the international symposium on "Early Man", held in
Philadelphia between 17 & 20 March 1937

[E] See 5.1.45.

[F] See Note B: 5.1.54.

5.1.54 HP/NAA Keith 19 December 1937

(a) Arthur Keith (1866-1955); (b) handwritten letter to Hrdlička at the Smithsonian Institution, on printed stationery: "Buckston Browne Research Farm, Downe, Farnborough, Kent"; (c) –.

Yesterday Ted McCown left for California [A]. . . . I did think I should have a M.S. to send to you by him but there have been so many delays that I have not even the illustrations finished [B]. . . . I may just mention briefly the chief conclusions I have come to about Swanscombe and Piltdown.

(1) They stand to each other as an early autombile does to a modern one – Piltdown being the early form.

(2) Swanscombe['s] absolutely intact occipital and left parietal gives a sure clue to all the points that have been in dispute in the reconstruction of Piltdown. The date of Swanscombe is uncertain – late Acheulian [C].

(3) There are many anthropoid features in the skull of Piltdown – as in the mandible – but these features are orangoid rather than chimpanzoid [D].

(4) This early development of humanity in England is of a kind as unlike the Neanderthal as can be . . ."

[A] Theodore D. McCown, see Note B: 5.1.45. McCown returned to the University of California, Berkeley.

[B] It is interesting to note, however, that Keith & McCown (1937) did find time to contribute a paper to the international symposium on "Early Man" held in Philadelphia in March, 1937. The proceedings of this symposium were edited by George Grant MacCurdy and subsequently published by Harvard University Press (1937). Furthermore, from all indications, Keith's Piltdown-Swanscombe manuscript was completed early in 1938, at which time he decided to submit it to the *Journal of Anatomy* rather than to the *American Journal Physical Anthropology* see Keith (1939).

[C] Compare this with Marston's viewpoint, see 5.1.47 and 5.1.51.

[D] Compare this with his earlier viewpoints (Keith 1925a, II: 637-660, 1931: 446-467). See also Note A: 5.2.13.

5.1.55 DF 116/50 Hinton 1938

(a) Martin A.C. Hinton (1883-1961); (b) copy of a typed draft of Hinton's "introduction" to the Swanscombe Committee Report [see Note B: 5.1.47]; (c) amendments written in ink by Hinton (see below).

The following is an extract from the Introduction of the Swanscombe Committee Report as amended by Hinton.

[In] (On) June 29, 1935, Mr. A. T. Marston, L.D.S. of Clapham, who had for some years visited the pit at regular intervals as a collector of palaeolithic implements, [was responsible for the discovery of] (obtained) [x/found] a fossil human occipital bone (which was first found by a workman) in the so-called Middle Gravels at (a) depth of 24 feet from the surface.

[ ] Words deleted from original by M.A.C.H; ( ) Words added by M.A.C.H; [x/] Words written and deleted by M.A.C.H.

The published version of the above passage reads:

"On June 29, 1935, Mr. A. T. Marston, L.D.S., of Clapham, who had for some years visited the pit at regular intervals as a collector of Palaeolithic implements, obtained a fossil human occipital bone in the so-called Middle Gravels at a depth of 24 feet (7 metres) from the surface" (Hinton et al. 1938:18).

In 1954, Kenneth Oakley, who had been a member of the original Swanscombe Research Committee, had his attention drawn to the wording of Hinton's first draft. In attempting to explain how the suggestion that the occipital bone was found by someone other than Marston had ever come to be made, Oakley could only say that the suggestion represented "an error (due to some misunderstanding) which we put right in the correction of the galley proof" (DF 116/50 Oakley to Christopher Hawkes, Keble College, Oxford 13 March 1954). There remains, however, the possibility that Hinton's first draft was a warning to Marston to desist from undermining Piltdown, see Spencer (1990) for further details and discussion of this episode. It should be noted that the Report of the Swanscombe Committee concluded that "there can be no doubt that the Swanscombe skull is an indigenous fossil of the gravels of the 100-ft. Terrace of the Thames. It is this the first completely authenticated skull from a known Acheulean horizon" (Hinton *et al.* 1938: 19). In addition to Hinton and Oakley, other members of the Committee included: Le Gros Clark, Christopher F.C. Hawkes, William B.R. King (1889-1963) and Geoffrey M Morant (1899-1964).

5.1.56 KP/RCS/Box KL2 Woodward 14 June 1938

(a) Arthur Smith Woodward (1864-1944); (b) handwritten letter to Arthur Keith on printed stationery: "Hill Place, Haywards Heath, Sussex"; (c) –.

Could you come someday in July to do the formal unveiling of a monolith memorial at Piltdown to Charles Dawson and the defunct lady? I am trying to arrange a little ceremony then or sometime later. If July is inconvenient, could you come at any time in August or September?

Keith replied that he could, and on 23 July unveiled the memorial to Dawson [A]. The inscription carved on the slender monolith (made of durable carboniferous sandstone from Yorkshire) reads:

> HERE IN THE OLD RIVER GRAVEL MR CHARLES DAWSON, F.S.A. FOUND THE FOSSIL SKULL OF PILTDOWN MAN 1912-1913
> THE DISCOVERY WAS DESCRIBED BY MR CHARLES DAWSON AND SIR ARTHUR SMITH WOODWARD IN THE QUARTERLY JOURNAL OF THE GEOLOGICAL SOCIETY [B]

[A] The text of Keith's speech can be found in *Nature* (1938) 142:196-197. The unveiling ceremony was followed by a reception held in the garden of Barkham Manor. Among the invited guests were: Brigadier General E.G. Godfrey-Faussett (Chairman of Council, Sussex Archaeological Society [SAS]); Elliot Curwen (Vice-Chairman, SAS, see Note A: 6.3.17); Miss Marion H. Cooper (Hon. Sec., SAS), Dr & Mrs F. Bentham Stevens (SAS); Mr & Mrs Walter H. Godfrey (Council, SAS); Arthur Hill (SAS); E. Cecil Curwen (SAS, see Note B: 6.3.17, 6.3.39); Mary S. Holgate (SAS); Wyndham Hulme (SAS); Scott Pitcher; Lady Chance (Leigh Manor); Dr Sidney Spokes (Lewes); Percival Bridgman; F.W. Mizeod (Worthing Archaeological Society); R.H. Burne (Keith's former assistant at the Royal College of Surgeons, see Keith 1950:291-292); Dr Frank Corner (see 2.3.13); Dr & Mrs Elliot Smith (son of late G.E.S.); Mrs Gordon (sister of Charles Dawson); Mr & Mrs John Kenward and Miss M. Kenward; Mrs Howell; Major & Mrs Holland (assisted Woodward at Piltdown in late 1920s and early 1930s); Dr & Mrs Lucas (Bramblehurst); Dowager Countess Brentford (Newick Park); Miss Shenstone (Sutton Hall); Rev. R.W. Burns-Cox; Miss Sylvia Seeley (Canadian School of Prehistory); and Sir Arthur & Lady Smith Woodward.

[B] The memorial was designed by Percival Bridgman of Lewes, see Fig. 5.2. The cost of the memorial was covered by private subscription. The first subscription was received from Henry Fairfield Osborn (5.1.22). The site was later recommended for preservation as a national monument, see 5.2.27 and Report of Wild Life Conservation Special Committee 1947, cmd 7122, p.105. Item GM 31.

Fig 5.2 Woodward at the unveiling of the Piltdown monument (1938). Courtesy of the Trustees of the British Museum (Natural History).

5.1.57 KP/RCS [SC II] Jones 11 February 1939

(a) Frederic Wood Jones (1879-1954); (b) typewritten letter to Arthur Keith on printed stationery: "Anatomy Department, The University, Manchester"; (c) – .

The following extract essentially summarizes the situation in palaeoanthropology as it appeared to many at the beginning of the Second World War.

. . . It seems to me that this business of human phylogeny is becoming highly complex. We seem to be getting so many dead ends hanging about – phyla that lead to nowhere – and all over the world at that. The South African series must be a blind side-line, and now you put Piltdown and Swanscombe off the main line – where are we to look for the real ancestral line? I am getting all mixed up.

5.2   After the War (1946-1952)

In the years immediately following the war, Alvan Marston (see Section 5.1) continued to promote the dualist cause ([1946, see fn 4; 1947] 1950, 1952), and it was largely in the context of this renewed attack on the Sussex chimaera that Kenneth Page Oakley, a geologist and palaeontologist at the British Museum (Natural History), began his investigations in 1947 that were to provide new insights into the controversy which ultimately were to lead to the exposure of the fraud some six years later.

At a meeting of the Geologists' Association in London during June of 1947, Marston had delivered a paper in which he reiterated his earlier arguments for the separation of the mandible from the Piltdown cranium (1936, 1937a, 1937b). Like Miller (1918) and Hrdlička (1922), he was convinced the Piltdown mandible and the associated canine belonged to a genuine fossil anthropoid ape. The cranial fragments on the other hand were regarded, from both an anatomical and a geological perspective, as having belonged to a relatively recent specimen. Compared to the Swanscombe skull, from a strictly anatomical viewpoint and contrary to the views of Keith (1939), Marston considered the endocranial morphology of the Sussex specimen a more advanced type than the one from Kent[1]. The case for downgrading the geological antiquity of the Piltdown cranium was also grounded in the comparison with the Swanscombe site.

The investigatory committee of the Royal Anthropological Institute had determined that the Swanscombe skull was an indigenous fossil of the 100-ft Terrace, belonging to the interglacial deposits of the Mindel-Riss (Oakley, in Hinton et al. 1938). Although the Piltdown gravels had originally been attributed to the 100-ft Terrace (Dawson & Woodward 1913a; Sollas 1924:183), this had been shown to be an erroneous correlation by Francis H. Edmunds (1893-1960) of the Geological Survey. In 1925, while surveying the region, Edmunds had determined that the true elevation of the Piltdown gravels was not 100-ft O.D. but rather below the 50-ft level (in White 1926: 68, fig 10). This finding, combined with the apparent survival of fragile turbinal and nasal bones in the Piltdown gravels (see Section 2.4), strongly supported the view, so Marston believed, that the mandible was adventitious and had been transported along with the other older fauna in the assemblage by natural processes from another locality and introduced into the deposit during its formation in either the Riss-Würm interglacial (i.e. Middle Pleistocene) or possibly even later[2]. To further support his case for the comparative modernity of the Piltdown cranial fragments, he claimed that their deep chocolate colour was misleading because they (unlike the mandible) had been treated with a bichromate preservative solution. Their original colour, like most post-glacial bone from this region, he contended, had been grey!

Although it was a matter of public record[3] that the first cranial fragments found at Piltdown had been treated by Dawson with a solution of potassium bichromate, there was every indication that later fragments, and in particular the occipital fragment found in situ by Woodward during the summer of 1912, had not been treated in this manner. The fact that its colour matched that of the other fragments, argued strongly against Marston's proposal. But while this aspect of Marston's presentation failed to gather support, his account of the anatomical and geological difficulties that continued to surround the Piltdown remains, elicited the interest of Oakley (see fn 4). In the discussion that followed Marston's presentation at the Geologists' Association meeting in 1947, Oakley recalled the work of Middleton (1844) and Carnot (1893) who had shown that the fluorine content of fossil bone increases with geological age, and suggested that the application of the fluorine estimation test to the Piltdown remains might throw light on their relative antiquity[4].

To test the validity of his hypothesis, Oakley chose to initially compare the much disputed Galley Hill remains with those of Swanscombe, both of which had been found in the same vicinity of Kent. The results were stunning and demonstrated quite conclusively that indigenous bones in the Middle Pleistocene gravels at Swanscombe contain around 2.0 per cent fluorine, whereas those from Upper Pleistocene gravels in the same region have around 1.0 per cent, and post-Pleistocene bones less than 0.3 per cent. The Galley Hill remains, although found in Middle Pleistocene gravels, proved to contain only small amounts of fluorine – the figures hovering in the region of 0.2 to 0.4 per cent. The conclusion was clear, the Galley Hill remains were not indigenous to the Middle Pleistocene, but an intrusive burial, probably dating, at the earliest, from the end of the Pleistocene. The results of this initial study were communicated by Oakley to Section H of the British Association in Brighton on 9 September 1948 [5].

Armed with these results, Oakley secured permission from the Museum authorities to extend his tests to the entire Piltdown assemblage (Letter 5.2.5), which were performed under the direction of C.R. Hoskins in the Government Laboratory, London. The preliminary results of these tests became available during the summer of 1949[6], and later summarized in an article published in *Nature* the following March (Oakley & Hoskins 1950). Briefly, all of the undoubted Villafranchian (i.e. Lower Pleistocene) fauna [namely *Elephas, Mastodon,* and *Rhinoceros*] in the assemblage were shown to have a fluorine content ranging from 1.9 to 3.1 per cent, while the post-Villafranchian fauna ranged from 0.1 to 1.5 per cent. The fluorine content of the teeth and bones of *Eoanthropus* I and II ranged from 0.1 to 0.3 per cent!

In his discussion of these results, Oakley argued that the wide range in fluorine content in the post-Villafranchian fauna was consistent with the view that the Piltdown gravels had been reconstructed on several occasions (see fn 7) and evidently had involved the introduction of new mammalian remains. Based on the available palaeontological evidence, he confessed it was impossible to determine whether the "final settlement" of the deposit had taken place in the Middle or early Upper Pleistocene times (Oakley & Hoskin 1950:382). Although the fluorine values of the various *Eoanthropus* remains clearly showed that they did not belong with the Villafranchian group, it appeared reasonable to assume that they belonged with the latest elements in the faunal mixture (i.e. the *Castor* remains[7]), Oakley said, and to "ascribe them to the period immediately preceding the final re-arrangement of the gravel, since which time free fluorine ions have apparently been remarkably deficient in the ground-water" (Oakley & Hoskins 1950:382). But while the timing of this event remained unclear, the results precluded the possibility of it having been earlier than the Middle Pleistocene. Furthermore, Oakley said, the results seemed to favour the conclusion that: "All the specimens of *Eoanthropus*, including the remains of the second skull found two miles away, are contemporaneous" (Oakley & Hoskins 1950:381).

Although Oakley continued to defend the integrity of the Piltdown remains (e.g. 5.2.15) it is evident from his continuing investigations (5.2.19, 5.2.23) that he was far from comfortable with the new situation he had created. Now, whether viewed from either a monistic (Broom 1950; Weinert 1953 [see also Letter 5.2.24]) or a dualistic perspective (Marston 1952, 1954a, 1954b; Montagu 1951a), the remains were a puzzling evolutionary anomaly (see introduction to Section 6.1). It was, however, another two years before this new dilemma was resolved.

NOTES

[1]   As indicated by Letter 5.1.54, Keith considered Swanscombe a derivative of Piltdown, that was evolving in the direction of anatomically modern Homo sapiens. In the Swanscombe Committee report, Geoffrey Morant (1899-1964) had shown that the metrical characters of the Swanscombe cranial bones were essentially indistinguishable from those of modern Homo sapiens (Hinton *et al.* 1938). But while the general form of this skull was undeniably modern, there were certain other features, including the very great thickness of the bones, which argued against its "recent" character.

[2]   In 1935 Arthur Hopwood had re-examined the entire Piltdown assemblage. Based largely on the condition and colouring of the specimens, he concluded that the human remains belonged with the derived

"Villafranchian" (i.e. Pliocene-Pleistocene boundary) remains. Also, it should be noted that many workers at this time regarded the Riss-Würm as being synonymous with the early Upper Pleistocene.

3   Indeed in 1935 when Hopwood had re-examined the Piltdown assemblage (see fn 5), he noted that: "Mr. Dawson soaked the first pieces in a solution of bichromate of potash to harden them! The remaining pieces were not so treated and retain their original colour." See also Letter 5.1.28.

4   From all accounts Oakley had chanced upon the references to the work of Middleton and Carnot during the war when he had been temporarily assigned to the Geological Survey to investigate sources of phosphate for use as a fertilizer. Later, in January, 1947, Oakley had attended the first Pan-African Congress on Prehistory and Pleistocene Studies held in Nairobi. During this conference Oakley became involved with L.S.B. Leakey and the problem associated with the remains he had found in the Kanjera-Kanam region in the early 1930s (5.1.44). Like Piltdown the antiquity of these African specimens was a matter of dispute. In an effort to resolve this issue, Oakley had suggested that fluorine analysis might offer a solution, and on returning to Britain he had arranged for the tests to be performed by the Home Office Forensic Science Laboratory. The results (see Oakley 1951) were disappointing, showing that the method "is not applicable where fluorine is excessively abundant." At the annual meetings of the British Association for the Advancement of Science in Dundee in August 1947, however, Oakley elaborated further on the method, noting that the fluorine content of bones from a limited area, such as at Piltdown or from contiguous sites, could, with reservations, be used to determine the contemporaneity or otherwise of fossils found in physical association (Oakley 1948). From the available evidence it is not at all clear to what extent Marston's agitations prompted Oakley to investigate the potential of the fluorine technique. In the minds of many contemporary observers, however, Marston was viewed as the catalyst – a notion Oakley later rejected claiming that the Kanjera-Kanam problem had been the prime-mover. It should be noted that Marston reopened his attack on Piltdown at a meeting of the Geologists' Association (London) on 5 July 1946. On this occasion he based his argument on Edmunds's earlier survey of the Piltdown site (see Marston 1950). This was followed by his presentation to the same organization in 1947 (see above text). For further discussion on this issue, see Spencer 1990.

5   The results of this investigation can be found in the collaborative paper by Oakley & Montagu published by the British Museum in 1949.

6   As indicated by Letter 5.2.9, Oakley had communicated these preliminary findings to the British Association meetings in Newcastle in early September; followed by a more complete summary presented first at a meeting of the Oxford University Anthropological Society on 2 November and then at a meeting of the Geological Society of London on 14 December 1949. It is interesting to note that just prior to these announcements, Marston had questioned, in a paper he read before the Royal Anthropological Institute on 6 June 1949, why the fluorine estimation test had not been extended to the Piltdown remains.

7   Specifically, Oakley had written: "The fluorine results are, in fact, so consistent with the known or probable relative dates of the mammalian fossil in the Piltdown mélange, that it now appears justifiable to regard *Eoanthropus* and *Castor fiber* as the latest elements in the mixture." This, Oakley noted, correlated with Dawson's earlier view: "Putting aside the human remains and those of the beaver [*Castor*], the remains all point to a characteristic land fauna of the Pliocene age; and though all are portions of hard teeth, they are rolled and broken. The human remains on the other hand . . . are not rolled, and the remains of the beaver are in a similar condition. It would therefore seem that the occurrence of these two individuals belong to one of the periods of reconstruction of this gravel" (Dawson & Woodward 1914a:86).

CORRESPONDENCE

5.2.1 DF 116/27 Kennard 17 May 1946

(a) Alfred S. Kennard (1870-1948); (b) handwritten letter to S. Hazzledine Warren, stationery embossed: "Benenden, 161 Mackenzie Road, Beckenham [Kent]"; (c)–.

See Letter 6.2.5 for details on Warren.

. . . Its a long time since I saw the Piltdown Pub[lication]s and my views were stated rather mildly [A]. Besides I hadn't the experience at Swanscombe which I have had since. I know in the past I have accepted flints as human which I would not now. But the Eo[lith]s to me were always natural [B]. . . I have always thought it was a great pity that someone didn't speak out about Piltdown and the unsatisfactory nature of the evidence. But ASW was an authority and who were you or I to challenge his conclusions backed as they would be by the Nat. Hist. Officials. I know Hinton was not satisfied but he had his job to think over [C]. However truth will out. . .

[A] Dawson & Woodward (1913a, 1914a, 1915a), and Woodward (1917).

[B] Kennard's somewhat sceptical views on the Piltdown implement are indicative of this posture (see Kennard, in Dawson & Woodward (1915a:149). Warren's antieolithophilic views were a matter of public record, see for example his attack on Reid Moir in 1921.

[C] For details on Hinton, see 6.3.18.

5.2.2 DF 116/36 Le Gros Clark 12 August 1946

(a) Wilfrid Edward Le Gros Clark (1895-1971); (b) typewritten letter to Clive Forster Cooper (1880-1947), Director of the British Museum (Natural History), on printed stationery: "Department of Human Anatomy, University Museum, Oxford"; (c) annotated by Cooper: "Answd. 18 August '46. Type specimens not allowed out of Museum – Trustees regulations. CFC"

This letter from Le Gros Clark at Oxford informed Forster Cooper of a pending crystallographic study of bone, and requested permission to extend their investigations to the Piltdown and Rhodesian specimens [A]. The work was to be done by Joseph S. Weiner, a South African physical anthropologist who had been trained in anthropology under Dart at the University of the Witwatersrand in Johannesburg. For further details on Weiner, see Harrison & Collins (1982). As indicated by Forster-Cooper's annotation, the Museum declined to co-operate.

[A] The Rhodesian [Kabwe] skull was first described by Woodward (1921) as "Homo rhodesiensis". Later, Pycraft (1928) reclassified the remains as "*Cyphanthropus rhodesiensis*"! For further details on this material, see Day (1986: 267–271).

5.2.3 DF 116/36 Harden 11 March 1948

(a) D[onald] B[enjamin] Harden (b 1903); (b) typewritten letter to Kenneth Oakley on printed stationery: "British Association for the Advancement of Science, Burlington House, London W.1"; (c) underlining in original by Harden.

At this time Harden was attached to the Department of Antiquities, Ashmolean Museum, Oxford and was Recorder for Section H of the British Association.

I am wondering whether you would have anything further to say about the results of your fluorine investigations of Piltdown man at the British Association meeting this year in Brighton [A]? I have had a letter from one Alvan Marston offering us a paper on Piltdown. For your confidential information he gives the following synopsis of his proposed paper:

"The paper would be in the nature of a complete debunking of the Eoanthropus status; would give <u>proof</u> that the mandible and canine tooth did not belong to Piltdown Man but to a fossil ape and as such could not be used for dating Piltdown Man; and would show that the age of the Piltdown deposits as judged by the Terrace Shelf on which they rest is not early Pleistocene but Upper Pleistocene.

The Piltdown cranium has no anthropoid features whatever, but each fragment when examined individually . . . would be shown to correspond closely with the actual man of today. [B]"

I have consulted our physical anthropologists here and their advice is that Marston's proposals do not seem to include anything very new, but if you could lead off with a fluorine paper and Marston be invited to give a short talk afterwards along the lines he suggests, we might have an interesting session [C]. . .

[A] In 1947, at the Dundee meetings of the British Association, Oakley had mentioned his intention of applying a fluoride estimation test to the Piltdown problem. For further details, see introductory notes to Section 5.2.

[B] Alvan Theophilus Marston, a London dentist and amateur archaeologist who discovered the Swanscombe skull in 1935, see Section 5.1. For further details on Marston's campaign against the Piltdown remains, see introduction to Section 5.2.

[C] According to the programme for the British Association meetings, Oakley did contribute a paper entitled "On the application of the fluorine test to Galley Hill". Marston's name does not appear in the programme.

5.2.4 DF 116/36 Le Gros Clark 20 July 1948

(a) Wilfrid Edward Le Gros Clark (1895-1971); (b) typewritten letter to Kenneth Oakley on printed stationery: "Department of Human Anatomy, University Museum, Oxford"; (c) –.

. . . I am extremely interested to hear the results of the fluorine analysis which you have so far got. They seem to me to be of quite outstanding importance. I don't think I had heard of the Galley Hill [A] before, which I suppose make it practically certain that the skull was not contemporaneous with the gravels in which it was found. With the results you have already obtained, you ought to be able to get permission without much difficulty for some bony material from the Piltdown fragments [B]. I should be very excited to hear the result of any analysis of these. . .

[A] For further details on the Galley Hill skull, see Note B: Letter 2.3.13. The results of the fluorine tests on this skull can be found in Oakley & Montagu (1949).

[B] See 5.2.5.

5.2.5 DF 116/36 Oakley 23 July 1948

(a) Kenneth Page Oakley (1911-1981); (b) carbon copy of typewritten letter to Le Gros Clark at Oxford; (c) letter initialled "K.P.O".

. . . The Keeper [A] is anxious that a re-examination of the Piltdown material (human and other) should now be undertaken, and the results published by the Museum. The staff of the Government Chemist's Laboratory is prepared to undertake further work along the lines of that carried out on the Galley Hill skeleton. They have now perfected a chemical technique for determining <0.1% F in 10 mg of bone, so it should be quite possible to apply it to the Piltdown specimens. The Keeper asks me to enquire whether you think that Dr. Weiner and his crystallographic associates would still be prepared to report on the crystalline structure of these (and other fossil human bones) [B] . . .

[A] Wilfred Norman Edwards (1890-1956), Keeper of Geology from 1938-1956. After 1956 the department was renamed Palaeontology.

[B] See 5.2.2.

5.2.6 DF 116/36 Le Gros Clark 24 July 1948

(a) Wilfrid Edward Le Gros Clark (1895-1971); (b) typewritten letter to Kenneth Oakley on printed stationery: "Department of Anatomy, University Museum, Oxford"; (c) letter signed "Le Gros".

I am very interested to hear that you have really got permission to analyse the Piltdown specimens. Weiner is in South Africa at the moment, but I will enquire with him whether he is prepared to make a crystallographic study at the same time . . .

5.2.7 AK/RCS/Box KL2 Oakley 21 September 1948

(a) Kenneth Page Oakley (1911-1981); (b) typewritten letter to Arthur Keith on printed stationery: "British Museum (Natural History), Cromwell Road, London S.W.7"; (c) –.

. . . I am now investigating a method of establishing the relative dating of fossil bones by their fluorine-content. Working in collaboration with staff at the Government Chemist's Laboratory, I have applied the test to the Galley Hill skeleton with striking result as you will see from the enclosed summary of results [A].

I wish now to apply the test to other human skeletal remains of doubtful antiquity. I should be grateful for any suggestions which you can make in this connection.

In particular I should like to find out the present whereabouts of the Halling Skeleton [B]. Do you happen to know? . . .

[A] It is conjectured that Oakley had sent Keith a copy of the paper he had read the Brighton BAAS meetings.

[B] This was a skeleton found in a brick earth terrace in the Medway valley at Halling, near Rochester, Kent, in 1912. Keith had described these remains in a report published in 1914 by the Royal Anthropological Institute and had contended that the skeleton belonged to an early "Palaeolithic Englishman" dating from the Upper Pleistocene. For further details on this find and his interpretation, see Keith (1914e, 1915:71, 1925a,I:114).

5.2.8 AK/RCS/ Box KL2 Armstrong 1 October 1948

(a) A. Leslie Armstrong; (b) handwritten letter to Arthur Keith on plain stationery: "27 Victoria Road"; (c) underlining in original by Armstrong.

Armstrong was an amateur archaeologist, see Keith's autobiography (1950:631). The following letter provides (presumably at Keith's request) a summary of the activities of Section H of the British Association meeting held at Brighton earlier in September.

. . . A paper of exceptional interest was that given by Dr Kenneth Oakley on "The Application of the Fluorine-test to the Galley Hill skeleton" [A]. I enclose an abstract (for your retention) of this paper, which gives the result of the tests. They are startling! How far they are to be relied upon, I don't know, and whether a fluorine test is to be deemed conclusive evidence in regard to dating? It is claimed that it is,·and that it will prove as important for bones as pollen analysis has for the dating of peat.

In regard to Galley Hill Man and other remains which it is proposed to test, it occurs to me that consideration should be given to the fact that the bones would almost certainly be treated soon after discovery with a strong solution of hot, perhaps boiling, size [B], or other preservative. I am not a chemist so am ignorant as to what affect [sic] this treatment might have upon the fluorine content, but it might perhaps lower that very considerably? Oakley has no doubt thought of this and perhaps experimented to test the affect [sic], but I am raising the question with him. He hopes to "test" the Halling Man, if he can locate the remains and he proposes to test the Piltdown jaw and skull fragments and the animal remains from Piltdown and see if that throws any light upon the suggestion that the Pliocene bones are derived. If the process is really reliable this investigation should prove valuable [C].
. .

[A] See Note A: 5.2.7. For further details on the Galley Hill Skull, see notes to Letter 2.3.13 and Oakley & Montagu (1949).

[B] "Size" is a gelatinous solution used in glazing paper and stiffening textiles etc.

[C] See 5.2.16.

5.2.9 DF 116/36 Wells 9 September 1949

(a) Lawrence Herbert Wells (1908-1980); (b) handwritten letter to Oakley on printed stationery: "University of the Witwatersrand, Medical School, Hospital Street, Johannesburg"; (c) underlining in original by Wells.

Wells was then Reader in human palaeontology at the Witwatersrand Medical School.

. . . The local papers during the last few days have been carrying more or less garbled accounts of your results on Piltdown and other fossils [A]. The one point I was really able to take hold of is that you definitely assign the Piltdown skull and jaw to one period. (The reports made you assign them to one individual, which doesn't sound quite right). So I take the position to be that it has not been found that they are not one individual. This throws the question of whether they are or are not back on to the morphologist. As I told you I have come round to taking Marston a bit more seriously than I used to. . .[B]

[A] A reference to Oakley's paper read to the BAAS meeting in Newcastle on the application of the fluorine estimation test to the Piltdown problem. As Oakley explained in a letter to J. Curnow dated 26 September 1949 (DF 116/36): "The F test has shown that (1) the mandible is of the same age as the cranium (2) *Eoanthropus* does not belong with the Lower Pleistocene elements in the Piltdown melange, but is among the least old in the Middle to Upper Pleistocene group . . ."

[B] On 14 June 1949, Marston had read a paper at the Royal Anthropological Institute in which he reiterated the arguments he had made in 1947 that called for a downgrading of the antiquity of the Sussex specimen (see introductory notes to Section 5.2, and Marston 1950:294). The paper was widely reported in the popular press. In the *Daily Mail* story (15 June 1949), Lawrence Wells is quoted as saying: " I think he [Marston] has made a case that has got to be answered. It is difficult in the light of what we now know of early types of man to give any satisfactory place in anthropological sequence to this Piltdown jaw." It is interesting to note that Weiner harboured a similar view which he shared with Oakley when the latter had presented these results in a lecture at the Oxford University Anthropological Society on 2 November 1949, see Weiner, *in* Harrison (1983).

5.2.10 DF 116/19 Broom September 1949

(a) Robert Broom (1866-1951); (a) a handwritten 5 page report made by Broom following a visit to the Natural History Museum in the Spring of 1949 [see DF 116/19 Broom 21 August and 29 October 1949]; (c) underlining in original by Broom, and as indicated below edited by both, Broom and Oakley.

This report is concerned with the so-called Barcombe Mills materials, see 2.3.21. A summary of Broom's report was later given by Oakley to Section H of the BAAS at its meeting in Newcastle on September 5, 1949. Following a brief synopsis of the Piltdown materials, Broom notes that the Barcombe Mills material was presented to the Museum in January 1917. Deleted from the text is the passage: "Dr K.P. Oakley came across the skull in the British Museum where it had lain undisturbed for some 30 years. He hopes to apply the Fluorine test and to be able to prove that the skull is of great antiquity and possibly contemporaneous with the other Piltdown skulls." This deletion was made by Oakley. Broom then goes on to state:

. . . The skull had been found by Dawson in gravel on top of the hill above Barcombe Mills railway station, north of Lewes. [*/I took a run down to Barcombe Mills; but rain came on and I was unable to go to this spot]. Piltdown deposits are found in this area, as noted by Dawson in 1912.

The frontal bone is large, wide and high. The inter-temporal measurement is 102 mm. The interorbital width is 28.5 mm. The frontal fragments of skulls 1 and 2 might readily have belonged to such a frontal. . . The only tooth we have is a degenerate molar which is possibly the 3rd lower right.

. . . The three skulls all probably belong to one species Eoanthropus dawsoni. If so, then [x/we must conclude] it seems probable that this large brained type of primitive man evolved on quite a different line from Homo, and did not pass through an Australopithecine stage. The simian shelf in the Piltdown jaw is possibly a parallel development and not an indication of any affinity with the chimpanzee and gorilla; and the brain a parallel development to what we find in the Homo line.

Smith Woodward probably considered the Barcombe Mills skull as a recent skull of no particular scientific value, and he made no reference to it in his little book "The Earliest Englishman" published in 1948 after his death. As it appears an antique skull and from Piltdown gravels, [x/ and thus a very early type of human skull], it seems worthy of rather intensive study in connection with the two previously known Piltdown skulls and also with the Swanscombe skull [A].

As a lawyer at odd moments in a few years discovered remains of these early human skulls in the Piltdown deposits [sic] , it seems probable that any good fossil hunter would make some wonderful discoveries in a few weeks [B].

[x/] Written and deleted by Broom.

[A] For a quite different assessment of the Barcombe Mills material, see the report by Ashley Montagu (1951b). Montagu considered the remains represented more than one individual and of a "neanthropic type." Although noting that the fluorine analysis conducted by Oakley & Hoskins (1950) was inconclusive, he felt that the "condition of the material is consistent with the suggestion that they are of Upper Pleistocene age" (Montagu 1951b:424). Also Montagu (1951a) did not support the monistic interpretation of the Piltdown remains.

[B] In September 1950 a new section of the Piltdown gravel terrace was opened up, see 5.2.18 for further details.

5.2.11 DF 116/37 Edmunds 28 November 1949

(a) Francis Herewood Edmunds (1893-1960); (b) handwritten letter to Oakley on printed stationery: "Geological Survey and Museum, Exhibition Road, South Kensington, London S.W.7."; (c) –.

It is not known if Edmunds's planned note on the Piltdown gravel had been initially prompted by Marston's agitations, or whether Oakley had requested a statement.

I return your most interesting note on Piltdown [A]. It would be most appropriate to place my note . . . in juxtaposition to your abstract [B]. . . I have amended the wording to a considerable extent, as a matter of polishing it up . . ."

[A] A reference to Oakley's preliminary report on the fluorine analysis of the Piltdown remains read before the Geological Society of London on 14 December 1949, and published in the Society's *Quarterly Journal* in 1950.

[B] Edmunds' "Note on the [Piltdown] gravel deposit" drew attention to his survey in 1925 which showed, contrary to the estimates of Dawson (see Dawson & Woodward 1913a) and Sollas (1924:183), the Piltdown terrace did not correlate with the 100-ft Terrace (in White 1926, fig 10). The true elevation was below 50-ft (Edmunds 1950).

5.2.12 KP/RCS/Box KL2 Oakley 3 January 1950

(a) Kenneth Page Oakley (1911-1981); (b) typewritten letter to Arthur Keith on printed stationery: "British Museum (Natural History), Cromwell Road, London"; (c) underlining in original by Oakley. See Letter 5.2.16.

I much appreciated your letter about the Galley Hill paper. I think it was very gracious of you to bother to write.

The fluorine content of all the undoubted Plio-Pleistocene remains in the Piltdown gravel is high (3.0%). The later types in the gravel show less than 1.6% F. and all the Eoanthropus material shows very little (0.2%). In other words Eoanthropus is one of the latest elements in the Piltdown melange. Some years ago F. H. Edmunds showed that the gravel itself belongs to the 50ft terrace group [A]. Thus, the balance of the evidence now favours a date for "Piltdown Man" as late as the last interlacial period [B].

You have shown how important isolation is as a factor in human evolution [C]. The so-called "simian shelf" is not found in the ancestors of modern apes or man (e.g. Proconsul [D] and Australopithecus) but is a secondary development in modern apes connected with an enlargement of the incisor teeth. Broom recently suggested that Eoanthropus may represent an isolated side-line in evolution, in which the brain became large as in Homo sapiens, while the jaws evolved in parallel with modern apes [E]. In this case, the later date of Eoanthropus, the more "modern-apelike" one might expect its jaws to be. It is amusing to reflect that the Pliocene ancestors of Piltdown Men may have had jaws which were less like those of modern apes, and more like those of man!

[A] For further details on Edmunds' 1925 study, see Note B: 5.1.47.

[B] See Oakley & Hoskins (1950).

[C] See Keith (1939) and Letter 5.1.54.

[D] See Note A: 5.1.43.

[E] See Broom (1950) and Letter 5.2.10.

5.2.13 DF 116/36 Keith 4 January 1950

(a) Arthur Keith (1866-1955); (b) handwritten letter to Oakley on printed stationery: "Buckston Browne Research Farm, Downe, Kent"; (c) –.

. . . Bringing Piltdown man down into the last Inter-glacial increases my interest in him – he has so much of the orang in his anatomy [A]. The simian shelf may be acquired independently – like the bony nasal ridge which demarcates the floor of the nasal outlets. Neanderthal man has acquired it in certain cases and so have many modern Europeans.

Are you quite sure the Straits of Dover are so recent formation? Could Piltdown be an insular race? or merely a peninsular one? Could not the late Pleistocene [?] have reached Britain across a frozen North Sea? – Still the Cromerian and Mauer fauna are so nearly the same it does look as if England was continental then. There is much that is obscure in the distribution of anatomical characters amongst the surviving anthropoids I think Mendelism helps us to explain the strange features of the Piltdown race [B].

[?] word unclear.

[A] This allusion to orang affinities is not a new observation, but can be found in his book *New Discoveries* published in 1931. On page 454 of this text, Keith notes: "I was moved to place the Piltdown occipital thus because of several other considerations: (1) the forehead, so far as it was known to us, was modelled on orang lines; . . ." Then, in a footnote Keith draws attention to the work of the Italian anthropologist Fabio Frassetto who was of the opinion that the Piltdown remains "represented a primitive race belonging to a genus of the orang type" (see Frassetto 1927:12). A similar view was expressed by the German palaeontologist Freidrichs (1932). See also Weidenreich (1937:149; 1943:216-220) and Note D: 5.1.54.

[B] See Letter 5.2.15 for Oakley's response.

5.2.14 DF 116/47 Pyddoke 7 January 1950

(a) Edward Pyddoke; (b) typewritten letter on printed stationery: "Sussex Archaeological Society, Barbicon House, Lewes"; (c) –.

Pyddoke was the Finance Officer and Curator of the Sussex Archaeological Society.

. . . I am no chemist but the only true conclusion seems to me to be that the jaw and braincase have lain in fluorine-charged waters for the same length of time. What were their ages at the time of being "swept together" with "bones and teeth of various degrees of antiquity" is surely not determined."

As this letter indicates Oakley's Piltdown results aroused considerable criticism, and many doubted the validity of the technique (e.g. Letters 5.2.8, 5.2.16, and 5.2.17).

5.2.15 DF 116/36 Oakley 10 January 1950

(a) Kenneth Page Oakley (1911-1981); (b) typewritten letter to Arthur Keith on printed stationery: "British Museum (Natural History), Cromwell Road, London"; (c) –.

A reply to 5.2.13.

. . . I think Britain was quite possibly isolated during the great interglacial when the sea-level was relatively high. The straits of Dover may have been cut during the intense erosion accompanying a low sea-level at the time of the second glaciation. It is not generally realized that the last link between Britain and the Continent, the link which existed during the Submerged Forest Period, was formed by the Dogger Bank lowlands. The Dover-Calais ridge had been breached at a much earlier date.

By the way I think that the tendency to regard Pekin Man as great interglacial stems from the confusion of geological terminology [A]. Thus Hopwood [B] and some other palaeontologists include the Cromer and Mauer faunas in the Middle Pleistocene, but these are patently older than Swanscombe . . .

[A] For a discussion of these difficulties, see Oakley (1964:133-144).

[B] See Hopwood (1935).

5.2.16 KP/RCS/Box KL2 Armstrong 13 January 1950

(a) A. Leslie Armstrong; (b) handwritten letter to Arthur Keith on printed stationery: "Chartered Surveyor of Richmond Lodge, Bowdon, Cheshire"; (c) underlining in original by Armstrong. The letter is pinned to Letter 5.2.12.

. . . I have perused Oakley's letter and return it herewith [A]. I am not very happy about the fluorine-content tests, or satisfied that we know sufficient about the matter to justify basing firm conclusions, at present, upon the results. . . Is it possible that the marked difference in fluorine content may be due in part to human bones absorbing fluorine less rapidly than animal bones; or being more repellent in some way; or having a lower saturation ratio? [B] Oakley tells me that the process of cleaning specimens and the application of preservatives cannot affect, or reduce, the fluorine content, and can be ruled out as an objection.

Geological Evidence. I cannot agree that "the balance of evidence now favours a date for Piltdown Man as late as the last interglacial period" . . . If the test is a really reliable one, then Eoanthropus is perhaps less ancient than we deemed him to be, but not, I think, so late as Oakley would place him.

How interesting it would be to know the fluorine content of the Swanscombe remains [C]; I presume that no such test is possible at the moment, however, unless Mr. Marston has greatly changed his views in regard to scientists . . .[D]

[A] A reference to Letter 5.2.12.

[B] For similar doubts, see 5.2.14.

[C] Evidently Armstrong was not aware that Oakley had already extended the fluorine test to the Swanscombe material (see Oakley & Montagu 1949). Regarding Piltdown, further information had been released on 5 September 1949 at the British Association meetings in Newcastle, followed by a presentation at the Geological Society of London in December, and the subsequent communication to Nature on 11 March 1950 (see Oakley & Hoskin 1950).

[D] At this junction Armstrong discusses at length the Piltdown artifacts. Later, after mentioning the possibility that Piltdown is a sideline in human evolution, Armstrong concludes: "How little we really know!".

5.2.17 DF 116/36 Marston 1 May 1950

(a) Alvan T. Marston (1889-1971); (b) typed letter to Kenneth Oakley on printed stationery: "74 South Side, Clapham Common, London S.W.4"; (c) –.

. . . I am not happy about your interpretation of the evidence [A].

When Smith Woodward said the mandible belonged to the skull, in the light of knowledge at the time (1912) the mistake was excusable: but when in 1913 and with utter disregard to Waterston's objections he assigned the canine tooth with D-shaped cross-section of the root to Man, he made a damned silly mistake which no palaeontologist worth his salt can be excused for making . . . However, the figures for the fluorine content of the Piltdown material have been published thanks to you both. It may have resulted in a sort of "Radio Parlour Game – Talk Yourself Out of This" – but the results do show that the figures 0.1 to 0.4 percent of Fluorine for the Piltdown skull and mandible compare directly with 0.2 to 0.4 per cent for Galley Hill which you have addressed as Holocene. . . [B]

[A] A reference to the Oakley & Hoskin (1950) paper published in *Nature* on 11 March. See introduction to Section 5.2. for background information.

[B] This dissatisfaction is clearly mirrored in the paper Marston published in the June (1950) issue of the *British Dental Journal*. Here Marston, reviewed the history of the debate from the perspective of his discoveries at Swanscombe. Although Marston's subsequent publications did not pursue this point, he did continue to agitate against the monistic viewpoint, see his 1952 paper also published in *British Dental Journal*.

5.2.18 DF 116/47 Wooddise 25 September 1950

(a) Thomas Wooddise (b 1893); (b) typewritten memorandum on plain stationery to W.N, Edwards, Keeper of Geology; (c) –.

Wooddise was Secretary of the British Museum (Natural History) from 1935 to 1959.

The Director approves the proposal that Mr. H.A. Toombs should go to Piltdown (as on Museum duty) for approximately a week commencing on 25th September to supervise excavations which are being undertaken there by the Nature Conservancy [A]; also that Dr. Oakley should visit Piltdown in the same connection for one day. . .

Assisted by a Mr. Rixon, Toombs opened up a new section of the gravel terrace, running east and west across the site. The excavation, however, failed to yield anything of significance. On completion of the excavations, the exposed beds were bricked in to safe guard them from erosion due to flooding; and to allow future examination of the famous strata this wall was also supplied with two small glass window-doors, measuring 2ft 3ins by 1ft 3ins, placed on either side of the trench at its western end. For further details, see Toombs (1952) report published in *South-Eastern Naturalist & Antiquary*, and Toombs' letter to Oakley describing his progress at Piltdown dated 28 September 1950 [DF 116/47].

[A] In 1952, the Nature Conservancy declared the site to be a Geological Reserve, see 5.2.27.

5.2.19 DF 116/44 Oakley 4 November 1950

(a) Kenneth P. Oakley (1911–1981); (b) carbon copy of letter to David B. Scott at the National Institutes of Health in Maryland; (c) –.

While I was in Chicago during the summer, Dr A. Dahlberg [A] suggested that I should ask you whether you would care to undertake metal-shadowing of Collodion replicas of the enamel teeth of the Piltdown skull [B]. . . We would be interested to know whether you think that your method of study is likely to throw any light on the two main problems raised by the Piltdown teeth: (i) whether they are human or anthropoid, (2) whether they belong to one individual or two.

[A] Albert A. Dahlberg (b 1908), an American dental anthropologist. While the exact itinerary of Oakley's American visit is unknown it appears that the primary objective of his visit had been to attend the Viking Fund [Wenner-Gren Foundation] summer seminar in physical anthropology, held in New York between June 19 and 24, and at which he read a paper giving details of the fluorine-dating method on 19 June 1950.

[B] This was a technique developed by Scott in collaboration with the electron microscopist R.W.G. Wyckoff in 1946.

5.2.20 DF 116/44 Scott 21 November 1950

(a) David B. Scott (b 1919); (b) typewritten letter to Oakley on printed stationery: "National Institute of Dental Research, National Institutes of Health [NIH], Bethesda, Maryland"; (c) –.

I should be glad to shadow and examine any replicas of the tooth surfaces from the Piltdown skull that you send over [A].

 . . . I hardly think that we could determine with positive assurance whether the teeth are human or anthropoid, especially at the present time, since our experience to date has been almost exclusively with human teeth. However, it might be possible to tell whether the teeth belong to one individual or two. . . [B]

[A] See 5.2.22.

[B] The remainder of Scott's letter is devoted to instructions regarding the preparation of the "collodion replicas" for study. For Oakley's response, see 5.2.21.

5.2.21 DF 116/44 Oakley 22 December 1950

(a) Kenneth P. Oakley (1911-1981); (b) carbon copy of typewritten letter to David Scott of NIH; (c) –.

. . . The replicas have been prepared, following your instructions as closely as possible [A] . . . I have included for comparison replicas of the canine tooth surfaces of gorilla and orang.

 I am not sure whether the fact that the Piltdown teeth have been slightly abraded by the action of river sand will make their surfaces difficult to interpret [B]. With this possible difficulty in mind I have also included for comparison a replica of the labial surfaces of a river-worn tooth of Homo sapiens. The lingual surface of this tooth is curious. The only area of unworn enamel available for replication on the Piltdown canine appears to have been freshened by sealing. . . .

[A] See 5.2.20.

[B] It is interesting to note that the abraded surface of the molars at this time was attributed to natural causes.

5.2.22 DF 116/44 Scott 12 February 1951

(a) David B. Scott (b 1919); (b) typewritten letter to Oakley on printed stationery: "National Institute of Dental Resarch, NIH, Besthesda, Maryland"; (c) –.

I have shadowed and examined the replicas you sent over. While there is much detail to be seen it is certainly difficult to visualize much of a relationship between the surfaces. I think we are quite limited by the fact that you are not able to make replicas of entire surfaces, and that only facial surfaces are replicated. I suspect that we might learn much more from proximal surfaces, provided you can make replicas which include the surface from the occlusal edge all the way to the cement-enamel junction. The region near the back of the tooth is often the most informative. If you can make such replicas, I shall be glad to carry on further.

Examination of the slides show that PI M1 and PI M2 are not readily recognizable as ancient teeth, since they show very little evidence of post-mortem damage. On the other hand both PC and PII M1 show considerable post-mortem damage, but that is about where the similarity seems to end [A]. Bar M showed a slight amount of post-mortem damage, but not nearly as much as PC or PII M1. GO and OR showed no clear cut evidence of damage.

The Piltdown and Barcombe surfaces showed very little primary structure, such as perikymata and rod ends. Most likely these details had been worn away ante-mortem.

The symbols used in Scott's letter were assigned by Oakley: PC = Piltdown canine; OR =left lower canine of orang [1948.10.25.1]; GO = Gorilla left lower canine [SS.28.4.1919]; PI M1 = first molar in Piltdown mandible; PI M2 = second molar in Piltdown mandible; PII M1= Piltdown II first lower left molar; Bar M= second right lower molar from Barcombe Mills collection.

[A] The true significance of these findings was not fully appreciated until it was discovered that these teeth (including the canine and isolated molar) had been artificially abraded.

5.2.23 DF 116/44 Oakley 27 February 1951

(a) Kenneth P. Oakley (1911-1981); (b) carbon copy of typewritten letter to David Scott at NIH; (c) –.

A reply to Letter 5.2.22.

. . . Your comments are most interesting to me, and indicate that this line of study may eventually be most rewarding. Having had no experience of your method of taking replicas, we regard the preparation of the ones we sent as a trial round. Of course one is rather handicapped by variable preservation in the case of fossil teeth. For instance, the surface of the Piltdown canine is obscured proximally by a thin film of iron oxide, and it is difficult to remove this without producing a surface which was largely artificial. However, since you are kind enough to offer to shadow and examine further replicas we will certainly proceed now to prepare another series. . .[A]

[A] From all indications this second series merely confirmed the findings revealed in Letter 5.2.22.

5.2.24 DF 116/36 Weinert 19 September 1951

(a) Hans Weinert (b 1877); (b) typewritten letter (in German) to Oakley on printed stationery: "Anthropologisches Institut der Universität Kiel". N.B. This letter was written in Heidelberg where Weinert was on vacation; (c) –.

Weinert was a well-known German anatomist and anthropologist.

. . . Your researches on the Piltdown findings seem to confirm my own view that the Eoanthropus I does not possess human age ["Anthropos-Alter"] . . . And that there exists only one Piltdown skull: namely Piltdown I. Only the small piece of the back skull bone comes from Piltdown II, which both by its position as by its shape does not have any special importance. The forehead bone and single molar which Dawson [sic] likewise describes as Piltdown II belong most certainly to the Piltdown I place of findings. In my latest works I have written on several occasions about this [A].
In my original work of '33 [B] I expressed myself still somewhat less definitely under the personal influence of Sir Arthur Smith-Woodward to whom I was indebted for his helpfulness. Sir Arthur declared he could give only the descriptions of the finds from Dawson because he had never seen the forehead bone and molar in situ. Abbé Breuil however, who was in London at the same time, said too that he was sure my suspicion was right and that Dawson had made a mistake [C]. . . I am surprised that my colleague Hopwood never mentioned . . . [my work] . . . even though I did my researches in his presence and in his room at the British Museum [D].

. . . Do I understand you rightly . . . that with your time reckoning of Eoanthropus you mean to say that it could not be older than Interglacial? In my opinion the finding belongs to the last Ice-time at the utmost; I would not be surprised if it belonged to the "Jundpalaeolithicum" [E]. All parts of Piltdown I belong to one cranium! It is quite impossible that brain-skull should belong to a man and the lower jaw to a fossil chimpanzee. Not to mention the orangutan. It is regretable that the highly respected Dr. Broom should take up again this story of the chimpanzee jaw which had been settled long ago [F]. . .

[A] See for example Weinert (1944:233 and 1951).

[B] In this paper Weinert had expressed the view that the frontal bone of Piltdown II really belonged to Piltdown I.

[C] It is interesting to note that later, in 1938, Breuil expressed some reservations about the Piltdown bone implement, which were later renewed by Oakley in his textbook *Man the Tool-Maker* (1949).

[D] Arthur Tindell Hopwood, see Letter 5.1.43.

[E] This term is synonymous with the Upper Pleistocene.

[F] It is not clear from this if Weinert is suggesting that Broom was advocating a dualist position, or merely that his discussion of the mandible's characters had resurrected the issue. However as indicated in 5.2.26 and his 1951 paper it appears that he was implying the latter. As these references indicate Weinert was advocating that the Piltdown jaw was not only Upper Pleistocene, but if correctly reconstructed, would be shown to be hominid and not at all ape-like. For details of Broom's 1950 report, see 5.2.10.

5.2.25 DF 116/36 Oakley 8 October 1951

(a) Kenneth P. Oakley (1911-1981); (b) carbon copy of typewritten letter to Hans Weinert at Keil; (c) underlining (in original) presumably by Oakley.

I was aware that you had independently reached the conclusion that Eoanthropus is Upper Pleistocene, but I must confess that I had not seen your paper of 1933 [A] . . .

As you know the remains of Eoanthropus occurred in a gravel terrace about 20 m[etres]. above the present river level. Since remains of neither Elephas primigenius nor Rhinoceros antiquitatus have been found on the Piltdown gravel, it is difficult to believe that the deposit is of Würm age. The associated fauna (beaver and red deer) suggests temperate conditions, but the height above the present river indicates that it dates from the 3rd interglacial rather than from an interstadial of Würm. However, it is quite possible that the gravel was laid down at the end of that interglacial, which would be nearer your own estimate of the antiquity of Eoanthropus . . .

[A] It is conjectured that Oakley was familiar with Weinert's opinions on Piltdown through his association with A.T. Hopwood, whom as indicated in Letter 5.2.24 was aware of Weinert's earlier work on Piltdown.

5.2.26 DF 116/36 Weinert 22 November 1951

(a) Hans Weinert (b 1877); (b) typewritten letter (in German) to Oakley on printed stationery: "Anthropologisches Institut der Universität Kiel"; (c) –.

In reply to Oakley's Letter 5.2.25, Weinert said:

. . . [M]ay I point out that in my 1933 monograph I did not express myself in disagreement with Dr Arthur Smith-Woodward so definitely as to say that there was Piltdown II. My real views are in my newer book and paper [A]. . . I find it very regretable that even now individual authors plead for a chimpanzee jaw for Piltdown I [B] . . .

[A] See Weinert 1951, 1953.

[B] A reference to Broom (1950) and possibly Marston (1950).

5.2.27 DF 116/47 Macfadyen 12 November 1952

(a) W.A. Macfadyen (b) typewritten letter to Oakley on printed stationery: "The Nature Conservancy, 91 Victoria Street, London S.W.1."; (c) –.

Thank you for your letter of 11 November 1952 enclosing a draft of Toombs's note "A new section in the Piltdown gravel" [A].

Confirming our telephone conversations this afternoon, The Nature Conservancy has no objection to the publication of the article in the S.E. Naturalist as proposed.

Since it has already passed the page proof stage so that minor alterations cannot be made, it is suggested that a footnote be added referring to "Geological Monument" in line 2: "The Nature Conservancy has declared it a Geological Reserve" [B].

[A] For further details, see 5.2.18.

[B] The published version of Toombs' text reads: "A 'witness section' in the Piltdown gravel has been preserved by Nature Conservancy as a permanent Geological Monument. The site (National Grid 51/439217) lies on the northwest side of the drive to Barkham Manor . . . ."

6 The Debunking of Piltdown

6.1 The Solution

Although the precise sequence of events leading to the exposure of the Piltdown forgery in the summer of 1953 have become hazy in the intervening years, a crucial turning point, so it appears, had been an international conference on human palaeontology held in London that July. Recalling this meeting, Joseph Weiner wrote, two years later, that:

The problems of fossil man were the subject of its deliberations. Java man, Neanderthal man, Rhodesian man, the South African prehumans [the australopithecines] – all these were given close attention. But Piltdown was not discussed. . . Yet, unofficially, the Dawn Man did manage an appearance. Most of those present had not seen the original fossil specimens, so on a tour of the Natural History Museum these were shown along with others housed there. The sight of the actual fragments provoked the familiar tail-chasing discussion. As always there were those who could not feel that the famous jaw really harmonized with the rest, but there were others who took the opposite view. The enigma remained'' (Weiner 1955:26).

According to Weiner (1955:26-35, see also Harrison 1983) it was in this context that his own earlier thoughts and doubts about the Sussex remains were resuscitated. Evidently, in 1949, when Oakley had given a talk to the Oxford University Anthropological Society about his recent application of the fluorine estimation test to the Piltdown problem, Weiner had expressed some concern with the seemingly anomalous nature of the results (see Note B: 5.2.9). As he later recounted, what had troubled him specifically at the time, was:

[that]. . . these first tests had shown. . .that the mandible was much younger than had been supposed, and so was the skullcap. This in itself struck me as extraordinary, that an ape-like fossil of such recent age could be found in England of all places towards the very end of the Pleistocene. What was even more incongruous, was that the similar dates given by the fluorine test. . . made it possible that all the fragments belonged to one individual. This to me was an astonishing finding, since a composite, 'primitive' man-ape would be even more incongruous at the end of the Pleistocene in England than two separate fossil individuals. . . (Weiner *in* Harrison 1983:47).

On returning to Oxford, he apparently continued to ruminate on this problem. Having dismissed, on strictly evolutionary grounds, the monistic interpretation as unacceptable, Weiner (1955:29-30), said his thoughts focussed increasingly on the problem of explaining the enigmatic Piltdown jaw. While recognizing that the fluorine results had supported the apparent antiquity of this specimen, Weiner was at a loss to find an adequate explanation for the presence of a fossil ape in Sussex at such a late date. He was, however, aware of the fact that the fluorine method of estimation had involved an experimental error of $\pm$ 0.2 per cent. Thus, although the fluorine content for the jaw had been recorded as 0.3 per cent, the actual value, he conjectured, "might in fact be less than 0.1 per cent, as in recent bone" (Weiner 1955:30-31). But in following this line of reasoning, Weiner was confronted by the problem of finding a plausible explanation of why the dentition of the Piltdown mandible failed to match that of any known modern ape. It was at this junction, so Weiner reports (1955:30-31), that he first considered the possibility that the Piltdown mandible was nothing more than that of a modern ape which had been deliberately remodelled and stained to simulate the appearance of a genuine fossil hominid. His subsequent experiments on chimpanzee molars, revealed how relatively easy it was to file and stain these teeth to approximate those of the Piltdown mandible. Thus, early in August, armed with this experimental data, Weiner took his forgery hypothesis to Professor Le Gros Clark under whom he worked at Oxford. Impressed by Weiner's arguments, Le Gros Clark immediately telephoned Oakley in London, who, after expressing some initial dismay (Weiner in Harrison 1983:47), finally concurred with the view that the forgery hypothesis warranted further study. It was also agreed that Museum be actively involved in the new investigations[1], and that in the interim period the entire matter should be kept secret.

During the next eighteen months, an exhaustive re-examination of the entire Piltdown assemblage was made, using a wide range of techniques, including an improved technique for estimating small quantities of fluorine. The results of the new fluorine tests provided immediate confirmation of Weiner's suspicion [2]. The cranial fragments were found to have an average fluorine content of 0.1 per cent; whereas the mandible had a level below 0.03 per cent (Weiner, Oakley, Le Gros Clark 1953:143). On the basis of these results, combined with the evidence demonstrating that some of the cranial material had been stained and the teeth artificially abraded, a preliminary report on these findings was issued on 21 November 1953. This report dismissed the Piltdown jaw as that of a modern ape which had been deliberately remodelled and stained to match the Piltdown I cranial fragments. Likewise, the Piltdown II remains were also rejected as forgeries. In fact it was conjectured that the frontal bone of Piltdown II belonged to Piltdown I (see 6.2.5, Note B: 6.2.11 and 6.2.13). At this time the status of the Piltdown I cranium was uncertain. Although the results clearly called for a downgrading of its antiquity, it was for the moment still regarded as a genuine fossil (see 6.2.13). Later, on 21 January 1955[3], a second and more detailed report was issued. This report revealed that the entire assemblage at Piltdown had been deliberately planted (Weiner et al. 1955)[4]. Specifically it was noted:

The mandible has been shown by further anatomical and X-ray evidence to be almost certainly that of an immature orang-utan[5]; that it is entirely Recent has been confirmed by a number of microchemical tests, as well as by the electron-microscope demonstration of organic (collagen) fibres; the black coating on the canine tooth, originally assumed to be an iron encrustation, is a paint (probably Vandyke brown); the so-called turbinal bone is shown by its texture not to be a turbinal bone at all, but thin fragments of probably non-human limb-bone; all the associated flint implements have been artifically stained; the bone implement was shaped by a steel knife; the whole of the associated fauna must have been "planted," and it is concluded from radioactivity tests and fluorine analysis that some of the specimens are of foreign origin. The human skull fragments and some of the fossil animal bones are partly replaced by gypsum, the result of their treatment with iron sulphate to produce a colour matching that of the gravel. Not one of the Piltdown finds genuinely came from Piltdown ... (de Beer in Weiner et al. 1955:228).

Following in the wake of this report, the taxon Eoanthropus was formerly discarded (see de Beer 1955:171-172).

In 1959 the Piltdown I cranium and mandible were submitted for radiocarbon analysis. This investigation showed that the mandible was of a geologically recent age: 500 ± 100 years, while the date of the cranium was found to be 620 ± 100 years (de Vries & Oakley 1959)[6].

NOTES

[1] Those taking part, and their respective contributions included:
(a) Le Gros Clark and Weiner [Department of Anatomy, University of Oxford]. Anatomical evidence: morphological, radiographic and experimental.
(b) Oakley [Department of Geology, British Museum (Natural History)]: Typology and staining of the Piltdown implements; fluorine content of other aspects of the composition of the Piltdown bones and teeth. Experimental work done by L.E. Parsons. It is interesting to note that Parsons was responsible for the preparation of a female orang jaw, simulating the various characteristics of the Piltdown specimen, see Weiner *et al.* 1953,fig 1, pl 8.
(c) G.F. Claringbull, M.H. Hey, and A.A. Moss [Department of Minerals, British Museum (Natural History)]: Detection of calcium sulphate in the Piltdown bones, and experimental evidence of its origin. Chemical detection of chromate on flint implements.
(d) S.H.U. Bowie & C.F. Davidson [Atomic Energy Division, Geological Survey]: Geochemical distribution of radioactive elements in the Piltdown assemblage; A.D. Baynes-Cope [Department of Government Chemist, London]: The fluorimetric determination of uranium in the Piltdown fossils. See report by Oakley to Gavin de Beer, 29 June 1954, DF 116/43. For further details, see Weiner *et al.* (1955), and fn 4.

[2] Further confirmation of the mandible's modernity was supplied by the test for nitrogen content, using an improved technique devised by Cook & Heizer (1952). Since the late 1940s these two American workers from the University of California had been investigating the nitrogen test as a possible means for determining the age of organic remains (see Cook & Heizer 1947). Where the fluorine test reflects the accumulation of this element in bone, the nitrogen test estimates the progressive loss of organic matter from a bone specimen during the fossilization process. For further details, see Weiner *et al.* (1953:143-144); Weiner *et al.* (1955:255-256); and 6.2.17.

[3] A preview of these results was given at a meeting of the Geological Society of London at Burlington House on 30 June 1954, see Note A: 6.3.46 for details.

[4] Besides Weiner, Oakley and Le Gros Clark, during the period from August 1953 through to June 1954, the Piltdown investigations had involved an impressive list of specialists: electron microscopy – J.T. Randall and A.V.W. Martin, Physics Department, King's College, University of London; chemical analysis – C.F.M. Fryd, Department of Government Chemist, London, and G. Weiler and F.B. Straus, Microchemical Laboratory, University of Oxford; spectographic analyses – E.T. Hall, Claringdon Laboratory, University of Oxford and H.L. Bolton & H.J. Dothic, Department of Government Chemist, London; pigment analysis of the canine – A.E.A. Werner & H.J. Plesters, Research Laboratory, National Gallery; soil analysis – C. Bloomfield, Counties Public Health Laboratory (see Weiner *et al.* 1955, and Report by Oakley to de Beer, 29 June 1954 DF 116/43).

[5] Using an immunological technique it was shown in 1982 that the mandible and canine tooth had belonged to an orangutan (see Lowenstein *et al.* 1982).

[6] Subsequent reanalysis of this material in 1964 confirmed the estimations of de Vries: cranium 620 ± 100 years, mandible 500 ± 100 years (Vogel & Waterbolk 1964).

CORRESPONDENCE

6.1.1 MSS WEI 4.19 Oakley 12 August 1953

(a) Kenneth Page Oakley (1911-1981); (b) copy of typewritten letter to Le Gros Clark at Oxford. The letter was written from Oakley's home: "Woolstone, Chestnut Close, Amersham, Bucks"; (c) underlining presumed to be in original and by Oakley.

On going over all the evidence that comes to mind immediately, I do agree that there is a distinct possibility that Weiner's idea is correct [A]. You may recall that in the paper I wrote with Hoskins in 1950 (7th page of reprint) we recorded: "Drill holes in the canine and in the molars of Eoanthropus revealed, most unexpectedly, that below an extremely thin ferruginous surface stain their dentine was pure white, apparently no more altered than the dentine of recent teeth from the soil" [B].

The F. content of the canine and molars in the type mandible was < 0.1% considering that the experimental error on small samples is ± 0.1%, this figure can be accommodated within the fluctuation which one expects in material whose mean F. content is 0.2%. But, on the other hand, I must confess that the colour of the dentine in depth, plus the negligible F. content, struck me as very odd.

In the first edition of "Man the Tool-Maker" p.70, I risked hinting that the "bone implement" was a forgery!. . . " [C]

[A] According to Oakley's records [DF 116/43] he first heard from Le Gros Clark about Weiner's forgery hypothesis on 6 August. Weiner, however, implies in his book, *The Piltdown Forgery* (1955:44) that he and Le Gros Clark met with Oakley at the Museum on 5 August to carry out a preliminary anatomical re-examination – but it is conjectured that this is a printing error. From all indications this meeting did not take place until September (see 6.1.5).

[B] See Oakley & Hoskins (1950:379).

[C] Oakley (1949: 70).

6.1.2 MSS WEI 4.19 Le Gros Clark 14 August 1953

(a) Wilfrid Edward Le Gros Clark (1895-1971); (b) handwritten letter to Joseph Weiner on printed stationery: "Department of Human Anatomy, University Museum, Oxford"; (c) underlining in original appears to have been executed by Le Gros Clark.

It now seems perfectly clear to me that the Piltdown canine <u>by itself</u> can only be understood if it is a fake. I don't see that any other interpretation is possible. I have been puzzled that an incompletely erupted canine could show such an extreme degree of wear [A], and had casually thought to myself that the open pulp cavity might really be due to post-mortem damage during fossilization. But this would not explain the <u>width</u> of the pulp cavity near the apex of the root – and I think, therefore, that Marston must be right on this particular point [B]. But I think one may say that it is <u>impossible</u> to have such extreme attrition in an incompletely erupted canine and that, therefore, it can <u>only</u> be a fake. This conclusion is, of course, reinforced by the position of the wear which finds no comparison in any known hominoid ape or man , recent or extant. Lastly, the abraded surface, though curved from above downwards – is quite flat from [?] backwards. I can't think of any natural occlusal relationship which could explain this. I thought I would pass on these comments to you before I leave on holiday. I hope you have good hunting at Piltdown [C].

[?] word unclear.

[A] For further details, see Le Gros Clark's report in Weiner et al (1953:142-143; 1955:234), see also Weiner (1955:32,33-34,46-49).

[B] See Marston (1952).

[C] See 6.1.4.

6.1.3 DF 116/37 Washburn 16 August 1953

(a) Sherwood L. Washburn (b. 1911); (b) typewritten letter to Oakley on printed stationery: "University of Chicago, Department of Anthropology"; (c) –.

At this time Washburn was professor of anthropology at Chicago. Later in 1958, Washburn moved to Berkeley where he remained until his retirement in the late 1970s.

. . . The Conference was fine and seeing all those fossils meant a great deal to me [A]. I was particularly intrigued by the condition of the Piltdown jaw [B]. If it is possible to get new photographs, taken to emphasize the pattern of the cracks, it is certainly worth a brief paper. Oddly enough, none of the other fossil jaws seem to be split in that way. Very comparable splitting appears in modern jaws which are a little decalcified and dry. I think I will try a few experiments in duplicating the condition. . . [C].

[A] For further details on this conference held in London during July 1953, see introduction to Section 6.1.

[B] Later, Oakley believed the crackled appearance of the jaw was because it, unlike the cranial fragments, was an ancient, sub fossil. This is revealed in a letter he drafted to Le Gros Clark following the publication of De Vries paper [with Oakley] on the C14 dating of the Piltdown remains in July, 1959:

Prior to de Vries carrying out his test I had come to the conclusion that the jawbone already looked ancient __before__ the forger began work on it. Why does it appear so crackled? The banding of the collagen fibres seen in electron-microscope photograph shows that the jawbone was __not__ boiled. Yet, until I had seen the Everett collection [D] (and heard about the old trophy skulls) I could not believe that anyone could conceivably get hold of an orang-utan jaw that was not modern. So you can see how exciting it was to me personally when I found that the Everett Collection contained so many ancient-looking (but in every other way modern) specimens! If de Vries' result had been 150/100 I should still advance the hypothesis that it was more likely 250 years old than 50. Claringbull [E], who saw the __silty__ condition of the innermost cancellae when we sawed out a deep strip from the mandible for analysis, is fully in sympathy with this view." [P.MSS KPO (Le Gros Clark File)].

The above letter is not dated, and from all indications it was not sent. Underlining in [?] original by Oakley.

[C] See 6.2.19.

[D] A collection of orangutan crania made by A. Hart Everett in the late 1800s. For details on this collection, see Everett (1879), Oakley (1959), Harrison (1959), and Spencer (1990).

[E] Gordon Frank Claringbull (b. 1911), a mineralogist, see his collaborative paper with Max H. Hey (b. 1904) on the "X-Ray Crystallography of the Piltdown Fossils" (*in* Weiner *et al.* 1955:268-270). Claringbull later became Director of the Museum (1968-1976).

6.1.4 MSS WEI 4.19 Weiner 17 August 1953

(a) Joseph Sydney Weiner (1915-1982); (b) carbon copy of typewritten letter to Le Gros Clark. Letter addressed: c/o International Students Seminar, Austrian College Society, Alpbad, Austrian Tyrol"; (c) –.

The opening paragraph of this letter deals with Weiner's recent visit to Piltdown, see 6.3.1 for further details.

. . . Thank you very much for your note about the canine [A]. I feel that your conclusions are inescapable and I would add that the mandible does seem to me to show where the socket for the canine would be – precisely as in a chimpanzee jaw which would make Smith Woodward's positioning of the canine impossible and must imply that the interlocking of the canine would then be incompatible with the wear of the molars. I shall now marshal all the "indictable" points in preparation for the meeting with Oakley [B].

[A] See 6.1.2.

[B] See Note A: 6.1.1.

6.1.5 P.MSS KPO (Weiner File) Weiner 17 August 1953

(a) Joseph Sydney Weiner (1915-1982); (b) typewritten letter to Oakley on printed stationery: "Department of Human Anatomy, University Museum, Oxford" (c) –.

. . . The Professor [A] has told me about your last letter to him about the Piltdown tooth and I am very pleased that you are interested in a review of the whole problem. I look forward very much to seeing you about it when I come back from Canada on September 18th. [B]

[A] Referring to Wilfrid E. Le Gros Clark.

[B] The primary purpose of this trip was to attend the XIXth International Physiology Congress in Montreal. While there Weiner read a paper, see Weiner & Macpherson (1953). See also Note A: 6.1.1.

6.1.6 MSS WEI 4.19 Oakley 7 September 1953

(a) Kenneth Page Oakley (1911-1981); (b) typewritten letter to Weiner at Oxford on printed stationery: "British Museum (Natural History), Cromwell Road, London S.W.7"; (c) annotated by Oakley: "Under separate cover".

. . . I look forward to reviewing the Piltdown material with you after my return. I expect to be away on September 17 and 18, so perhaps you could make your call here during the week beginning September 21? [A]. I hope you have enjoyed your Canadian trip?
I thought you might like to have the accompanying papers [B].

[A] See Note A: 6.1.1.

[B] See Oakley's annotation (above),placed at the foot of the letter. Exactly what he sent Weiner is not known, probably reprints of his earlier work on the application of the fluorine technique.

6.1.7 MSS WEI 4.19 Oakley 10 September 1953

(a) Kenneth Page Oakley (1911-1981); (b) typewritten letter to Le Gros Clark at Oxford on printed stationery: "British Museum (Natural History), Cromwell Road, London S.W.7"; (c) annotated by typist: "Department of Geology"; and a handwritten note by Weiner at foot of letter in reference to matter raised in a later paragraph not cited.

. . . Now that I have examined the X-ray of the canine tooth I too begin to doubt whether Weiner can be right [A]. (I will send you a print of this X-Ray). The pulp cavity is tightly packed with sand grains. I shall be sending Washburn new plates of the jaw in the course next two weeks, and I might then suggest that he joins us in preparing a statement [B]. I think I shall wait until we hold our first meeting. . .

[A] It is not clear from this letter exactly what the problem was. One possibility is that they are referring to the original radiograph of the canine used to illustrate Underwood's (1913) article (see Note A: 1.3.13), which showed what appeared to be a patch of secondary dentine – a reaction to excessive wear. This evidence had been used by Underwood (1916) to counter Lyne's (1916) argument for the immaturity of the specimen. According to Lyne the excessive wear pattern of the tooth did not correlate with its age; he contended it had only recently erupted. New radiographs showed no evidence for a secondary dentine deposit, see Weiner *et al.* (1953:142); Le Gros Clark (*in* Weiner *et al.* 1955:234); and Weiner (1955:48). Similarly the new radiographs of the mandible resolved earlier misconceptions about the Piltdown molars.

[B] As indicated by Letter 6.1.3, Washburn was actively interested in the Piltdown problem. As later developments indicate it was decided, however, to keep the exposure an entirely British affair.

6.1.8 DF 116/44 Le Gros Clark 5 October 1953

(a) Wilfrid Edward Le Gros Clark (1895-1971); (b) handwritten letter to A.T. Hopwood at the Natural History Museum, on printed stationery: "Department of Anatomy, University Museum, Oxford"; (c) underlining in original by Le Gros Clark.

I wonder if you could help me with the curious Piltdown puzzle. It is a question of the artificial staining of the bones. Smith Woodward stated that only the <u>earlier</u> pieces of the skull had been stained with *bichromate by Dawson (on the mistaken impression, one gathers that this would harden the specimens). But how is it, then, that the later specimens – particularly the small occipital fragment found by Smith Woodward in situ, are also similarly stained? Would the later specimens, including the jaw, have been brought directly to the Museum, or would they have been in Dawson's hands for some time first? If the latter was the case, it is of course possible that Dawson may have also stained them first to make them match the others? I thought perhaps you may remember, or know of, the exact circumstances.*

As noted in the introduction to Section 6.1, Alvan Marston had drawn attention to this same question in 1947 (see Marston 1950), and had cited Hopwood's study of the Piltdown fauna in 1935. For further details, see 6.1.12, and the introduction to Section 5.2 (and particularly fn 4 & 6). It should be noted that Hopwood did not join the Museum until 1924, the year after Woodward retired.

6.1.9 MSS WEI 4.19 Weiner 7 October 1953

(a) Joseph Sydney Weiner (1915-1982); (b) typewritten letter to Oakley on printed stationery: "Department of Human Anatomy, University Museum, Oxford"; (c) annotated by ? Oakley: "E606" [in margin of 2nd paragraph] (see Note B).

I am sorry that I was not able to stay for Hall's last analysis [A]. One or two small points occur to me. If the "worked" flints are, as you believe, not really implements then I suppose there should be quite a lot more of this type of flint with light patina at Piltdown. Don't you think it would be worthwhile taking some hydrochloric acid down and testing the various kinds of stone? I probably could arrange to do this, but the present owner I think would have to have some document to show that I have the official approval of the British Museum.

. . . Dawson says that one only [sic] of the worked flints came from layer two, is this the one which is chromium stained? [B]

In view of the fact that this chromium staining is beginning to look really odd, I feel that we ought to have Hall's analysis applied at least to the frontal bone of site two. There should be no reason at all for chromium staining of this bone. It would be worth trying, as the fragment could so easily belong to skull number one. There is also a staining of the isolated molar, which Woodward says is heavily stained with iron oxide, and what about the colour of the bone implement which is said to be "much mineralized with oxide of iron" and to have a yellowish brown surface but much less darkly stained than the bones?. . . .

[Postscript]: "I enclose Hall's report. The Professor thinks we ought not to delay very much longer getting out a published statement [C]."

[A] A reference to the work of E.T.Hall in the Clarendon Laboratory at Oxford University. At this time Hall was working on his doctoral research which had involved the development of an X-ray spectographic method of analysis (Hall 1953). Hall's spectographic analysis confirmed that all the cranial fragments recovered prior to May 1912 had been stained with bichromate; whereas those found after this date had not been treated in this way. Hall's method also revealed that the mandible also contained chromate. This seemed to indicate to Weiner and his co-workers that the mandible had been treated in order to match it with the cranial fragments (see Weiner 1955:52, 147-150). As indicated by the above letter, Hall's technique was also applied to the stone tool assemblage from Piltdown. This study showed, with one exception, that all the Piltdown flints were ferruginous. The "Palaeolith" No E606 (see Note B) was the single exception.

[B] Specimen E606, found *in situ* by Teilhard de Chardin in 1912, was regarded by Dawson & Woodward (1913a, pl XVI,2,2a) as exhibiting the best workmanship of the flints recovered from the site. Hall's spectographic analysis, however, showed that this specimen had been treated with chromate! For further details, see Oakley (*in* Weiner *et al.* 1955:243-246).

6.1.10 P.MSS KPO (Weiner File) Weiner 14 October 1953

(a) Joseph Sydney Weiner (1915-1982); (b) typewritten letter to Oakley on printed stationery: "Department of Human Anatomy, University Museum, Oxford"; (c) –.

I have spoken with the Professor and I think that he is in agreement that the statements should be prepared, one for "Nature" and the other for the Bulletin [A], and should be ready for this meeting on Friday morning. He is drafting a "Nature" statement and will include your points when we receive your report. Meanwhile, I shall prepare something of rather a more detailed account of the background to the full investigation, but Le Gros hardly thinks that his dental data will need much amplification, anyway we can settle the form of the bulletin article when we meet.

[A] This idea was evidently dropped in favour of the *Bulletin of the British Museum (Natural History)* having exclusive rights on the story. From all accounts, Lionel J.F. Brimble (1904-1965) joint-editor of *Nature* was informed of the pending revelations and apparently concurred with the idea of the results appearing exclusively in the Museum's *Bulletin*. Later, however, Brimble, speaking to the Royal Society of Edinburgh on "Science and the Press" on 11 January deplored the Museum's decision to give an exclusive release to *The Times*, rather than have an open press conference. For further details, see *Manchester Guardian* 12 January 1954.

6.1.11 MSS WEI 4.19 Oakley 27 October 1953

(a) Kenneth Page Oakley (1911-1981); (b) typewritten letter to Weiner on printed stationery: "British Museum (Natural History), Cromwell Road, London S.W.7"; (c) annotated by Oakley, see Note A.

. . . R. Wood [sic] refers to "a number of objects", but it is only one in which we are interested. Do you think if we offered [A] for the inscribed flint it would be acceptable. . . On reading the letters written by C.D. to A.S.W. in 1912, I can see no hint that the latter was shown any of the skull fragments before May 24, or that he [had] visited the site [B]. It looks to me as though his first visit to the gravel pit was still pending on 27 May. True it was being considered at the end of March, but evidently A.S.W. had suggested postponement. On 19th April, Woodward received letter proposing visit to Hastings via Lewes, but he has written across it "Regret cannot" [C]. Dawson's letter of 12 May indicates that Woodward had been abroad on holiday since 19 April [D].

Have you evidence that he visited the R.C.S. on May 12th? [E] Possibly he wanted to see what the Ipswich skeleton was like.

The revised figure for the % F in the occipital (II) has just come in, and confirms the statement in your first draft! The % is only 0.05% (compared with 0.1 in the frontal). We must alter that in the proof [F].

[A] An asterisk is inserted here, and refers to a handwritten note by Oakley at the foot of the letter. The script is small and impossible to read except for the number either "603" or "608", but it is evident from the context of the letter that Oakley is offering a flint tool from the Museum's Piltdown collection in exchange for the inscribed flint in the Morris cabinet owned by a Mr Frederick Wood, see 6.3.2.

[B] See Letters 1.2.2-1.2.9.

[C] See Letter 1.2.5.

[D] See Letter 1.2.7. For details of Woodward's trip, see 1.2.5.

[E] See Note B: 1.2.7.

[F] The figure recorded in Weiner *et al.* (1953:143) for the Piltdown II occipital is 0.03 per cent, and not 0.05 per cent., as noted.

6.1.12 MSS WEI 3.17 Hopwood 29 October 1953

(a) Arthur Tindell Hopwood (1897-1969); (b) handwritten letter to Le Gros Clark at Oxford on printed stationery: "British Museum (Natural History), Cromwell Road, London S.W.7"; (c) –.

Hopwood was a mammalogist and palaeontologist in the Department of Geology. During the 1930s Hopwood had made a study of the Piltdown assemblage, with particular emphasis on the fauna (see 5.1.28).

Your letter about Piltdown and bichromate made me think that a few simple experiments would be more useful than memories half forgotten. Accordingly I took two fragments of bones from the Middle Pleistocene and dabbed patches with a strong, nearly saturated solution of bichromate. The results are enclosed. I am told that the treated parts will darken in time but are not likely to become chocolate brown. On the other hand, fresh bone so treated should become brown relatively quickly because the organic matter reduces the bichromate to "chromium chromate". This I am now testing on a piece of antelope rib, but it will be weeks before any result is known.

I very much doubt whether Woodward knew how long Dawson had the material before handing it over, certainly I have no information. The whole new development seems fantastic to me and I have impressed upon Edwards with the need for the greatest care and circumspection. Above all you and I must see that everything is done to keep our dear old friends Elliot Smith and Keith from becoming a target from the gibes of the "smart Alecs" of today.

This letter was written in response to Le Gros Clark's earlier communication, Letter 6.1.8. For Le Gros' reply to Hopwood's concern for "old friends" involved in the pending scandal, see 6.1.13.

6.1.13 DF 116/44 Le Gros Clark 30 October 1953

(a) Wilfrid E Le Gros Clark (1895-1971); (b) handwritten letter to A.T. Hopwood on printed stationery: "Department of Human Anatomy, University Museum, Oxford"; (c) annotated by Le Gros Clark: "Confidential".

The following is a response to Hopwood's earlier Letter 6.1.12.

. . . The whole of this business about the Piltdown mandible and canine is really very sad indeed, and I feel very regretful it turned out this way. But I do hope that the manner in which the results have been expressed will be sufficient to deflect any uninformed criticism against Elliot Smith, and others. Anti-evolutionists may try to make the most of it – but they really don't count. But I share with you your feelings of distress.

6.1.14 MSS WEI 4.19 Oakley 2 November 1953

(a) Kenneth Page Oakley (1911-1981); (b) typewritten note to Weiner at Oxford on printed stationery: "British Museum (Natural History), Cromwell Road, London S.W.7."; (c) –.

We expect the proofs to arrive here late tomorrow afternoon. In this case I might come up to Oxford with them on Wednesday morning, and at the same time bring the rest of the P[iltdown]. fragments for Hall to run over with his instrument, if he could spare the time. At any rate, I will try and give you a ring on the phone say about 4.30 tomorrow and let you know how things stand . . .

6.1.15 MSS WEI 4.19 Oakley 6 November 1953

(a) Kenneth Page Oakley (1911-1981); handwritten note to Weiner at Oxford on printed stationery: "British Museum (Natural History), Cromwell Road, London S.W.7."; (c) –.

We thought it would be wise to have a handout in readiness for the gentlemen of the press when the news bursts. Would you and the Professor approve of the enclosed drafts?"

For a copy of the press release, dated Saturday, 21 November 1953, see DF 116/45.

6.2 The Reaction

The story of the forgery was released via *The Times,* on Saturday, 21 November 1953, and made immediate headlines in the popular press throughout the world. In *The Times* the story was heralded as an "Elaborate Hoax", while in less conservative newspapers such as *The Star* (a London evening newspaper) the news was presented as "The Biggest Scientific Hoax of the Century" – a theme reiterated in the Sunday (weekly) newspapers such as *The People*, which ran the story under the headline "Great Missing Link Hoax Rocks Scientists."

As the following correspondence indicates, the international scientific community, while registering some shock, was, by and large, relieved to hear that the enigmatic remains had finally been dispatched. There were, however, a few scientists, most notably Alvan Marston, who found it difficult to accept and adjust to the new reality. Besides resisting the fact that the jaw was a deliberate forgery, Marston also bitterly resented the emerging view in the popular press that Dawson had perpetrated the Piltdown hoax[1]. But while many observers tended to regard the exposure of the forgery as a triumph for modern science, in some quarters, such as at the Nature Conservancy, the news of the forgery was greeted with some embarrassment, and it was anticipated that there might be criticism that it was protecting a fraudulent site (see 6.2.8). Although this attack never came, the fact that for nearly forty years a faked specimen had gone undetected in the Natural History Museum did not pass unnoticed. In fact, the same day Marston launched his protest at the Geological Society of London [2], several Members of Parliament tabled a motion of "no confidence in the Trustees of the British Museum." The motion, however, after some lighthearted discussion, was eventually withdrawn [3].

NOTES

[1] See particularly: *The Times* Saturday, 21 November 1953; *Evening Standard* Saturday, 21 November 1953; *The People* Sunday, 22 November 1953; *News Chronicle* Monday, 23 November 1953; *Daily Express* Monday, 23 November 1953 (see Note A: 6.1.10). In addition to Marston, Charles Dawson's stepson, Capt F.J.M Postlethwaite also strongly protested the insinuations against Dawson, see his letter to *The Times* Wednesday, 25 November 1953, p 9.

[2] On Wednesday, 25 November, 1953 at an evening meeting of the Geological Society of London, Oakley and Weiner presented a summary of their Piltdown investigations. Among those in the audience was Alvan Marston, who used the occasion to publicly criticize the results of Weiner, Oakley and Le Gros Clark, and to protest against recent insinuations in the press that Dawson had perpetrated the forgery (e.g. the *Daily Express* (23 November 1953), story entitled: "Did Charles Dawson Give Mr Piltdown His Fake Jaw?"). Some reports of this meeting suggest that it had been upset by outbursts from Marston and his supporters who were denied an opportunity to speak. It appears that Marston was given an opportunity to comment on the forgery, but when he began presenting his case in defence of Dawson, he was ruled out of order by William B.R. King (1889-1963), who was presiding over the meeting. See Section 6.3 for further details on Marston's continuing dissatisfaction.

[3] This motion was tabled by W.R.D. Perkins and five other members: George Lambert, Montgomery Hyde QC, Brigadier Terence H. Clarke, Frederick Gough and Thomas Price. The Speaker of the House [W.S.

Morrison] questioned the seriousness of the motion, noting: "I shall have to consider it, but speaking for my co-statutory trustees, the Archbishop of Canterbury, and the Lord Chancellor, I am sure that they, like myself, have many other things to do besides examining the authenticity of a lot of old bones (loud laughter)." To which the Leader of the House [Capt Crookshank] replied: ". . . Brigadier Clarke's question was awkward because his predecessor, Mr [James Chuter] Ede, was also a trustee and he himself was ex officio. (Laughter.) But, as he told the House two years ago, the Government had found so many skeletons to examine when they came into office that they had not found enough time to extend his researches into skulls. (Laughter.)" This brought Mr F. Beswick, the Labour M.P. for Uxbridge to his feet saying: "What has happened to the Dentists Bill?" Crookshank replied: "I have no announcements to make on that, beyond the fact that it is not a fake. (Laughter.)" At this point Brigadier Clarke asked to withdraw his name from the motion "in view of the excellent answer which I have received"! (Based on a report in *The Times* 26 November 1953).

CORRESPONDENCE

6.2.1 DF 116/36 Wells 21 November 1952*

(a) Lawrence H. Wells (1908-1980); (b) typewritten letter to Oakley on plain stationery: "26 Greenbank Drive, Edinburgh 10"; (c) *based on the text of the letter, the date is clearly a typographical error, and should be 1953.

A copy of Oakley's letter to Wells has not been preserved. For further details on Wells' earlier interest in the Piltdown case, see Letter 5.2.9. At this time Wells was Senior Lecturer in Anatomy at Edinburgh University. Later, in 1956, he became Professor of Anatomy at the University of Cape Town, where he remained until his retirement in 1973.

Your letter containing the inside story of Piltdown arrived this morning, just before the story hit the headlines in the local evening papers. I am glad to be able to feel that ever since I heard Marston speak at the R[oyal] A[nthropological] I[nstitute] [A] I had found the Piltdown jaw increasingly difficult to stomach. As I think I mentioned to you once, the major difficulty to me in accepting M's thesis was that it seemed to involve us in finding a Third Interglacial ape in Britain. I suppose, if one could have looked at it quite objectively, the idea of a modern intrusion would have presented itself as the only logical solution, but I feel that Weiner deserves the highest credit for having spotted the indication of faking. The other significant point is that if this interpretation had been put forward earlier it could not have been substantiated by analysis and must have remained a matter of controversial opinion . . .

[A] Marston's paper, "On Piltdown Man," was read on 14 June 1949. For further details, see Note B: 5.2.9.

6.2.2 DF 116/37 Straus 21 November 1953

(a) William L. Straus (1900-1981); (b) typewritten "aerogramme": "Laboratory of Physical Anthropology, The Johns Hopkins University, Baltimore, Maryland"; (c) underlining in original by Straus.

Straus was at this time president of the American Association of Physical Anthropologists.

. . . I see in this afternoon's "Baltimore Evening Sun", which came into my hands just a few minutes ago, a first-page story about the report in the <u>Bulletin of the British Museum</u> by yourself, Le Gros Clark & Weiner in re the Piltdown remains. Naturally, this excites me very much. My congratulations on solving this riddle that has plagued our science for so many years. . .

. . . As one of those who refused to accept the association of cranium and jaw, I am naturally pleased that the matter is now settled. . .

I am sure that Gerrit Miller, who I believe is still alive though an extremely old man, must feel vindicated. . .

Straus later wrote an excellent summary of the "solution" for *Science*, published in February 1954.

6.2.3 DF 116/25 Oakley 21 November 1953

(a) Kenneth Page Oakley (1911-1981); (b) typewritten report: "Visit to Sir Arthur Keith at 'Homefield' Downe [Kent]"; (c) underlining in original by Oakley. The report bears his signature: "Kenneth P Oakley."

Prior to the release of the news of the forgery, Oakley had written to Keith on 14 November, saying: "Weiner of Oxford and I have some news about one of the Pleistocene men which we think is of outstanding interest that we would like to tell you about in person. I wondered whether you would be free and willing to see us if we called on you next Saturday afternoon" [DF 116/25]. Keith replied that he would be happy to receive them. The following is Oakley's account of this visit to Keith's home on Saturday, 21 November 1953. For Weiner's version of the same meeting, see 6.3.5.

Dr Weiner drove Margaret [A] and me to Downe in the afternoon. Keith greeted us very warmly on the landing. . . He took us into his bedroom-study. We all sat down while Weiner and I expounded our Piltdown findings to Keith. "You may be right, Weiner, and I must accept it, but it will take me a little while to adjust to it." (He told us by the way that he was engaged in tracing Darwin's mental evolution from his own writings. Darwin did not alter any of his fundamental views or opinion after the age of 60) [B].

We got Keith talking about the early days of the Piltdown controversy. He said that Dawson came and apologized to him for giving the skull to Woodward to describe, saying that he had had a long association with Woodward through taking fossils to him. He said too that he regretted Elliot Smith's attack on Keith [sic]. [C]

Keith admitted that he certainly doubted the mandible at first, but then the flat wear on the teeth seemed after all to accord well with the temporo-mandibular joint. Also there were in his opinion "orang-like features" in the frontal region of the cranium [D]. He had noted that the molars in Tasmanian skulls commonly showed a precisely similar flat wear. (The fine Tasmanian collection at the R[oyal].C[ollege].S[urgeons]. had been destroyed during the war) [E]. The finding of the canine finally convinced him of the reality of <u>Eoanthropus</u>, for it was ape-like yet not worn as it would be in an ape. We asked him if he was not surprised by the number of specimens yielded by the Piltdown pit. "Yes," he said, "I felt they kept on finding things with which to confute me!" Dawson had seemed to him a quiet, respectable, honest man [F]. "I had the impression," said Keith, "that he wanted to make a big discovery."

Keith gathered from Dawson that all the specimens had been dipped in bichromate of potash [G]. He had always regarded the colour of the mandible as one due to that treatment. We argued with him about the difficulty of believing that the mandible would have been dipped after it had been dug out of the gravel in Woodward's presence, particularly as the other pieces found during the excavations had not been. Keith seemed a bit impatient at our labouring of the point about staining. "That evidence is of trifling value. You have the <u>composition</u>, Oakley, we hadn't."

He recalled the Lewes bank clerk, Morris, and that there was 'some commotion' over his ideas on eoliths. But any remarks that he may have made to Keith about Dawson would have fallen on deaf ears, he said. He vaguely remembers that Morris seemed jealous of Dawson, but he would have discounted any criticisms of Dawson at that time [H].

Keith had a number of letters from Dawson, but they were all destroyed a few years ago [I]. He thought that Dawson must have told him that he removed the first fragment of the skull in 1908. (Weiner had asked him about this. The only record of the year is in Keith's <u>Antiquity of Man</u> [J]).

[A] Oakley's wife, Edith Margaret Oakley (1920-1987).

[B] This work was entitled: *Darwin Revalued*, and later published in 1955.

[C] For further details, see introduction to Section 2.3 and Note D: 3.1.13.

[D] See 5.1.54 and 5.2.13.

[E] In May 1941, during a German bombing raid, the Royal College sustained a number of direct hits which resulted in the destruction of 67,000 specimens, which included well-over two-fifths of the original Hunterian collection.

[F] See 6.3.5.

[G] For background information on this issue, see introduction to Section 5.2 and 6.1.8; Note A: 6.1.9; and 6.1.12.

[H] See 6.3.6.

[I] Keith's destruction of the Dawson correspondence appears to have been thorough. Between 1983 and 1986, Keith's private and professional papers, housed in the Library of the Royal College of Surgeons of England, were catalogued by Spencer. This work failed to unearth any surviving correspondence between Keith and Dawson.

[J] See Keith (1925a, II: 491). Here Keith cites the opening passage in Dawson & Woodward's (1913a:117) paper, but has inserted the date 1908!

6.2.4 DF 116/40 Warren 21 November 1953

(a) Samuel Hazzledine Warren (1872-1958); (b) handwritten letter to Oakley on stationery embossed: "Sherwood, Forest View Road, Loughton, Essex"; (c) –.

Warren was a well-known amateur geologist and prehistorian. He was responsible for discovering the Clacton spear in 1911, and for describing in 1927 the Palaeolithic industry which he dubbed "Clactonian" (a term subsequently adopted by many workers to describe a Mousterian-like flake tool industry of the Third Glaciation). For further information on Warren, see Letter 5.2.1.

I am much interested in the report in The Times on the Piltdown skull – this reads as if the use of bichromate of potash were a new discovery. There was no secret about this at the time, and the intention was stated to be to harden the bone by the crystallisation of the salt on drying out. My impression was that the skull had received the same treatment. Smith Woodward knew all about this, and many students at the time (besides myself) expressed disapproval at the staining affect. . .

See introductory notes to Section 3.2 , and Letter 3.1.23 for Warren's views on the Piltdown implement.

6.2.5 DF 116/37 Watson 22 November 1953

(a) David Meredith Seares Watson (1886-1973); (b) handwritten letter to Gavin de Beer on printed stationery: "12 Preston Way, Harrow Middlesex"; (c) –.

Many thanks for your letter of warning about the Piltdown skull. Its an extraordinary story, but it fits some peculiarities of the history of the discovery of the bones.
    I remember, when I first saw the fragments, saying to someone presumably C.W. Andrews [A] that they were most unusually dark brown in colour and hearing that Dawson had had bits for some years? [and] before he disclosed them had treated them with Potassium permanganate as a preservative! [B] It then seemed an incredible treatment, perhaps now we know why this treatment was made. . .

[A] Charles William Andrews (1866-1924), a vertebrate palaeontologist who worked in the Department of Geology of the Natural History Museum from 1892 till his death in 1924.

[B] The idea that Dawson had stained the bones with permanganate was a popular misconception, see 6.3.2.

6.2.6 DF 116/37 Howells 22 November 1953

(a) William White Howells (b. 1908); (b) typewritten letter to Oakley on printed stationery: "Department of Sociology and Anthropology, University of Wisconsin, Madison"; (c) –.

Howells was at this time editor of the *American Journal of Physical Anthropology*.

. . .This is quite the most staggering news in anthropology that I can remember reading, and the notion of the jaw being an actual hoax is so extraordinary . . . So . . . the jaw is only a piece of villainy, even though this is shocking. Are you shielding anybody from the obloquy he deserves? . . .

See Note A: 6.2.10 for Oakley's view's on this latter question.

6.2.7 DF 116/37 McCown 23 November 1953

(a) Theodore D. McCown (1908-1969); (b) handwritten letter to Oakley on printed stationery: "Department of Anthropology, The University of California, Berkeley, California"; (c) –.

. . . My own specific unease about the jaw dates from January 1936, before Keith undertook his "final" reconstruction of the Piltdown skull [A]. I drove him to London to the BM. I do not remember now whether you or Hopwood arranged for us to spend a morning with the originals. I had never handled the specimens before and after examining some of the cranial parts, picked up the mandible and had the strangest sensation that it didn't "feel" right. Like a "good" scientist, I fought down a feeling which I could not objectify. So, until there was proof of faulty association, I have accepted the parts as contemporary and probably related. Certainly, I never would have thought of faulty association as being deliberate [B].

[A] See Keith (1939) and Note A: 5.1.54.

[B] Later, on receiving a reprint of the Weiner *et al.* paper, McCown replied: "My most grateful thanks . . . It is a model of clarity and scientific restraint" (DF 116/37 McCown 9 December 1953).

6.2.8 DF 116/47 Macfadyen 23 November 1953

(a) W.A. Macfadyen; (b) typewritten letter to Oakley on plain stationery: "The Nature Conservancy, 91 Victoria Street, London, S.W.1."; (c) –.

Mr Nicholson suggests that in view of the publicity [Piltdown site] has received, some of it tendentious, the B.M. should, in a press statement, make it quite clear that the scientific value of the skull fragments and of the site remains unimpaired in spite of the false jaw and teeth.

He feels that the Nature Conservancy may possibly be attacked or criticised in the House as having made a Nature Reserve of a fraudulent site (an impression that could be drawn, I understand from certain of the Press articles), and it would be very helpful for us to be able to quote an authoritative B.M. statement in refutation.

See Letters 6.2.9 and 6.2.13.

6.2.9 DF 116/47 Oakley 24 November 1953

(a) Kenneth Page Oakley (1911-1981); carbon copy of typewritten letter from Oakley to W.A. Macfadyen of "The Nature Conservancy"; (c) –.

A reply to Letter 6.2.8.

The Director [A] has decided to hold a Press conference next week at which he will make a statement about the increased scientific value of the Piltdown cranium now that the removal of the mandible makes its status quite clear. You may have noticed that the leader in The Times today emphasises the continuing value of the skull [B].

[A] Gavin Rylands de Beer (1899-1972).

[B] This leader opened with the following statement: "Now that Dr. J.S. Weiner, Dr. K.P. Oakley, and Professor Le Gros Clark have demonstrated that the jaw of the Piltdown skull is that of a modern ape, though the fragments of the cranium are from a genuine human fossil, it is important to consider how the discovery of this curious imposition affects the present understanding of the evolution of man. . . " And concluded with the note: "Now, it becomes clear that the genuine parts of it [Piltdown] – the cranial fragments – are much nearer to the general development of modern man, and indeed are from one of the two earliest skulls which are certainly those of *Homo sapiens*, the other being that found at Fontéchevade in 1948." (*The Times*, 25 November 1953). For details on the Fontéchevade material, see Vallois (1949a) and Oakley, Hoskins & Henri-Martin (1951).

6.2.10 DF 116/37 Oakley 24 November 1953

(a) Kenneth Page Oakley (1911-1981); (b) carbon-copy of letter to David Meredith Seares Watson (1886-1973) at his home in Harrow, Middlesex; (c) –.

A reply to Letter 6.2.5.

. . . We feel confident that the tooth of the second find comes from the jaw of the first find, and that the frontal bone of the second find belongs to the skull of the first. Added together they do not make more than one skull and this is presumably why there was included with the second find a modern occipital bone which duplicated the genuine occipital bone of the first find and provided "evidence" of two individuals; this bludgeoned our poor friends into accepting the whole thing as genuine.

As you will have noticed we are extremely careful not to name the suspected hoaxer. All the more because recent information suggests that the person most likely to be suspected may not in fact have been the hoaxer [A].

[A] By this, Oakley is presumed to be implying Dawson. As indicated by Oakley's correspondence in Section 6.3, he was at this time leaning toward Teilhard as a possible suspect.

6.2.11 DF 116/37 Vallois 25 November 1953

(a) Henry Victor Vallois (1889-1981); (b) typewritten letter to Oakley on printed stationery: "Musée de l'Homme (Muséum National d'Histoire Naturelle), Palais de Chaillot, Paris"; (c) –.

Vallois was a qualified supporter of the Piltdown remains, which along with the remains from Fontéchevade he had used to promote his version of the so-called Presapiens theory of human evolution (Vallois 1949b, 1952, 1954). Cognisant of this, on the eve of the announcement of the forgery, Oakley had written Vallois:

I am sorry that on account of "official secrecy" it was not possible for me to tell you when I wrote last week that we have now proved that the mandible of Eoanthropus, and the canine, are those of a modern ape (chimpanzee or orang) faked to simulate fossil specimens. If it is possible will you please add this statement as a postscript to the Catalogue [A]? I enclose a draft of the appropriate wording [B].

Replying to the above letter, Vallois wrote:

. . . Je ne croix pas du reste qu'il y ait un gros incovénient, en ce sens que la bombe atomique que vous venez de faire éclater dans le ciel anthropologique y a fait un tel bruit que dans le monde entier maintenant on est averti! . . .

[A] *Catalogue des Hommes Fossiles* edited by Vallois and the American geologist and prehistorian Hallam Movius [b 1907] at Harvard. This Catalogue was first issued in 1952. Oakley also contacted Movius by cable, the message read: "Eo dawsoni mandible and canine proved modern fakes. Postscript for catalogue in post to you and Vallois" (DF 116/37). Movius' reaction can be gauged by an interview he gave to the *Harvard Crimson* (Vol CXXXI, No 49. November 29, 1953). "[There is] nothing like this in the history of palaeontology . . . Researchers in this field are normally honest, virtuous people," he told the Harvard reporter. "I am only guessing," he said, "but I think the joker was one of the technicians in the British Museum who had an ambition to fool the experts." See also Movius' congratulatory reply to Oakley's cable (DF 116/37 Movius 30 November 1953).

[B] Oakley's postscript reads:

While this catalogue was in press it was reported that a critical re-study of all the Piltdown material has shown that the mandible and canine tooth are those of a modern ape (chimpanzee or orang) faked to simulate fossil specimens. The cranium of Piltdown I is a genuine fossil of Upper Pleistocene age. The frontal fragment reported as Piltdown II is also a fossil, but probably it originally belonged to the cranium Piltdown I. The isolated molar referred to Piltdown II has been artificially abraded and almost certainly came from the mandible recorded under Piltdown I. The occipital bone of Piltdown II was evidently faked and introduced in an attempt to prove to A.S. Woodward and others the existence of a second Piltdown skull.

6.2.12 DF 116/37 Fleure 26 November 1953

(a) Herbert John Fleure (1877-1969); (b) handwritten note to Oakley on plain stationery: "145 Canfield Gardens [London] N.W.6"; (c) –.

Fleure was a well-known British anthropologist.

. . . It is a great relief to me that we no longer have to face the combination of skull and jaw. . . I did not know Dawson, but from all I heard, I can't think he was the cheat. . . I'm very sorry that the exposure of the fraud comes when Keith is in very frail old age (80 I'm told), but glad that Marston's objection to any link between skull and jaw is so fully confirmed.

6.2.13 DF 116/47 de Beer 27 November 1953

(a) Gavin Rylands de Beer (1899-1972); (b) carbon copy of letter to E.M. Nicholson of The Nature Conservancy, on printed stationery: "British Museum (Natural History), Cromwell Road, London S.W.7"; (c) annotated by de Beer: "Copy for information to Mr. W.N. Edwards [Keeper of Geology]".

Gavin de Beer was Director of the British Museum (Natural History) from 1950-1960. See Letter 6.2.9.

In accordance with our telephone conversation yesterday I have much pleasure in confirming that it was with the recommendation of the British Museum (Natural History) that the Nature Conservancy took steps to preserve the site of the Piltdown finds, the scientific importance of which as the source of portions of the authentic brain-case is in no way lessened by the recent discoveries relating to the mandible and the teeth.

If and when we give a press view of an exhibit which we hope to prepare we shall make a point of including the importance of the site with that of the brain-case.

6.2.14 MSS WEI 4.19 Oakley 27 November 1953

(a) Kenneth Page Oakley (1911-1981); (b) handwritten note to Weiner at Oxford on printed stationery: "British Museum (Natural History), Cromwell Road, London S.W.7"; (c) –.

. . . In a letter I have had from Le Gros this morning, he still seems worried about our having crossed swords with Marston at the Geol[ogical]. Soc[iety]. [A] but most of the people present with whom I have spoken think that it was really quite salutory and that we shall now hear less of Marston in the press![B]

[A] For further details of this incident which took place at Burlington House, on the evening of 25 November, see the introduction to Section 6.2, and footnote 2.

[B] Contrary to Oakley's expectations, Marston was not appeased and in February 1954 once again attacked Oakley and company at a session of the Geological Society of London. For further details, see Letter 6.3.37.

6.2.15 DF 116/31 Teilhard de Chardin 28 November 1953

(a) Pierre Teilhard de Chardin (1881-1955); typewritten letter to Oakley on plain stationery: "The Wenner Gren Foundation, 14 East 71st Street, New York". (c) annotated by Teilhard, see Note A. Underlining in original by Teilhard.

I congratulate you most sincerely on your solution of the Piltdown problem. Anatomically speaking, "Eoanthropus" was a kind of monster. And, from a palaeoanthropological point of view, it was equally shocking that a "dawn-man" could occur in England. Therefore I am fundamentally pleased by your conclusions, in spite of the fact that, sentimentally speaking, it spoils one my brightest and earliest palaeontological memories. . . But now the psychological riddle remains.

Of course nobody will even think of suspecting Sir Arthur Smith-Woodward. But to a lesser degree this holds for Dawson too. I knew pretty well Dawson, since I worked with him and Sir Arthur three or four times [A] (after a chance meeting in a stone-quarry near Hastings in 1911) [B]. He was a methodical and enthusiastic character, entirely different from, for instance, the shrewd Fradin of Glozel. And, in addition, his deep friendship for Sir Arthur makes it almost unthinkable that he should have systematically deceived his associates for several years [C]. When we were in the field I never noticed anything suspicious in his behaviour. The only thing which puzzled me, one day, was when I saw him picking up two large fragments of the skull out of a sort of rubble in a corner of the pit (these fragments had probably been rejected by the workmen the year before) [D]. I was not in Piltdown when the jaw was found. But, a year later, when I found the canine, it was so inconspicuous amidst the gravels which had been spread on the ground for sifting that it seems to me quite unlikely that the tooth could have been planted. I can even remember Sir Arthur congratulating me on the sharpness of my eyesight.

I am quite unable to suggest [to] you any satisfactory explanation of the puzzle. But I feel that there is something wrong in the hypothesis of a hoax. Don't forget three things:

a) The pit at Piltdown was a perfect dumping-place for the neighbouring farm and cottage.

b) During the winter the pit was flooded.

c) The water, in Wealdian clays, can stain (with iron) at a remarkable speed. In 1912, in a stream near Hastings, I was unpleasantly surprised to see a fresh-sawed bone (from the butcher's) stained almost as deep a brown as the human remains from Piltdown. Under such conditions would it have been impossible for some collector who had in his possession some ape bones, to have thrown his discarded specimens into the pit? The idea sounds fantastic. But, in my opinion, no more fantastic than to make Dawson the perpetrator of a hoax.

As far as the fragments of Piltdown Locality 2 are concerned, it must be observed that Dawson never tried to emphasize them particularly, although (if I am correct) these specimens were announced <u>after</u> the finds in Locality 1 were complete. He just brought me to the site of Locality 2 and explained [to] me that he had found the isolated molar and the small pieces of skull in the heaps of rubble and pebbles raked at the surface of the field [E]. Now, if there had been a hoax, one would normally expect to see a rise in the tempo of the discoveries: something still better than the jaw and the canine. But this was not the case.

This letter was in response to Oakley's communication written on 19 November (DF 116/32), warning Teilhard that: "By the time that this reaches you, you probably will have heard the dramatic revelation that you and Woodward were "hoodwinked" at Piltdown!" Oakley then went on to say: "We should greatly appreciate it if you would send us some comments on these findings. We would particularly like to be able to file in our archives any recollections of yours which might throw light on this inexplicable hoax." [F]

[A] Inserted here are two vertical parallel lines, and in the left hand margin, Teilhard has written: "at Piltdown".

[B] This date is incorrect. As indicated in Note B: 1.1.10 it appears that Teilhard first met Dawson sometime during the summer of 1909.

[C] Teilhard expressed a similiar view to *The Times* correspondent in New York (26 November 1953), saying "it was virtually impossible to believe that Dawson, and still less Woodward, could have been guilty of a hoax. . . "

[D] It is conjectured that the event Teilhard describes took place on 2 June, see notes appended to Letter 1.2.9. From all indications, while Teilhard knew of the Piltdown site (see notes to Letter 1.2.5), he had not visited it before this date. After the session on 2 June, it is not at all clear how many times, if at all, he visited the site again during 1912.

[E] Correlating this statement with what was then known about the discovery of the Piltdown II specimens, combined with the knowledge of Teilhard's movements between 1912 and 1917, did much to reinforce the case for Dawson's involvement in the forgery (see Note B: 6.3.32). Furthermore, in light of Teilhard's growing reluctance to discuss the case, and his confused chronology led Oakley and Weiner to suspect that Teilhard was withholding information. For further discussion of the emerging suspicion of Teilhard's involvement in the forgery, see Section 6.3.

[F] According to a note made by Oakley, appended to a letter dated 10 May 1979 (in P. MSS.KPO: Minton File), he had "received 2 letters" from Teilhard in November 1953. Oakley's typewritten note is dated "24.v.79". See also Speaight (1967) and Bowden (1977). Oakley however does not indicate the timing of these letters. If there had been a second letter from Teilhard in November, it is clear from the text of 6.2.15 that it must have been written after the 28th!

6.2.16 DF 116/37 Armstrong 29 November 1953

(a) A. Leslie Armstrong; (b) handwritten letter to Oakley on stationery embossed: "Richmond Lodge, Bowdon, Cheshire"; (c) –.

Armstrong was a surveyor by profession and as indicated earlier (see Letters 5.2.8 and 5.2.16), a keen amateur archaeologist and a friend of Arthur Keith.

Thank you very much for the Bulletin. The press ("gutter") campaign is a disgusting business, especially Marston's share in it. . . [A]

[A] Evidently a reference to Marston's recent outburst at a meeting of the Geological Society of London on 25 November that had been widely reported in the press, see Note A: 6.2.14.

6.2.17 DF 116/37 Heizer 30 November 1953

(a) Robert Fleming Heizer (1915-1979); (b) handwritten letter to Oakley on printed stationery: "Department of Anthropology, University of California, Berkeley, California"; (c) –.

Heizer was an American archaeologist with a professional interest in the problems of dating palaeontological material – an interest he had inherited from his earlier connection with Aleš Hrdlička (1869-1943), see Spencer (1979).

Everyone is much interested in the announcement concerning the Piltdown mandible. . . I am sending on the last efforts of Sherburne Cook and myself on bone dating [A]. We have closed down our experiments with a feeling that we have not contributed very much except to explore some blind alleys.

[A] See introduction to Section 6.1 (particularly footnote 2), and see Heizer & Cook (1954).

6.2.18 DF 116/37 Briggs 30 November 1953

(a) Lloyd Cabot Briggs (b. 1909); (b) typewritten note to Oakley on printed stationery: "Maître en Recherches en Anthropologie Nord-Africaine de l'Université de Harvard, 7 rue Pierre Viala, Alger"; (c) signed: "Beaver".

Many thanks for your latest bombshell – on Piltdown. My! you really are getting things all tidied up nicely!"

6.2.19 DF 116/37 Washburn 4 December 1953

(a) Sherwood L. Washburn (b. 1911); (b) typewritten letter to Oakley on printed stationery: "Department of Anthropology, University of Chicago"; (c) –.

. . . Naturally, I will not continue to work on the jaw [A] as the less said on Piltdown from now on, the better [B]. We had a chimpanzee jaw partially decalcified and had been boiling a human jaw. I suspect that Mr. X (Dawson??) probably boiled the chimpanzee jaw for a considerable period of time and was producing a little decalcification which led to the splitting and formation of the split-line pattern when the jaw dried . . . [C] Have you looked over G.S. Miller's 1915 account on the jaw recently? He almost had the correct solution and points out that "deliberate malice" could hardly have produced a more difficult combination of parts. I really think that he might have solved the problem then if he had studied the originals rather than casts. . .

[A] See 6.1.3.
[B] Later, in December, Washburn published a brief summary of the hoax in the *American Anthropologist*.
[C] For further details, see Note B: 6.1.3.

6.2.20 DF 116/37 Trevor 7 December 1953:

(a) J.C. Trevor (1908-1967); (b) handwritten letter to Oakley on printed stationery: "Faculty of Archaeology & Anthropology, Downing Street, Cambridge"; (c) –.

"Jack" Trevor was a physical anthropologist at the Duckworth Laboratory, University of Cambridge.

Miles Burkitt [A] seems to have got me wrong and also to have misled you. I told him over the phone that Friedrichs had identified the Piltdown jaw as an orang-like fossil ape [B]. I don't know of any German who said it was a fake.
. . . [A]lthough one finds it more than easy to be wise after the event . . . I have long been an unbeliever. What decided me agin' . . . the association was the first fluorine test, which scouted the antiquity yet supported the contemporaneity. . . [C]

[A] Miles Crawford Burkitt (1890-1971), an anthropologist at Cambridge, see his book *Our Earlier Ancestors* (1926), and contribution to the volume edited by Elliot Smith in 1931 for the Royal Anthropological Institute entitled *Early Man, his Origin, Development and Culture*. See also his congratulatory postcard to Oakley, from "Merton House, Cambridge" (DF 116/37 Burkitt 23 November 1953).

[B] A reference to a paper published in 1932 by the German anatomist Heinz F. Friedrichs, who in arguing against the monist interpretation of the Piltdown remains, argued for the modernity of the cranial fragments, and the view that the mandible was that of a fossil ape. He also noted the orang affinities of the latter and proposed that it should be renamed: "*Boreopithecus dawsoni*. Friedrichs was a former student of Franz Weidenreich (see Note F: 5.1.49).

[C] Trevor later concocted the theory that Woodward had been the forger, see his letter to Oakley (marked "STRICTLY PRIVATE AND CONFIDENTIAL"), dated 13 February 1967 (DF 116/26) and unpublished manuscript of "Note to the Editor of Nature" (DF 116/26). For further details and a discussion of Trevor's theory, see Spencer (1990).

6.2.21 KP/RCS/SC II Hooton 20 December 1953

(a) Earnest Albert Hooton (1887-1954); (b) typewritten letter on plain stationery: 13 Buckingham Street, Cambridge, Mass."; (c) –.

Hooton was professor of physical anthropology at Harvard. While at Oxford (1910-1913), as a Rhodes Scholar, Hooton had come under the influence of Robert Marett (see 2.3.59) and more particularly Arthur Keith at the Royal College of Surgeons. Indeed Hooton's ideas of human evolution developed closely along the lines of those espoused by Keith. The following letter clearly reveals Hooton's thinking in this regard. Also it is interesting to note that Hooton did not write to either Oakley or Weiner on the matter discussed below.

. . . I am sure that you must have found the Piltdown business distressing and tragic, as I have. It is more difficult for me to believe that Sir Arthur Smith Woodward or Dawson would have perpetrated a fraud than to believe that an apelike jaw goes with a human brain-case. In fact I refuse to believe it (the fraud) as far as Woodward at least was concerned. I never knew Dawson. These fluorine tests may or may not be accurate. You note that Oakley has gone back on the published tests of three years ago in which he claimed the same amount of fluorine in the mandible as in the rest of the skull. Also it is hard to accept the evidence about the grinding down of the teeth. Of course Oakley and Le Gros Clarke are very reliable men and I suppose we must accept their verdict. The whole thing has a most disastrous effect in destroying public confidence in the integrity of science and has been seized upon by the anti-evolutionists. Doubtless you are reluctant to discuss the matter and I have been also. Have refused to give out interviews. I have seen so many reversals of opinion on matters supposed to have been settled – e.g. the eolithic business – that I am inclined to hold back and suspend judgement. . .

6.3   Inquest 1953-1954

Between the summers of 1953 and 1954, Joseph Weiner, with the co-operation of Kenneth Oakley and other staff members of the British Museum (Natural History), and the assistance of two colleagues from Oxford (Geoffrey A Harrison and Derek F. Roberts), mounted an intensive inquiry aimed at identifying the perpetrator of the forgery. The general results of this enquiry were later incorporated into Weiner's book *The Piltdown Forgery* which was published early in 1955.

   The following correspondence reveals not only the source of specific information embedded in Weiner's book, but also captures the spirit and extent of the inquiry. Although the inquiry failed in its primary goal, the information gathered was not without importance. In addition to providing considerable insight into the private and public relationships of both major and minor participants in the Piltdown affair, the enquiries also provided information useful in the reconstruction of events between 1912 and 1917.

As indicated in the introduction to Section 6.2, Charles Dawson, was, at the time regarded as the prime suspect. Although favourably inclined to this hypothesis, Weiner nevertheless admitted that the case against the Sussex solicitor was largely circumstantial and clearly "insufficient to prove beyond all reasonable doubt" that he had been the culprit (Weiner 1955:204). Also it is clear that both Weiner and Oakley harboured some uneasy suspicions about Teilhard de Chardin's involvement in the affair, but as with Dawson there was little in the way of evidence to support a case against him. In fact, as the letters in this section reveal, they also had some lingering doubts about several other individuals, and in particular Lewis Abbott. But despite the continuing investigations of both Weiner and Oakley, after 1955, they were unable to advance the case against either Abbott or Teilhard de Chardin (see Spencer 1990).

Following in the wake of Weiner's book, there have been a number attempts made to establish the identity the Piltdown forgers (e.g. Essex 1955; Vere 1955, 1959; Millar 1972; van Esbroeck 1972; Halstead 1978; Langham 1978; Gould 1980; Matthews 1981; Winslow & Meyer 1983; Costello 1985; Daniel 1986; Blinderman 1986a, 1986b), but without exception the respective cases developed by these investigators have been based exclusively on suspicion rather than evidence.

CORRESPONDENCE

6.3.1 MSS WEI 4.19 Weiner 17 August 1953

(a) Joseph Sydney Weiner (1915-1982); (b) carbon copy of a typewritten letter to Le Gros Clark, addressed: "c/o International Students Seminar, Austrian College Society, Alpbad, Austrian Tyrol"; (c) annotated by Weiner in top right corner "Anthropology Laboratory [Oxford]".

. . . The second visit to Piltdown and Lewes has yielded on the whole only a little more positive information confirmatory of what I heard on the first occasion [A]. I was able to obtain, and have now in the department, the written statements by Harry Morris in which he makes his allegations against C.D. [B]. I have also the allegedly stained flint which he says he extracted from C.D.'s collection. This flint certainly does not appear in any of Geological Magazine papers. There are also other papers I collected. There is no doubt that H.M. [Morris] was eolithically obsessed and is not at all a strong witness. Nevertheless his allegations can be put to the test for he "challenges the South Kensington Museum authorities to test" all the other implements and this of course can be done. Morris makes an allegation about the canine tooth having been planted but it sounds more like gossip. I heard the same allegation spontaneously from two different sources in Lewes [C].

We [D] had one episode of the most fantastic and exciting kind which fizzed out. It was this: The present owners of Castle Lodge, Lewes, Drs Nicholl jnr. and snr. were extremely helpful. They confirmed the generally low opinion which seems to be held of C.D. in Lewes, again on the score of the eviction of the Society from Castle Lodge [E]. It was in discussion with Nicholl jnr. that he suddenly said that he remembered as a boy of 8 that while the floor in the back dining room was being relaid for dry rot "two monkey skulls were found under the floor." You can imagine that this was startling indeed, yet on the following day no one else could be found to corroborate it [F]. Neither Nicholl senior, the old nurse, the gardener, nor even the foreman who had done work 20 years ago, but it may have happened while the family was away and there was a locum who, Nicholl jnr. thought may have actually had the skulls. The locum is now in Transjordania and although I shall write to him, this now seems a slender hope. Nicholl jnr. is keen to help us and will allow us to search the large lofts in the house at any time.

We were told by a clerk that there no papers of C.D.'s at Uckfield and that the lofts had all been cleared out during the war for salvage [G].

We saw quite a number of other people including the daughter, Miss Kenward, of the then tenant of Barkham Manor. She remembered (but not in a really distinct way) all the discoveries and the great delight of Smith Woodward when the canine was found. Her picture of Dawson is one of admiration . . . [H].

I feel that your conclusions are inescapable and I would add that the mandible does seem to me to show where the socket for the canine would be – precisely as in a chimpanzee jaw which would make Smith Woodward's positioning of the canine impossible and must imply that the interlocking by the canine would then be incompatible with the wear of the molars. . .

[A] The timing of Weiner's first visit to Piltdown is uncertain. Although a later letter from Mabel Kenward (6.3.58) suggests it had been in the spring (prior to the London Conference, see introduction to Section 6.1), this seems unlikely. Professor Geoffrey A Harrison (Oxford University), who assisted Weiner in his inquiries (see Note D), is convinced the first visit had been sometime toward the end of July or the beginning of August (personal communication).

[B] For further details on Harry Morris, see Weiner (1955: 154-158) and Spencer (1990). See also 6.3.2 and 6.3.14.

[C] As indicated by Weiner (1955:154) this is probably a reference to A.P. Pollard (6.3.3) and Louis Francis Salzman (1878-1971). Salzman was medieval historian and a prominent member of the Sussex Archaeological Society, see Note E.

[D] In making his Piltdown inquiries (1953-54), Weiner was assisted by Geoffrey Ainsworth Harrison and Derek F. Roberts.

[E] Since 1885 the Sussex Archaeological Society (SAS) had apparently maintained a small museum at the "Castle Lodge" of Lewes Castle. In 1903, however, when the owner of "The Lodge", the Marquess of Abergavenny, decided to sell, the SAS made no move to bid for the property. Instead it was acquired by Dawson. From all indications the SAS was under the impression that Dawson was acting as their agent. The source of this information was evidently Salzman, see Note C. Subsequently Weiner learned of this incident from a number of other informants, some of whom were convinced Dawson had "hoodwinked" the SAS. It is clear that this incident accounts for some of the hostility directed against Dawson by some of the informants. Salzman was also the source of other incriminating evidence against Dawson, see Note I: 6.3.30.

[F] Although Weiner pursued this lead (MSS WEI 3.17 PCJ Nicholl 2 February 1954), his inquiries ultimately led nowhere.

[G] Confirmed by G. Denton of Dawson, Hart & Co, Uckfield (personal communication).

[H] See Note A: 6.3.58

6.3.2 MSS WEI 3.17 Weiner 18 August 1953

(a) Joseph Sydney Weiner (1915-1982); (b) carbon copy of typewritten letter to A.P. Pollard of Lewes; (c) –.

. . . Mrs Frederick Wood of Ditchling [A] was extremely helpful to us and has kindly allowed us to take away on loan the papers of Harry Morris about which you told me. The flint was also there and altogether we are delighted to have this very important material. The main difficulty is that there is no indication at all as to when Mr. Morris made these written statements. They may have been made at any time from 1913 to 1916. It appears from one of his statements that someone else may have known from Mr. Morris about these matters. I wonder if you could suggest who else was likely to be in Mr. Morris's confidence . . . [B]

[A] Ditchling is a moderately large village, situated west of the county town of Lewes, Sussex.

[B] As indicated in a later letter (MSS WEI 3.18 Weiner 24 August 1954), Weiner had learned of Pollard's story via a circuitous route and was anxious to confirm his story (see 6.3.3) and to find the person to whom Pollard had spoken with about Morris's hypothesis in the early 1940s (6.3.12). From all indications Morris's hatred for Dawson was real, and revealed on a number of occasions, see Letter MSS WEI 3.17 Mabel Kenward 29 January, 1955: "Morris hated Dawson (and all scientists) -- and would have shouted this news [i.e. Dawson's complicity] from the housetops."

The note in Morris's cabinet, which Weiner found on 13 August 1953 reads:

Judging from an overheard conversation there is every reason to suppose that the canine tooth found at PDown was imported from France! [C] I challenge the S.K. Museum authorities to test the implements of the same portions as this stone which Dawson says were "excavated from the Pit!" They will be found [to] be white if hydrochlorate [sic] acid be applied. H.M. Truth will out.

The note is written on an index card, not dated (DF 116/17) and underlining in the original. Also on two other cards found in Morris's cabinet are the following messages: (1) *Stained with permanganate of potash and exchanged by D. for my most valued specimen! – H.M.* (DF 116/17); (2) *Dawson's Farce: "Let not light see my black and deep desires/ The eye wink at the hand; yet let that be. Which the eye Fears when it is done – to see!" Macbeth Act I, 3* (DF 116/17. N.B. underlining in original).

Finally, it should be noted that on Morris's flint is written: *stained by C. Dawson with intent to defraud (all). – H.M.* This particular implement is shown in plate 9 of Weiner's book (1955).

[C] An idea that is later echoed by Hinton (6.3.49) and Essex (6.3.45).

6.3.3 MSS WEI 3.17 Pollard 20 August 1953

(a) A.P. Pollard; (b) handwritten letter to Oakley at Oxford on printed stationery: "65 The Avenue, Lewes, Sussex"; (c) –.

Pollard was an Assistant Surveyor of Sussex County Council.

. . . I have gathered a few more details concerning the date of the written statement and it is just remotely possible I have been able to find a man with whom Morris was associated with at the time [A] If Dr Roberts [B] cares to call I shall be glad to give him such information as I have. . .

[A] Weiner believed this person to be a Major Marriott (see Weiner 1955:155, 161-62 and 6.3.24). For further references to Marriott see 6.3.6, 6.3.21 and 6.3.41.

[B] See Note D: 6.3.1.

6.3.4 P.MSS KPO (Weiner File) Weiner 26 October 1953

(a) Joseph Sydney Weiner (1915-1982); (b) typewritten letter to Oakley on printed stationery: "Department of Human Anatomy, University Museum, Oxford" (c) annotated by Oakley: "Mr. Edwards: If there is difficulty about purchasing the Morris flint officially I could buy it on behalf of Trechmann for 'his cabinet' which is virtually ours. I wonder if ASW kept day to day diary. KPO 27.X.53." Underlining in original by Weiner. [A]

. . . The analysis of Dawson's correspondence in relation to the order of the finds makes an intriguing and rather baffling story [B]. If only we could get hold of Smith Woodward's replies to Dawson, I wonder if Lady S.W. recovered the correspondence from Mrs Dawson or whether S.W. kept the copies [C]? One thing I should like to know is just when S.W. first saw the pieces – we know that he received them in London on May 24th, and first heard about the "portion of a human skull" on February 12th.

Between those dates there seems every likelihood that he went to see the gravel bed, and also passed through Lewes on a second occasion [D]. If so, the frontal of Piltdown two could <u>not have been seen by</u> <u>him at that time</u>, *though there is just a chance that Dawson found some of the fragments after February 12th. If we knew what it was S.W. saw before May 24th, I think we might understand the curious visit to the Royal College of Surgeons on May 12th! [E]*

[A] See Note A: 6.1.11.

[B] Exactly when Weiner began thinking about writing his book on the forgery is not known. However, as indicated by Letter 6.3.64 by the summer of 1954 he had completed a rough draft. The book was published by Oxford University Press, and was released early in February 1955.

[C] Subsequent enquiries failed to recover these letters. After Dawson's death in December (1916) and again in January (1917), Woodward had made enquiries about "pieces of skull", see 4.2.22 and 4.2.24. As indicated in Note B: 4.2.22, this led to the recovery of the Barcombe Mills material. Also, in a later letter from Mrs Dawson (DF 100/42 18 March 1917) and her daughter, Gladys Postlethwaite (DF 100/42 1 October 1917), it is evident that Woodward was sent, on several occasions during 1917, miscellaneous "manuscript" materials. Whether this material contained Woodward's correspondence remains unknown, but if it did then clearly Woodward chose not to preserve it. Indeed, the only surviving correspondence from Woodward to Dawson appears to be 4.1.37. The occurrence of this letter in Dawson's collection of reprints, seems to suggest that unlike Woodward, Dawson was not methodical in the preservation of his correspondence. It should be noted that after Hélène Dawson's death in May 1917, "The Castle Lodge" was sold.

[D] See Letters 1.2.1 through 1.2.9, and Oakley's assessment of the situation in Letter 6.1.11.

[E] For further details on this incident, see Note B: 1.2.7.

6.3.5 DF 116/25 Weiner 21 November 1953

(a) Joseph Sydney Weiner (1915-1982); (b) typewritten report: "Visit to Sir Arthur Keith, at his cottage, Downe, Kent. Based on notes made on Sunday evening, November 22nd 1953"; (c) signed: "J.S. Wiener." In Weiner's copy of this report (MSS WEI 2.8), several small editorial changes have been made (see below for details).

In response to Oakley's letter, dated 14 November 1953, Keith agreed to a meeting with Oakley and Weiner to discuss the results of their Piltdown investigations. For Oakley's account of the same meeting, see 6.2.3.

We arrived by car at about 2.35 pm. We found Keith more or less confined to his bedroom-study in which he had collected all of his most important books and papers. He did not look very well, he was pale and rather pinched looking and shaky and had a cough. I had never seen him before. I was immediately taken with him. As the interview went on, I became aware of certain elan and exuberance (though faint) in his manner. He was extremely charming and seemed very anxious for understanding and, indeed, sympathy over the whole matter of the Piltdown problem. He was certainly rather bewildered with it all, but for the most part seized on the points we made without real difficulty.

He started by saying that he had seen it all in "The Times" [A], and was glad for us to come down and hoped we had some specimens to show him. Oakley first took out the borings and told him about the smell of burning during drilling [B], but Keith only showed [*/a] strong interest when Oakley brought out a cast of the mandible. He said firmly that he had handled many chimpanzee and orang mandibles and he could not see that he would have been so easily deceived, in fact, he was not certain that filing down would have produced this appearance. Had we filed both orang and chimpanzee? I said no, only chimpanzee, but it had produced a very similar appearance [C], to which he said, "If you say so, Dr Weiner, I accept it." He then started to justify his old attitude and began an historical account.

After dwelling on the skull reconstruction, he went on to say that juxtaposition of the pieces and the flat wear made any other possibility unthinkable, [x/despite his scepticism]. Oakley and I heartily agreed with this [*/1]. Oakley brought out a picture of Keith's own reconstruction from the "Illustrated London News," in which the jaw even in 1913 was figured as completely human [D]. Keith then told us of his astonishment at the canine at the time, but again felt that he had to accept it on the wear. I asked whether the canine wear could not have been artificial, to which he did not reply. I then told him of the open cavity and the lack of secondary dentine, and Oakley showed him the picture. Although he said nothing, he seemed taken aback. I then told him that there was no iron in the canine. He expressed [x/great] astonishment, and Oakley then told him of the extreme whiteness under the thin dark layer. I asked him how often he had actually seen the original specimens. "A great deal", he said, "Smith Woodward was very good in that way later on", and then he began telling us of the first time when he saw it, but broke off when he realised [*/I imagine] we had probably already read about it in the autobiography. He then began to say, "You fellows have the evidence", and then once again he talked of the justifiability of his old views, but brought in the fact that Oakley had of course queried the date some years ago. Oakley then told him of the latest fluorine figures, but I was not sure that he actually took in their significance.

When we got on to the chromate, and [sic] Keith said that he knew the jaw had been stained and explained that it was for preservation. How had he learnt of the chromate staining? Dawson had told him, in fact, he had lots of correspondence from Dawson, and then he admitted that most of it, if not all, had been destroyed by himself in a bonfire some years ago [E]. I then pointed out that [*/Smith] Woodward had not known that the mandible was not stained [sic]. He expressed surprise at this, but when asked if he thought whether all the pieces had been stained, he said, "Most certainly," to which Oakley then replied that the two pieces found in the gravel in Smith Woodward's time were not stained. This definitely surprised him. We then went back to the teeth, and I pointed out [*/some of the] various identical features; the lack of congruity, and the inside more worn than the outside. He agreed this was very odd, and Oakley pointed out the lack of wear in the talonid basin, to all of which he merely said that he had seen flat wear of the same sort in Tasmanians.

I then picked up the jaw and said to him, "The jaw, you know, contained practically as much nitrogen as a fresh bone, and the calvarium contains very little." He was completely taken aback, and then asked Oakley how much nitrogen there actually was in Middle Pleistocene bones. Oakley said there could be even .5%, but that the mandible was of the order of 4%. Then we mentioned the iron staining; that it was superficial in the mandible, but went completely through the cranial fragments. Keith fell silent and leaned back thoughtfully and said, "You are making a reflection on a Christian gentleman." We said we realised that this was unfortunately so. And so he talked about Dawson, that he was "an open, honest chap," that he had talked to him often [F]. "When did you first see him?" we asked. Keith said, "The first time was when he came to see me to apologise for not being in a position to give me the material because I was the only man with any real experience, and he appreciated that but because of his long association with Smith Woodward he felt it was not possible." When was this occasion? Keith thought and said, "Before the famous meeting in 1912", and then suddenly he said, "No, it was afterwards, at the time when I was on bad terms with Smith Woodward." He seemed to me puzzled that in fact it had been after the meeting (and Oakley and I did tell him that we knew that Dawson had written to Smith Woodward in May, 1912, about his pleasure of having discovered the twelfth dorsal vertebra and photographed it under the very nose of Keith) [G].

Did Keith know that Dawson was disliked in Lewes? – No, he was not aware of that. Was it because he was a landlord's agent? asked Keith. I said that that was not the reason I could advance, and then told him about the purchase of Castle Lodge. He did not like to hear this, I thought, and only shook his head.

Did he remember Harry Morris? He thought for a long time at first and then eventually said, "Well, well, out of all those names that comes back to me. Was he a palaeolithic man?" Yes, he was. "Was he a bank clerk at Worthing?" asked Keith.. "Yes, a bank clerk at Lewes". "It comes back to me," said Keith, "I think I had many talks with him." [H] I reminded him of the exhibition at the R.C.S. which *he had arranged for Morris [I]. He did not seem to remember this, but repeated that he now recollected him quite definitely. So we told him of Morris' allegation against Dawson, and showed him what Morris had written, and after a pause, he said, "Yes, I do remember there was some commotion." "Was this about eoliths and the starch controversy?" I asked, but he could not remember, although he repeated that he had a vague recollection of some commotion, and as to allegations he would certainly have paid no attention at the time. Then Oakley told him of the stained flint, at which Keith gave a sort of twisted [*/feeble] laugh. Then I asked him how he had obtained the 1908 date, as Woodward nowhere quotes it [J]. He was surprised at this,[*/2] [*/and] said that he himself had not put it in the first edition. He said he was fairly sure that Dawson must have told him this date.*

I asked him whether he was not puzzled at the queer succession of events in 1912, '13, and '15, and then he said, "Well, yes, I almost felt it was to confute me personally", and made some reference [*/ again] to his earlier reactions and scepticism. Oakley showed him his old reconstruction [*/where it seemed] [*/which made] clear that he remained sceptical for long.

We felt that the discussion was more or less at an end, and I think Oakley at this point commented on Keith's wonderful flexibility in listening to the new evidence. Keith then started talking about the biography on Darwin he was writing and his method of work, and brought up the point, after some disquisition, that Darwin, to his surprise, was in fact very inflexible in his views, certainly in his later years. Then he said, "I am sure you are right, you fellows, you have the evidence, you have the composition, Oakley, we did not have the composition." After he had given us his autograph, we left, with Keith giving us helpful advice about returning etc. We left about 3.50 p.m. He was rather tired but not, I think, [*/very] agitated. [*/I noticed that] Throughout the discussion he kept on forgetting Smith Woodward's name and had to be reminded.

[x/] Word deleted (DF 116/25); [*/] Word(s) inserted (DF 116/25).

The following corrections appear in Weiner's copy of this report (MSS WEI 2.8):

[*/1] : . . . "despite his sceptism at which point. . ."

[*/2] : . . . "especially when I said . . ."

[A] The story in *The Times* (21 November 1953) was presented under the title: "AN ELABORATE HOAX."

[B] This observation was made while drilling the jaw for a sample to re-determine the fluorine content, see Oakley in Weiner *et al.* 1955:255.

[C] This was subsequently done, see introductory notes to Section 6.1, fn 1b, and 6.3.51.

[D] See *Illustrated London News*, 16 August 1913.

[E] See Note I: 6.2.4.

[F] See Letter 6.3.6.

[G] See Note E: 6.3.4.

[H] See Letter 6.3.6.

[I] See Weiner (1955:159, 184). For further details, see under "Annotations" in the *Lancet* (13 March 1915, p 562) which refers to Morris's "fine collection of eoliths lately exhibited in the Museum of the Royal College of Surgeons . . ."; and Spencer 1990.

[J] See Note J: 6.2.4.

6.3.6 MSS WEI 3.17 Keith 22 November 1953

(a) Arthur Keith (1866-1955); (b) typewritten letter to Weiner on printed stationery: "Homefield, Downe, Farnborough, Kent"; (c) words enclosed in [] indicate corrections made to typescript in Keith's hand.

This letter was written in reference to the visit of Oakley and Weiner on 21 November 1953, see 6.3.5.

It was passing kind of you and Oakley to make the journey to Downe and to explain so convinvingly [sic] the treachery of my old friend Charles Dawson. I'm glad Smith Woodward will never know of it but if you have any means of getting in touch with Dawson do rub it into him that after 40 years you have found him out. . . . After you left I went searching amongst my old papers and found a sort of journal I made entries [*/in] from time to time in my earlier years at the College of Surgeons from 1908 on. I have a full acc[oun]t of my first sight of the Piltdown material a week before the famous meeting on December 18, 1912, an acc[oun]t. of the meeting, then one of a visit my wife and I paid to Piltdown a week after the meeting, and then the first relevant note under the date of Jan. 28, 1913: the "above mentioned Charles Dawson came to see me" at the RCS Museum and I add "A clever level-headed man"; so that must [*/have been] my first personal meeting with him. Of the exhibits in our museum the one he was most interested in was the Heidelberg jaw; his ambition, he told me then or later, was to find the skull of then Heidelberg man.

The next relative entry is under a Saturday for July 1913. I was one of about 100 members of the Geol[ogists] Assoc[iation] which had accepted Dawson's invitation to visit Sussex sites, including Lewes and Piltdown. We met at Tunbridge Wells and motored via several places to Lewes. My particular companion was Mr Willett introduced to me by Dawson; Lewis Abbott was everywhere; in Lewes I was besieged [*/by a] Capt. Marriot, who was then I think in charge of the gaol at Lewes; I had been in correspondence with him [*/before] and he urged upon me the merits of his friend, Morris the bank clerk. We went with Morris to his (Morris's) small lodging – two rooms – crammed to overflowing with eoliths and some palaeoliths. I noted that "Morris is turning sour because of scepticism" [A]. I don't remember any mention of Dawson by him or Marriott but I remember very well my own thoughts about Dawson's acclamation and poor Morris's neglect. All amounting to very little but interesting because of your discovery. . .

[*/] Word(s) inserted by Keith.

[A] See Weiner (1955:159-60). For further details on the Geologists' Association excursion to Piltdown in 1913, see 2.3.19 and 2.3.21.

6.3.7 MSS WEI 2.8 Edmunds 24 November 1953

(a) Francis Hereward Edmunds (1893-1960); (b) typewritten copy of letter to Oakley; (c) letter is marked "Private & Confidential".

Edmunds was responsible for the revision in the estimated elevation of the Piltdown gravel terrace, see 5.2.11.

I have been most interested in reading your account of the Piltdown problem both in the Bulletin and in the less official account of "The Times". There are one or two points which I may be able to add a little in support of the extreme probability that the Piltdown fossils are frauds. It is perhaps unprofitable to try and trace the origin of the forgery in public, so that I have marked this "Private and Confidential".

As you will remember, in 1924, I had the job of doing some mapping in the Lewes area, in the course of which I mapped terraced gravels along the Ouse. To me these showed that the Piltdown terrace belonged to a 50-ft. terrace and not to a 100-ft. This was shown in a diagram published as Fig 10 in the Geological Survey Memoir of the Lewes sheet (1926) [A].

While I was in the district I made the acquaintance of a jeweller who owned a shop in Hastings, one W.J. Lewis Abbott, whose name was not unknown in the geological world of 40 years ago. He himself told me that he had worked with Dawson on the Piltdown skull and that the skull had been in his possession in his house six months before Smith Woodward saw it; and I gathered from him that he had soaked it in bichromate to harden it. I have every reason to believe that those statements were matters of fact. This has some bearing on the view as to who was the author of the forgeries you have detected. It seems to me unlikely that Dawson, a solicitor, would have either the knowledge or the ability to make skilful forgeries; although that is only an opinion as I never met Dawson [B]. Abbott certainly had the knowledge, skill, tools and opportunity to do so. He certainly tried to pull a fast one over me, by offering me errati [sic] of various types of rock, plus photograph of section, to show a boulder clay at 150 ft. O.D. just outside Hastings! Unfortunately I could not make the photograph fit the countryside.

As to motive, I also have my opinions, but they don't matter.

[A] See Note B, 5.2.11.

[B] See 6.3.9.

6.3.8 MSS WEI 3.17 Keith 25 November 1953

Arthur Keith (1866-1955); (b) handwritten letter to Weiner on printed stationery: "Buckston Browne Research Farm, Downe, Farnborough, Kent"; (c)–.

This letter is related to issues raised by the visit of Oakley and Weiner on 21 November 1953, see 6.3.5

Lewis Abbott died Aug[ust] 1933 aged 80. He was a jeweller (expert on precious stones) and watchmaker in Hastings but giving his time to Prehistory his business fell apart and before his death very poor. The Royal Society set aside £100 of its Charity Fund to help him and I went to Hastings on August 9, 1933 and paid £25 of the Royal Society money to meet his immediate needs. I found him moribund and see from my Diary I wrote a note on him for the "Times" published Sat[urday]. Aug[ust]. 12 [19]33 [A].

He was really self-educated and not an able thinking man. He had explored and reported on a late paleo floor near Hastings and was supposed to be an authority in all [matters] relating to [?] (Pliocene and post-[? Pliocene] recent) Geology of South England. I see in my notes a question as to the reliability of his own bibliography. He was pushy and self-opinionated – but poor chap!

[?] word unclear.

[A] For another obituary on Abbott, see Dewey (1934).

6.3.9 MSS WEI 2.8 Lang 30 November 1953

(a) William Dickson Lang (1878-1966); (b) typed copy of "Extract from letter" to W.N. Edwards; (c) underlining by Weiner.

Lang was former Keeper of Geology (1928-1938).

. . . Like you, it never entered my head that there was any faking in the matter, nor can I remember such a suggestion having been made. . . All I can offer is what J. Jackson [A] told me this morning. . . . A Miss Morey [B] . . . told him that, when she was with a South-Eastern Naturalists's Meeting at the house of Abbott, at Hastings, after Dawson's death, Abbott told the company that Dawson at first thought the Piltdown Skull was of the nature of an iron-stained concretion, but that he, Abbott, had persuaded him that it was a genuine bone.

[A] The identity of this individual is unknown (see Note B). This name is not underlined in the original.

[B] The name "Miss Morey" is circled, presumably by Weiner. In a letter to Errol White (later Keeper of Geology, see Note C: 6.3.18), Lang repeated the substance of this letter:

. . . Miss Morey (I think the name was) (one of the family with whom he [J.F. Jackson] was connected with the Shanklin Museum [? Isle of Wight]) told him that a visit with the South-Eastern Naturalists to Abbott's house at Hastings, Abbott had told them either that he found the Piltdown skull and gave it to Dawson, or he saw Dawson with it, and in either case persuaded Dawson that it was an interesting fossil and not to be thrown away, as Dawson was inclined to do . . . (MSS WEI 3.19 Lang 14 December 1953).

[C] For further details on the connection between Abbott and Dawson regarding the Piltdown cranial fragments, see 1.2.11, 1.2.13 and 2.3.28.

6.3.10 MSS WEI 4.19 Edwards 7 December 1953

(a) Wilfred Norman Edwards (1890-1956); (b) handwritten letter to Weiner on printed stationery: "British Museum (Natural History), Cromwell Road, London S.W.7."; (c) –.

Edwards was Keeper of Geology (1938-1955).

. . . By an extraordinary coincidence a housekeeper-companion who lives with us at home was visiting friends near St. Albans and met there a Capt. G. St. Barbe who once lived in Sussex [A]. She remarked that he might be interested in the Piltdown Case and he at once replied that he was indeed, and that as he knew a lot about it would like to unburden himself to somebody! I have of course written and asked him to come and see me. It seems that he regarded Dawson as the prime mover, and puts it down to overwhelming ambition. . .

[A] For further details on St. Barbe, see 6.3.13.

6.3.11 DF 116/35 Smith 3 December 1953

A.J. Smith; (b) handwritten letter to Oakley on printed stationery: "52 Alexandra Road, Leamington Spa, Warwickshire"; (c) the letter is marked "Confidential" and addressed to "Dr.K.P. Oakley, Geology Department, Oxford University."

From all indications this was an unsolicited letter. Smith is mentioned by Weiner in his book (1955:95).

. . . When I was in Sussex in 1924-29 I met, in my official capacity, the County Public Analyst, Dr. Woodhead, of the Mount, Lewes, now since dead [A]. One day, having called upon him with a water sample from a well near Piltdown and having mentioned my interest in the finding of the skull, he told me that he had been present with Mr. Dawson at its great discovery and on subsequent visits to the gravel pit. Mr. Dawson was a friend of his and the fact that he had not been mentioned in any account of the finding of the fragments was because he should not have been there at that time! My recollections of Dr. Woodhead was that he had a nice sense of humour and as he had a fully equip[p]ed laboratory, was able to examine bones and other pathological material, causes me to wonder. No more than that.

[A] Samuel Allinson Woodhead (1872-1943), for biographical details, see Wright (1943). Smith's letter precipitated an inquiry from K.P. Oakley to the Sussex County "Analytical Laboratory" at Lewes (DF 116/32 Oakley 22 December 1953), see 6.3.19 for reply.

6.3.12 MSS WEI 3.17 Shepherd 7 December 1953

(a) Walter Shepherd; (b) typewritten copy of letter addressed to KP Oakley: "Downs Edge, Washington, Sussex"; (c) annotated by Weiner: "Pollard".

See Letter 6.3.2.

. . . My friend [A] assures me that during the last war he went with Pollard on a car run which took them to Piltdown.

Pollard insisted on conducting him to the place where the bones were found, and then chuckled and said that he knew for a fact that Dawson had faked the jaw. He didn't say how he knew . . . This was in 1941. . .

[A] This individual was later identified as a Mr F.W. Thomas, a journalist, who lived at Seaford, Sussex. In a letter addressed to Weiner, dated 29 August 1954 (MSS WEI 3.17), Thomas confirmed the story of the trip to Piltdown (circa 1941), adding:

. . . [Pollard later told me] . . . that he knew that some of the flints were faked, and who faked them and how. I think, but this I am not sure of, there was a mention of bichromate of potash. Would that be for "ageing" [sic]? Sometime later, after the war, I told these things to Shepherd. . .

6.3.13 MSS WEI 4.19 Edwards 12 December 1953

(a) Wilfred Norman Edwards (1890-1956); (b) handwritten letter to Weiner on printed stationery: "British Museum (Natural History), Cromwell Road, London S.W.7."; (c) –.

See Letter 6.3.10.

Capt. Guy St. Barbe (formerly St. Barbe Watkins) came to see me yesterday [A], and I enclose a summary of his rather rambling story, based on what my secretary could take down as he talked.

St. Barbe is obviously quite genuine, but himself admits that his memory is failing especially for names and dates – he seemed to be about 70, and was seriously wounded in the 1914-18 war. He was not at all clear about the dates of his visits to Dawson. . .

Following this, Weiner interviewed St. Barbe at his home in St Albans, Herts. See 6.3.21 and 6.3.22 for further details.

[A] See MSS WEI 2.8 for transcript of Edward-St. Barbe interview (Friday, 11 December 1953).

6.3.14 MSS WEI 4.19 Weiner 14 December 1953

(a) Joseph Sydney Weiner (1915-1982); (b) carbon copy of letter to W.N. Edwards; (c) –.

A reply to information relayed by Edwards to Weiner in Letter 6.3.13.

What St. Barbe told you links up with Morris, who was also a close friend of Marriott [A]. I have tried to find out about Marriott, and have ascertained that there are no letters of his now to be seen; but his daughter wrote to say that her father had privately always expressed his certainty of the fraudulent nature of the Piltdown material, and she added that her father was a man not given to expressing his opinions unless he felt very strongly and was certain of his position. . . If St. Barbe visits you again perhaps you would ask him about Morris . . . perhaps [he] . . . would know how it was that Morris was able to obtain one of the dubious flints from Dawson himself (Morris said that he had exchanged something very valuable for it) . . .[B]

[A] See Letter 6.3.24 for further details on the Morris-Marriott connection.

[B] See transcript of the Weiner-St. Barbe interview conducted in January 1954 (6.3.21), see Weiner (1955:165-7).

6.3.15 DF 116/32 Oakley 22 December 1953

(a) Kenneth Page Oakley (1911-1981); carbon copy of typewritten letter to Teilhard de Chardin in New York City; (c) –.

Many thanks for your interesting letter of Nov. [A] I am sorry not to have replied before, but I have not only been overwhelmed by correspondence on Piltdown, but in bed for 10 days with 'flu.

I think you will agree now that you have read our report that it is no accident that the ape's jaw was found at Piltdown. The grinding of the teeth and the chemical staining are sufficient evidence of fraudulence.

We now find that the pointed flint which was found in the layer just overlying the dark gravel has been stained with dichromate! Naturally it now occurs to us that the Villafranchian mammalian teeth were planted.

We should be grateful for any further recollections which might throw light on the curious happenings at Piltdown forty years ago. . . [B]

[A] Contrary to Note B: 6.2.15 this statement would seem to imply that Oakley had only received a single communication from Teilhard during November.

[B] See 6.3.32.

6.3.16 P.MSS KPO Weiner 22 December 1953

(a) Joseph Sydney Weiner (1915-1982); (b) typewritten letter to Oakley at his home (Amersham), on printed stationery: "Department of Human Anatomy, University Museum, Oxford"; (c) –.

Sorry to have been somewhat tardy with my piece for the A.J.P.A. I return your original manuscript along with enclosed draft of both yours and my contribution [A]. . .

I am not sure whether I have sent you the notes I made on Vere's broadcast [B] . . . I have also written to Vere . . . asking him outright if he had any private information to account for the fervour with which he defended Dawson, seeing that his arguments are, on the whole, so untenable. . .

I dare say that Le Gros will be writing to you about the turbinates [C]. It is hardly to be doubted that these things are not turbinates at all, but bits of shaft of long bones not necessarily human. So much for Marston's "claim" to have dated the skull by these "fragile" turbinates!! [D] . . .

[A] See Weiner & Oakley (1954). This article was published in the March issue of the *American Journal of Physical Anthropology*.

[B] Francis Vere, who subsequently wrote several works on the Piltdown mystery. His talk on Piltdown was broadcast by the BBC on 8 December 1953. Vere was convinced that Dawson had been a victim (see Vere 1955).

[C] For further details on his assessment of the so-called turbinal bones, see Le Gros Clark (*in* Weiner *et al*. 1955:234-242).

[D] At the close of his 1950 paper, Marston had written:

In my 1949 paper I gave reasons why the turbinate bone had undergone neither fluviate nor solifluvial transport, and did not belong to the period of the gravel spread. In Widdowson's "Dental Anatomy" Vol 2, Human and Comparative, 1939, I called attention to the preservation of the frail turbinate bone and nasal bones and said "the Piltdown human remains belong to a later period than those in which they are found" (Marston 1950:299).

6.3.17 MSS WEI 3.17 Grinsell 22 December 1953

(a) Leslie Valentine Grinsell (b 1907); (b) copy of letter to Oakley. Grinnell's address was: "Department of Archaeology, The City Museum, Bristol"; (c) –.

Grinsell is a well-known British archaeologist and former Curator of Archaeology at the Bristol City Museum (1952-1972), see Fowler (1972).

. . . I know that Dr. Eliot Curwen [A] was very reluctant to say anything at all [about Dawson and the Piltdown affair]; or rather, while prepared to say it in a whisper, would not have been prepared to write it down. [B]

. . . I remember clearly, however, that one evening when I was about to leave Curwen's house at 1. St. Aubyns [C], either 1929 or 1930, we were talking about Piltdown and Dawson, and he warned me that he "mixed things" and I received the impression that Dawson left the Sussex Archaeological Society at their own request [D]. . . Curwen certainly did not say that Dawson "cooked" the Piltdown find, but he did indicate that he had "mixed" other things, if not Piltdown. . . [E]

[A] Eliot Curwen (1865-1951), a prominent figure in Sussex archaeological circles. According to Thomas (1972:13-14), Grinsell met Curwen through his earlier interaction with H.S. Toms (1874-1940), the Curator of the Brighton Museum. Curwen is of interest, since around 1911, he obtained some fossils from workmen at a brickearth site near Brighton which included a molar of *Ursus arvernensis*. The investigations of 1953-54 led to the discovery that this tooth had a radioactivity that was not only higher than any of the other specimens from this site, but also of any British Pleistocene fossils (barring of course the Piltdown specimens E620 and

596). For further details, see Oakley in Weiner *et al.* (1955: 248-249), and Spencer (1990). From all indications (6.3.24) there was no connection between Curwen and Morris.

[B] Weiner later directed the same question to Curwen's son, E. Cecil Curwen, see Letter 6.3.39.

[C] Located in Lewes, Sussex. At this time Grinsell had just embarked on a career in Barclays Bank (Thomas 1972:13).

[D] Recently Grinsell has indicated (in a personal communication) that this "impression" was based on incorrect information, see notes to Letter 6.3.39.

[E] See 6.3.39.

6.3.18 MSS WEI 3.17 Hinton 29 December 1953

(a) Martin Alister Campbell Hinton (1883-1961); (b) handwritten letter to Le Gros Clark at Oxford on printed stationery: "Glaisters, Wrington, Bristol"; (c) –.

Hinton joined the staff of the Natural History Museum in 1921. He became Deputy Keeper of Zoology in 1927 and was Keeper from 1936 until his retirement in 1945. See Note B.

. . . Of course, I had not the slightest intention of attributing any personal reluctance to Smith Woodward. I have no doubt he would show the specimens to anyone interested quite freely. But the fact remains that when Barlow's casts became available they were used as far as possible by everybody, including Smith Woodward and Pycraft who could dispense with handling the originals.

It is a pity that S[mith]. W[oodward]. was so secretive before his paper was read. Had he talked to Old Thomas [A] or even to me [B] I do not think Eoanthropus would have been invented [C].

With regard to the faker of the jaw and canine tooth I do not know who he was; but suspect he was a local man who thought it very amusing to pull Dawson's leg. Kennard (who died a little time ago) always said he knew who had done it [D]. But he never mentioned names. The thing or rather 2 things I am quite certain of is that neither Dawson or Kennard were guilty. Neither possessed the inclination to do such a thing or the necessary knowledge. . .

This was in reponse to a letter from Le Gros Clark, evidently prompted by Hinton's letter published in *The Times* on 4 December 1953: "Piltdown Man Forgery: Investigators' access to fragments." See also Hinton's letter to de Beer (6.3.49) and Weiner (1955:137). In this latter reference Weiner dismissed the notion that Woodward had denied "free-access" to the Piltdown materials. Later, Hinton repeated essentially the same story to Weiner (MSS WEI 3.17 Hinton 11 May 1955):

I have no knowledge of Kennard's suspicion of a hoax and no names were ever mentioned by him to me. I never suspected a hoax myself but I have never handled the original material. Had I done that I am pretty sure the recent bones would not have deceived me.

But from the beginning I was sure a false association had been made by Smith Woodward [see 4.2.2] – he had lined up the jaw of a chimpanzee (I still regard it as that and not Gorilla) with a human skull and "Eoanthropus" was a vile compound. . . .

To which he added in a later paragraph:

"I think the original discovery of the skull by the workmen was very likely genuine – but the rest was a practical joke which succeeded only too well. . ."

[A] Michael Rogers Oldfield Thomas (1858-1929), former curator of mammals at the British Museum (Natural History).

[B] Prior to joining the Museum in 1921, Hinton had been a clerk in a London law office. From 1905 until his appointment he had been a regular visitor with research privileges in the zoology department. For further discussion of Hinton and his involvement in the Piltdown affair, see Spencer (1990).

[C] Commenting on Hinton's letter in *The Times*, W.D. Lang [6.3.9] in a letter to Errol J. White, said:

I saw Hinton's letter and it read as if he thought that had he had the material handed to him, he would have detected the fraud. But perhaps he didn't mean that. In any case, I think S. Woodward was right in letting only anthropological specialists . . . see the stuff for detailed handling, and Hinton was not one to be included, for all his eminent work on Voles! I should say that his letter cuts very little ice . . .

[D] See 5.2.1 and 6.3.22.

6.3.19 DF 116/35 Wright 31 December 1953

(a) Reginald F. Wright; (b) typewritten letter to Oakley on printed stationery: "The Analytical Laboratory, Wraysbury, 1 Offham Road, Lewes"; (c) –.

(MSS WEI 3.19 Lang 14 December 1953). White (b.1901) was Keeper of Geology from 1955-1966. A reply to Oakley's enquiry, see Note A: 6.3.11. Wright was the Public Analyst for Sussex County.

I am afraid I have no record here of any analysis carried out by the late Dr. S.A. Woodhead (who died in 1943) on any part of the Piltdown skull [A]. I should imagine that if such an analysis was made it would have been while Dr. Woodhead was Principal of the Uckfield Agricultural College. Unfortunately, this College is no longer in existence. . . . I know Dr. Woodhead knew Dawson, and I remember him telling me about Dawson's work in connection with the discovery of the skull, so I should imagine that if any analysis was made it would probably be at Dawson's request [B]. I will endeavour to locate Woodhead's two sons in case either of them can supply the information you require. . .

[A] Wright wrote Woodhead's obituary (1943).

[B] The implication here is that Woodhead's analysis of the Piltdown materials had been unofficial. This being the case, the subsequent publication of the results by Dawson may have caused Woodhead some embarrassment which could have contributed to the tension between the two men reported by L.S.F. Woodhead (6.3.40/II) and Costello (1985). For further information on the Dawson and Woodhead connection, see 6.3.25, 6.3.29, and the transcript of the interview with Woodhead: 6.3.40/II.

6.3.20 DF 116/38 Warren 1 January 1954

(a) Samuel Hazzledine Warren (1872-1958); (b) handwritten letter to Oakley on stationery embossed: "Sherwood, Forest View Road, Loughton, Essex"; (c) –.

See Warren's earlier communication: 6.2.4.

. . . I can quite understand that you have had rather too much over Piltdown.! I saw that Marston was quite abusive in "Picture Post" [A]. I agree with you that the Crag fossils were suspect – and also that hacked bone [B]. . . Have you ascertained if the hacked bone was treated with chromate? The stained flint is very telling. We know that Dawson used chromate, which looks bad, but we must hope that someone else heard about it and used it to pull his leg.

[A] On 19 December 1953 the London based magazine *Picture Post* ran a story by Marston under the title: "Missing Link – But he wasn't a fake, says Alvan T. Marston FDS."

[B] A reference to some of the components of Reid Moir's materials (see 5.1.1) and to the Piltdown bone implement (Dawson & Woodward 1915a).

6.3.21 MSS WEI 2.8 St.Barbe 4 January 1954

(A) Guy St. Barbe; (b) typewritten summary of interview conducted by Weiner at St. Barbe's home in St. Alban's, Herts; (c) attached to this transcript is the annotated questionnaire used by Weiner at the interview.

This interview was conducted in the presence of Weiner's assistant, Geoffrey Ainsworth Harrison.

. . . *He and Major M[arriott] had decided at the time to say nothing of their suspicions for the sake of Dawson's wife . . . W[einer] asked whether Marriott told anyone else. B[arbe] said [that M] . . . may have told somebody else . . . before . . . they had agreed to keep the thing to themselves.[B]. . . .B. did not know Morris at all. He in fact hardly knew the people in Lewes and was not a member of the S[ussex]. A[rchaeological]. S[ociety]. He lived near Uckfield at Coombe Place.*

B's contacts with Dawson began entirely for professional reasons. The Dawsons came to garden parties, and in this way Dawson learnt that B was interested in archaeological matters, and had collected flints, including Red Crag implements [A]. . . W[einer] asked whether B knew Kennard and he said that he had met him but never told him about Dawson. Hinton . . . was the only one he had ever told . . . after Dawson died . . . when B worked with the Bristol Spelaeological Society and Hinton took an interest in their activities. . . In one of these [local] caves B. found the Slaughterford skull [B] which he refered to Keith. . .

When B told Hinton about Dawson, Hinton commented on Dawson's very great ambition . . . B could not say whether Hinton had ever told Kennard . . .

. . .[H]e [Barbe] did not think that Dawson himself had the ability to do the . . . forgery. . . . B went on to mention that the jeweller [Abbott] of Hastings has been put to him as a possibility.

W[einer] asked whether he thought that Dawson was well off and B said he appeared to be a thriving family solicitor, and was surprised when W[einer] mentioned that his widow had had to apply for a pension. B suggested that D had probably been "bled white" by some blackmailer. "Perhaps Abbott may have put the screw on old Dawson." [C]

Then B described how extremely frightened Dawson was when B surprised him in his office staining bones. There were perhaps 20 dishes, 6 inches in diameter, full of brownish liquid. Dawson, when he had calmed down, explained that he was interested in staining bones [D] . . . On a second occasion B came into Dawson's office and found he was staining flints and stones. He remembers saying to D that he could not believe that flint would take up much stain. . . He and Marriott discussed [this and]. . . they believed Dawson was "salting the mine."

W: *When you surprised Dawson had you already been to the Piltdown site?*

B: *Yes, on my own. He remembered that there was somebody working there, behind the hedge.*

W: *Was Woodward already digging at the site?*

B: *Yes, I think it must have been.*

W: *Do you know whether the jaw had been found at the time you surprised D?*

B. made it clear that previous to the "surprise" visit . . . he had been shown the cast of the skull and jaw by Dawson. . . He thought the "surprise" visits were after the big announcement . . . perhaps 6 months [but] . . . before August 12th . . . After the second surprise visit he had occasionally encountered Dawson at the Country Club but only to say good morning, Dawson avoided him, he thought.

W: *Asked whether D had been staining teeth as well as bones.*

B: *Could not remember . . .*

W: *"Can you remember anything about the finding of the canine tooth, or . . . any new announcements at Piltdown?"*

B: *"Yes, I remember several new things being found which Marriott and I discussed and decided that he was salting the mine.". . .*

W: *"How had B got to know Marriott?"*
       B. said socially, through garden parties etc. . .
W: *Did B know that D was interested in eoliths and had he read a paper in 1915 on the subject. B*
said no.

W said that D had used starch models for his theories about eolith fractures. B said that he did not know about that. W asked whether D had been staining starch as well as bone and stone. B said that he was quite sure that it was not starch that he saw being stained in Dawson's office. . . [B knew nothing] about the business of the house which brought D into disrepute with the local society . . . [B did not know] Miss [Mabel] Kenward . . . [nor did he know Dawson's friends] John Lewis . . . [and] Elliot Curwen. . . [E]

[A] See Note B: 6.3.20.

[B] See Note B, 6.3.26

[C] While the idea that Abbott had been black-mailing Dawson has its attractions, there is no firm evidence to substantiate the rumour (see Note B: 4.1.11). The only direct reference to Dawson's financial situation during the period 1913-16, appears in Letter 2.3.26.

[D] As indicated in 2.3.14 and 2.3.21, Dawson had been conducting an number of experiments with colour simulation and hardening techniques.

[E] See 6.3.22 for Weiner's assessment of this interview.

6.3.22 P.MSS KPO Weiner 5 January 1953

(a) Joseph Sydney Weiner (1915-1982); (b) typewritten letter to Oakley on printed stationery: "Department of Human Anatomy, University Museum, Oxford"; (c) letter marked: "Private and Confidential"; annotated by Weiner: "Thank you for yours of 4.1.54. Could I have Essex's information sometime please [see 6.3.23]."

I saw Barbe yesterday and my secretary took down shorthand notes of the conversation which lasted some two hours. I think that Barbe is pretty reliable and he does not seem to have embroided or improved upon his story at all since he saw Edwards [A].
* . . . Meanwhile the points that will probably interest you the most are these:*
*   1) It is absolutely certain that Hinton (whom he referred to as Martin Hinton or Martin and whom he says he knows intimately) was his only confident [sic] [B]. He knows Kennard but never told him a thing. He thinks it just possible that Hinton told Kennard though he felt that Hinton was more likely to say nothing as he, St. Barbe, had asked him to keep the information absolutely private and he thought Hinton was the sort of man to do so.*
*   2) The surprise visits of Barbe and Marriott to Dawson's office [C] undoubtedly took place after the discoveries had been announced because Barbe had previously been shown on a previous visit the plaster reconstruction of cranium and jaw by Dawson. It does appear that these visits took place just before the canine was discovered. [D]*

[A] See 6.3.13.

[B] See 6.3.18, and 6.3.49.

[C] See 6.3.21.

[D] This is supported by Dawson's reported experimental activities during the early Spring and Summer of 1913, see his letters to Woodward (2.3.14 and 2.3.21). See also Oakley's transcript of his interview with St. Barbe (6.3.31).

6.3.23 DF 116/23 Edwards 7 January 1954

(a) Wilfred Norman Edwards (1890-1956); typewritten letter to Weiner on printed stationery: "British Museum (Natural History), Cromwell Road, London S.W.7."; (c) letter marked "Private & Confidential."

. . . Oakley has, I understand, told you something of Essex's visit. It was a difficult and not a very satisfactory interview. Essex [A] is nearly stone deaf and his hearing apparatus was out of order. Most of his supposed evidence was elaborate surmise; he was pretty hopeless on dates and it was not clear whether he had worked out his theories since the Piltdown exposure of last November or how much he had suspected forty years ago. Briefly he is convinced that Teilhard de Chardin was the hoaxer and he did not think anyone else was involved.

[A] Robert Essex was a schoolmaster at Uckfield Grammar School during the Piltdown period. At the time of Weiner's investigations, Essex was at Bootham School, a boarding school for boys in York, where he taught biology. As indicated by Edwards' letter, Essex was convinced of Teilhard's involvement in the hoax. Later, in 1955, Essex went public with his theory, though it failed to attract much attention. See 6.3.27 for subsequent developments concerning Essex.

6.3.24 MSS WEI 3.17 Pollard 10 January 1954

(a) A.P. Pollard; (b) handwritten letter addressed to J.S. Weiner, on printed stationery: "65, The Avenue, Lewes, Sussex"; (c) underlining in original by Pollard.

This letter is in reply to specific questions from Weiner (see MSS WEI 3.17 Weiner 5 January 1954).

. . . Harry Morris did <u>not</u> obtain his information from Major Marriott [A], as he had begun his research. . . sometime <u>previous</u> to 1911. . . He made the acquaintance of Marriott <u>afterwards</u>. . . He [Morris] knew from the geological formation of the gravel at Piltdown that it was <u>not</u> palaeolithic or pre-p[alaeolithic] but transitional between P and Neolithic. . .[I] know nothing of Lewis Abbott. . .[and]. . . No mention was made by Morris. . . to the late Eliot Curwen. . .

For background information on the connection between Pollard and Morris, see 6.3.1.

6.3.25 DF 116/35 Woodhead 10 January 1954

Leslie S.F. Woodhead (1907-1969); (b) typewritten letter to Oakley on printed stationery: "Kingmere, Oval Way, Ferring, Worthing, Sussex"; (c) –.

Following the lead from Wright (6.3.19), Oakley made contact with Samuel Woodhead's eldest son, Leslie Woodhead [A], who was a general practitioner in Worthing, Sussex.

. . . Dr. S.A. Woodhead was my Father and he died in 1943. At the time of the finding of the Piltdown skull he was at the [Agricultural] College at Uckfield and he was Public Analyst for East Sussex at that time and he was working by himself. None of the records at that time are to be found as the Lab closed down in Uckfield in 1916 and opened in Brighton and later at Lewes.

My Father was a close friend of Charles Dawson and knew far more about the finding of the skull than anyone other than Charles himself. It was Dad's wish that his name should not be connected with it as he always hated to be in the public eye unless it was very necessary due to his work. I have kept quiet till now because of his wish but I think the time has come to tell you what very little I know from what Dad used to tell me about it. Charles Dawson brought the skull to Dad as soon as he found it and realised it was something out of the ordinary. They went back together to look for the missing parts and Dad was actually there when the jaw was found and Dad HIMSELF found the eye tooth which was on the path by the side of the digging. I can assure you that Dad would never have been a party to any kind of fraud or hoax, call it what you will. . .

For further details on the Woodhead connection, see 6.3.29.

[A] Woodhead had two sons, Leslie (1907-1969) and Lionel (b 1911).

6.3.26 P.MSS KPO Weiner 12 January 1954

(a) Joseph Sydney Weiner (1915-1982); (b) typewritten letter to Oakley on printed stationery: "Department of Human Anatomy, University Museum, Oxford"; (c) annotated by Weiner: "I return T de C's letter herewith."

. . . Hinton has not written to reply to Le Gros Clark's second letter [A] in which Le Gros Clark mentioned that we had information from St. Barbe though without saying that St. Barbe had told us of his connection with Hinton. It looks as if a visit to Hinton will be necessary, because it is obviously desirable that Barbe's knowledge of Dawson's dealings before our disclosures should be confirmed. According to him, he told Hinton what we knew in the 1920's when Hinton took some interest in the activities of the Bristol Spelaeological Society in which Barbe participated (it was one of those Bristol caves in which Barbe found the Slaughterford skull and referred it to Keith) [B] . . . Like Le Gros and myself, you will have heard from the British Association people about a Piltdown meeting. Le Gros is not very keen but will do it if you and I will. My first reaction is very much against the proposed table of the session – "The Piltdown Problem" and a change will be necessary as far as I am concerned . . . I think it would be quite appropriate to have a further session even though this will very likely bring out Marston, but then there will additional ammunition (if your Villafranchian idea comes off). I shall wait to hear what you feel about this meeting before making any further moves. . . [C]

[A] Prompted by Hinton's letter 6.3.18.

[B] The Slaughterford skull was discovered at Guy's Rift (Wiltshire) near Bristol in the early 1920s, see Hewer (1925). For a description of the skull, see Buxton (1925). According to Hewer (1925:483) the Guy's Rift site (discovered by St. Barbe in 1922) was excavated in 1924-1925 by the Bristol Spelaeological Society at the request of Keith. Apparently his interest in the site had been aroused by St. Barbe's earlier discoveries. However, when Weiner wrote Keith about this matter (MSS WEI 3.17 Weiner 18 December 1953), Keith replied that he could not remember either St. Barbe or the skull (MSS WEI 3.17 Keith 22 December 1953).

[C] Unbeknown to Weiner at the time Marston was about to launch another attack, see 6.3.33 and 6.3.37.

6.3.27 DF 116/23 Essex 12 [January] 1954

(a) Robert Essex; (b) handwritten letter to W.N. Edwards and Oakley on printed stationery: "Bootham School, York". The letter is dated July 12, 1953 – but as Essex later noted in a letter to Edwards dated 18 January 1954 (DF 116/23) this was a mistake; (c) annotated by Oakley: "Cornwell says this was a slip. He had no inside information. K.P.O. 13.1.54." Underlining in original by Essex.
This letter was evidently written following an interview with Edwards earlier in January, see 6.3.23.

I have just been reading Chambers Encyclopaedia Vol.9 p 36: "In 1912 the discovery was announced. Further systematic research yielded – half a jaw bone with <u>three molars in position</u>." The article was written by Ian W. Cornwell Sec. Institute of Archaeology, University of London. You see the implication? Dawson's jaw had two teeth. The one I saw had <u>three in position</u>. How did Ian Wolpan Cornwell get his information from T. de C.? [A]. In fact where else could he have got it? It shows either T. de C.'s memory is bad or he is still playing pranks.

Incidentally I have just found that Dawson's Clerk, who showed me the three toothed jaw, died in 1938, but I am hoping to get some more information since there are still two men there whom I knew in 1912 . . .

[A] As indicated by Oakley's annotation, Cornwell admitted that this was a typographical error, and that he had no inside information. Essex, however, was not to be deterred and continued to pursue the notion that Teilhard had perpetrated the Piltdown fraud, see 6.3.44.

6.3.28 MSS WEI 4.19 Edwards 16 January 1954

(a) Wilfred Norman Edwards (1890-1956); (b) typewritten letter to Weiner on printed stationery: "British Museum (Natural History), Cromwell Road, London S.W.7."; (c) –.

. . . I have written to Essex asking the suggested questions, and have also asked whether he had met or knew anything about Pelletier. I should surmise that Essex had not seen Miss Kenward after Nov.21 and before he came to us, but we'll see what he says. . .

See 6.3.44.

6.3.29 DF 116/35 Woodhead 16 January 1954

(a) Leslie S.F. Woodhead (1907-1969); (b) typewritten letter to Oakley on printed stationery: "Kingmere, Oval Way, Ferring, Worthing, Sussex"; (c) –.

A reply to further questions posed by Woodhead's earlier letter to Oakley, see 6.3.25.

. . .[T]here are no letters or documents of Dad's of that data and all I can go on is memory which is of course rather vague after all this time although I was always very interested in it and Dad would talk about it at times. He was always very definite about the fact that it was not long after Dawson brought the skull to show him that he and Dawson went back and found the jaw – a matter of days at the most NOT months. Again the tooth was found within a day or so of the jaw – on a Saturday as a matter of fact.

My Mother does remember that a Priest found a tooth a year or so later but could not remember his name. This must of course be the Father Teilhard de Chardin you mention in your letter . . . [Y]our suggestion about the reason Dad wished to remain anonymous because he suspected that there might have been malpractice regarding the jaw may be right . . . There is however no proof of this in any form . . . I am quite certain that Dad was not CERTAIN of the fraud for if he was, then nothing would have stopped him from making it known . . . It does seem strange to me that no records of any kind about any analysis are to be found at Lewes . .

For futher details on the Dawson-Woodward connection and the implication of this new information, see notes appended to 6.3.40/II.

6.3.30 MSS WEI 4.19 Edwards 21 January 1954

(a) Wilfred Norman Edwards (1890-1956); (b) typewritten letter to Weiner on printed stationery: "British Museum (Natural History), Cromwell Road, London S.W.7."; (c) letter marked "Private & Confidential".

Lady Woodward came to see me on Tuesday, and Oakley joined us for lunch. . . Herewith a summary of the talk:
. . . (1) At the time of the Piltdown investigations Lady Woodward was much occupied with her two children and had little to do with those concerned. She only met C.D. [Dawson] a few times altogether and he had never visited their house [A]. . . T. de. C. [Teilhard de Chardin] she scarcely knew at all [B] – she knew nothing of Postlethwaite, Woodhead or Kennard, nor anything of A.S.W.'s relations with Hinton. She remembered Corner only as a big man who was a bit of a character and who collected everything [C]. On the other hand L.A. [Lewis Abbott] was "an honest jeweller of Hastings" who collected everything, and also an amateur geologist from whom A.S.W. had purchased her 21st birthday brooch [D], her engagement ring, and other jewellery which she still wore. (So A.S.W. had known L.A. for a very long time).
(2) Lady W. was present when the nasal and turbinal were found, and was called over to help in their extraction because her fingers were more delicate than A.S.W.'s or C.D.'s. . .[E]
(3) She was unable to resolve the apparent inconsistency involved in her recollection. . .that C.D. would never reveal, even to A.S.W., exactly where he [Dawson] found the second skull etc. . .

(4) She had a slightly fuller story of how T. de C. found the canine. Dawson threw a pebble on to a heap of spread material and suggested that T. de C. should sit there and look things over [F].

(5) She dismissed as invention the story ascribed to the Norfolk M.P. . . . [G]

(6) She confirmed another story: that a successor who occupied C.D.'s house had occasion to take up some floor boards and that a skeleton (said to be ape) was found underneath. Lady Woodward had recently talked to Miss Kenward about this, and the latter remembered the story. . . [H]

(7) L.F. Salzman. . . wrote to one Vidler, a close friend of Lady Woodward's son-in-law, Hodgson, that he didn't trust C.D. because C.D. had once tried to damage him by circulating a forged letter . . . [I]

(8) Shane Leslie "forced himself" on Lady Woodward, together with Lady Demestriadi . . . and told the Vere Cole story, which she rejected as impossible. [J]

Finally, I have had a letter from Essex . . . [who had not originally suspected a hoax, and merely thought that he was the first to see the jaw. [K]

Later, on 11 February, Weiner interviewed Lady Woodward at her home in Brighton [6.3.40/I], and followed up on a number of questions raised during the session with Edwards and Oakley.

[A] This appears to be accurate. Dawson's surviving correspondence gives no indication that he ever stayed at the Woodward residence while in London.

[B] Her recollection on the matter of Teilhard, however, is open to question. In addition to staying over-night at Woodward's home on 25 September 1913 and signing his name on Lady Woodward's celebrated cloth (see annotations to Letter 2.3.35), Teilhard is also known to have travelled with the Woodwards in America (5.1.41). Also, while Teilhard's letters were sporadic during the 1920s and 1930s, they all invariably contain greetings to "Lady Smith Woodward" that are indicative of a closer relationship than that conveyed in this interview.

[C] See 2.3.13 for further details on Frank Corner.

[D] See Note A: 1.2.11 for details regarding Woodward's association with Abbott.

[E] Prior to this it was inferred from Dawson & Woodward (1914a:85) that these remains had been found by Dawson in the presence of Woodward. Although Dawson (Ibid:85) noted that the fragile turbinals "had been pieced together satisfactorily by Mrs Woodward", it was not known that she had been present when they were discovered.

[F] In his book *The Earliest Englishman*, Woodward recounted this event, somewhat differently:

". . . We [Dawson and himself] had washed and sieved much of the gravel, and had spread it for examination after washing by rain. We were then excavating a rather deep and hot trench in which Father Teilhard, in black clothing, was especially energetic; and as we thought he seemed a little exhausted, we suggested that he should leave us to do the hard labour for a time while he had comparative rest searching the rain-washed spread gravel" (Woodward 1948:11).

[G] The details of this are unknown.

[H] For further details on this story, see 6.3.1.

[I] The details of this incident were later related by Salzman to Weiner (MSS WEI 3.17 Salzman 18 February 1954). According to Salzman he strongly believed that Dawson had circulated printed cards to members of the Society of Antiquaries urging the election of "Salzman, historian and critic." Candidates for office in the Society, Salzman explained, are not allowed to canvas. Informed by a colleague of the situation, Salzman immediately reported to the president of the Society that he was not responsible and that he was sure it was the work of a "misguided friend." To which Salzman added: "That this was the work of Charles Dawson was obvious." Salzman believed that Dawson held a grudge against him because of his critical review of Dawson's book *History of Hastings Castle* (1.1.21). Also Salzman noted that a former friend of Dawson, "John Lewis FSA", had implied that Dawson had been involved. Dawson and Lewis had been friends since the 1890s, and had collaborated on a number of local excavations for the Sussex Archaeological Society. According to Weiner (1955:179), around 1911, Dawson had a serious quarrel with Lewis which terminated their friendship. The details of this quarrel are not known.

[J] John Randolph Shane (b 1885), the Irish journalist and writer.

[K] See DF 116/23 Essex 18 January 1954. Here Essex claimed that he had been amongst the first to see the jaw. He then went on to recall what he knew about Father Félix Pelletier. Essex felt that Pelletier did not share Teilhard's enthusiasm for geology and palaeontology. In Essex's opinion, he much preferred being in the local pub. See 6.3.44-45.

6.3.31 MSS WEI 2.8 St. Barbe 27 January 1954

(a) Guy St. Barbe; (b) typewritten summary of an interview conducted by Kenneth Oakley at St. Barbe's home at St. Alban's. Herts; (c) underlining in original by Oakley.

Captain St. Barbe spoke of "bowling him over" (i.e. bowling D[awson] over) when he burst into his office on two occasions before the 1914-18 war. 1910 was the earliest possible year during which this could have happened. . . B. then said D. showed him the cast of the reconstructed skull on one occasion therefore it must have been later than 1912. D. was surprised in his office on three occasions [A]. First by B. who noted a strong smell as of a chemist shop and several dishes containing dark-coloured fluid, in some of which <u>bones</u> were being boiled. Second, by Marriot [sic] who also noticed <u>bones</u> being boiled in dark fluid. Third, by B again when D was apparently boiling <u>flints</u>. D. was very agitated and explained that he was experimenting with a view to finding out how bones and flints become stained. He said on one occasion, "I'm trying iodine." His agitation was very obvious on each occasion. B. was not expected in D.'s office on either of these occasions, when he "burst in", because he was in the habit of calling upon him on the spur of the moment in regard to matters concerning his estate. B. said that being of an artistic temperament, it would not have occurred to him that it might be inconvenient to do this, "even on Christmas Day!" B. reported that he was sure that these two visits were made when <u>D had his office in Lewes</u>. D. appeared to be interested only in darker-coloured flint's in B.'s collection, and it is quite likely that D.had used flints from that collection. [B]

[A] St. Barbe's recollections in this regard tally closely with what he told Weiner earlier, see 6.3.21.

[B] At the bottom of this report, Oakley has typed the following note:

Evidence of salting in excavation at Beaufort Park

L.V.Grinsell [6.3.17] has drawn my attention tothere being references to the work of Charles Dawson in E. Straker, "Wealden Iron" [London: Bell, 1931], including on pp 335-7 a reference to the possible "salting" of an excavation in Beaufort Park, of which Straker considered Dawson may have been the victim.

6.3.32 P.MSS KPO Teilhard de Chardin 29 January 1954

(a) Pierre Teilhard de Chardin (1881-1955); typewritten letter to Oakley on plain stationery: "The Wenner-Gren Foundation, 14 East 71st Street, New York"; (c) the letter is annotated by Teilhard, and the underlining in the original are typed.

This letter was written in response to Oakley's specific questions (see 6.3.15 and another letter written on 26 January) relating to Teilhard's mention of the Piltdown II site in his earlier letter of 28 November 1953 (6.2.15).

Well received your letter of January 26th.

Concerning the point of "history" you ask me, my "souvenirs" are a little vague. Yet, by elimination (and since Dawson died <u>during</u> the first war, if I am correct) my visit with Dawson to the second site (where two small fragments of skull and the isolated molar were supposedly found in the rubbish) must have been late July 1913 [A]. I cannot remember whether Smith-Woodward was with Dawson and me, this particular day. But the possibility is not excluded.

In those times I [had] heard of Lewis Abbott, but I don't think I ever met him. . . .

The following postscript is handwritten:

When I visited the site No. 2 (in 1913?) the two small fragments of skull and the tooth <u>had</u> already been found, I believe. But your very question makes me doubtful. . . . Yes, I think definitely they <u>had</u> been already found, and that is the reason why Dawson pointed to me the little heap of raked pebbles as the place of the discovery [B].

[A] In margin Teilhard has written: "/certainly <u>not</u> in 1914/".

[B] It is conjectured (Spencer 1990) that Teilhard was confusing Piltdown II with the material found at the Barcombe site (see Letters 2.3.14 and 2.3.21). The latter remains were "found" in late June or early July 1913. Teilhard returned to England on 1 August 1913 (see 2.3.35). It is interesting to note in this regard that Weiner later received a letter from a Rev. H.J.T. Johnston of Cambridge (see MSS WEI 4.19 Weiner 4 March 1954), who claimed that Dawson (then in "failing health") had shown him cranial fragments (? Piltdown II) and the site where they were discovered. Weiner believed Johnson had been shown the Barcombe material, but as indicated by Lankester's 1915 letter (4.1.39) it could well have been Piltdown II.

6.3.33 DF 116/38 Marston 1 February 1954

(a) Alvan T. Marston (1889-1971); (b) typewritten letter on printed stationery: "74 Southside, Clapham Common, London S.W.4."; (c) –.

Will you tell me what was the colour of the Piltdown flint (Reg. No. 606) before the test was made on it which revealed the effects of chromate treatment?

The area subsequently treated by acid to remove the stain, was localized or did it extend over the whole flint?"

For further details on this request, see 6.3.35.

6.3.34 MSS WEI 4.19 Oakley 1 February 1954

(a) Kenneth Page Oakley (1911-1981); (b) typewritten letter to Le Gros Clark at Oxford on printed stationery: "British Museum (Natural History), Cromwell Road, London S.W.7"; (c) annotated by Oakley [B].

The enamel of M1 was cracked at the anterio-internal cusp, but whether a splinter broke away during the faking it is not possible to be certain. On cleaning the tooth with spirit and benzene we found that a splinter of enamel at this corner had been replaced by wax! Parsons [A] now remembers that when the original mould was being made there was a hullabaloo in the workshop because a small splinter of enamel had been pulled off by the jelly and was lost [B] . . .

[A] See introduction to Section 6.1, fn 1.

[B] Handwritten footnote: "Days were spent in sieving dust, but all in vain!"

6.3.35 DF 116/38 Oakley 2 February 1954

(a) Kenneth Page Oakley (1911-1981); (b) carbon copy of type written letter to Alvan T. Marston; (c) underlining typed.

A reply to Marston's letter, 6.3.33.

The colour of the Piltdown flint (E. 606) is the same now as before the test was made. The method used (X-ray spectography) did not require the removal in solution of any part of the stain. Independently of the test a small area (circa 1cm. diam.) of the flint was treated with dilute hydrochloric acid, which rapidly dissolved the stain over that area.

For further details, see notes to Letter 6.3.37.

6.3.36 MSS WEI 4.19 Weiner 2 February 1954:

(a) Joseph Sydney Weiner (1915-1982); (b) carbon copy of typewritten letter to Oakley at the British Museum; (c) –.

. . . I shall make a few alterations in the St. Barbe report to incorporate your additions and send it to him for his comments and signature [A] . . . I have written to Woodhead [B] . . . Hall [C] came in to show me his D. Phil. thesis section on the Piltdown affair. He has been able to make a calibration with different intensities of iron and chromium on some bones I lent him, and he has re-expresses [sic] his results on the Piltdown fragments as a concentration per square centimetre of bone surface. What I had not realised (what comes out from his results and is evident on the original figures) is that the chromium stained flint is the only one, I believe, with an extremely low iron staining. Doesn't this confirm that chromium was deliberately used rather than iron to get a "certain colour" as you suggested?

I have just seen Straker's [D] book in the Bodelian and I am a bit disappointed to find that it in fact refers only to the figurines which Baines, at Hastings, showed me and told me was extremely dubious [E]. . .

[A] See 6.3.21.

[B] See 6.3.40.

[C] See Note A: 6.1.9.

[D] See Note B: 6.3.31.

[E] J. Mainwaring Baines, Curator of the Hastings Museum and Art Gallery. At this junction Weiner and Oakley were interested in items belonging to the Dawson collection held by the Hastings Museum. Subsequently, however, Weiner discovered that Baines was in the process of studying the history of Hastings Castle, and had in his possession the manuscript of William Herbert, the antiquarian who had carried out excavations at the castle in 1824. Although Dawson indicates that he had relied heavily on the Herbert's manuscript in the preparation of his *History of Hastings Castle* (1909), Baines believed Dawson had essentially plundered the work (MSS WEI 3.17 Baines 19 February 1954). For further details on this, see report of an interview with Baines in *The Times* 15 November 1954, under the title: "Plagiarism in History", and Weiner (1955:176-177).

6.3.37 DF 116/38 Marston 3 February 1954

(a) Alvan T. Marston (1889-1971); (b) typewritten letter to Oakley on printed stationery: "74 Southside, Clapham Common, London S.W.4"; (c) –.

For background information on the following letter, see 6.3.33 and 6.3.35.

. . . I have asked and received permission to exhibit the results of my own experiments on the chromate treatment of flint at the next meeting of the Geological Society of London . . .

Marston's presentation to the Geological Society took place on 25 February 1954. Here Marston explained that his exhibit was prompted by a note published by Oakley and Weiner in *Nature* 12 December 1953 (p 1110), in which it was asserted that the Piltdown flint E606 was "recovered *in situ* from the layer immediately overlying the skull horizon." Marston pointed out that the provenance of the skull was undetermined (Marston 1954b:xlv). He then went on to note that Oakley and Weiner had claimed that the E606 specimen [6.1.9] had been deliberately stained with chromate in order to deceive those working at Piltdown. Marston thought otherwise and to illustrate his argument he showed an exhibit of modern and ancient bones which had been treated with various chemicals. In concluding his presentation, Marston said there was "no need, no purpose, no motive, over forty years ago, to fake the colour of E606." He suggested that perhaps the presence of chromium on E606 was due to residual trace element in the Piltdown gravels (Marston 1954b:xlvi). Following Marston's delivery, Oakley presented the results of recent investigations of the geochemist, Alfred Allinson Moss at the Natural History Museum and E.T. Hall at Oxford. This work, Oakley said, had revealed the probable artificiality of the staining of most of the Piltdown flints that had been recorded as implements. The stains of most of the alleged worked flints he said proved to ferruginous which dissolved in dilute hydrochloric acid, whereas specimen E606, was found to contain chromium. Oakley then went on to note that no significant traces of chromium had been detected in the Piltdown gravels (Oakley 1954:xlvi-xlvii).

6.3.38 DF 116/32 Oakley 9 February 1954

(a) Kenneth Page Oakley (1911-1981); carbon-copy of typewritten letter to Teilhard in New York City; (c) –.

A reply to Letter 6.3.32.

. . . *What you tell me rather confirms the impression I have that Dawson withheld information from Woodward. Thus according to the records we have here he said nothing to Woodward about having found the specimens at the second site until 1915! . . .*

6.3.39 MSS WEI 2.8 Curwen 11 February 1954:

(a) E.Cecil Curwen (d 1967); (b) typewritten summary of interview with Curwen by Joseph S. Weiner and Geoffrey A. Harrison at Curwen's home in Hove, Sussex.

E.C. Curwen is the son of Eliot Curwen (1865-1951), the Sussex archaeologist and antiquarian.

J.S.W. asked whether Curwen was aware of his father's doubts about C.D[awson]. He said he was not . . . He had only learned of the general hostility at the last general Council meeting of the S.A.S. at which most outspoken were Bentham Stephens . . . and Margery. He only joined the society in 1916 and he was not aware that C.D. had dropped out in 1914 . . . [A]

[A] Charles Dawson, along with his wife, and Gladys Postlethwaite (his step-daughter) are listed separately as members of Sussex Archaeological Society in the 1914. From all indications Dawson retained his membership until his death in 1916.

6.3.40 MSS WEI 2.8 Woodward (I)/Woodhead (II) 11 February 1954

I: (a) Lady Maud Smith Woodward (1874-1963); (b) typewritten summary of interview conducted by Joseph Weiner and Geoffrey A. Harrison in Brighton, Sussex on Thursday 11 February; (c) underlining in original by Weiner.

See Edwards' interview, 6.3.30.

D[awson]. was not really very friendly with W[oodward]. who did not regard him really as a man of science. He was at their home for tea but never for dinner (name embroidered on table cloth with other visitors) . . . W never stayed over Castle Lodge [A], nor did she. D was a "magpie" of collector . . . D seemed quite well off though she understood that Mrs. Dawson was left not well provided for [B].

. . . She used to go along [to Piltdown] quite often but was not active in the work. She was certain that the pit was never a rubbish dump. She could not remember that Woodhead was helping at that time, and in fact did not remember him or when the chemical analysis was done. Abbot [sic] was probably about. Teilhard was there very frequently . . . As regards site II, she was firm that D[awson] would not [sic] give details of the exact spot, that her husband was most anxious about it, and that D's illness made his enquiries fruitless, and that he spent much time searching for site II specifically. . . [I]t seemed to her that her husband regarded site II as something that D. had imagined, it "existed in Dawson's imagination." She knew that D. was rather queer in his last illness. . .

[A] Dawson's correspondence, however, suggests otherwise. In Letter 2.3.50, Dawson writes: "I am sorry that I can not put you up this weekend. . ."

[B] Two letters (DF 100/42, dated 7 January 1917 (4.2.22) and 18 March 1917) from Hélène Dawson indicates that she was financially pressed, and that Woodward had promised to assist her in obtaining a civil pension. As indicated in Note C: 6.3.4 Mrs Dawson died 25 May 1917.

II: (a) Leslie S.F. Woodhead (1907-1969); (b) typewritten summary of interview conducted by Weiner and Harrison at Woodhead's surgery at Goring (Worthing), Sussex on Thursday, 11 February; (c) transcript edited by Weiner.

L[eslie]. W[oodhead]. said that C[harles]. D[awson]. had been a friend of his father for a long time until his father's (second) marriage in 1906 [?]. He, L.W. was the second child and the date of his birth, 13th December 1907, was only a few weeks before his father made a search for further fragments, within days of the finding of the first piece. His mother had never liked D. and he was sure that after the marriage things "cooled off" with D. (his mother had a poor opinion of C.D. on the score of his "personal behaviour"). He was quite certain that his father had found a jaw soon after the first discovery. His father had last told him this in 1933, just before L.W. went to Malaya. They were motoring in the district at the time. He was sure that his father claimed to [*/have found] [x/find] find the jaw and also an eye-tooth. The eye-tooth was found by his father working on his own on the day following the finding of the jaw [A]. L.W. realized all this conflicted with Dawson's own statement in the Hastings Journal [B]. He volunteered the statement that Dawson was a collector of lots of things including antique furniture which he believed he restored [C]. L.W. asserted that his father would, out of loyalty, prefer to say nothing, even if he had suspected something early on. L.W. inferred that the cooling off might have indicated some possible suspicion in his father's mind. . . [D]

[*/] Word(s) inserted or deleted [x/] by Weiner.

[?] word unclear.

[A] For a possible explanation of this, see Note A: 2.3.49 and 6.3.29.

[B] See Dawson's article in the *Hastings & East Sussex Naturalist* (1913) and (1915).

[C] See Weiner (1955:178).

[D] Later in 1985, Peter Costello published a paper in *Antiquity* in which he developed a case against Woodhead. See Note C: 1.1.1 for further details.

6.3.41 MSS WEI 2.8 Clarke 12 February 1954

(a) E. Clarke (1872-1954); (b) typewritten summary of interview with Clarke by Joseph S. Weiner and Geoffrey A. Harrison; (c) –.

. . . [B]oth [Clarke and his wife] remembered the Dawsons well. Mr. C[larke] thought that Dawson was quite a friendly and hospitable man and he was personally on good terms with him. He spontaneously told us however that Dawson had certainly perpetrated a "bit of sharp practice" when he acquired Castle Lodge [A]. . . Clarke regarded this quite cynically as not unexpected type of commercial behaviour.

He and his wife had dined with the Dawsons before Woodward [S.W.] came into the picture [x/ although] they knew [/ at the time] that [*/S.W. at the B.M]. was being contacted [B].*

After dinner Dawson said to Clarke that he had something of interest to show him in his cellar, to which Mrs. Dawson said something to the effect that she did not know what was going on. He would not let her into the secret. "I sometimes think he is a Dr. Crippen" [C]. Both Clarke's remembered this clearly. In the cellar . . . Dawson showed Clarke several pieces of bone. They were dry. Both JSW and GAH understood him to say that there were more than two pieces of bone. C. could not say that the cellar was equipped as a workshop although it was large enough for that purpose. He did not see any bottles of chemicals or tools. . .

Clarke saw Dawson within a few months of his death. He met him one day on Lewes station and noticed that he looked anxious. Dawson then said that the doctors in London had given him a very bad verdict. Clarke said Dawson had died of anaemia but a doctor friend of his some years later had told him that the cause of death from the description was more likely to have been leukaemia. "My white cells are multiplying too rapidly [D]." . . . He had known Major Marriott extremely well and regarded him as complete crank. . . He remembered Morris, slightly, as a crank [E].

[x/] word(s) deleted or [*/] added by Weiner.

[A] See Note E: 6.3.1.

[B] See Note C: 1.2.2.

[C] [Hawley Harvey] Crippen (1862-1910), a notorious convicted murderer who poisoned his wife and then dismembered her body (which he buried in their house), before making an unsuccessful attempt to flee with his mistress to the United States.

[D] For further details on Dawson's illness, see introduction to Section 4.2.

[E] See 6.3.2.

6.3.42 MSS WEI 2.8 Wade 12 February 1954

(a) Major G. Wade; (b) typewritten summary of interview conducted by Joseph Weiner and Geoffrey A. Harrison; (c) –.

Wade's identity and relationship to Dawson is not clear. Wade at this time lived at Farnham, near Aldershot (Hants).

Major Wade considered that the gravel diggers were capable of perpetrating any fraud for the sake of money. He had previous experience of gravel diggers in his own district of transferring fossil animals and flints from one strata to another . . .

Weiner acknowledges Wade's assistance in the preface of his book (1955:vii). According to Weiner (1955:106), Wade was a close friend of Reginald Smith (see Section 1.3)

6.3.43 DF 116/32 Oakley 16 February 1954

(a) Kenneth Page Oakley (1911-1981); (b) carbon copy of typewritten letter to Teilhard in New York City; (c) –.

An interesting piece of information has now come in. A Mr Woodhead has told us that his father was present when Dawson found the (or a?) Piltdown jawbone and that it was in 1908 or thereabouts! [A] Apparently Woodhead was an official analytical chemist in Sussex at the time. Do you remember anything about him? It seems extraordinary that Dawson only mentions him once, as having analysed a piece of the skull.

Do you remember Dawson telling you that he had dipped the bones in potassium dichromate?

For Teilhard's response, see 6.3.47.

[A] See 6.3.40: Interview II.

6.3.44 MSS WEI 3.17 Essex 17 February 1954

(a) Robert Essex; (b) handwritten letter to Weiner on printed stationery: "Bootham School, York"; attached is a handwritten, 5 page memorandum [A]; (c) underlining in original by Essex.

. . . I am certain, in the light of what I know now, that Charles Dawson, before he was taken ill in 1915 – suspected Teilhard – I am <u>certain</u> he suspected a hoax. The thing that started him off on his suspicions was a remark about the <u>16" cricket bat</u> [B] – I saw the look on his face and from then on his manner seemed change. However, soon after he became ill. I left England and didn't get back until 1927. . .

[A] Replies to Weiner's specific questions. Weiner had requested information on Woodhead and several local personnages, including Saxby (lecturer in Husbandry at Uckfield Agricultural College); Goody (a botanist) also from the Agricultural College; A. Farr (owner of local Chemists (Pharmacy) shop; Wakeford, Jenner and Eade (solicitor clerks: Dawson & Hart); Pierre Teilhard de Chardin; M.C. Burkitt; Abbé Breuil and Father Pelletier (see DF 116/23 for typed copy of this memorandum).

[B] See 6.3.45 for further details. From all indications this implement was first likened to a cricket bat by Reginald Smith of the British Museum (Dawson & Woodward 1915a:148)

6.3.45 MSS WEI 3.17 Essex 19 February 1954

(a) Robert Essex; (b) handwritten letter on printed stationery: "Bootham School, York"; (c) –.

. . . To explain the 16" cricket bat . . . [standing outside of Dawson's office in Uckfield discussing Piltdown was a group consisting of]: Charles Dawson, John Montgomery [JM], who was my headmaster [Uckfield Grammar School], myself, and one or two interested "outsiders" and a second group which included Father Teilhard. . . Charles Dawson remarked that he couldn't remember seeing anything quite like the "sixteen inch bat" which was found in the rubble heap on the Piltdown site – [supposed to be cut from the femur of a very large extinct elephant type]. "But I have" said John Montgomery. "Oh!" said Dawson, "Where?" "In the Dordogne," said J.M. Dawson's eyebrows went up and he looked round to see where Teilhard was standing and for a few seconds seemed deep in thought – From that position he suddenly swung back and apologized for his lapse – then said he must get back to work . . .

For an elaboration of this scenario, see Essex (1955) and Head (1971). It should be noted that Weiner did not incorporate any of Essex's testimony into his book (1955). On 18 January 1960, Oakley interviewed Essex (see DF 116/23 for transcript) in which he reiterated his case against Teilhard.

6.3.46 MSS WEI 4.19 Oakley 26 February 1954

(a) Kenneth Page Oakley (1911-1981); (b) typewritten letter to Weiner at Oxford on printed stationery: "British Museum (Natural History), Cromwell Road, London S.W.7."; (c) –.

The following letter relates essential details of Oakley's encounter with Marston at the Geological Society of London on 25 February 1954 (see 6.3.37).

Marston gave a rambling account of his experiments on staining flints, which did not seem to have much bearing on the problem at Piltdown. (1) He doubted if Kr is present on E 606; (2) if it is, then it was stained for some unknown reason in the B.M. labs; or there was some chromium (sic) in the Piltdown gravel which became concentrated patchily [A].
  . . . I have been comparing the histology of the various Piltdown cranial bones by means of thin sections. There are some puzzling features which I should like to discuss with you and Le Gros. I could bring them to Oxford one day next week. [B]

[A] Despite the evidence, Marston continued to insist that Oakley and his co-workers were wrong, and on 30 June 1954 at another meeting of the Geological Society of London, he repeated his arguments. At this same meeting, Oakley, Weiner, Le Gros Clark , Gavin de Beer and other members of the Piltdown investigatory team reviewed the results of their various researches, which completely neutralized Marston's previous arguments. A summary of this meeting was widely publicized, see particularly *Nature* (10 July 1954, p 81).

[B] From all indications the histology of the Piltdown cranial fragments indicated that while their structure and thickness could be matched with recent crania, the thickening of the diploe was not considered normal. In fact there was every indication, so Oakley believed, that Shattock's (1913:46) view "that certain details of the Piltdown calvaria . . . suggest the possibility of a pathological process having underlain the thickened condition" might be correct. For further details, see Oakley, in Weiner et al (1955: 257-259). It should be noted, however, that while there is support for this pathological interpretation, the evidence is not conclusive. In this light, Montagu (1960), later argued that the thickening may have been artificially induced by boiling in a solution of sodium hydroxide.

6.3.47 DF 116/31 Teilhard de Chardin 1 March 1954

(a) Pierre Teilhard de Chardin (1881-1955); (b) typewritten letter to Oakley on plain stationery: "Wenner-Gren Foundation, 14 East 71st Street, New York 21"; (c) –.

Well received your letters of February 9 and 16 [A]. I know unfortunately nothing about Mr. Woodhead – and in 1908 I did not know Dawson [B]. Nor did Dawson tell me anything about a possible use made by him of potassium dichromate [C]. You know at the time, I was a young student in theology, not allowed to leave much his cell of Ore Place (Hastings), and I did not know anything about anthropology (or even prehistory); my chief passion was the Wealdian bone-beds and their fossil teeth content. . .

Anyhow, I hope that next summer we shall have ample time to discuss, not only Piltdown, but much more interesting Africa [D].

[A] See Letters 6.3.38 and 6.3.43.

[B] As indicated by Letters 1.1.8 and 1.1.10, Dawson and Teilhard first met in 1909.

[C] From all indications (Note D: 1.1.10), Teilhard had been supplied by Dawson with a dichromate solution prepared by Frank Barlow, for use on their palaeontological specimens.

[D] See 6.3.55.

6.3.48 MSS WEI 2.8 Sargent 2 March 1954

Henry.J. Sargent (1891-1983); (b) typewritten summary of interview by Kenneth Oakley, at the Bexhill Museum, Bexhill-on-sea, East Sussex; (c) reported initialled by Oakley: "K.P.O".

Sargent had been Curator of the Bexhill Hill Museum since 1920.

. . . [Sargent] knew C[harles].D[awson]. [and] he recalls that he met him one day in Hastings (circa 1911 or 12) and that C.D. produced out of his pocket a small piece of very thick skull bone. It was rather carelessly wrapped in a piece of newspaper. C.D. said that he was going to take it to the B.M.(N.H.). Sargent remembers that it was dark brown and of pointed form [A]. C.D. was in the habit of visiting Hastings on Saturdays . . .

[A] Sargent's dating of this event coincides (approximately) with the incident related to Weiner by Clarke, see 6.3.41. Likewise, Sargent's note on the distinctive colour of the remains is not insignificant, but to what extent his memory in this regard had been influenced by recent accounts in the newspapers is debatable.

6.3.49 DF 116/24 Hinton 17 March 1954

(a) Martin Alister Campbell Hinton (1883-1961); (b) handwritten letter to Gavin De Beer on plain stationery: "Glaisters, Wrington, Bristol"; (c) –.

This letter was in response to an earlier one from de Beer, dated 27 February 1954 [DF 116/24] in which he notes that Weiner had interviewed him, and as indicated below, Hinton had suggested that some of the Piltdown fauna may have been imported from France – which picks up on the theme echoed by Essex [6.3.45] and Morris's cards (Note B: 6.3.2).

My suggestion to Weiner that Montpellier might be the source of the fossils was a pure spur of the moment guess [A]. . . . The temptation to invent such a "discovery" of an ape-like man associated with late Pliocene Mammals in a Wealden gravel might well have proved irresistible to some unbalanced member of old Ben Harrison's circle at Ightham [B]. He and his friends (of whom I was one) were always talking of the possibility of finding a late Pliocene deposit in the Weald and even a Miocene stream deposit on the Kentish Plateau (crest of the North Downs). I spent the long vacation of 1902 and the Easter and part of the long vacation of 1906 in searching the water partings in the Weald near Ightham and the ridge between the combes of the North Downs for traces of gravels deposited by pre-existing streams. But I was not successful; at least I found nothing that would give any clear evidence of such remote antiquity. Old Ben and I had many a walk to likely spots and F.J. Bennett [C] was a keen searcher at the same time.

Weiner told me that an officer of the Geological Survey had established that the Piltdown deposit is only 50 feet above the bed of the nearest stream [D]. On the face of it that would look as though the gravel could not be very old – not as old as the 100 ft. Terrace. But it would depend upon whether the gravel lies on a water-parting or not; it might be a deposit belonging to an older system and by reason of the development of a later system it could be brought into relation with a quite modern stream cutting into the ridge by headward erosion. I put this point forward as a warning to any person reviewing the facts without a great deal of field experience, that there is necessity to take full notice of the topography as well as the levels before coming to a conclusion.

My view is that the above fraud has been proved to have been perpetrated at Piltdown it would be wise to disregard the whole story. The skull which seems to be a fossil may have been brought there too as well as the spurious jaw, the Pliocene and early Pleistocene Mammalia and the flint implements . . . I now regard the whole discovery with the deepest suspicion [E].

[A] The date of Weiner's implied visit to Hinton, is uncertain, but clearly had taken place sometime between 13 & 27 February, when de Beer contacted Hinton. The only record of the interview is a series of questions (without annotations) listed under Hinton's name on a single sheet (undated), see MSS WEI 2.8.

[B] Benjamin Harrison (1837-1921), who along with Joseph Prestwich (1812-1896), had established a case for the validity of an eolithic tool industry in southeast England during the early 1890s.

[C] Francis J. Bennett (b1845).

[D] A reference to Francis H. Edmunds's survey in 1924, see 5.2.11 and 6.3.7.

[E] Hinton repeated this position in his letter to Weiner dated May 11, 1954 (MSS WEI 3.17). Indeed, after this time, until his death, Hinton appears to have promoted the view that the forgery had been an inside job (e.g. P.MSS KPO: Glyn Daniel 23 January 1973).

6.3.50 DF 116/24 de Beer 22 March 1954

(a) Gavin Rylands de Beer (1899-1972); (b) carbon copy of a letter to Martin Hinton in Bristol.

This copy contains a number of editorial changes, and evidently a first draft which was not sent.

A reply to Letter 6.3.49.

I was delighted to receive your letter of 17 March because of what you tell me about the Piltdown affair corresponds so closely with what we have discovered in the course of our very thorough investigation of the evidence.

. . . We were particularly interested in your suggestion that the fossils had been stained to match the human skull and spurious jaw, because we ourselves only obtained proof of this a few days before your letter arrived. The chemical composition of the two teeth which were at first referred to <u>Stegodon</u> is in one way so peculiar that we hope that we shall, before the end of our research be able to establish their origin [A].

Could you suggest where the anonymous hoaxer might have obtained rareties such as these two teeth? It occurs to us as being possible that there was a dealer in fossils from whom they could have been purchased. This is suggested to us by a letter from Dawson to Woodward written on 1st March 1913 [B] . . . Do you recall anyone in Sussex who might have been disposing of such specimens (presumably foreign)?

We were very sorry to hear that you are so troubled by your eyes.

The middle two paragraphs from the above "draft" are inserted at the end of the following letter (carbon copy), and is initialled "GR de B."

I am very sorry to learn of your trouble with your eyes; it makes me rather ashamed of having put you my conundrum; but all the more grateful to you for your kind and valuable answer.

Coming into the Museum from outside, I had no inkling of anything "phoney" about the Piltdown finds, but as we now have independent scientific evidence, based on newly devised methods, which confirms everything that you say in your letter, it is plain to me that at the time there must have been a body of knowledge on the subject which you are probably the only surviving possessor. Let me hasten to say that I appreciate to the full how very very delicate your position must have been, because obviously, after this hoax had got well ahead, and out of hand, your loyalty to the Museum would have prevented you from wanting to make opposition which would have amounted to public exposure, in which you might even have been disbelieved, for at that time there were no methods of establishing the facts as at present. On the other hand, your scientific conscience must have been subjected to strain. Marston is going about saying that he has seen a letter from you to Corner advising him not to pay too much attention to the finds, and if I had been in your position at the time, I should have done the same for my friends.

The Museum is, of course, not concerned to discover or reveal the identities of the hoaxers (for more than one must have been involved), but only to pursue the scientific analysis of the specimens to the full. I wonder therefore if I might trespass on your kindness to ask you if you can help me with the following puzzle? . . . [C]

[A] See Oakley in Weiner *et al.* (1955: 247–253).

[B] See 2.3.6.

[C] If Hinton did reply to de Beer's letter it has not been preserved in the collection. It is interesting to note, however, that Hinton did respond to Weiner's enquiries regarding Kennard and the question of "access" (see Notes to 6.3.18). But, this letter, dated 11 May 1954, did not elaborate on the question of the source of the Piltdown fossils.

6.3.51 MSS WEI 4.19 Oakley 29 March 1953

(a) Kenneth Page Oakley (1911-1981); (b) handwritten note to Weiner at on Oxford on printed stationery: "British Museum (Natural History), Cromwell Road, London S.W.7." (c)

I wondered if you would care to draft a short section on experimental grinding of ape teeth for inclusion in our report? Parsons [A] now has the orang jaw which we selected and will begin grinding the two molars as soon as possible.

I find that Carborundum was first produced in 1891. Our chief carpenter has a carborundum stone which he brought 40 years ago!

[A] See Note C: 6.3.5.

6.3.52 MSS WEI 3.17 Weiner 21 May 1954

(a) Joseph Sydney Weiner (1915-1982); (b) carbon copy of letter(s) sent to Professor H.H. Swinnerton of Nottingham [cf 6.3.53], Professor A.H. Cox of Rhiwbina, Wales, and S. Hazzledine Warren [6.3.54]; (c) –.

. . . The late Mr. A.W. Oke, F.G.S. wrote a letter to a Brighton newspaper in 1926 in which he threw doubt on the reported circumstances of the finding of the Piltdown fragments [A]. In this letter Mr. Oke makes it plain that at the meeting of the Geological Society on December 2nd, 1914, when Dawson and Woodward exhibited the unique bone implements [sic], there was hostile and sceptical comment [B]. He says, that Mr. Dawson could not stay to answer any questions on that occasion, and left to catch his train . . . As you were present on that occasion I wonder if you can recollect how the discussion actually went

[A] Alfred W. Oke, is listed as a member of the Sussex Archaeological Society, living in Hove. He is also known to have been a member of a number of other scientific societies in the south eastern counties. Weiner (1955:142,164,173) found Oke's letter in a file pertaining to A.S. Woodward located in the University College Library, London. A recent search of Woodward's papers at UCL, however, failed to recover this letter (?clipping). According to Weiner, Oke's letter is dated 30 December (? 1926) and refers the reader to H.J. Osborne White's monograph: "The Geology of the Country near Lewes" (1926) in which the Piltdown gravels and *Eoanthropus* are considered (pp 63-69). From this work, Oke cites the following passage:

The skull-fragments, jawbone, and teeth of Eoanthropus dawsoni *exhibit simian traits, which are so pronounced in the jawbone as to warrant the ascription of the elderly female (?) individual to whom, in Smith Woodward's opinion, all these relics belonged, to a distinct genus of Hominidae. The discovery of the skull-fragments and the jaw bone at different times, in excavated material yielding other mammalian remains, leaves room for doubt whether they actually formed parts of the same being: more than one zoologist of standing has maintained that the jawbone is that of a chimpanzee; but at present the balance of opinion favours Smith Woodward's interpretation (p. 66)*

[B] For further insight into this, see Swinnerton's response, 6.3.53.

6.3.53 MSS WEI 3.17 Swinnerton 1 June 1954

(a) H.H. Swinnerton; (b) typewritten letter to Weiner on plain stationery: "17 Burlington Road, Nottingham"; (c) –.

A reply to Weiner's inquiries, 6.3.52.

. . . The meeting [A] to which you refer is one of the few out of a great many of which I clearly remember being present . . . Being a provincial fellow . . . I did not know many of the speakers even by sight.

I can quite confidently say there was no hostile comment . . . There was candid discussion, that is what such meetings are for. It is possible that Mr. Oke was not accustomed to such discussion and mistook disagreement for hostility. The general impression produced upon my mind was that there was doubt upon two issues. First there was doubt about the precise position of the skull in the deposits. It was first found by workmen extracting the gravel . . . [Thus] . . . it is not surprising therefore that some speakers were more sanguine and others less – but none hostile. I may say that I was sufficiently interested to go and see the site myself. . .

The second doubt lay in the interpretation of the fragments . . . Woodward's reconstruction was . . . doubted and candidly criticised. After all Woodward was not a human anatomist. . . [T]he impression created on my mind was that Woodward himself had streaks of doubt about the jaw. In deciding that this jaw belonged to this skull the geologically minded investigator would naturally be more influenced by the stratigraphical association than would the pure anatomist . . . The bone implement [B]. I recollect that Woodward pointed out the features, weighed the pros and cons and on the balance seemed in favour of its genuineness. Over this again there was candid discussion, some believed but others doubted. Hostility – no. . .

[A] Referring to the meeting of 18 December 1912, when the Piltdown remains were first unveiled.

[B] The bone implement (Woodward & Dawson 1915a) was first discussed on 2 December 1914.

6.3.54 MSS WEI 3.18 Warren 12 June 1954

(a) Samuel Hazzledine Warren (1872-1958); (b) handwritten letter to Weiner on printed stationery: "Hadleigh Hotel, Marine Parade, Clacton-on-Sea"; (c) –.

A reply to Weiner's inquiries, 6.3.52. For further details on Warren, see notes to 6.2.4.

. . . I have been trying to think back to the Geol. Soc. discussion on the hacked bone from Piltdown, but I cannot remember anything useful [A]. . . I do not think I heard of Mr. Oke's letter [B], and I am bound to admit that I cannot remember any adverse comments at the meeting. . .

[A] For a report of what Warren said about the bone implement on 2 December 1914, see notes to Section 3.2.

[B] See 6.3.52 for details.

6.3.55 DF 116/31 Teilhard de Chardin 29 June 1954

(a) Pierre Teilhard de Chardin (1888-1955); (b) handwritten note to Oakley on printed stationery: "Etudes, Paris 15, rue Monsieur (7)"; (c) underlining in original by Teilhard.

. . . I shall be in London between August 6 and 10 (leaving the 10). – Hope to find Leakey! and you (!?), – and Desmond Clark, by chance . . .[A]

[A] As indicated by two letters Oakley received in September [DF 116/31], Teilhard was anxious to discuss J. Desmond Clark's work at Twin River.

6.3.56 MSS WEI 3.17 Kenward 1 July 1954

(a) Mabel Kenward (1885-1978); (b) handwritten letter to Weiner at Oxford on stationery embossed: "Little Sharpes, Piltdown, Uckfield, Sussex"; (c) underlining in original by Kenward.

I would like to ask the present day scientists this simple question – how do they suggest that the Piltdown "fakes" were buried underneath and in hard gravel the top soil of which had not been removed. I am prepared to take an oath that where the cranium was dug the ground had not previously been moved. I can only suggest that a necromanser of the dark ages – faked and buried the remains in order to hoax future credulous scientists.

6.3.57 MSS WEI 3.17 Weiner 3 July 1954

(a) Joseph Sydney Weiner (1915-1982); (b) carbon copy of letter to Mabel Kenward of Piltdown; (c) –.

. . . From the accounts given by Charles Dawson in two different papers at least, it seems quite clear that the gravel was dug from the pit at least five, and possibly as much as ten years before the piece of cranium was uncovered. Charles Dawson stressed over and over again that a great deal of the gravel was loose at all times when the pieces of cranium came to light. He describes how these pieces were found in "spoil heaps". There is little doubt that during the time that Woodward was engaged in the excavations, as well as before, the gravel was, to use Dawson's expression, in a "disturbed" condition [A].

I know that this whole business is in some ways a sad affair, but it is important to realize that, in the last five or six years, Piltdown man had almost completely lost his scientific standing long before this hoax was uncovered.

[A] From this it is evident that Weiner regarded the so-called "coconut" story with great suspicion, and was now convinced that the cranial fragments had been deliberately planted. In recounting the confused and often conflicting details related to the "coconut" story (see Introduction 1.2), Weiner concluded in his book: ". . . the origin of the coconut story sinks into obscurity" (1955:129) – a remark that drew a sharp and immediate response from Miss Kenward, see Letter to the Editor, *The Daily Telegraph* (23 February), 1955.

6.3.58 MSS WEI 3.17 Kenward 4 July 1954

(a) Mabel Kenward (1885-1978); (b) handwritten letter to Weiner at Oxford on stationery embossed: "Little Sharpes, Piltdown, Uckfield, Sussex"; (c) –.

A reply to Weiner's letter, 6.3.57.

I take great exception to your letter of the 3rd inst. in reply to mine to you. In the letter you definitely imply that I am lying when I tell you the ground where the cranium of the Piltdown skull was dug [sic], had not been uncovered before. My Father – man of the highest integrity saw his workman strike with a pick the skull which was lying buried in untouched gravel, and thereby shattering it in all directions. I have nothing to say about the subsequent finds, which it is claimed had been "planted". . . I also resent very much that you came last spring [A] and questioned me about Mr Dawson without telling me the object of your visit . . .

[A] See Note A: 6.3.1.

6.3.59 MSS WEI 4.19 Oakley 21 July 1954

(a) Kenneth Page Oakley (1911-1981); (b) handwritten note to Weiner at Oxford on printed stationery: "British Museum (Natural History), Cromwell Road, London S.W.7."; (c) –.

The following was in preparation for Teilhard's pending visit to the Natural History Museum, see 6.3.55.

Many thanks for sending the T. de C. questionnaire [A]. Leakey and Sonia Cole [B] have gathered data from scattered sources. The dates you need are:
  Born 1881
  Jersey 1901-05 (Philosophical studies)
  Cairo 1906-08 (lecturer in physics and chemistry)
  Sussex 1908-12
  Paris 1912–> apart from visit to England in 1913.
  They expect that the visit next month is for the confession.

[A] Copies of Weiner's "questionnaire" and the accompanying letter (?date) have not been located in the BMNH Piltdown archive. However, from a subsequent letter, written to Le Gros Clark, it appears that Weiner had posed 3 questions, see 6.3.63 for details.

[B] Louis B. Leakey (1903-1972) of Olduvai Gorge fame and a science writer, Sonia Cole, who later became Leakey's biographer. Leakey was convinced that Teilhard had been the perpetrator – though his reasons are not clear from the documents pertaining to this period. From all indications Leakey had threatened to publish his views but on each occasion was deterred. A veiled reference to Leakey's theory can be found in his book (co-authored with M. Goodall) *Unveiling Man's Origins* (1969). See also DF 116/32 Leakey 15 September 1972, in which he outlined to Oakley a possible scenario; and G. Daniel's editorial, *Antiquity* (1975) XLIX:165-167. Eventually, however, Leakey's cause was taken up by Stephen J. Gould (1980). For criticisms levelled against Gould's case and his reponse, see Gould (1981).

6.3.60 MSS WEI 4.19 Le Gros Clark 5 August 1954

(a) Wilfrid Edward Le Gros Clark (1895-1971); handwritten letter to Weiner on printed stationery: "Department of Human Anatomy, University Museum, Oxford"; (c) –.

Sorry to bother you on holiday. What do you think about Kenneth's suggestion re Marston.? I think it might be a good idea to note this reference, if only to stop him from continuing to [? word] and try and get credit for himself. But I can't remember just what reference you did make to Marston in your section. . .

Exactly what publication of Marston's had been suggested by Oakley is not known, and evidently this is in reference to Weiner's introduction to the collection of papers planned for the *Bulletin of the British Museum (Natural History)* on "Further Contributions to the Solution of the Piltdown Problem" (Weiner *et al.* 1955). Weiner's contribution to the foregone cites Marston's 1952 paper (1955:252,253). In the reference section, the 1952 paper is listed along with that of 1950 (Weiner *et al.* 1955:286).

6.3.61 MSS WEI 4.19 Oakley 9 August 1954

(a) Kenneth Page Oakley (1911-1981); (b) handwritten note to Weiner at Oxford on printed stationery: "British Museum (Natural History), Cromwell Road, London S.W.7"; (c) underlining in original by Oakley.

The following letter relates details of Teilhard's visit.

I am afraid that nothing new emerged as a result of the interviews today or yesterday. But you should know of the following:

(1) T. de C. and his friend Mrs. de Terra came to tea with us at Amersham. Possible visit to Swanscombe discussed; M de T[erra] said "No chance I suppose of seeing Piltdown?" T. de C. "No, no Mrs. de Terra – sore subject!" [A]. Nothing more was said about Piltdown that day.

(2) T. de C. was awaiting me at the Museum when I arrived this morning at 10.15. (Thus I did not have a chance to prime Edwards or de Beer). He spoke only of African work, but I slipped in your question about writing to him. He said "Yes by all means." Then Edwards came into the room. Again he spoke only of Africa, and of joint interest there. E[dwards] said, "Ah ha. Yes I'm trying to wean Oakley from Piltdown too. I expect that amused you quite a lot" (clapping hand on T. de C.'s arm with jovial chuckle)? "Well not really, you see, it was a souvenir of my youth and so to me it was rather sad." "Indeed," said E., "I can well imagine your feelings" (in rather harsh sarcastic tone). T. de C. " . . .but as I was saying to Oakley these mandibles found by Arambourg at Palikao [B] . . . most important . . ." Then he talked rapidly about discoveries in Patagonia and the need for more work on dating earliest evidence of man in the Americas. Edwards left, and suggested that I should take T. de C. to see de Beer. I did that, left them alone for 10 minutes while I sought Hopwood [C]. On returning to de

Beer's room, I found T. de C. and the Director in animated conversation (in French); the former busy disclaiming much knowledge of Dawson, and rapidly getting onto the subject of the disappearance of the Pekin skulls. He terminated the Piltdown conversation saying: "They have done great work in clearing it up." Having deposited T. de C. with Hopwood I found Edwards, placed your manuscript in his hands and suggested that he should try to see T. de C. again with this as an excuse. A clerk took a message to Hopwood's room, that the Keeper would like to see T. de C. for a moment before he left. At 12.20 he came into E.'s room accompanied by H, saying "I have only a moment . . . an appointment at 12.30, you know." E[dwards] then said "Weiner has completed the MS of a book on P[iltdown] and concludes that D[awson] was wholly responsible for the fraud. Do you think that is wise, is it perhaps going too far" I gather that T. de C. then spent 15 minutes telling E[dwards] what he told us, that he scarcely knew D[awson], "as a <u>man</u>, not at all," so he could not express an opinion about his character, but "didn't it seem more likely that the pit had been a rubbish hole and that the fossils etc. had been thrown there? Do you know there was a case like that in France a few years ago, the most extraordinary things were found in association, just a collection that had been dumped!" Edwards tried to pull him back to the point, and then T. de C. said: "Yes, Weiner told me about the book Saturday, he spent about an hour, with his questions, he seemed quite <u>worked up</u> about this business – yes, and Oakley too!" Hopwood: "Yes, I have told Oakley, it is not worth <u>bothering</u> too much about it." "Well, well, I told Weiner," said T. de C., "if he <u>likes</u> I will look at the proof of his book, but I really must go now."

I have read the above to Edwards who agrees with my reporting. The only additional point is that he [T. de C.] said to E: "I was a mere youth at the time, little more than a boy [D]. . . [E]

[A] Mrs Rhoda de Terra of New York City.

[B] Camille Arambourg (1885-1969), a French palaeoanthropologist. A reference to the hominid remains found by Arambourg and R Hoffstetter in July 1954 at Ternifine, near the village of Palikao, situated 10 miles east of Oran, Algeria. For further details, see Day (1986:143-147).

[C] Arthur Tindell Hopwood (1897-1969).

[D] In 1912, Teilhard was 24 years old!

[E] For details of Weiner's reaction to this information, see 6.3.62 and 6.3.63.

6.3.62 MSS WEI 4.19 Le Gros Clark 9 August 1954

(a) Wilfrid Edward Le Gros Clark (1895-1971); (b) handwritten letter to Weiner at Oxford on printed stationery: "Moor Park Hotel, Chagford, Newton Abbot [Devon]; (c) underlining in original by Le Gros Clark.

Many thanks for your letter [A]. You do not say whether T. de C. even gave any of his fossil specimens to Dawson, or what his reactions were to the suggestion that Dawson could inevitably be regarded as the perpetrator. But perhaps you were not able to press those points. I am frankly puzzled by his attitude. If T. de C. had <u>no</u> hand in the forgery, why should he be <u>embarrassed</u>? If he knows something about the perpetrator (but was not himself implicated), surely he could say so – or at any rate make clear that he is not able to divulge matters which he regards as confidential? To say that he only knew Dawson slightly when he had so many contacts with him – helped him in his excavations – stopped in his house, seems rather ridiculous. On the other hand, I cannot imagine him ultimately planning the forgery. The more I come to think of it, the more attractive is the idea represented in Kipling's story [B]. I hope you are developing this idea in your book, as a counter to all the evidence against Dawson. He knew he had deadly enemies, that he was an ambitious man with [?words] the Royal Society [C], and that he became mentally affected in the last year of his life [D]. It thus seems to me not impossible that someone (?Lewis Abbott) may have deliberately planted the material and then tortured him with threats of exposure just at the moment when he was achieving the summit of his fame [E]. Anyhow – it makes a very intriguing story for speculation. . .

[A] A copy of this letter is not present in Weiner's Piltdown files.

[B] Some months earlier Weiner's attention was drawn to a short story written by Rudyard Kipling, "Dayspring Mishandled", which was published in 1932. The story deals with a forged manuscript. It should be noted that Kipling, who lived in Burwash, Sussex, was an active member of the Sussex Archaeological Society and was on friendly terms with Sargent at the Bexhill Museum. Weiner (1955:118) conjectured that perhaps Kipling's story was a tangential reference to Dawson and his dubious activities [see 6.3.63].

[C] See 3.1.6, 6.3.10, and 6.3.21.

[D] See 6.3.40: Interview I.

[E] See 6.3.21.

6.3.63 MSS WEI 4.19 Weiner 17 August 1954

(a) Joseph Sydney Weiner (1915-1982); (b) carbon copy of typewritten letter to Le Gros Clark in Devon [see (b) 6.3.62]; (c) –.

. . . It is true that we unfortunately did not ask T. de C. point blank whether he gave Dawson any specimens, but we did ask him where it was that Dawson might have got them, and whether he regarded Dawson as a collector of such specimens, or whether Pelletier could have given him the specimens. To all of which he simply said he did not know and that he hardly knew C.D. etc. etc. . . His reaction to an indictment of Dawson was tested by Edwards on the Monday, and I think by de Beer also (in French). He offered only the comments that the thing could be explained by the dumping of a collection of specimens by some collector in the gravel pit. On Monday and on Sunday when he went to tea with Oakley it was quite evident that the subject of Piltdown was an embarrassing one to him. He preferred to keep off the subject and, in fact, avoided answering some of Edwards' questions by turning to Oakley.

As I think I told you the thing that obviously bothered him was my reference to Dawson's public statement of his association with T.de C. going back to 1909. When I got back to Swansea after the meeting I wrote him a letter (which should have reached him before he saw Oakley although he made no mention of it), and asked him three definite questions [B] – whether Dawson was in error in saying that they had worked together actively on fossil plants and on fossil mammals of the Weald; whether Dawson was also in error in saying that this close association had started in 1909; finally how it was that he was invited in 1913 to work at Piltdown again, seeing that he came straight from Dieppe to Lewes and stayed the night at Dawson's home. The line I took in putting these questions was simply that I regarded all of C.D.'s actions as indicating a deliberate attempt to involve him right from the beginning. I also made the point that if, as T. de C. said, his first meeting with Dawson in the quarry was the occasion also of his learning that Dawson had already found several things at Piltdown then it was quite obvious that Dawson had several pieces in his possession by 1909, whereas he admitted only to one piece a cranium [sic]

. . . I am trying to find out a little more about the circumstances under which Kipling came to write the story [A]. Do you think the title curious? "Dayspring" is poetical for the break of day or the dawn!

[A] See Note B: 6.3.62.

[B] ? Weiner's "questionnaire" mentioned by Oakley in Letter 6.3.59.

6.3.64 MSS WEI 4.19 Oakley 21 August 1954

(a) Kenneth Page Oakley (1911-1981); (b) handwritten note to Weiner on printed postcard: "Woolstone, Chestnut Close, Amersham, Bucks"; (c) –.

. . . I have much enjoyed reading your M.S. [A] which is excellent. I have made suggestions and corrections in pencil on the copy which is at the Museum ready to be sent to you on Monday. . .

[A] *The Piltdown Forgery* (1955).

6.3.65 MSS WEI 3.17 Teilhard de Chardin 30 September 1954

(a) Pierre Teilhard de Chardin (1881-1955); (b) typewritten letter to Weiner at Oxford on plain stationery: "14 East 71st Street, New York 21"; (c) annotated by Weiner: " Copy note for Cuénot: 18/5/59" [A]. Underlining in original by Teilhard.

This was Weiner's last communication with Teilhard, who died of a heart attack on 10 April (Easter Sunday), 1955.

. . . *I have very little to add to what I could tell you, in the course of our conversation with Oakley. Except that, for the dates, I think you must rely on the Dawson letters. "A la réflexion," it is quite possible that the meeting in the Hastings stone-quarry (in which, I* think, *I heard of the Piltdown skull fragments for the first time) should have happened as early as 1909 (?)[B]. Dawson did* not *use to come with Pelletier and me in the stone quarries or in the cliffs (I don't remember distinctly that he should have come even once) [C]. But, as I tell you, he acted (after we met him) as an "intermediare" between us and Woodward and Seward (fossil plants) [D].*

In 1913, my staying overnight in Lewes (and the trip to Piltdown) was pre-arranged *[E]. But I can absolutely not remember whether the "initiative" came from me or from Dawson. In fact the occasion (meaning my going to Hastings, in order to spend my vacations at Ore Place) was so "naturelle" for a meeting (after a year I had spent in Paris, with Boule) that it could not have been missed.*

I have never kept a single letter from Dawson. Too bad. . .

Footnote by Teilhard:

Once, I remember, Dawson brought Sir Arthur to Ore Place to see my fossil specimens. Before my first visit to Piltdown I believe [F].

[A] Claude Cuénot, who wrote Teilhard's biography (1958).

[B] Teilhard's correspondence reveals that Dawson showed him some of the Piltdown materials in April 1912, see notes to Letter 1.2.5. His recollection, on this occasion, that he first met Dawson in 1909 is correct, see 1.1.8 and 1.1.10.

[C] From all indications Dawson did accompany Teilhard on at least one excursion, see notes to Letter 1.1.29.

[D] See Letters 1.2.1, 1.2.5. and 1.2.19.

[E] See Note A: 2.3.35.

[F] Woodward's visit to Ore Place (Hastings) occurred in July 1912, see notes to 1.2.12.

6.3.66 DF 116/38 Gunner 11 January 1954*

(a) A Gunner; (b) typewritten letter to Oakley on printed stationery: "The Midhurst & District Natural History Society"; (c) *the context of the letter indicates that the date of this letter is 1955 and not 1954.

. . . *Sir Arthur Keith must have died a little broken hearted as he like so many others had one way or another cashed in on [Piltdown]. . . [A] I do agree about my friend Marston. He has taken all this very badly. And refuses to be comforted. But as you may know some feel that he has had a raw publications deal throughout, and so was driven into a kind of underworld; his papers appearing first in one and then in another journal of obscurity. He could have been accepted into a more cordial circle?*

[A] Keith died on 7 January 1955.

Manuscript Sources

1. BRITISH MUSEUM (NATURAL HISTORY)

Materials relating to the Piltdown episode held by the Natural History Museum are located in three major collections of the Palaeontology Library. In addition to these sources, several letters from Martin Hinton's papers have been employed. This latter collection is housed in the Library of the Department of Zoology.

Library of Palaeontology
DF 100-116   Archives of the Department of Palaeontology
MSS WEI   Joseph S. Weiner Papers
P.MSS KPO   Kenneth P. Oakley's Piltdown Files

Library of Zoology
MHP/DM-BMNH   Martin A. C. Hinton Papers

2. THE ROYAL COLLEGE OF SURGEONS OF ENGLAND

KP/RCS   [Sir] Arthur Keith Papers

The Keith collection is extensive, containing numerous letters (some bound), diaries, manuscripts and reprints. Contrary to expectations Keith did not keep a Piltdown file. What letters have survived and pertain to the Piltdown episode are scattered throughout the collection. Their location is indicated either by a Box number and/or File number.

3. THE SMITHSONIAN INSTITUTION

GMP/SIA   Gerrit Smith Miller Papers

The Miller correspondence is located in the Smithsonian Institution Archives, Washington, D.C. The location of the letters from this source are indicated by Box and File number.

HP/NAA   Aleš Hrdlička Papers

The Hrdlička Papers are located in the National Anthropological Archives, U.S. Museum of Natural History, Smithsonian Institution, Washington D.C. This extensive collection is organized in box-files arranged in alphabetical order.

4. AMERICAN MUSEUM OF NATURAL HISTORY

HFO/AMNH   Henry Fairfield Osborn Papers
WKG/AMNH   William King Gregory Papers

The papers of Osborn and Gregory are located in the Library of the American Museum in New York City. When these collections were originally consulted (1975-76) they had not been organized and catalogued, hence the present location of the various letters employed might present a problem.

5. INSTITUT ROYAL DES SCIENCES NATURELLES DE BELGIQUE

    RP/IRSNB   A. Louis Rutot Papers

The Rutot collection is located in Brussels at the Royal Institute of Natural Sciences.

6. MISCELLANEOUS SOURCES

    CDR/HPL   Charles Dawson Reprints

Letter 4.1.37 is preserved in a bound collection of Dawson's reprints (Call No: S373.3) held by the Hastings Public Library.

    LP/WBD
    LP/AHP   Ian Langham Papers

Several letters collected by the late Dr Ian Langham have been employed in this volume, namely Letters 2.3.71 [LP/WBD] and 3.1.13 [LP/AHP]. Because their origin is uncertain and had not been confirmed at the time of going to press, their correct source has not been indicated. Langham's papers (LP) are presently located in the Department of History, University of Sydney, New South Wales, Australia.

    RWP/UC   Richard West Papers

In 1967, Letter 4.2.5 was found by Professor Richard West (Department of Botany, Cambridge University), who provided Weiner with a copy [see MSS WEI 3.17 Weiner 18 July 1967] and it appears to have been subsequently misplaced. The letter printed in this volume is a transcription from a new copy supplied by West.

    SPC/   Spencer Private Collection

Letter 5.1.17 [Sollas to Woodward] was found among a collection of reprints presented to Spencer by Sir Arthur S. Woodwards's daughter, Mrs Margaret Hodgson.

Literature Cited

Abbott, W.J.L. 1892a. The section exposed in the foundations of the new Admiralty offices. *Proc Geol Assoc* **12**:346-356.

Abbott, W.J.L. 1892b. A new reading of the Highgate Archway section. *Proc Geol Assoc* **13**:84-90.

Abbott, W.J.L. 1893. Excursion to Basted and Ightham [Kent]. *Proc Geol Assoc* **13**:157-163.

Abbott, W.J.L. 1894. Plateau man in Kent. *Nat Sci* (London) **4**:257-266.

Abbott, W.J.L. 1895. The Hastings kitchen middens. *J Anthropol Inst* (London) **25**:122-145.

Abbott, W.J.L. 1897a. Worked flints from the Cromer Forest Bed. *Nat Sci* **7**:89-96.

Abbott, W.J.L. 1897b. Plateau man in Kent. *Nat Sci* **4**:257-266.

Abbott, W.J.L. 1898. Authenticity of Plateau implements. *Nat Sci* **8**:111-116.

Abbott, W.J.L. 1911. On the classification of the British Stone Age industries, and some new and little known, well-marked horizons and cultures. *J Roy Anthropol Inst* **41**:458-481.

Abbott, W.J.L. 1913. Prehistoric man: The newly discovered link in his evolution. *Hastings & St Leonard's Observer* (Feb 1).

Abbott, W.J.L. 1915. Pliocene deposits of the southeast of England. *Proc Prehist Soc E Anglia* **II**:175-194.

Andrews, C.W. 1906. *A Descriptive Catalogue of the Tertiary Vertebrata of the Fayum, Egypt.* London: British Museum (Natural History).

Andrews, C.W. 1915. *Discovery of a skeleton of* Elephas antiquus *near Chatham. Nature* **96**:232,332, 398.

Andrews, C.W. & C.F. Cooper. 1928. *On a Specimen of* Elephas antiquus *from Upnor.* London: British Museum.

Anthony, R. 1913. Les restes humains fossiles de Piltdown (Sussex). *Rev Anthropol* (Paris) **23**:293-306.

Barrell, J. 1917. Probable relations of climatic change to the origin of the tertiary ape-man. *Sci Monthly* **4**:16-26.

Beer, G. de. 1955. Proposed rejection of the generic and specific names published for the so-called "Piltdown Man". *Bull Zool Nomencl* **11**(6): 171-172.

Bennett, F.J. 1901. The earliest traces of man. *Geol Mag* (London) **VIII**:427.

Black, D. 1925. Asia and the dispersal of primates. *Bull Geol Soc China* **4**:133-183.

Black, D. 1926. Tertiary man in Asia: The Chou Kou Tien discovery. *Nature* **118**:733-734.

Black, D. 1927a. The lower molar hominid tooth from the Chou Kou Tien deposit. *Palaeontol Sinica* **7**. 24 pp.

Black, D. 1927b. Further hominid remains of lower Quaternary age from the Chou Kou Tien deposits. *Nature* **120**:954.

Black, D. 1929. Sinanthropus pekinensis: The recovery of further fossil remains of this early hominid from the Chou Kou Tien deposit. *Science* **70**:674-676.

Black, D. 1934. On the discovery, morphology, and environment of *Sinanthropus Pekinensis*, *Phil Trans Roy Soc London* **123**:57-120.

Blinderman, C. 1986a. The Piltdown problem solved. *J Irreprod Results* **31**:2-6.

Blinderman, C. 1986b. *The Piltdown Inquest.* New York: Prometheus.

Boaz, N.T. 1982. American research on Australopithecines and early *Homo*, 1925-1980. *In*: F. Spencer (Ed), *A History of American Physical Anthropology, 1930-1980*. New York: Academic Press. pp 239-260.

Boule, M. 1911-13. L'Homme fossile de la Chapelle-aux-Saints. *Annales Paléontol* (Paris) **6**:111-172 (1911); **7**:21-56, 85-192 (1912); **8**:1-70 (1913).

Boule, M. 1913. L'Homo néanderthalensis et sa place dans la nature, *Congr Intnl Anthropol Archéol préhist*, C-R XIV th session (Genève 1912). Tome **II**: 392-395.

Boule, M. 1915. La paléontologie humaine en Angleterre. *L'Anthropologie* (Paris) **26**:1-67.

Boule, M. 1917a. The jaw of Piltdown. *L'Anthropologie* (Paris) **28**:433-435.

Boule, M. 1917b. [Review of WK Gregory (1916a)]. *L'Anthropologie* (Paris) **28**:157-159.

Boule, M. 1920. The Piltdown jaw. *L'Anthropologie* (Paris) **29**:566-568.

Boule, M. 1921. *Les hommes fossiles*. First edition. Paris: Masson.

Bowden, M. *Ape-Men: Fact or Fallacy?* Bromley, Kent: Sovereign Publ.

Bowler, P.J. 1986. *Theories of Human Evolution. A Century of Debate, 1844-1944*. Baltimore: Johns Hopkins University Press.

Branco, W. 1898. Die menschenähnlichen Zähne aus dem Bohnerz der schwäbischen Alb. *Jahr d Ver f Vaterland Natur Würtemberg*. **54**:1-144.

Breuil, H. 1931. Le feu et l'industrie lithique et osseuse à Choukoutien. *L'Anthropologie* **42**:1-17.

Breuil, H. 1938. The use of bone implements in the Old Palaeolithic. *Antiquity* **12**:56-67.

Bridgland, D.R. *et al.* 1985. New information and results from recent excavations at Barnfield Pit, Swanscombe. *Q. Newsl.* **46**:25-39.

Broom, R. 1918. The evidence afforded by the Boskop skull of a new species of primative man (*Homo capensis*). *Anthropol Papers Amer Mus Nat Hist (New York)* **23**:67-79.

Broom, R. 1925a. Some notes on the Taungs skull. *Nature* **115**:569-571.

Broom, R. 1925b. On the newly discovered South African man-ape. *Nat Hist* (New York) **25**:409-418.

Broom R. 1950. Summary of a note on the Piltdown skulls. *Adv Sci* **6**:344.

Burkitt, M.C. 1921. *Prehistory: A study of early cultures in Europe and the Mediterranean basin*. London: Cambridge University Press.

Burkitt, M.C. 1931. Lecture on early man. In: *Early Man, His Origin, Development and Culture. Lectures delivered before Royal Anthropological Institute*. London: Benn.

Buxton, L.H.D. 1925. Report on calvarium from Guy's Rift [Wiltshire]. *Proc Spel Soc (Univ Bristol)* **2**: 235-237.

Carnot, A. 1893. Recherches sur la composition générale et la teneur en fluor des os modernes et des os fossiles de différents ages. *Ann Mineral* (Paris) **3**:155-195.

Churchward, A. 1922. *Origin and Evolution of the Human Race*. London: Allen & Unwin.

Claringbull, G.F. & M.H. Hey. 1955. The X-ray crystallography of the Piltdown fossils. *In*: Weiner *et al.*, Further contributions to the solution of the Piltdown problem. *Bull Br Mus Nat Hist* (Geol) **2** (6): 268–70.

Clark, W.E. Le Gros, see Le Gros Clark, W.E.

Collyer, R.H. 1867. The [Foxhall] fossil human jaw from Suffolk. *Anthropol Rev* (London) **V**:331-339

Cook, S.F. & R.F. Heizer. 1947. The quantitative investigation of aboriginal sites: Analyses of human bone. *Amer J Phys Anthropol* **5**:201-220.

Cook, S.F. & R.F. Heizer. 1952. The fossilization of bone: Organic components and water. *Rep Univ Archeol Surv* (Berkeley) **17**:1-24.

Cooper, C.F. 1945. Arthur Smith Woodward, 1864-1944. *Obit Not Fellows Roy Soc (Lond)* **5**:79-112.

Costello, P. 1985. The Piltdown hoax reconsidered. *Antiquity* **59**:167-171.

Cuénot, C. 1958. *Pierre Teilhard de Chardin: les grandes étapes de son évolution.* Paris: Libraire Plon.

Cunningham, D.J. 1895. Dr Dubois' so-called missing-link. *Nature* **51**:428-429.

Cunnington, W. 1897. Authenticity of Plateau man. *Nat Sci* **8**:327-333.

Cunnington, W. 1898. On some palaeolithic implements from the Plateau gravels and their evidence concerning "Eolithic" man. *Quart J Geol Soc Lond* **LIV**:291.

Curwen, E.C. 1929. *Prehistoric Sussex.* London: Homeland Association.

Daniel, G. 1986. Piltdown and Professor Hewitt. *Antiquity* **60**:59-60.

Dart, R.A. 1925a. *Australopithecus africanus,* the man-ape of South Africa. *Nature* **115**:615.

Dart, R.A. 1925b. The word *Australopithecus* and others. *Nature* **115**:875.

Dart, R.A. 1925c. The Taungs skull. *Nature* **116**:462.

Dart, R.A. 1926. Taungs and its significance. *Nat Hist* **26**:315-327.

Dart, R.A. 1929. A note on the Taungs skull. *S Afr J Sci* **26**:648-658.

Dart, R.A. 1934. The dentition of *Australopithecus africanus. Folia Anat Japonica* **12**:207-221.

Davies, H.N. 1904. [The Cheddar skeleton]. *Quart J Geol Soc Lond* **LX**:335.

Dawkins, W.B. 1916. The antiquity of man and the dawn of art in Europe. *Edinburgh Rev* **224**:80-98.

Dawson, C. 1897. Discovery of a large supply of natural gas at Waldron, Sussex. *Nature* **57**:150-151.

Dawson, C. 1898a. On the discovery of natural gas in east Sussex. *Quart J Geol Soc Lond* **54**:564-571.

Dawson, C. 1898b. Natural gas in Sussex. *Proc SE Union Sci Soc* pp 73-80.

Dawson C. 1898c. List of Wealden and Purbeck-Wealden fossils. *Brighton Nat Hist Soc Rep 1898* pp 31-37.

Dawson, C. 1909 [1910]. *History of Hastings Castle.* 2 vols. London: Constable.

Dawson, C. 1913. The Piltdown skull. *Hastings & E Sussex Nat* **2**:73-82.

Dawson, C. 1915. The Piltdown skull. *Hastings & E Sussex Nat* **4**:144-149.

Dawson, C. & A.S. Woodward. 1912. On the discovery of a Palaeolithic human skull and mandible in a flint-bearing gravel overlying the Wealden (Hastings Beds) at Piltdown, Fletching (Sussex). *Abs Proc Geol Soc Lond* (1912-13). pp 20-27.

Dawson, C. & A.S. Woodward. 1913a. On the discovery of a Palaeolithic human skull and mandible in a flint-bearing gravel overlying the Wealden (Hastings Beds) at Piltdown, Fletching (Sussex). *Quart J Geol Soc Lond* **69**:117-151.

Dawson, C. & A.S. Woodward. 1913b. On the discovery of Palaeolithic human skull and mandible in a flint-bearing gravel overlying the Wealden (Hastings Beds) at Piltdown, Fletching (Sussex). *[Abstract] Geol Mag* **5**(10):42-44.

Dawson, C. & A.S. Woodward. 1913c. Supplementary note on the discovery of a palaeolithic human skull and mandible at Piltdown (Sussex). *Abstr Proc Geol Soc Lond* pp 28-29.

Dawson, C. & A.S. Woodward. 1914a. Supplementary note on the discovery of a Palaeolithic human skull and mandible at Piltdown (Sussex). *Quart J Geol Soc Lond* **70**:82-90.

Dawson, C. & A.S. Woodward. 1914b. Supplementary note on the discovery of a palaeolithic human skull and mandible at Piltdown (Sussex). [Abstract] *Geol Mag* **6**(1):44-45.

Dawson, C. & A.S. Woodward. 1914c. On a bone implement from Piltdown (Sussex). *Abstr Proc Geol Soc Lond* . pp 15-17.

Dawson, C. & A.S. Woodward. 1915a. On a bone implement from Piltdown (Sussex). *Quart J Geol Soc Lond* **71**:144-149.

Dawson, C. & A.S. Woodward. 1915b. On a bone implement from Piltdown (Sussex) [Abstract] *Ann Mag Nat Hist* **15**:337.

Dawson, C. & A.S. Woodward. 1915c. On a bone implement from Piltdown (Sussex). [Abstract] *Geol Mag* **2**:45.

Dawson. W.R. (Ed) 1938. *Sir Grafton Elliot Smith: A biographical record by his colleagues.* London: Cape.

Day, M.H. 1986. *Guide to Fossil Man* 4th ed. Chicago: University of Chicago Press.

Dewey, H. 1934. WJ Lewis Abbott (Obituary). *Proc Geol Soc Lond* **90**:50-51.

Dubois, E. 1896. On the Pithecanthropus erectus: a transitional form between man and the apes. *Sci Trans Roy Dub Soc* **6**:1-18.

Dubois, E. 1899. Remarks upon the brain-cast of *Pithecanthropus erectus*. *Proc XIV Intnl Congr Zool* (Cambridge 1898). pp 78-95.

Duckworth, W.L.H. **1912.** *Prehistoric Man.* Cambridge: University Press.

Duckworth, W.L.H. 1913. [Discussion of Piltdown skull]. *In*: Dawson & Woodward 1913a:149.

Duckworth, W.L.H. 1925. The fossil anthropoid ape from Taungs. *Nature* **115**:236.

Edmunds, F.H. 1926. Fig 10 in H.J.O. White (1926).

Edmunds, F.H. 1935. *The Wealden District.* London: HMSO.

Edmunds, F.H. 1950. Note on the gravel deposit from which the Piltdown skull was obtained. *Proc Geol Soc Lond* **106**:133-134. [see *Abst Proc Geol Soc* No 1457 (1950):39-40].

Edmunds, F.H. 1955. The geology of the Piltdown neighbourhood. *In*: Weiner *et al.*, Further contributions to the solution of the Piltdown problem. *Bull Br Mus Nat Hist* (Geol) **2**:273-275.

Elliot, G.F.S. 1914. Prehistoric man. *Proc Roy Phil Soc Glasgow* **45**:17-27.

Elliot, G.F.S. 1915. *Prehistoric Man and His Story.* London: Seeley, Service.

Elliot Smith, G. 1913a. Preliminary report on the [Piltdown] cranial cast. *In*: Dawson & Woodward (1913a) pp 145-147.

Elliot Smith, G. 1913b. The Piltdown skull. *Nature* **92**:131;267-268;318-319.

Elliot Smith, G. 1914. On the exact determination of the median plane of the Piltdown skull. *In*: Dawson & Woodward (1914a) pp 93-97.

Elliot Smith, G. 1916. New phases of the controversies concerning the Piltdown skull. *Proc Manchester Lit Phil Soc* **60**: xxviii-xxix.

Elliot Smith, G. 1917a. The problem of the Piltdown jaw: human or sub-human? *Eugenics Rev* **9**:167.

Elliot Smith, G. 1917b. Primitive man. *Proc Brit Acad* **7**:1-50.

Elliot Smith, G. 1924. *The Evolution of Man: Essays.* London: Humphry.

Elliot Smith, G. 1925a. The fossil anthropoid ape from Taungs. *Nature* **115**:235.

Elliot Smith, G. 1925b. The London skull. *Brit Med J* **II**:853.

Elliot Smith, G. 1925c. The London skull. *Nature* **116**:678-680,819-820.

Elliot Smith, G. 1930a. Early man in China. *Nature* **125**:448-449.

Elliot Smith, G. 1930b. The ancestry of man. *Bull Geol Soc China* **9**:191-194.

Elliot Smith, G. 1930c. A new basis for the study of human evolution. The first complete brain-case of one of our earliest ancestors. *Illustrated London News* **176**:210-211.

Elliot Smith, G. 1930d. The revelatory brain-case of *Sinanthropus* **176**:769-771, 810.

Elliot Smith, G. 1931a. Human palaeontology. Review of "New discoveries relating to the Antiquity of Man." by Sir Arthur Keith. *Nature* **127**:963-967.

Elliot Smith, G. 1931b. *The Search for Man's Ancestors.* London: Watts.

Elliot Smith, G. & J.I. Hunter. 1924-25. The reconstruction of the Piltdown skull. *Proc Anat Soc* (London) **59**:38-40.

Esbroeck, G. van. 1972. *Pleine Lumière sur l'Imposture de Piltdown*. Paris: Les editions de Cedre.

Essex, R. 1955. The Piltdown plot: A hoax that grew. *Kent & Sussex J* (July-Sept). pp 94-95. Reprinted in Bowden (1978).

Etheridge Jr, R. & A.S Woodward. 1891. On the occurrence of the genus *Belonostomus* in the Rolling Downs Formation of Central Queensland. *Trans Roy Soc Vict* **II** (2): 1-6.

Everett, A.H. 1879. Second quarterly report on the Bornean cave exploration. *Rep Brit Assoc Adv Sci (Sheffield)*. pp 149-155.

Fleagle, J.G. & W.L. Jungers. 1982. Fifty years of higher primate phylogeny. *In*: F Spencer (Ed), *A History of American Physical Anthropology 1930-1980*. New York: Academic Press. pp 187-230.

Fowler, P.J. 1972. *Archaeology and the Landscape. Essays for LV Grinsell*. London: Baker.

Frassetto, F. 1918. *Lezioni di antropologia* . Vol I. Milano.

Frassetto, F. 1927. New views on the "Dawn Man" of Piltdown (Sussex). *Man* (London) **27**:121-124.

Friedrichs, H.F. 1932. Schaedel und Unterkiefer von Piltdown (*Eoanthropus dawsoni* Woodward) in neuer Untersuchung. *Z Anat u Entw Gesch* (Berlin) **98**:199-266.

Gaster, C.T.A. 1929. Chalk zones in the neighbourhood of Shoreham, Brighton and Newhaven. *Proc Geol Assoc* (London), **XL**.

Geikie, J. 1894. *The Great Ice Age & Its Relation to the Antiquity of Man* 3rd ed. London: Stanford. [see also *J Geol* [Chicago] **3**:241, 1894].

Giuffrida-Ruggeri, V. 1913. [Review of Dawson & Woodward 1913]. *Arch Antropol Etnol* (Firenze) **43**:184-186.

Giuffrida-Ruggeri, V. 1918. Unicità del philum umano con pluralità dei centri specifici. *Rev Ital di Paleontol* (Perugia) **24**:1-15.

Giuffrida-Ruggeri, V. 1919. La controversia sul fossile di Piltdown e l'origine del philum umano. *Monitore Zool Ital* **30**:7-18.

Gould, S.J. 1980. The Piltdown conspiracy. *Nat Hist* (New York) **89**:8-28.

Gould, S.J. 1981. Piltdown in letters. *Nat Hist* (New York) **90**:12-30.

Gregory, W.K. 1914. The dawn man of Piltdown, England. *Amer Mus J* **14**:189-200.

Gregory, W.K. 1916a. Studies on the evolution of the Primates (Parts I & II). *Bull Amer Mus Nat Hist* **35**:239-355.

Gregory, W.K. 1916b. Note on the molar teeth of the Piltdown mandible. *Amer Anthropol* **18**:384-387.

Gregory, W.K. 1922. *The Origin and Evolution of the Human Dentition*. Baltimore: Williams & Wilkins.

Gregory, W.K. 1927a. [On Hesperopithecus]. *Science* **66**:579-581.

Gregory, W.K. 1927b. The origin of man from the anthropoid stem – when and where? *Proc Amer Phil Soc* **66**:439-463.

Gregory, W.K. 1928a. The upright posture of man: A review of its origin and evolution. *Proc Amer Phil Soc* **67**:339-377.

Gregory, W.K. 1928b. Reply to Professor Wood-Jones's note: "Man and the Anthropoids". *Amer J Phys Anthropol* **12**:253-256.

Gregory, W.K. 1929a. Is the pre-dawn man a myth? *Human Biology* **1**:153-166.

Gregory, W.K. 1929b. *Our Face From Fish to Man*. New York: Putnam.

Gregory, W.K. 1930a. A critique of Professor Osborn's theory of human origins. *Amer J Phys Anthropol* **14**:133-164.

Gregory, W.K. 1930b. A critique of Professor Wood Jones's paper: "Some landmarks in the phylogeny of the primates". *Human Biol* **2**:99-108.

Gregory, W.K. 1934. *Man's Place among the Anthropoids*. Oxford: Clarendon.

Gregory, W.K. 1938. Man's place among the primates. *Palaeobiologica* **6**:208-213.

Gregory, W.K. 1949. Franz Weidenreich 1873-1948. *In*: S.L. Washburn & D. Wolffson (compilers), *Anthropological Papers of Franz Weidenreich 1939-1948.* New York: Viking Fund. pp 251-267.

Gregory, W.K. & M. Hellman. 1926. The crown patterns of fossil and recent human molar teeth and their meaning. *Nat Hist* (New York) **26**:300-309.

Gregory, W.K. & M. Hellman. 1938. Evidence of the Australopithecine man-apes on the origin of man. *Science* **88**:615-616.

Grist, C.J. 1910. Some eoliths from Dewlish, and the question of origin. *J Roy Anthropol Inst.* XL:192.

Haddon, A.C. 1913. *Eoanthropus dawsoni. Science* **37**:91-92.

Hall, E.T. 1953. Analysis of archaeological specimens: a new method. *Times Sci Rev (London)* **9**:13.

Halstead, L.B. 1978. New light on the Piltdown hoax. *Nature* **276**:11-13.

Hammond, M. 1982. The expulsion of the Neanderthals from human ancestry: Marcellin Boule and the social context of scientific research. *Soc Stud Sci* **12**: 1-36.

Hammond, M. 1988. The shadow man paradigm in paleoanthropology, 1911-1945. *In*: G.W. Stocking Jr (Ed): *Bones, Bodies, Behavior. Essays in Biological Anthropology.* History of Anthropology No 5. Madison: University of Wisconsin Press. pp 117-135.

Harrison, B. 1899. Plateau implements (eoliths). *Trans SE Union of Sci Soc.* p 12.

Harrison, G.A. 1983. J.S. Weiner and the exposure of the Piltdown forgery. *Antiquity* **57**:46-48.

Harrison, G.A. & K. Collins. 1982. Joseph Sydney Weiner (1915-1982). *Ann Human Biol* **9**(6):583-592.

Harrison, T. 1959. The Piltdown forgery: A.H. Everett and Niah. *Sarawak Mus J* **IX** (13-14):147-150.

Haward, F.N. 1912. The chipping of flint by natural agencies. *Proc Prehist Soc E Anglia* **I**: 185.

Head, J.O. 1971. Piltdown mystery. *New Scient* (London) **49**:86.

Heizer, R.F. & S.F. Cooke. 1954. Comments on the Piltdown remains. *Amer Anthropol* **56**:92-94.

Hewer, T.F. 1925. Guy's Rift, Slaughterford, Wiltshire. *Proc Spel Soc (Univ Bristol)***2**:229-234

Hewitt, J.T. 1898. Note on natural gas at Heathfield Station (Sussex). *Quart J Geol Soc Lond* LIV:572-574.

Hill, J.P. 1932. The developmental history of the primates. *Phil Trans Roy Soc* ser B, **221**:45-178.

Hinton, M.A.C. 1909. On the fossil hares of the ossiferous fissures of Ightham, Kent, and on the recent hares of the *Lepus variabilis* group. *Sci Proc. Roy Dublin Soc* **12**:225-265.

Hinton, M.A.C. 1914. On some remains of rodents from the Red Crag of Suffolk and from the Norfolk Forest-Bed. *Ann Mag Nat Hist* **13**:186-195.

Hinton, M.A.C. *et al.* 1938. Report on the Swanscombe Committee. *J Roy Anthropol Inst* **68**:17-98.

Hooton, E.A. 1916. The evolution of the human face and its relation to head form. *Dental Cosmos* **58**:272-281.

Hopwood, A.T. 1933. Miocene primates from Kenya. *Linn Soc Lond* **38**:437-464.

Hopwood, A.T. 1935. Fossil elephants and man. *Proc Geol Ass Lond* **46**:46-60.

Hrdlička, A. 1914. [On Piltdown] *In*: The most ancient skeletal remains of man. *Ann Rep Smithsonian Inst (1913)* pp 500-509.

Hrdlička, A. 1916. The most ancient skeletal remains of man. 2nd ed. Smithsonian Institution. Washington DC. 63p .

Hrdlička, A. 1917. Suggestions to the new national army by the anthropological committee of the National Research Council. *Proc Nat Acad Sci* **III**:526-528.

Hrdlička, A. 1921. The peopling of Asia. *Proc Amer Philo Soc* (Philadelphia) **60**:535-545.

Hrdlička, A. 1922. The Piltdown jaw. *Amer J Phys Anthropol* **5**:337-347.

Hrdlička, A. 1923. Dimensions of the first and second molars with their bearing on the Piltdown jaw and on man's phylogeny. *Amer J Phys Anthropol* **6**:195-216.

Hrdlička, A. 1924. Critical notes on the Foxhall jaw. *Amer J Phys Anthropol* **7**:420-424.

Hrdlička, A. 1925. The Taungs ape. *Amer J Phys Anthropol* **8**:379-392.

Hrdlička. A. 1930. The skeletal remains of early man. *Smithsonian Miscell Coll* **83**:1-379.

Hürzeler, J. 1954. Contribution à l'odontologie et à la phylogénèse du genre *Pliopithecus* Gervais. *Ann Pal* **40**:1-63.

Irving, A. 1912. Implements of man in the Chalky Boulder Clay. *Nature* **90**:3-4.

Irving, A. 1914. Some recent work on later Quaternary geology and anthropology, with its bearing on the question of "pre-Boulder Clay man". *J Roy Anthropol Inst* **44**:385-393.

Johnston, H.H. 1916. [Review of H.F. Osborn's *Men of the Old Stone Age*] *Geogr J* **48**:349-350.

Jones, Frederic Wood, see Wood-Jones, F.

Keith, A. 1911. *Ancient Types of Men.* New York: Harper.

Keith, A. 1913a. The present problems relating to the origin of modern races. [Introductory address to Winter session in medicine, University of Birmingham]. *Lancet* **2**:1050-1053.

Keith, A. 1913b. The Piltdown skull and brain cast. *Nature* **92**:197-199;292;345-346.

Keith, A. 1914a. The reconstruction of fossil human skulls. *J Roy Anthropol Inst* **44**:12-31.

Keith, A. 1914b. The significance of the discovery at Piltdown. *Bedrock* **2**:435-453.

Keith, A. 1914c. Soldiers as anthropologists. *Nature* **94**:391-392.

Keith, A. 1914d. Book review of H.E. Balch's *Wookey Hole: Its Caves and Cave Dwellers*. *Nature* **94**: 395-397.

Keith, A. 1914e. Report on the human and animal remains found at Halling, Kent. *J Roy Anthropol Inst* **44**:228-260.

Keith, A. 1915. *The Antiquity of Man.* London: Williams & Norgate.

Keith, A. 1916. Lo schema dell'origine umana. *Rev Antropol* **20**:1-20.

Keith, A. 1921. *Human Embryology and Morphology.* London.

Keith, A. 1925a. *The Antiquity of Man.* 2nd edition. London: Williams & Norgate.

Keith, A. 1925b. The fossil anthropoid ape from Taungs. *Nature* **116**:11.

Keith, A. 1925c. The new missing link. *Brit Med J* **1**: 325-336.

Keith, A. 1925d. The Taungs skull. *Nature* **116**:11.

Keith, A. 1925e. The Taungs skull. *Nature* **116**:462-463.

Keith, A. 1929. *The Antiquity of Man.* 7th imp. London: Williams & Norgate.

Keith, A. 1931. *New Discoveries Relating to the Antiquity of Man.* New York: Norton.

Keith, A. 1938-39. A re-survey of the anatomical features of the Piltdown skull with some observations on the recently discovered Swanscombe skull. *J Anat* (London) **75**:234-254.

Keith, A. 1950. *An Autobiography.* London: Watts.

Keith, A. 1955. *Darwin Re-Valued.* London: Watts.

Keith, A. & G.G. Campion. 1922. A contribution to the mechanism of growth of the human face. *Dental Rec* **42**:61-88 [also in *Intnl J Orthodont* **8**:607-633.

Keith, A. & F.H.S Knowles. 1911. A description of teeth of palaeolithic man from Jersey. *J Anat Physiol* (London) **6**:12-27.

Keith, A. & T.D. McCown. 1937. Mount Carmel man: His bearing on the ancestry of modern races. *In*: G.G MacCurdy (Ed), *Early Man* [International Symposium, Academy of Natural Sciences, Philadelphia, March 1937]. Philadelphia: Lippincott. pp 41-52.

Kipling, R. 1932. Dayspring Mishandled. *In: Limits and Renewals.* London: Macmillan. pp 3-33.

Klaatsch, H. 1899. Der gegenwärtige Stand der Pithecanthropus-Frage. *Zool Centralbl* **6**:217-235.

Kleinschmidt, O. 1922. Realgattung *Homo sapiens (L). Eine naturgesch Monogr d Menschen Berajah Zoogr infinita*. pp 1–30.

Kollman, J. 1895. Discussion of Dubois' Pithecanthropus, *Z Ethnol* **27**:740-744.

Langham, I. 1978. Talgai and Piltdown – the common context. *Artefact* **3** (4):181-224.

Langham, I. 1984. Sherlock Holmes, circumstantial evidence and Piltdown man. *PAN [Phys Anthropol News]* **3**(1):1-14

Lankester, E.R. 1912. On the discovery of a novel type of flint implements below the base of the Red Crag of Suffolk. Proving the existence of skilled workers of flint in the Pliocene age. *Phil Trans Roy Soc* (London) **102** (B):283-336.

Lankester, E.R. 1913. [Discussion of the Piltdown skull]. *In*: Dawson & Woodward 1913a:147-148.

Lankester, E.R. 1915. *Diversions of a Naturalist*. London: Methuen.

Lankester, E.R. 1921. A remarkable flint from Piltdown. *Man* No 32: 59-62.

Leakey, L.S.B. 1927. Stone Age man in Kenya Colony. *Nature* **120**:85-86.

Leakey, L.S.B. 1928. The Oldoway skull. *Nature* **121**:499.

Leakey, L.S.B. 1933. The status of the Kanam mandible and the Kanjera skulls. *Man* (London) **33**:200-201.

Leakey, L.S.B & M. Goodall. 1969. *Unveiling Man's Origins*. London: Methuen.

Leakey, L.S.B; A.T. Hopwood & H. Reck. 1931. Age of the Oldoway Bone Beds, Tanganyika. *Nature* **128**:724.

Le Gros Clark, W.E. 1955. An anatomical study of the Piltdown teeth and the so-called turbinal bone. *In*: Weiner *et al.* (1955). Further contributions to the solution of the Piltdown problem. *Bull Br Mus nat Hist* (Geol) **2**(6):234-242.

Lewin, R. 1987. *Bones of Contention: Controversies in the search for human origins*. New York: Simon & Schuster.

Lowenstein, J.M., T.I. Molleson; S.L. Washburn. 1982. Piltdown jaw confirmed as orang. *Nature* **299**:294.

Lubbock, J. [Lord Avebury]. 1913. *Prehistoric Times: As Illustrated by Ancient Remains and the Manners and Customs of Modern Savages*. London: Williams & Norgate.

Lull, R.S. 1917. *Organic Evolution*. New York: Macmillan.

Lyne, W.C. 1916. The significance of the radiographs of the Piltdown teeth. *Proc Roy Soc Med* (London) **9**:33-62.

Marriott, R.A. 1918. The Downs and the escarpments of the Weald: A new view of their geological history. *Sci Progr* **12**:591-608.

McCown, T.D. & A. Keith. 1939. *The Stone Age of Mount Carmel. Vol II: The fossil human remains from the Levalloiso-Mousterian*. Oxford: Clarendon Press.

MacCurdy, G.G. 1913. Ancestor hunting: the significance of the Piltdown skull. *Amer Anthropol* **15**:248-256.

MacCurdy, G.G. 1914. The man of Piltdown. *Amer Anthropol* **16**:331-336.

Manouvrier, L. 1895. Deuxième étude sur le *Pithecanthropus erectus* comme précurseur présumé de l'homme. *Bull Soc Anthropol* (Paris) ser 4, **6**:12-47.

Marsh, O.C. 1895. On the *Pithecanthropus erectus, Dubois*, from Java. *Amer J Sci* **49**:144-147.

Marston, A.T. 1935. [Note on discovery of the Swanscombe occipital fragment]. *Nature* **136**:637.

Marston, A.T. 1936a. Preliminary note on a new fossil human skull from Swanscombe, Kent. *Nature* **138**:200-201.

Marston, A.T. 1936b. Chimpanzee or man? The Piltdown canine tooth and mandible versus the human specific characteristics of the straight canine and the fused alveolar-maxillo-premaxillary suture. *Brit Dental J* pp 216-221.

Marston, A.T. 1937a. The Swanscombe skull. *J Roy Anthropol Inst Grt Brit & Ire* **67**:339-406.

Marston, A.T. 1937b. The case of the Piltdown jaw. *Discovery* (London) **18**:13-15.

Marston, A.T. 1946-47. Piltdown man: with reference to the ape mandible and canine tooth. [Two unpublished papers read at the meetings of Geologists' Association of London] cited in Marston 1950:298.

Marston, A.T. 1950. The relative ages of the Swanscombe and Piltdown skulls, with special reference to the results of the fluorine estimation tests. *Brit Dental J* **88**:292-299.

Marston, A.T. 1952. Reasons why the Piltdown canine tooth and mandible could not belong to Piltdown man. *Brit Dental J* **93**:1-14.

Marston A.T. 1954a. Comments on "The Solution of the Piltdown Problem." *Proc Roy Med Soc* **47**:100-102.

Marston,A.T. 1954b. [On exhibit of chromated flints]. *Proc Geol Soc Lond* No 1508. pp xlv-xlvi.

Matthew, W.D. 1916. Note on the association of the Piltdown jaw. *Bull Amer Mus Nat Hist* **35**:348-350.

Matthews, L.H. 1981. Piltdown man: The missing links. *New Scientist* (London) **90**: 280-282, 376, 515-516, 578-579, 647-648, 710-711, 785, 861-862; **91**:26-28.

Middleton, J. 1844. On fluorine in bones, its source, and its application to the determination of the geological age of fossil bones. *Proc Geol Soc Lond* **4**:431-433.

Millar, R. 1972. *The Piltdown Men.* London: Gollancz.

Miller, G.S. Jr. 1915. The jaw of the Piltdown man. *Smithsonian Misc Coll* No 65. pp 1-31.

Miller, G.S. 1918. The Piltdown jaw. *Amer J Phys Anthropol* **1**:25-52.

Miller, G.S. 1929. The controversy over human "missing links". *Smithsonian Report (1928)* (Washington DC). pp 413-465.

Mitchell, P.C. 1915. An application of the rules of zoological nomenclature. *Nature* **96**:480.

Moir, J.R. 1910. The flint implements of sub-Crag man. *Proc Prehist Soc E Anglia* **I**:17-24.

Moir, J.R. 1911. The natural fracture of flint and its bearing upon rudimentary flint implements. *Proc Prehist Soc E Anglia* **II**:171-184.

Moir, J.R. 1912. The Piltdown skull. *The Times* (December 25th) p 8.

Moir, J.R. 1913a. A defence of the "humanity" of the Pre-River Valley implements of the Ipswich district. *Proc Prehist Soc E Anglia* **I**:368-374.

Moir, J.R. 1913b. Pre-palaeolithic man. *Bedrock* **II**(2):165-176.

Moir, J.R. 1915. A series of mineralised bone implements of a primitive type below the base of the Red and Coralline Crags of Norfolk. *Proc Prehist Soc E Anglia* **2** (ii):116-131.

Moir, J.R. 1916a. On the evolution of the earliest palaeoliths from the rostro-carinate implements. *J Roy Anthropol Inst* **XLVI**:197-220.

Moir, J.R. 1916b. Pre-Boulder Clay man. *Nature* **98**:109.

Moir, J.R. 1918. Pre-Palaeolithic man in England. *Sci Progr* **12**:465-474.

Moir, J.R. 1924. The human jaw-bone found at Foxhall. *Amer J Phys Anthropol* **7**:409-416.

Moir, J.R. 1927. *The Antiquity of Man in East Anglia.* London: Cambridge University Press.

Moir, J.R. 1935. *Prehistoric Archaeology & Sir Ray Lankester.* Ipswich: Adlard.

Moir, J.R & A. Keith. 1912. An account of the discovery and characters of a human skeleton found beneath a stratum of chalky boulder clay near Ipswich. *J Roy Anthropol Inst* **42**:365-379.

Mollison, T. 1924. Neuere Funde und Untersuchungen fossiler Menschenaffen und Menschen. *Z Anat u Entw Gesch* (Berlin) **25**:696-771.

Montagu, A.M.F. 1951a. The Piltdown mandible and cranium. *Amer J Phys Anthropol* **9**:464-470.

Montagu, A.M.F. 1951b. The Barcombe Mills cranial remains. *Amer J Phys Anthropol* **9**:417-426.

Montagu, A.M.F. 1960. Artificial thickening of bone and the Piltdown skull. *Nature* **187**:174.

Munro, R. 1913. *Prehistoric Britain.* London: Home University of Modern Knowledge Ser.

Newton, E.T. 1895. On a human skull and limb-bones found in the Palaeolithic terrace-gravel at Galley Hill, Kent. *Quart J Geol Soc Lond* **51**:505-527.

Newton, E.T. 1897. The evidence for the existence of man in the Tertiary period. *Proc Geol Assoc* **XV**:63.

Oakley, K.P. 1948. Fluorine and the relative dating of bones. *Adv Sci* **4** (16):336-337.

Oakley, K.P. 1949. *Man the Toolmaker*. British Museum (Nat Hist), London.

Oakley, K.P. 1951. The fluorine-dating method. *Yrbk Phys Anthropol* **5**:44-52.

Oakley, K.P. 1954. [On the Piltdown flint implements]. *Proc Geol Soc Lond* No 1508. pp xlvi-xlvii.

Oakley, K.P. 1959. Comments on results [Vries & Oakley 1959]. *Nature* **184**:225-226.

Oakley, K.P. 1964. The problem of man's antiquity. An historical survey. *Bull Br Mus nat Hist* (Geol) **9**(5):85-155.

Oakley, K.P. & M.F. Ashley Montagu. 1949. A reconsideration of the Galley Hill skeleton. *Bull Br Mus nat Hist* (Geol) **1** (2):25-48.

Oakley, K.P., B.G. Campbell & T.I. Molleson (Eds) 1975. *Catalogue of Fossil Hominids.* Part III: Americas, Asia, Australasia. London: British Museum (Natural History), pp 203-204.

Oakley, K.P. & C.R. Hoskins. 1950. New evidence on the antiquity of Piltdown man. *Nature* **165**:379-382.

Oakley, K.P. C.R. Hoskins & G. Henri-Martin. 1951. Application du test de la fluorine aux crânes de Fontéchevade (Charente). *L'Anthropologie (Paris)* **55**:239-247.

Obermaier, H. 1916. *El hombre fosil.* Madrid: Com invest paleontol prehist Mem No 9.

O'Donoghue, C.H. 1918. Review of Lull's "Organic Evolution". *Sci Progr* **13**:162-163.

Osborn, H.F. 1915. *Men of the Old Stone Age: Their Environment, Life and Art.* New York: Scribners.

Osborn, H.F. 1916. Review of the Pleistocene of Europe, Asia and northern Africa. *Ann NY Acad Sci* **26**:215-315.

Osborn, H.F. 1921a. The Dawn Man of Piltdown, Sussex. *Nat Hist [New York]* **21**:577–590.

Osborn, H.F. 1921b. The Pliocene man of Foxhall in East Anglia. *Nat Hist* (New York) **21**:565–576.

Osborn, H.F. 1922. Hesperopithecus, the anthropoid primate of western Nebraska. *Nature* **110**:281–283.

Osborn, H.F. 1924. Where did man originate? *Asia* **24**:427.

Osborn, H.F. 1926. Why Central Asia? *Nat Hist* (New York) **26**:263-269.

Osborn, H.F. 1928a. *Man Rises to Parnassus: Critical Epochs in the Prehistory of Man. 2nd edition.* Princeton: Princeton University Press.

Osborn, H.F. 1928b. Recent discoveries relating to the origin and antiquity of man. *Palaeobiologica* **1**:189-202.

Osborn, H.F. 1930. The discovery of Tertiary man. *Science* **71**:1-7.

Osborn, H.F. 1942. *The Proboscidea. A monograph of the discovery, evolution, migration and extinction of the mastodonts and elephants of the world.* Vol 2. New York.

Osborn, H.F. & W.K. Gregory. 1923. The Dawn Man. [An authorized interview] *McClure's Mag* (New York) **55**(1):19-28.

Ovey, C.D (Ed). *The Swanscombe Skull.* Roy Anthropol Inst Occ Papers No 20. London: Royal Anthropological Institute.

Penck, A. & Brückner, E. 1900. *Die Alpen im Eiszeitalter.* 3 vols. Leipzig.

Pilgrim, G.E. 1915. New Siwalik primates and their bearing on the evolution of man and Anthropoidea. *Rec Geol Surv India* **45**:1-74.

Pilgrim, G.E. 1927. A *Sivapithecus* palate and other primate fossils from India. *Palaeontol Indica* **14**:1-24.

Piveteau, J. 1957. *Traité de Paléontologie. Tome VII: Primates: Paléontologie humaine.* Paris: Masson.

Plenderith, H.J. 1934. *The Preservation of Antiquities.* London: Museums Association.

Pocock, R.I. 1920. [External genitalia of the Cebidae]. *Proc Zool Soc Lond* pp 91-113.

Prestwich, J. 1889. On the occurrence of palaeolithic flint implements in the neighbourhood of Ightham, Kent: Their distribution and probable age. *Quart J Geol Soc Lond* **XLV**:270-297.

Prestwich, J. 1891. On the age, formation and successive drift stages of the valley of Darent; with remarks on the palaeolithic implements of the district, and on the origin of its chalk escarpments. *Quart J Geol Soc Lond* **XLVII**:126-163.

Prestwich, J. 1892. On the primitive characters of the flint implements of the chalk plateau of Kent. With notes by B. Harrison and de B. Crawshay. *J Anthropol Inst* [London] **XXI**:246.

Prestwich, J. 1895. The greater antiquity of man. *Nineteenth Century Mag.* p 617.

Puccioni, N. 1913. Appunti intorno al fragmento mandibolare fossile di Piltdown (Sussex). *Archivo Antropol Etnol (Firenze)* **43**:167-175.

Puccioni, N. 1914. Morphologie du maxillaire inférieur. *L'Anthropologie* (Paris) **23**:291-321.

Pycraft, W.P. 1916. [Discussion of W.C. Lyne (1916)] *Proc Roy Soc Med* (London) **9**:58.

Pycraft, W.P. 1917. The jaw of Piltdown man: A reply to Mr Gerrit S. Miller. *Sci Progr* **11**:389-409.

Pycraft, W.P. 1918. Discussion of Piltdown II [Woodward 1917]. *Quart J Geol Soc Lond* **73**:9.

Pycraft, W.P. 1928. Description of the remains. In: F.A. Bather (Ed). *Rhodesian Man and Associated Remains.* London: British Museum (Natural History). pp 1-51.

Ramström, M. 1916. Om underkäken i Piltdown fyndet *Eoanthropus. Svenska Läkaressällskapets Handl* **42**:1223-1256.

Ramström, M. 1919. Der Piltdown-Fund. *Bull Geol Inst* (Upsala) **16**:261-304.

Ramström, M. 1921. Der Java-Trinil *Pithecanthropus* oder können die *Eoanthropus* und *Pithcanthropus.* Funde uns zuverlässige Aufschlüsse über die Anthropogenesis geben? *Upsala Läkareförenings Förhandl* **26**:1-37.

Reed, CA. 1983. A short history of the discovery and early study of the Australopithecines: The first find to the Death of Robert Broom (1924-1951). In: K.J. Reichs (Ed), *Hominid Origins: Inquiries Past and Present.* Washington, DC: University Press of America. pp 1-70.

Reid-Moir, J., see Moir, J.R.

Rutot, A. 1900. Les industries paléolithiques primitives. Note sur la découverte d'importants gisements de silex taillés dans les collines de la Flandre occidentale. Comparaison de ces silex avec ceux du Chalk-Plateau du Kent. *Bull Mém Soc Anthropol* [Bruxelles] **XVIII**. Mém No 1.

Rutot, AL. 1914. Essai de reconstitution plastique de quelques races humaines primitives. *Ann: Congr Fédér Archéol Hist Belgique 1913* **XXIII**. pp 195–207.

Rutot, AL. 1919. *Un Essai de Reconstitution Plastique de Races Humaines Primitives.* Mém Beaux-Arts Acad Roy Belgique. Bruxelles.

Savage, R.J.G. 1963. Martin Alister Campbell Hinton, 1883-1961. *Biog Mem Fellows Roy Soc Lond* pp 155-170.

Schoetensack, O. 1908. *Der Unterkeifer des Homo heildelbergensis aus den Sanden von Mauer bei Heidelberg.* Leipzig: Englemann.

Schultz, A.H. 1927a. Observations on the growth of a gorilla fetus. *Eugenical News* **12**:37-40.

Schultz, A.H. 1927b. Studies on the growth of a gorilla and other primates with special reference to the fetus of the gorilla, preserved at the Carnegie Museum. *Mem Carnegie Mus* **11**:1-87.

Schmitz-Moormann, K. 1981. The Stephen Jay Gould hoax and the Piltdown conspiracy. *Teilhard Rev* **16**(3):7-15.

Schwalbe, G. 1899. Studien ber *Pithecanthropus erectus Dubois* . *Z Morphol Anthropol* **I**:16-228.

Schwalbe, G. 1914. Kritische Besprechung von Boule's werk: "L'homme fossile de la Chapelle-aux-Saints." *Z Morphol Anthropol* **16**:227-610.

Scott, D.B & R.W.G. Wycoff. 1946. Shadowed replicas of tooth surfaces. *US Pub Health Repts* **61**:697-700.

Seligman, C.G. & F.G. Parsons. 1914. [Cheddar man and his civilization]. *J Roy Anthropol Inst* **XLIV**:241.

Sera, G.L. 1917. Un presto Hominida miocenico: *Sivapithecus indicus. Natura* **8**:149-173.

Sergi, G. 1914. *L'Evoluzione oragnica e le origini umane.* Torino. pp 192-198.

Seward, A.C. 1913. A contribution to our knowledge of Wealden floras with especial reference to a collection of plants from Sussex. *Quart J Geol Soc Lond* **69**:85-116.

Shattock, S.G. 1914. Morbid thickening of the calvaria; and the reconstruction of a bone once abnormal; a pathological basis for the study of the thickening in certain Pleistocene crania. *Proc XVIIth Intnl Congr Med London 1913* Sect 3, pt 2:3-46.

Sicher, H. 1937. Zur phylogenese des Menschilichen Kierfergelenkes nebst Bemerkungen über den Schädelfund von Piltdown. *Z Stomatol* (Wien) **35**:269-275.

Smith, F.H. & F. Spencer (Eds). 1984 *The Origin of Modern Humans: A World Survey of the Fossil Evidence.* New York: Alan Liss.

Smith, Grafton Elliot, see Elliot Smith.

Smith Woodward, A., see Woodward, A.S.

Sollas, W.J. 1895. *Pithecanthropus erectus* and the evolution of the human race. *Nature* **53**:150-151.

Sollas, W.J. 1915. *Ancient Hunters and their Modern Representatives.* 2nd ed. London: Macmillan.

Sollas, W.J. 1922. A method for the comparative study of the human skull, and its application to *Homo neanderthalensis. Proc Roy Soc* ser B, **94**:134-137.

Sollas, W.J. 1924. *Ancient Hunters and Their Modern Representatives.* 3rd edition. London: Macmillan.

Sollas, W.J. 1925. The Taungs skull. *Nature* **115**:908-909.

Speaight, R. 1967. *Teilhard de Chardin: A Biography* . London: Collins.

Spencer, F. 1979. *Aleš Hrdlička MD (1869-1943): A Chronicle of the Life and Work of an American Physical Anthropologist.* 2 volumes. London: University Microfilms International.

Spencer, F. 1984. The Neandertals and their evolutionary significance: A brief historical review. In: F.H. Smith and F. Spencer (Eds), *The Origins of Modern Humans : A World Survey of the Fossil Evidence.* New York: Liss. pp 1-49.

Spencer, F. 1990. *Piltdown: A Scientific Forgery.* London: British Museum (Natural History) and Oxford University Press.

Spurrell, H.G.F. 1917. *Modern Man and His Forerunners.* 1st ed. London: Bell.

Stearn, W.T. 1981. *The Natural History Museum at South Kensington. A history of the British Museum (Natural History) 1753-1980.* London: Heinemann.

Straus, W.L. 1954. The great Piltdown hoax. *Science* **119**:265-269.

Sutcliffe, W.H. 1914. A criticism of some modern tendencies in prehistoric anthropology. *Mem Proc Manchester Lit Phil Soc* **57**:1-25.

Symington, J. 1915. On the relations of the inner surface of the cranium to the cranial aspect of the brain. *Edinburgh Med J* **14**:85-100.

Symington, J. 1916. Endocranial casts and brain form: a criticism of some recent speculations. *J Anat Physiol* (London) **50**:111-130.

Taylor, R.M.S. 1937. (By title only) The dentition of the Piltdown fossil man *(Eoanthropus dawsoni)* from a new aspect. *Rep Australian & New Zealand Ass Adv Sci* **23**:201,245. [For the complete text of this paper, see Taylor 1978].

Taylor, R.M.S. 1978. *The Piltdown paper* [see Taylor 1937]. Variation in Morphology of Teeth: Anthropologic and Forensic Aspects. Springfield, Illinois: Thomas, pp 362-370.

Teilhard de Chardin, P. 1920. Le cas de l'homme de Piltdown. *Rev des questions scientifiques* (Bruxelles) 77:149-155.

Teilhard de Chardin, P. 1965. *Lettres d'Hastings et de Paris, 1908-1914*. Preface by H. de Lubac, annotations by A. Demoment & H. de Lubac. Paris: Aubier.

Teilhard de Chardin, P. 1967. *Letters from Paris, 1912-1914*. New York: Herder.

Teilhard de Chardin, P. 1968. *Letters from Hastings, 1908-1912*. New York: Herder.

Teilhard de Chardin, P. & W.C. Pei. 1931. The lithic industry of the *Sinanthropus* deposits in Choukoutien. *Bull Geol Soc China* 11:315-358.

Terra, H. de. 1936. Late Cenozoic history in India. *Nature* 137:686-688.

Terra, H. de, P. Teilhard de Chardin & T.T. Patterson. 1936. Joint geological and prehistoric studies of the late Cenozoic in India. *Science* 83:233-236.

Thacker, A.G. 1913. The significance of the Piltdown discovery. *Sci Progr.* 8:275-290.

Thacker, A.G. 1916. [Note on Miller (1915)] *Sci Progr* 10:468.

Thomas, N. 1972. Leslie Valentine Grinsell, field archaeologist. *In*: P.J. Fowler (Ed), *Archaeology and the Landscape*. London: Baker. pp 13-36.

Tilney, F. 1928. *The Brain from Ape to Man* . 2 vols. New York: Hoeber.

Tobias, P.V. 1984. *Dart, Taung and the Missing Link*. Johannesburg: Witwatersrand University Press.

Tobias, P.V. 1985. The former taung cave system in light of contemporary reports and its bearing on the skull's provenance: early deterrants to the acceptance of *Australopithecus*. *In*: P.V. Tobias (Ed), *Hominid Evolution: Past, Present and Future*. New York: Liss. pp 25-40.

Todd, T.W. 1914. The ancestry of *Homo sapiens*. *Cleveland Med J* 13:460-469.

Tomes, C.S. 1914. *A Manual of Dental Anatomy*. 7th ed. London.

Toombs, H.A. 1952. A new section in the Piltdown gravel. *S East Nat* 57:31-33.

Topley, W. 1875. *Geology of the Weald*. Mem Geol Surv Eng. London: HMSO.

Trinkaus, E. 1982. A history of *Homo erectus* and *Homo sapiens* Palaeontology in America. *In*: F. Spencer (Ed), *A History of American Physical Anthropology, 1930-1980*. New York: Academic Press. pp 261-280.

Underwood, A.S. The Piltdown skull. *Brit Dental J* 56:650-652.

Underwood, A.S. 1916. [Discussion of W.C. Lyne (1916). *Proc Roy Med Soc* (London) 9:55-56.

Vere, F. 1955. *The Piltdown Fantasy*. London: Cassell.

Vere, F. 1959. *Lessons of Piltdown*. London: The Evolution Protest Movement.

Virchow, R. 1895. Pithecanthropus erectus. *Z Ethnol* 27:435-440.

Vallois, H.V. 1949a. L'homme fossile de Fontéchevade (Charente). *C-R Acad Sci (Paris)* 228:598-600. [see also *Amer J Phys Anthropol* (1949) 7:339-362].

Vallois, H.V. 1949b. L'origine de l'Homo sapiens. *C-R Acad Sci (Paris)* 228:949-951.

Vallois, H.V. 1952. Monophyletism and polyphyletism in man. *S Afr J Sci* 49:69-79.

Vallois, H.V. 1954. Neanderthals and Praesapiens. *J Roy Anthropol Inst* 84:111-130.

Vallois, H.V. & H.L. Movius (Eds). 1952. Catalogue des Hommes Fossiles. *XIX Congrs Géologique International, Algiers.* 5.

Vogel, J.C. & H.T. Waterbolk. 1964. Groningen radiocarbon dates [Piltdown series]. *Radiocarbon* 6:368.

Volz, W. 1896. Ueber *Pithecanthropus erectus Dub*. Eine menschenähnliche übergansform aus Java. *Jahres-Berl schles Ges vaterl. Cultur Stiz d zool bot Sect* 74:5-8.

Vram, U.G. 1913. Le reconstruzioni dell' *Eoanthropus dawsoni*, Woodward. *Boll Soc Zool Ital* (Roma) 2:192-198.

Vries, de H. & K.P. Oakley. 1959. Radiocarbon dating of the Piltdown skull and jaw. *Nature* 184:224-225.

Waldeyer, W. Discussion of Dubois' Pithecanthropus. *Z Ethnol* **27**:88.

Walkhoff, H. 1913. Entstehung und Verlauf der phylogenetischen Umformung der menschlichen Kiefer seit dem Tertiär und ihre Bedeutung für die Pathologie der Zähne. *Deutsche Monatsschr Zahnheilk* **31**:947-979.

Warren, S.H. 1905. [On eolith problem]. *J Anthropol Inst* (London) **XXVI**:349-357.

Warren, S.H. 1914. The experimental investigation of flint fracture and its application to problems of human implements. *J Roy Anthropol Inst* **44**:412-449.

Warren, S.H. 1921. A natural 'Eolith' factory beneath the Thanet Sand. *Quart J Geol Soc Lond* **76**:238-253.

Warren, S.H. 1928. The study of comparative flaking in 1927. *Man*. January 1928.

Washburn, S.L. 1954. The Piltdown hoax. *Amer Anthropol* **55**:259-262.

Waterston, D. 1913. The Piltdown mandible. *Nature* **92**:319.

Weidenreich, F. 1937. The dentition of *Sinanthropus pekinensis*: a comparative odontography of the hominids. *Palaeontol Sinica* (Peiping) **101**: v + 180 pp.

Weidenreich, F. 1943. The skull of *Sinanthropus pekinensis*: a comparative study on a primtive hominid skull. *Palaeontol Sinica* **127**: xxi +298 pp.

Weiner, J.S. 1955. *The Piltdown Forgery*. London: Oxford University Press.

Weiner, J.S. & R.K. Macpherson. 1953. A comparison of the responses to heat of unacclimatized young males in Britain with those of individuals in the tropics. *Proc XIXth Intntl Physiol Congr, Montréal*. pp 874-875.

Weiner, J.S. & K.P. Oakley. 1954. The Piltdown fraud: Available evidence reviewed. *Amer J Phys Anthropol* **12**:1-7.

Weiner, J.S. Oakley, K.P. & W.E. Le Gros Clark. 1953. The solution of the Piltdown problem. *Bull Br Mus nat Hist* (Geol) **2**:141-146.

Weiner, J.S. et al. 1955. Further contributions to the solution of the Piltdown problem. *Bull Br Mus nat Hist* (Geol) **2**(6):225-287.

Weinert, H. 1933. Das Problem des *Eoanthropus* von 1951. *Stammesentwicklung der Menschheit*. Bruanschweig: Vieweg.

Weinert, H. 1953. Der Fossile Mensch. *In*: A.L. Kroeber (Ed), *Anthropology Today*. Chicago: University of Chicago Press. pp 101-119.

Werth, E. 1909. Das geologische Alter und die stammesgeschichliche Bedentung des Homo heidelbergensis. *Globus* **XCVI**:229-232.

Werth, E. 1916. Auflösung des Eoanthropus dawsoni. *Z Ethnol* **48**:261-264.

Werth, E. 1918. Das Problem des tertiaren Menschen. *Sitz Gesell natur* (Berlin) pp 1-32.

Werth, E. 1928. *Der Fossile Mensch: Grundzuge einer Paläanthropologie*. Berlin: Borntraeger.

White, H.J.O. 1926. *The Geology of the Country near Lewes*. Mem Geol Surv England & Wales. Expl Sheet 319. London. HMSO.

Winchell, N.H. 1917. The antiquity of man in America as compared with Europe. *Bull Minnesota Acad Sci* **5**:121-151.

Winslow, J. & A. Meyer. 1983. The perpetrator at Piltdown. *Science*. **83** (4):32-43.

Wislocki, G.B. 1936. [External genitalia of Cebidae]. *Human Biol* **VIII**:309-347.

Wood Jones, F. 1918. *The Problem of Man's Ancestry*. London: SPCK.

Wood Jones, F. 1919a. The origin of man. *In*: A. Denby (Ed), *Animal Life and Human Progress*. London: Constable. pp 101-131.

Wood Jones, F. 1919b. On the zoological position and affinities of *Tarsius. Proc Zool Soc Lond*. pp 491-494.

Wood Jones, F. 1928. Man and the anthropoids. *Amer J Phys Anthropol* **12**:245-252.

Wood Jones, F. 1929. Some landmarks in the phylogeny of the primates. *Human Biol* **I**:214-228.

Woodward, A.S. 1882. On the occurrence of oxide of Manganese (Wad) in the Yoredale rocks of east Cheshire. *Chem News* (London) **45**:241-243. (See also *Proc Manchester Lit Phil Soc* **21**:115-124.)

Woodward, A.S. 1889-1901. *Catalogue of the Fossil Fishes in the British Museum (Natural History)*. Part I (1889), Part II (1891), Part III (1895), Part IV (1901). London: British Museum Natural History.

Woodward, A.S. 1890. [with C.D. Sherborn] *A Catalogue of British Fossil Vertebrata*. London: British Museum (Natural History).

Woodward, A.S. 1898. *Outlines of Vertebrate Palaeontology for Students of Zoology*. Cambridge.

Woodward, A.S. 1911. On some mammalian teeth from the Wealden of Hastings. *Quart J Geol Soc Lond* **67**:278-281.

Woodward, A.S. 1912. Note on a maxilla of *Triconodon* from the Middle Purbeck Beds of Swanage. *Proc Geol Assoc* **23**:100-101.

Woodward, A.S. 1914. [Note on Piltdown excavations in 1914]. *Nature* **94**:5.

Woodward, A.S. 1914. On the lower jaw of an anthropoid ape (*Dryopithecus*) from the Upper Miocene of Lérida (Spain). *Quart J Geol Soc Lond* **70**:316-320.

Woodward, A.S. 1915. *A Guide to the Fossil Remains of Man in the Department of Geology and Palaeontology in the British Museum (Natural History)*. London: British Museum (Nat Hist).

Woodward, A.S. 1916. [Obituary] Charles Dawson F.S.A., F.G.S. *Geol Mag* **3** (6):477-479.

Woodward, A.S. 1917. Fourth note on the Piltdown gravel with evidence of a second skull of *Eoanthropus dawsoni*. *Quart J Geol Soc Lond* **73**:1-10.

Woodward, A.S. 1921. A new cave man from Rhodesia, South Africa. *Nature* **108**:371-372.

Woodward, A.S. 1922. A supposed ancestral man in North America. *Nature* **109**:750.

Woodward, A.S. 1923. Presidential address. *Proc Linn Soc Lond*. pp 27-34.

Woodward, A.S. 1933. The second Piltdown skull. *Nature* **131**:86.

Woodward, A.S. 1948. *The Earliest Englishman* . London: Watts.

Woodward, H. 1915. Eminent geologists: Arthur Smith Woodward. *Geol Mag* (London) **6**(2):1-5.

Wooldridge, S.W. 1949. The Weald and the field sciences. *Adv Sci* **6** (21):3-11.

Wright, G.F. 1889. *The Ice Age in North America and Its Bearing Upon the Antiquity of Man*. New York.

Wright, G.F. 1892. *Man and the Glacial Period*. New York.

Wright, R.F. 1943. Samuel Allinson Woodhead (Obituary). *The Analyst [J Soc Publ Analysts]* **68**:297.

Wright, W. 1916. [Review of Keith's *Antiquity of Man* (1915)]. *Man* **16**:124-127.

Wymer, J. 1955. A further fragment of the Swanscombe skull. *Nature* **176**:426-427.

Subject Index

Name Index